# Education and the Kyoto School of Philosophy

*Scope of the Series*

*Contemporary Philosophies and Theories in Education* signifies new directions and possibilities out of a traditional field of philosophy and education. Around the globe, exciting scholarship that breaks down and reformulates traditions in the humanities and social sciences is being created in the field of education scholarship. This series provides a venue for publication by education scholars whose work reflect the dynamic and experimental qualities that characterize today's academy.

The series associates philosophy and theory not exclusively with a cognitive interest (to know, to define, to order) or an evaluative interest (to judge, to impose criteria of validity) but also with an experimental and attentive attitude which is characteristic for exercises in thought that try to find out how to move in the present and how to deal with the actual spaces and times, the different languages and practices of education and its transformations around the globe. It addresses the need to draw on thought across all sorts of borders and counts amongst its elements the following: the valuing of diverse processes of inquiry; an openness to various forms of communication, knowledge, and understanding; a willingness to always continue experimentation that incorporates debate and critique; and an application of this spirit, as implied above, to the institutions and issues of education.

Authors for the series come not only from philosophy of education but also from curriculum studies and critical theory, social sciences theory, and humanities theory in education. The series incorporates volumes that are trans- and inner-disciplinary.

The audience for the series includes academics, professionals and students in the fields of educational thought and theory, philosophy and social theory, and critical scholarship.

For further volumes:
http://www.springer.com/series/8638

Paul Standish • Naoko Saito
Editors

# Education and the Kyoto School of Philosophy

## Pedagogy for Human Transformation

 Springer

*Editors*
Paul Standish
Centre for Philosophy of Education
Institute of Education
University of London
London, UK

Naoko Saito
Graduate School of Education
Kyoto University
Kyoto, Sakyo-ku, Japan

ISBN 978-94-007-4046-4      ISBN 978-94-007-4047-1 (eBook)
DOI 10.1007/978-94-007-4047-1
Springer Dordrecht Heidelberg New York London

Library of Congress Control Number: 2012936066

Printed on acid-free paper

Springer is part of Springer Science+Business Media (www.springer.com)

# Contents

**Part II    Thinking of Education around the Kyoto School of Philosophy**

# Notes on Contributors

**Andrea English** is an Assistant Professor at Mount Saint Vincent University in Halifax, Canada. She spent many years teaching and researching in Germany at Humboldt University of Berlin. Her primary research interests include Continental philosophy of education, especially Herbart, critical theory, John Dewey and American pragmatism, and theories of teaching and learning, including the notion of 'negative experience' in education.

**Steven Fesmire** is a Professor of Philosophy at Green Mountain College in Vermont, United States. His book *John Dewey and Moral Imagination: Pragmatism in Ethics* (Indiana University Press, 2003) focused on developing an adequate philosophical psychology of wise moral deliberation. His current research focuses on the wider sphere of human interactions with complex natural systems. The concept of 'ecological imagination' is at the center of this research. As a Fulbright Scholar at Kyoto University and Kobe University in 2008–2009, Fesmire pursued a qualitative study of ecological imagination through the lenses of the Kyoto School of philosophy and American pragmatism.

**Nobuo Kazashi** is Professor of Philosophy at Kobe University in Japan. He received his Ph.D. from Yale University, and he specializes in phenomenology, pragmatism, modern Japanese philosophy, and peace studies. He was the recipient of the 6th William James Prize from the American Philosophical Association in 1991. Based in Hiroshima, he has been involved in peace activities and is a founding member of ICBUW (International Coalition to Ban Uranium Weapons). Among his publications in English are: 'The Musicality of the Other: Schutz, Merleau-Ponty, and Kimura', *Prism of the Self*, 1995; 'Bodily Logos: James, Nishida, and Merleau-Ponty', *Merleau-Ponty: Interiority and Exteriority,* 1999, and his publications in Japanese include: *Nishida's Philosophy of History*, ed. 1998; *The 21st Century of Philosophy: First Steps from Hiroshima,* 1999; A *World without Uranium Weapons: The ICBUW Challenge*, co-ed., 2008.

**Chae Young Kim** is Professor of Religious Studies at Sogang University, Korea. His research areas are theory of religion, psychology of religion, and religious education, with particular reference to William James and Bernard Lonergan. He has published several co-authored books and numerous articles and is the translator into Korean of William James' *The Varieties of Religious Experience: A Study in Human Nature* (Hangilsa, 2000). He also has published several articles in English: 'William James, Che Je-U and Religious Experience', *Journal of Dharma* (2009), 'William James and Bernard Lonergan on Religious Conversion', *The Heythrop Journal* (2010), and 'Bernard Lonergan's Approach to Religious Value in a Pluralistic Age', *Gregorianum* (2012).

**Bas Levering** (University of Utrecht, Netherlands) has taught Philosophy and History of Education at the University of Utrecht since the beginning of the 1970s. Since 2004 he has been Professor of Pedagogy at the Fontys Professional University in Tilburg, Netherlands and guest Professor of Pedagogy at the University of Ghent in Belgium (2009–2011). He published numerous books and articles on philosophy of science and ethics. His book *Childhood's Secrets. Intimacy, Privacy and the 'Self' Reconsidered* (New York, 1996), co-authored by Max van Manen is in eight languages now. Levering's most recent book *Praktische pedagogiek als theoretisch probleem (Practical Pedagogy as theoretical problem)* is a collection of his methodological studies. He is European Editor of the *International Journal of Qualitative Methods* and Editor in Chief of a Dutch pedagogical magazine.

**Tadashi Nishihira** is Professor in the Graduate School of Education at Kyoto University. His research interests have focused upon studies of Human Personality, Life-cycle, and Spirituality. His main publications (in Japanese) include: *Philosophy and Psychology of E.H. Erikson* (University of Tokyo Press, 1993); *Spiritual life-cycle in the work of Jung, Wilber, and Steiner* (University of Tokyo Press, 1997); *Inquiries into the Psychology of Religion* (co-editor) (University of Tokyo Press, 2001); *Philosophical investigation into Zeami's teaching of Exercise and Expertise* (University of Tokyo Press, 2009); and the Japanese translation of E.H. Erikson's *Young Man Luther* (Misuzu shobo, 2002) *and Identity and Lifecycle* (Seishin shobo, 2011). His recent interests are in the Japanese traditional wisdom of human transformation.

**Takuo Nishimura** is Professor of Philosophy of Education, Nara Women's University, Japan. His major works include *Concepts of Aesthetic Education; Japanese and European Perspectives* (2007, ed. by Y. Imai & Ch. Wulf), *Expressive Activities of Children and the Task of Teachers* (1998, in Japanese) and *Pedagogy of Narrative* (2003, in Japanese).

**Steve Odin** has taught in the Philosophy Department at the University of Hawaii in Manoa, Honolulu, Hawaii, from 1982 to the present. He has also been a Visiting Professor at Boston University (1989), Tohoku University in Sendai Japan (1984–1985) and Tokyo University (2003–2004).

**Naoko Saito** is Associate Professor in the Graduate School of Education at Kyoto University. Her primary areas of scholarship are philosophy of education and American philosophy. Her main interests are in the work of John Dewey, Ralph Waldo Emerson, Henry David Thoreau and Stanley Cavell. Her main publications include *The Gleam of Light: Moral Perfectionism and Education in Dewey and Emerson* (New York: Fordham University Press, 2005), the Japanese translation of Stanley Cavell's *The Senses of Walden* (Tokyo: Hosei University Press, 2005) and *Stanley Cavell and the Education of Grownups* (New York: Fordham University Press, 2011), co-edited with Paul Standish.

**Paul Standish** is Professor of Philosophy of Education at the Institute of Education, University of London. He has published widely in the philosophy of education. Recent books include*: The Therapy of Education* (2006), co-authored with Paul Smeyers and Richard Smith*, The Philosophy of Nurse Education* (2007), co-edited with John Drummond, and *Stanley Cavell and the Education of Grownups* (2011), co-edited with Naoko Saito. From 2001 to 2011 he was Editor of the *Journal of Philosophy of Education*.

**Lynda Stone** is Professor of Philosophy of Education at the University of North Carolina at Chapel Hill. Her research interests include poststructuralist perspectives, John Dewey, feminism, and curriculum issues. She has an emerging interest in social ethics and is currently working on a book provisionally entitled *Mirror for Our Ethics: Discourses on Youth, Schooling, and Philosophy*. She is co-editor, with Jan Masschelein, of the book series *Contemporary Philosophies and Theories in Education*, in which this volume appears. Currently she is president of The John Dewey Society.

**Shoko Suzuki**, Dr. Phil., is Professor at the Graduate School of Education Kyoto University, Member of The Science Council of Japan, and Academic Unit-Leader of Global Center of Excellence Program 'Revitalizing Education for Dynamic Hearts and Minds' in Kyoto University. She was engaged in research at the University of Cologne from 1982–1989 and held a Guest Professorship at the Free University of Berlin in 2009–2010. Her publications include: 'Takt in Modern Education'. Muenster, New York: Waxmann, 2010, *Mimesis, Poiesis, and Performativity in Education*, Waxmann, (ed. with Christoph Wulf: 2007), Brush Calligraphy. Mimesis and Poiesis in *Rinsho* (Imai, Y. & Wulf, Chr. eds., 'Concepts of Aesthetic Education. Japanese and European Perspectives', Waxmann, pp. 149–161, 2007).

**Tsunemi Tanaka** is now Professor at the School of Letters, Mukogawa Women's University, in Japan. Formerly, 1995 till 2012, he was Professor in the Center for the Promotion of Excellence in Higher Education at Kyoto University; from 2006 he was Director of the Center. He received his doctorate in education from Kyoto University. He research is in the philosophy in education, the history of educational thought and university pedagogy. His books include *Towards the Clinical Theory of Human Becoming* (Keisou Shobo, 2003), *The Development of Educational Anthropology* (Hokuju Shupann, 2009) (both in Japanese). His studies have focused particularly on the work of Motomori Kimura, Kitaro Nishida, and Akira Mori, and on the topics of the pedagogy of the Kyoto School and *hyogen* (expression).

**Satoji Yano**, Ph.D., is Professor of Clinical-Philosophical Pedagogy at Kyoto University. He has taught and published widely on anthropological and philosophical studies on education. He is the author of *Education from the Perspective of Gift and Exchange*.

# Contributors

**Andrea English**  Faculty of Education, Mount Saint Vincent University, Halifax, NS, Canada

**Steven Fesmire**  Philosophy and Environmental Studies, Green Mountain College, Poultney, VT, USA

**Nobuo Kazashi**  Graduate School of Humanities, Kobe University, Kobe, Japan

**Chae Young Kim**  Department of Religious Studies, College of Humanities, Sogang University, Seoul, South Korea

**Bas Levering** Faculty of Social Sciences, Utrecht University, Utrecht, The Netherlands

**Tadashi Nishihira**  Graduate School of Education, Kyoto University, Kyoto, Japan

**Takuo Nishimura**  Faculty of Letters, Nara Women's University, Nara, Japan

**Steve Odin**  Department of Philosophy, University of Hawai`i at Manoa, Honolulu, HI, USA

**Naoko Saito**  Graduate School of Education, Kyoto University, Kyoto, Japan

**Paul Standish**  Institute of Education, University of London, London, UK

**Lynda Stone**  School of Education, University of North Carolina at Chapel Hill, Chapel Hill, NC, USA

**Shoko Suzuki**  Graduate School of Education, Kyoto University, Kyoto, Japan

**Tsunemi Tanaka**  School of Letters, Mukogawa Women's University, Nishinomiya, Japan

**Satoji Yano**  Graduate School of Education, Kyoto University, Otsu, Japan

# Chapter 1
# Sounding the Echoes –
# By Way of an Introduction

**Paul Standish**

A haunting scene in Kon Ichikawa's 1955 film *Kokoro* shows two men treading
water in the sea. One, the older man, has swum out by himself. From the shore, the
other, a young man, sees him – waiting, possibly floundering, apparently beyond
earshot… The young man sees him and swims out. We see the older man's head
bobbing above the surface, and the water dense and opaque beneath. When they are
close, the two men look into each other's eyes, but between them there is a distance,
an absence that is not going to be filled.

We see the man as if floundering, but not because he cannot swim. And we see
water, closer to us, but not as we might see if it we were there: we see water bobbing
against a pane of glass, water in cross-section. We see a cinematically coded illusion
of immersion; a glass screen marks our separateness.

This scene occurs towards the middle of the film, by which time we have learned
something of this relationship, though much of the past remains submerged at present,
its significance murky and wavering, and the future is suspended before us. But we
have been told enough to know that the older man will be referred to by the younger
as *sensei* – which is to say 'teacher', but teacher in a sense that is broader, wider, and
more resonant in Japanese than that term's significance in English: the term incorporates the associations of mentor, guide, older friend, for example – or in some
ways those of *maître* in French. So this is the story of an educative relationship
between friends, where one is significantly older than the other. We might recall
dialogues of Plato, where we see Socrates in relationships of this kind. In a Japanese
context, this will carry connotations of respect for learning and authority, and for
superior age, with a sense of indebtedness for the gift that the teacher bestows.

P. Standish (✉)
Institute of Education, University of London, 20 Bedford Way, WC1H 0AL London, UK
e-mail: p.standish@ioe.ac.uk

P. Standish and N. Saito (eds.), *Education and the Kyoto School of Philosophy*,
Contemporary Philosophies and Theories in Education 1,
DOI 10.1007/978-94-007-4047-1_1, © Springer Science+Business Media Dordrecht 2012

Satoji Yano's paper, Chap. 16 of this volume, eloquently explains the importance and the ramifications of this, demonstrating in the process the power of the notion of indebtedness in Japanese ways of thinking.

The story proves to be rather more complex, however. The *sensei* in the story turns out to be someone whose early educational ambitions have been blighted by his being cheated of an inheritance. It is telling also that the reclusive life of learning he subsequently commits himself to, so it seems, is not given any substance in the film: we do not know what he is studying, and his commitment to this comes to seem more like a withdrawal, from his marriage and from the world.

But the image is there also at the start of the film, even as the titles are in view, prompting us to speculate further as to its significance. The film, released in 1953, was made in the decade following the devastation and defeat of Japan during the Second World War, and it is difficult not to see here something of the struggles of re-connection following trauma. The film is based on the novel of the same name by Soseki Natsume published in 1914, giving us a date that together with that of the film seem to embrace or frame the period during which the Kyoto School was moving through its most flourishing and most influential phases. Rapid industrialization and change during the time that the novel surveys, starting roughly in the middle of the Meiji era but encompassing its ending in 1912, make this a time during which intergenerational relationships and structures of subjectivity figured in people's consciousness in unprecedented ways and the understanding of inheritance and loyalty were newly tested. This was plainly a time of rapid change for Japan – at political and military levels, ultimately with disastrous consequences, but also in terms of the national psyche.

Although the film was not particularly well received at the time of its first release in Japan, it quickly gained recognition abroad, and it is now regarded as a key work in Ichikawa's *oeuvre*. It is appropriate to acknowledge, however, some of the ways in which the film departs from the novel, ways that realize an autonomy for the film but that risk distorting the achievements of the book. The inevitable economies the film effects in terms of the events of the story are used to make less explicable the behaviour of the central character, and the departure from its narrative structure in turn makes this character into someone whose actions are heartless and cruel, and whose motivations are harder to fathom – without recourse, that is, to a more psychoanalytic reading. Such a reading prompts explanation in terms of layers of repression, including the repression of homosexual desire, with correlates in suggestions of impotence and sadism. Yet this is scarcely evident in the book.

Insofar as *Kokoro*, the novel and the film, are to be seen as speaking to the larger disturbances of the respective ages of their production, this invites a reading in terms of a sense of loss of inheritance, with the suggestion also that one has somehow been cheated of this, that one has been deprived or that something has been denied, or perhaps that a promise has not been honoured. If the uncomfortable allegorical associations of the story are pressed, this is to figure the young man's attraction to the *sensei* in terms of the (willing) turn to Western culture during the Meiji era and the (forced) adoption of Western practices following the Second World War. But to the extent that this is a cogent reading, it is important to register also the nature of the limitations of the *sensei* himself. As has been pointed out, there is an uncertainty about his credentials as a *sensei*. Just what is his expertise, his field of study? How genuinely is he moved by this – and how far is it, as implied above, a kind of impotent retreat from the world, compounded with its own forms of negativity, resentment, and denial? This would be a semblance of education; to see through this would be an education in itself. Any suspicion of this or disillusionment on the part of the younger man is at most hinted at in both novel and film. But the reader is positioned similarly in terms of what these works have to teach, and the heart of the matter proves to beat to a rhythm that is other and less vibrant than one initially expects. To the extent that the *sensei* can be symbolic in this way, these works reflect a wariness about the relation to the West, and a latent scepticism about the quality of some of its attractions. This is an ambivalence that has characterised the Japanese reception of Western thought and practices.

The year 1911 saw the first translation into Japanese of a complete work by Nietzsche, *Thus Spake Zarathustra*. And although the vast and sometimes contradictory nature of Nietzsche's work had led to widely divergent readings in Japan, what must have been clear was that here also, in this supreme work of a German thinker, was an account of the vacuousness at the heart of Western bourgeois culture. Indeed sometimes Nietzsche was perceived to be writing in an Eastern vein. In his contextualisation of a discussion of the reception of the early thought of Nietzsche in Japan, Graham Parkes (1991) highlights the significance of the ending of the prohibition of Christianity that had come with the Meiji Restoration, with the new attention to the inner life that this allowed, as well as the gradual turn, towards the end of the nineteenth century, away from philosophies of positivism and utilitarianism in the direction of German *Bildung*. But into this picture must also be brought the new nationalism that came with victory in the war against China, a war that was in part a response to aggressive Western colonialism. The elements of Confucian tradition – the ideas of the 'family state' (*kazoku kokka*) and 'national morality' (*kokumini dotoku*), as well as the divinity of the Emperor as the father of the nation-family – were diametrically opposed to any form of individualism. In this context, the rapid development of the school and university systems reflected the ways that education was seen as essential to the inculcation of 'national morality'. Yet there were tensions here with the policy, during the Meiji era, of sending to the West such young intellectuals as Soseki himself in order to 'discover' what was going on, in terms of literature, the arts, science, and therefore education. These are some of the contradictory forces at work in the complex context that needs to be considered.

We have approached the Kyoto School in this somewhat oblique way, by suggestion rather than by a straightforwardly synoptic introduction, partly because of a wariness about how this book might be received. The forms of thinking realised in the Kyoto School, and the distinctive manner of the various forms of its philosophising, do not amount to a systematic philosophy offering readily identifiable viewpoints on either the standard questions of philosophy or the perennial problems of education. Any quick attempt to rush into this book looking for the 'Kyoto School's position on *x*' will block from the start the kind of reading and reception these authors need, rather in the manner that a cinematic coding, uncritically viewed, can lull the viewer into an illusion of unusual clarity. One needs rather to dwell with these ideas, in their variety, and to block from the start too quick an impulse to translate and assimilate. But equally it would be a mistake to give any quarter to that familiar tendency in Western receptions of the East towards indulgence in a kind of voyeuristic mystification. Such fantasies are similarly obstructive to insight and understanding. Furthermore, as will become apparent, any simple dichotomisation of East and West can scarcely do justice to the complex interweavings of thought that contribute to the Kyoto School's achievement. Hence, it is with some caution that we venture here a more direct account of what it is that entitles us to speak of the Kyoto School as a phenomenon in the development of philosophical thought. What does the term encompass, and how coherent is the grouping of thinkers and lines of thought to which it refers? A collection of essays entitled *The Thought of the Kyoto School*, edited by Ryosuke Ohashi (2004), has examined the controversial history even of the *name* 'Kyoto School'. And the deflationary tone of the following remarks from one of its principal thinkers, Keiji Nishitani (1900–1990), is clearly pointed: 'The name "Kyoto School" is a name journalists used in connection with discussions that friends of mine and I held immediately before and during the war' (NKC XI, 207; see Heisig 2001, p. 277). Is it reasonable to go further by way of identification than these guarded, even defensive remarks would seem to allow?

John Maraldo has explored this question at some length, and drawing on representative commentaries, he suggests six characteristics that might be regarded as typical, and in the paragraphs that follow we shall loosely follow the structure these provide, expanding upon them freely in the light of the purposes of the present collection. Plainly this is not an attempt at some kind of definitive classification, and, equally plainly, the criteria proposed are not entirely discrete, feeding into one another in various ways. Maraldo uses the list as a means of exploring how each of these criteria has figured in the promotion of the philosophical significance of the Kyoto School or in the disparagement of the political ideology with which it is in some respects associated (Maraldo 2005, pp. 33–38). For present purposes the list provides a useful heuristic for examining some salient features.

Two fairly obvious factors are emphasised initially by Maraldo: the connection with Kitaro Nishida (1870–1945) and with Kyoto University. Nishida's prodigious work at Kyoto University was a point of attraction and a lasting source of influence for many of those thinkers who subsequently became associated with the name 'Kyoto School'. It is important to acknowledge, however, that the name was not one that was self-consciously adopted by Nishida or by its other main luminaries. What brought them together was not any shared 'position' but rather a philosophical dynamic of intense mutual interest – a dynamic that enabled the emergence of interesting *differences* of thought. Moreover, it is as well to acknowledge the point made by Jun Tosaka (1900–1945) that there would be no Kyoto School had it not been for the critical appropriation by Hajime Tanabe (1885–1962) of Nishida's thought: without this, there would simply by Nishida and his followers. And although, Nishida and Tanabe were later to find differences with each other that severed their relationship, it was a feature of the School generally that critical exchange was accepted and encouraged. It is worth drawing attention also to the fact that, with no rival 'schools' of thought developing in Japan, at that time or, for that matter, since, there was nothing in contradistinction to which there was motive to self-identify. In fact, the very idea of a 'school of thought' itself needs to be brought into question: the Western presumption of a universal discourse of philosophy, within which distinct schools might emerge, is to some extent alien to those Japanese ways of thinking that inspired the Eastern reception of Western philosophy by the principal philosophers who are our concern.

A third factor to which Maraldo draws attention, and as these remarks begin to show, is the seriousness with which Japanese and Eastern intellectual traditions were taken. This is a point of central importance, especially given the way that *academic* philosophy had been established in Japan. When, in the late nineteenth century and after the period of Japan's closure to the outside world (1600–1868), an early envoy to the West, Amane Nishi (1829–1927), 'imported' philosophy, there was no ready-made translation for the term, and he constructed the name *tetsugaku* (哲学). Of course, the kinds of questions that philosophy addresses had been a part of Japanese traditions of thought in one way or another, but philosophy as an institutionalised academic subject did not exist. Much turns on this. And it is important that the path for philosophy in Japan was laid not just by the reading of the canonical texts that were taken to define the subject but also by the very forms of expression, the language, in which they were written. In order to understand the originality of the Kyoto School, it is necessary to realise the ways in which aspects of this importation laid a course for philosophy in substance and, crucially, in style. In this respect, it is interesting to register two things. First, as Heisig has helpfully pointed out, the texts of the Kyoto School present fewer problems to the translator than might be imagined (see Heisig 2001, pp. 17–21). This is so in part because the terms they use have been chosen to correspond with a philosophical vocabulary that is fundamentally European. But there are moments in this correspondence that are critical, as we shall see. Second, then, and in the light of this, it is the achievement of the Kyoto School that within this idiom they were able to assert and develop lines of thinking that were distinctly Japanese, in ways that are adumbrated below.

The thought to entertain here then is that the putative universality of Western thought is related to the presumptions of European languages. This universality was an attraction to Nishida and his followers in many respects, but the vocabularies it generated also proved problematic in some ways. Central to that thought, and hence to philosophy, is some notion of the human subject, which finds its most unavoidable form in the everyday recurrence of 'I' but which is there also in some of philosophy's inaugural moments. *Cogito ergo sum*. What is this 'I' that thinks and has being? What is the nature of the human subject whose relation to the objects of experience is the abiding preoccupation of epistemology? In finding a way of talking about these things in Japanese, Nishi made a decisive step. There is a differentiation in Japanese around this concept that English, for example, fails to register. That is, with no single word quite translating 'subject', one is forced to choose between *shukan* (主観) and *shutai* (主体), a problem now familiar to translators. Inevitably in philosophy and social science this is a peculiarly pivotal term, and so the cross-cultural consequences of this translational problem should be plain enough. Nishi's adoption of the former, preferring it as the equivalent of 'epistemological subject', inevitably helped to define the way that Japanese philosophy subsequently developed. According to Naoki Sakai (1997), Nishi had bemoaned the lack of systematic reasoning in Japan, and the emphasis on *shukan* was presumably intended to answer to that lack. The contending term *shutai* by contrast, became less visible in philosophy, but it is worth saying something further about this, for this will take us back to Maraldo's criteria.

His fourth criterion has to do with the complex relationship of the philosophers in question to Marxism and to politics. To clarify this it is worth making reference to the ethics and anthropology of Tetsuro Watsuji (1889–1960), developed in the 1930s and 1940s. Watsuji himself relates his own thinking to Marx's dissatisfactions with eighteenth century materialism, a metaphysics that divided the world into objects of knowledge, on the one hand, and epistemological subjects, on the other. It was against this that Marx emphasised the idea of *praxis*, where the subject is understood as (bodily) engaged in activities and hence socially and historically located. The second *kanji* forming the written expression for *shutai* (体) refers to the body, and this helps to show the way that it turns us back to notions of practical engagement and hence brings us closer to Marx. Watsuji implies that *shukan* is the mode of subjectivity of 'the West' and *shutai* that of 'the East'. This is, however, more problematic than it seems. To classify in this way, as Naoki Sakai has attempted to show, is to objectify the other and, hence, to identify oneself by contrast. And this ends up by reiterating the patterns of Western classification, with the result that to identify *shutai* as the *defining characteristic* of subjectivity in the East is ironically self-defeating. So these are questions about what can be understood by identity itself, and they suggest differences between the West and the East the understanding of which is likely to be foiled by enthusiasms for identification that are left unchecked! This applies to the individual human subject, to be sure, but also to peoples and nations.

The upshot of this is that these critical decisions concerning translation both opened up possibilities for thought and suppressed certain elements in Japanese ways of thinking and doing, and of self-conception. And it was partly in recognition of this that the philosophers of the Kyoto School retained a certain ambivalence towards the West. Thus, there is neither simple rejection nor simple acceptance toward Western philosophy and the West in general, and this extends to an ambivalence towards Western modernity, with modernization understood very much as Westernization. The unilateral globalization of Western modernity, which seemed in many respects inevitable, led to the idea of 'overcoming modernity' – an overcoming that would take place not by retreating from Western modernity, but by going *through* and beyond it. Hence the need for an existential sea-change. And this was understood both as requiring a move away from the ontological preoccupations of the West and as a means of recuperation of traditions of East Asian thought – perhaps of Mahâyâna Buddhism, in particular.

It is precisely the relation to Buddhism (and to religion, more generally) that Maraldo identifies as a fifth criterion. But it would be easy to get this wrong.

Nishida practised Zen meditation in his late twenties, but he continued this for less than a decade, although in the lives of some of his colleagues – Nishitani, for example – connections with Buddhism were more explicit. There are connections and disconnections with Martin Heidegger here that we shall shortly consider, but to lay the way for this, it will be better first to say something about the sixth feature Maraldo identifies: the notion of Absolute Nothingness. In his *Die Philosophie der Kyoto-Schule* (1990), Ohashi advances the view that the philosophers who might reasonably be associated with the Kyoto School are united in that they developed their philosophy with an idea of 'nothingness' as a basis. Kiyoshi Miki (1897–1945), for example, in his *The Logic of Imagination*, writes of nothingness as both transcending 'the subjective and the objective and enveloping them,' and in a later echo of this, the film-maker Yasujiro Ozu had *mu* (nothingness) inscribed on his grave-stone. But how is this notion to be understood? *Mu* is written with a single character, that is, not with the additional mark that would signify the negation of being, and it is a notion that is, for the most part, alien to Western thought, which tends to be drawn by the binary of positive and negative. But something like this *is* there in Plato's account of *khora* in the *Timaeus* and in Jacques Derrida's discussion of that text. And there is a connection with aspects of Heidegger's thought – in particular with his notion of the 'clearing', the opening that allows things to come into presence even as it simultaneously conceals others. This is to be understood as of a different order from determinate things, with their presence or their absence: it is a no-thingness.

Now the connection with Heidegger's thought is salient in various respects. There is no doubting the resonances that many have found between his work and Eastern thought. During the 1920s and 1930s a number of Japanese scholars visited Germany to study with him, the most significant of whom for present purposes was undoubtedly Tanabe; and the influence was far from one-sided. Thus, we find that *Sein und Zeit* (1927) was translated no less than six times into Japanese before the first translation into English, over the course of decades in which Heidegger was drawing upon and appropriating a range of East Asian sources (for an interesting and well developed discussion, see Parkes 1987). But for all the similarities between, on the one hand, Heidegger's account of Being, with the key place it gives to forms of nullity, and, on the other, the preoccupation on the part of the Kyoto School with *mu*, Heidegger's thought remains burdened with ontology, in spite of the various attempts in his later work to move away from direct enquiry into Being. What is realised in the thought of the Kyoto School is of a different order. In fact, Nishida came to view Heidegger's work in a negative light, describing its deficiencies specifically in terms of a failing of the sense of the religious (see Rigsby 2010).

The parallel with Heidegger also leads into the troubled terrain of the political. It is likely to be difficult for people in the West – especially in countries where philosophy is constructed in the popular imagination as ivory-tower, abstract, and irrelevant – to credit the fact that Nishida's views on public and political, even military issues were eagerly awaited and sometimes actively sought. But this public promi-nence came at a price: while at one time Nishida was under investigation in virtue of the left-leaning views he was at one time supposed to hold, his later partial absorption into the establishment, along with other members of the Kyoto School, was tainted with the excesses of Japanese nationalism. The legitimation that Nishitani attempted to give to his own political commitments involved a critique of the hypocrisy of Western imperialism in tandem with a vision of the leading role Japan might play. Japan would not be a colonising power. Modernity would be overcome through Japan's becoming not an aggressive empire but a 'nation of non-ego': the empire it would build would be a self-negating and compassionate one, enabling other nations to form their own identities. Naivety and error in judgement are surely evident here, failings in some respects shared by other members of the Kyoto School. But there are limits in the parallels with Heidegger's notorious political interventions, not to mention his subsequent obfuscating reticence about speaking of such matters. While, in both cases, it is possible to find elements in the philosophy that might be said to be vulnerable to adoption by objectionable forms of politics, there is nothing in the actions of the Kyoto School members that matches the iniquities of Heidegger's life in this respect.

Contemporary liberal scorn for such things is reasonable enough, but it also has its dangers, and the idea of overcoming modernity certainly should not be consigned to the errors of history. For our contemporary, globalised, neoliberal world manifests problems in ways of being and thinking that are, to some extent, the targets of both Heidegger and the Kyoto School writ large. Hence, we should take little comfort from fantasies, in the not too distant past, of the 'end of history'. It is in this more critically cautious, perhaps more humble way that the thought of the Kyoto School may be best approached. Perhaps, in conclusion, it is salutary to attend to the following, carefully measured words of Heisig:

> Kyoto School philosophy, therefore, should be understood neither as Buddhist thought forced into Western garb, nor as universal discourse (which the West happened to have invented or discovered) dressed up in Japanese garb. Rather, it is best understood as a set of unique contributions from the perspective of modern Japan – that is, from a Japan that remains fundamentally determined by its historical layers of traditional culture at the same time as being essentially conditioned by its most recent layer of contact with the West – to a nascent worldwide dialogue of cross-cultural philosophy (Heisig 2001).

To reiterate a point made earlier, it would be a fallacy to suppose that such dialogue would involve cultures that were otherwise self-contained and discrete – as if cultures were ever quite like that. To think along these lines in relation to the Kyoto School would further ignore the extent to which its originality was cultivated and articulated in the idiom of Western philosophy. But there is also an invitation to think here of the ways in which those same Western traditions were not without their Eastern sources.

The thoughts that have been entertained above, and the introduction to the Kyoto School we have tried to offer, are intended to lay the way for a consideration of the various strands of influence that are to be found in traditions of educational thought found in Japan. There is no doubting the originality and the depth of the best of the Kyoto School's work, and while we can reasonably aspire to highlight salient aspects of that originality for its pertinence to education, it would be rash of us to imagine that a collection such as the present one can satisfactorily plumb that depth.

We do, however, at least hope to tread water in these complex seas. But we do not thereby expect to expose in all transparency some set of 'positions' lying beneath the surface (as if, say, behind a glass screen), any more than we would expect to understand the human psyche primarily in terms of psychology's explicit developmental stages. It is not so much immersion that we seek, then, but rather the achieving of buoyancy of a kind, such that ideas can flow where once their currents were stopped and echoes be sounded where, in the past, nothing was heard.

There is a further sense in which the traffic of influence is by no means one way, for it would be completely erroneous to try to conceive of the Japanese heritage in which (Western) philosophy somehow took root without acknowledging the educational and other disciplinary practices that had so much defined the culture from which the members of the Kyoto School came. It is beyond the scope of this introduction to detail the ramifications of the thinking of the Kyoto School in the work of those more explicitly concerned with education, whether in theoretical or in more obviously practical ways. It is in part the purpose of this book to bring to light, in its various chapters, insights that are sometimes peculiarly Japanese that emerge in their writings, and our contributors have answered admirably to this task. But what they have also succeeded in doing is to take forward the ideas of the Kyoto School, as well as pertinent contemporaneous developments in thinking, into the work of education today. Indeed some can rightly be seen as the true inheritors of the best of that thought and as educationalists who have been developing it in unique ways.

In the light of this, let us then move to the contents of the collection and to a brief account of the chapters that follow.

\* \* \* \* \* \* \* \* \* \* \* \* \* \* \*

The book has two parts. Part I, 'Thinking of Education in the Kyoto School of Philosophy,' includes eight chapters whose purpose is to provide an account of this philosophical tradition, with a special focus on educational implications drawn from the idea of human becoming. The seven chapters that comprise Part II, 'Thinking of Education around the Kyoto School of Philosophy,' bring the consideration of the implications of this philosophy further into contact with other traditions, East and West, especially in relation to the idea of human becoming.

In Chap. 2, 'Pure Experience and Transcendence Down,' Paul Standish discusses Nishida's philosophy of mind and experience and some fairly obvious lines of influence that Nishida drew from his scholarship in Western philosophy, as well as pointing to aspects of Nishida's departure from this and to his originality. He develops his discussion especially in relation to the thought of Martin Heidegger and Jacques Derrida. The particular issues that Standish highlights are, first, nothingness and place, and second, language, silence, and transcendence. He offers some critical remarks on the idea of human becoming as elaborated in the tradition of the Kyoto School and examines tensions between this and the idea of a 'transcendence downward', as found in the philosophy of Stanley Cavell and American transcendentalism.

In Chap. 3, 'The Philosophical Anthropology of the Kyoto School and Post-War Pedagogy,' Satoji Yano attempts to trace and clarify the development of the anthropology of the Kyoto School, specifying its inception in the pre-war period under the influence of Kitaro Nishida and Hajime Tanabe and its post-war maturation. This anthropology was developed in Japan through an actively critical re-reading of Heidegger, in the course of Nishida's and Tanabe's philosophies and through their wider influence. The Kyoto School found its unique path of development as a dialectical anthropology, based upon an ontic-ontological understanding of the human being as a historical and social agent. More specifically, it was a distinctively Japanese anthropology, whose focus was on community, nation, culture, body, race and history. An anthropology of education based upon the Kyoto School directly contributed to the development of education, though this ended up more in service of the nationalistic, spiritual movement of the times than as a realization of its philosophical inspiration. The pedagogical anthropology that was established at the end of the Second World War has left much unsaid, whether consciously or unconsciously, in respect of its continuity with prewar and mid-war thinking about education. Yano argues, however, that prewar and mid-war pedagogical insights have been inherited in a variety of ways by studies in pedagogy in the postwar period.

In Chap. 4, 'The Kyoto School and J. F. Herbart,' Shoko Suzuki is engaged in a comparative examination of the Kyoto School and the German educational philosopher Johann Friedrich Herbart (1776–1841). The Kyoto School, and in particular its progenitor, Nishida, were deeply influenced both directly and indirectly by Herbart, who is commonly known in the German-speaking world as the 'father of modern pedagogy.' Suzuki refers, in particular, to Nishida's focus on Herbart's monolithic realism and to his emphasis on refinement of the sense of touch in his practice-based theory of learning. In Nishida's philosophy, this can be compared to the 'logic of place.'

Chapter 5 is Tsunemi Tanaka's 'A Genealogy of the Development of the Clinical Theory of Human Becoming.' The emergence of a new discipline along these lines, 'Clinical Theory', is to be found within the pedagogy of the Kyoto School. The School was in some ways a local development of German philosophy, but it received that tradition in its own Japanese context, where Buddhist thought and the social hardships of poverty and illness prevailed. The Kyoto School itself became known as a factory of philosophical study, also producing its own pedagogy, which began with Motomori Kimura's (1895–1946) 'Ichida no Nomi' ('One Carving of a Chisel') (1933) and culminating with Akira Mori's (1915–1976) theory of *Seimei Tuzumihashi (The Human Lifecycle as an Arch Bridge)* (1977). The Clinical Theory of human becoming was conceived in the context of the unfolding and eventual dissolution of the pedagogy of the Kyoto School. This is one of the supporting beams in the unique structure of Japan's educational theory – a beam that was hewn from native Japanese timber but cut and turned according to the templates of Europe and America.

In Chap. 6, 'The Kyoto School and the Theory of Aesthetic Human Transformation: Examining Motomori Kimura's Interpretation of Friedrich Schiller,' Takuo Nishimura provides an account of the theory of aesthetic human transformation of the Kyoto School and considers its relevance for current philosophy of education. Schiller's *Aesthetic Letters* is a text that is open to a broad range of interpretations, and how a thinker approaches it is a touchstone for his understanding of 'the aesthetic'. Kimura's interpretation of Schiller is of the school that identifies the 'purity' of the *schone Seele* with 'absolute nothingness' – where everything is generated and from which every act is received and affirmed. We can reinterpret Kimura's definition of human nature, 'expressive-formative existence' as the self-awakening of 'absolute nothingness', as showing us an alternative understanding of the human subject, which embraces but transcends the subjectivity of the Western modern self, to which various lines of postmodern thought have reacted. In the later part of his discussion, and in response to Standish's comments in a special panel during the International Network of Philosophers of Education meeting in Kyoto, 2008, Nishimura gives further consideration to the relevance of the Kyoto School for our current philosophy of education, especially concerning the conception of 'practice'.

In Chap. 7, 'Metamorphoses of "Pure Experience": Buddhist, Enactive and Historical Turns in Nishida,' Nobuo Kazashi brings into relief the hallmark characteristics of Nishida's philosophy by tracing the transformations his initial conception of 'pure experience' came to undergo through his endeavours, spanning over 30 years, to provide it with logical and historical dimensions, which concretized in such seminal notions as the 'logic of place' and 'acting-intuition.' He aims to draw out their educational implications by considering their philosophical import in relation to the basic tenets of Jamesian radical empiricism, characterized by its emphatic advocacy of pluralism, as well as other related thoughts, such as James Gibson's ecological psychology and George H. Mead's social behaviourism.

In Chap. 8, 'William James, Kitaro Nishida, and Religion,' Chae Young Kim develops an experimental sketch which compares the religious thought of these two thinkers. In tackling issues having to do with the dynamism that one finds in the growth and spread of religion and as this life is being expressed in today's new pluralistic religious situation, Kim argues that, among the modern thinkers in the East and the West, one can turn to the thought of William James (1842–1910) and Kitaro Nishida (1870–1945) for direction and guidance on how an authentically appropriate study of religion can be conducted within our new contemporary situation. In order to do this, he focuses on their religious writings, in particular James's Gifford Lectures, *The Varieties of Religious Experience: A Study in Human Nature,* and in Nishida's first and last works, *An Inquiry into the Good* and *Nothingness and the Religious World.* Kim concludes that in the work of James and Nishidas, one finds a pioneering attempt to attend to religion as an inner reality within the human self. By appropriating this subjectivity, one works with and from a philosophical foundation which would allow one to mediate diverse religious meanings within a global pluralistic world. This keen awareness of human subjectivity invites us to attend to the relation which exists between religion and education in a context which looks at how one might create a deep sense of humanity that could elicit a sense of participatory citizenship as this would exist in a global manner within our current pluralistic religious world.

In Chap. 9, 'Ecological Imagination and Aims of Moral Education Through the Kyoto School and American Pragmatism,' Steven Fesmire argues that in order to clarify and develop aims for moral education that contribute to moral coherence and are relevant to the globalized effects of our choices and policies, we need global philosophical dialogue. This must tap intellectual resources in such a way that we can reinvest our social and natural interactions in such a way as to avoid those moralistic or authoritarian forms of instruction that impede human becoming and freeze growth. The Kyoto School of modern Japanese philosophy and the classical pragmatist tradition in American philosophy can help us better to perceive the relational networks in which our finite lives are embedded. In the first section of the chapter, Fesmire explores relational thinking in the Kyoto School and American pragmatism to help develop, in the second section, a concept of 'ecological imagination.' In the final section, he draws on the account thus provided to clarify some appropriate aims for contemporary moral education.

In Chap. 10, 'Martinus Jan Langeveld: Modern Educationalist of Everyday Upbringing,' Bas Levering focuses on Langeveld's theoretical work. Though not directly related to the Kyoto School, Langeveld's philosophy and pedagogy influenced Japanese scholars, including those in Kyoto. Thus, Shuji Wada, one of his former students from Utrecht in the 1960s, saw to it that Langeveld's *Beknopte Theoretische Pedagogiek* was translated into Japanese. After a brief introduction to his life and work, Levering explains Langeveld's outlook on his subject in terms of the idea of pedagogy as practical science. On the strength of this, Langeveld's pedagogical theory and its links with anthropology and developmental psychology are explained. His particular use of the phenomenological method is examined next, showing how this connects with situation analysis: the analysis of what those who are responsible for bringing up children are to do. Finally, Levering offers an assessment of Langeveld's relevance for today.

In Chap. 11, 'Zeami's Philosophy of Exercise and Expertise,' Tadashi Nishihira considers certain elements in the thought and practice of Zeami (1363–1443). Commonly acknowledged as a master of traditional Japanese wisdom, Zeami wrote theoretical texts on theatre performance and *Keiko* – which translates as exercise, or the development of expertise, through lessons, practice, or discipline. Nishihira draws attention to the relationship between three processes described in Zeami's texts, all relating to the development of the skill of the actor: (A) the acquisition of skill, that is, the process of construction; (B) the unlearning of skill, that is, the process of deconstruction; and (C) the birth of renewed skill, that is, the process of reconstruction. According to Zeami's text, through this process of reconstruction the actor acquires the perspective of 'double eyes,' which refers to the birth of a new awareness. Nishihira takes Zeami's framework to offer a way of rethinking our current understanding of development and expertise. Postmodern philosophy is often considered to be the philosophy of deconstruction, and the value of 'progress' has, it is said, been completely undermined. In light of such deconstructionist thought, we have to look for a different understanding of 'development.' Nishihira presents Zeami's insight, and the idea of double eyes in particular, as one possible way forward. Double eyes is a defining concept in Eastern philosophy, and it encapsulates the richness of Zeami's theoretical text.

In Chap. 12, '"We Are Alone, and We Are Never Alone": American Transcendentalism and the Political Education of Human Nature,' Naoko Saito discusses the philosophy of Henry D. Thoreau, the nineteenth century American transcendentalist. Thoreau is known as a nature writer. The work by which he is best known, *Walden* (1854), is a record of the time he spent living in the woods at Walden Pond, a period of nearly two years. Lawrence Buell, in his *The Environmental Imagination: Thoreau, Nature Writings, and the Formation of American Culture* (1995) presents Thoreau's view on nature from the perspective of environmentalism and in the light of its implications for nature politics. Its underlying assumption is of a dichotomous picture between, on the one hand, the natural and the biological, and, on the other, the social, the cultural, and the conventional. A shift is called for, Buell claims, from homocentrism to biocentrism. Saito's discussion questions this Buellian politics of the environment and tries to destabilize its assumptions of coexistence between man and nature. In order to show why this is problematic and to present an alternative vision of environmentalism and political education, she discusses Stanley Cavell's reading of Thoreau, a reading conditioned by ordinary language philosophy. Cavell's Thoreau redirects the reader away from biocentrism and towards humanism, and provocatively turns political education away from anodyne aspirations concerning coexistence and towards a qualified acceptance of isolation. Political education is then seen as a matter of learning how to be a 'neighbour,' of nature and other people, bridging the private and the public – a political education for the perfection of human nature. To be a neighbour in this sense, Saito argues, asks for something other than mere coexistence. These are matters of obvious relevance to the Kyoto School.

In Chap. 13, 'Whitehead on the "Rhythm of Education" and Kitaro Nishida's "Pure Experience" as a Developing Whole,' Steve Odin uses the philosophy of education developed by Alfred North Whitehead as a framework by which to illuminate the idea of 'pure experience' articulated by Nishida. A consideration of Whitehead's idea of mental cultivation through a 'rhythm of education' in three phases provides the basis of an interpretation of Nishida's concept of pure experience as a threefold developing system of consciousness. Using the contemporary Japanese scholarship of Kunitsugu Kosaka, Odin then argues that, for Nishida, pure experience is a self-developing system of consciousness that unfolds by a Hegelian dialectical process consisting of three moments. According to Kosaka, Nishida's Zen-tinged concept of pure experience as a spontaneously developing system of consciousness unfolds in three dialectical stages. Odin goes on to emphasize how, for both Whitehead and Nishida, the development of consciousness in three moments itself culminates in practical wisdom as the *use* of knowledge in everyday life, thereby establishing a *continuity of action and knowledge*. Finally, the point is underscored that, for both Whitehead and Nishida, mental cultivation is aimed toward practical wisdom as an awakening to the vivid qualitative flow of pure or immediate experience, itself functioning as the unifying source of all value-realization in ordinary experience of everyday life, including all cognitive as well as aesthetic, moral and religious values.

Lynda Stone's 'A Different Road: The Life and Writings of Soseki Natsume as a Struggle for Modern Accommodation', Chap. 14 of the volume, extends the focus of our concerns but in such a way as to provide a broader context for issues and themes that recur in these essays. Her discussion begins with reference to a woodblock print by the modern master, Un'ichi Hiratsuka. This sets the scene for a reflection on the writings of Soseki's exploration in his novels of the profound changes Japan underwent during the Meiji restoration. She examines especially the figures of the teacher in Soseki's work, the theme with which we started, and through these brings out such matters as accommodation and the semblance of a Western lifestyle, shifts in generational relationships, and tensions between urban and rural life. Her reading is oriented by questions concerning the reception of other cultures that are plainly central to the ambitions of this book.

In Chap. 15, 'Negativity, Experience and Transformation: Educational Possibilities at the Margins of Experience—Insights from the German Traditions of Philosophy of Education,' Andrea English discusses the idea of negativity and human experience. The negativity of experience arises in our encounters with difference and otherness, and locates the moments in which we begin to learn from disillusionment, struggle and suffering. The questions that English asks in this paper relate to the difficulties and possibilities surrounding the relationship between the self and the other in education. How does the learner experience the world and learn to interact with other human beings? What is the teacher's role in the learner's process of experiencing and learning about the world? Can and should the teacher guide or even *interrupt* this process? Here, English seeks to answer these questions by examining the educational meaning of negativity, especially to the extent that this plays a constitutive role in transformational encounters between the self and the other. To do this, English turns to the German traditions of philosophy of education. As she seeks to show, the discourse in German educational philosophy in the nineteenth and twentieth centuries, and in its more recent developments, provides fruitful grounds for furthering the conversation around cross-cultural concerns about education. In looking to the future of cross-cultural dialogue on this topic, English discusses the indispensable need for inquiry into how we might continue theoretically and practically to approach negativity as a permanent blind spot that marks human experience.

A further paper by Satoji Yano constitutes the final chapter of the collection. In 'The Sense of Indebtedness to the Dead, Education as Gift Giving: Tasks and Limits of Post-War Pedagogy,' he attempts to elucidate the underlying force that has been driving post-war pedagogy in Japan by bringing together two perspectives: first, the 'theory of the gift,' and second, the idea of a communal indebtedness to the dead. It is argued that the giving of gifts brings about an experience of dissolution: the codes of community based on utility are disturbed. Yet such practices restore the sense of solidarity and fraternal love among the members of a nation as a community: they can intensify devotion to the nation state as a historical reality, understood as transcending the finite life of the individual. With the acknowledgement of this there arises the sense of indebtedness. Yano considers post-war education and pedagogy that has been influenced by this sense of indebtedness to the dead from the perspective of 'gift giving as an event', culminating in a reflection on the impossibility and possibility of education as gift-giving.

\* \* \* \* \* \* \* \* \* \* \* \* \* \* \* \*

This book has grown in part out of initiatives taken in Kyoto. In 2008 a symposium on the Kyoto School took place as part of the biennial conference of the International Network of Philosophers of Education. In 2009 further papers were presented at a research colloquium involving members of the Institute of Education, London, and the Graduate School of Education, Kyoto University, with Nara Women's University. We are grateful to those who participated on these occasions. We would also like to thank our other contributors, all of whom showed enthusiasm in being recruited to this project, as well as Jan Masschelein and Lynda Stone, the series editors, for their encouragement in taking this forward to publication.

# References

Heisig, J. (2001). *Philosophers of nothingness*. Honolulu: University of Hawai'i Press.
Maraldo, J. (2005). *Obei no shiten kara mita Kyotogakuha no yurai to yukue* [The whence and whither of the Kyoto School from a Western perspective] (A. Yurika, Trans.) (pp. 31–56). Fujita/Davis 2005.
Ohashi, R. (Ed.). (2004). *Kyotogakuha no shiso* [The thought of the Kyoto School]. Kyoto: Jinbunshoin. (Contains five chapters that critically examine past and present images of the 'Kyoto School,' and seven chapters that explore the potential of Kyoto School thought in various areas of contemporary philosophy.)
Parkes, G. (Ed.). (1987). *Heidegger and Asian thought*. Honolulu: University of Hawaii Press.
Parkes, G. (1991). Early reception of Nietzsche's philosophy in Japan. In G. Parkes (Ed.), *Nietzsche and Asian thought*. Chicago: Chicago University Press.
Rigsby, C. A. (2010). Nishida on Heidegger. *Continental Philosophy Review, 42*(4), 511–553.
Sakai, N. (1997). *Translation and subjectivity: On 'Japan' and cultural nationalism*. Minneapolis: University of Minnesota Press.

# Part I
# Thinking of Education in the Kyoto School of Philosophy

# Chapter 2
# Pure Experience and Transcendence Down

**Paul Standish**

Where are we to begin? Let me begin with some aspects of the philosophy of Kitaro Nishida, which, it seems to me, cannot fail to be of importance for education. Nishida's thought is not readily amenable to the tidy divisions to which at least analytical Western philosophy is drawn – say, between ethics and epistemology, or ontology and metaphysics, or between philosophy and religion. Indeed, it is Nishida's view that philosophy is to be understood in terms of a unification of the sciences and of the unifying power of the true, the good, and the beautiful. His originality is commonly taken to lie in the way that he brought a distinctively Japanese element – deriving from Buddhism in certain respects – to his scholarship and engagement in Western philosophy. His connections with and commitment to Buddhism can easily be misrepresented, however, while his immersion in the philosophical literature of the West can scarcely be denied. As an *entrée* into the questions that concern us, and bearing in mind these reservations, I propose to concentrate on Nishida's philosophy of mind. Inevitably this brief exploration will extend beyond this initial intent.

## Mind, Matter, and the Methodology of Doubt

Nishida addresses the familiar question of how thought relates to things in the world. Is the mind a blank slate (*tabula rasa*) upon which things make their impressions, as the (philosophical) empiricist says? Or do things exist as things only insofar as they are perceived: *esse est percipi* (to be is to be perceived), as the (philosophical) idealist

P. Standish (✉)
Institute of Education, University of London, 20 Bedford Way,
WC1H 0AL London, UK
e-mail: p.standish@ioe.ac.uk

P. Standish and N. Saito (eds.), *Education and the Kyoto School of Philosophy*,
Contemporary Philosophies and Theories in Education 1,
DOI 10.1007/978-94-007-4047-1_2, © Springer Science+Business Media Dordrecht 2012

says. Nishida's objection to both of these explanations is that they assume too much. He writes: 'To understand true reality and to know the true nature of the universe and human life, we must discard all artificial assumptions, doubt whatever can be doubted, and proceed on the basis of direct and indubitable knowledge' (Nishida 1990, p. 38). This still falls short, however, of the critical thinking that is needed:

> Highly critical thinking, which discards all arbitrary assumptions and starts from the most certain, direct knowledge, and thinking that assumes a reality outside the facts of direct experience are in no way compatible. Even such great philosophers as Locke and Kant fail to escape the contradiction between these two kinds of thinking. I intend to abandon all hypothetical thought and to engage in what I call critical thought. When we survey the history of philosophy, we see that Berkeley and Fichte also take this approach (p. 42).

We tend to believe, he argues, that there are two types of experiential facts – phenomena of consciousness and phenomena of matter – but actually there is only one: phenomena of consciousness. This remark might make us think that he must be committed to a kind of idealism. But in fact his position is different, for the idealist tends to posit, without evidence, that there is a thinking being that has these thoughts, whereas in fact all we can be sure of is that there is experience. The idea of a thinking being is an assumption we make on the basis of this experience, but this assumption leads us astray. Hence, adopting a term previously used by the philosopher-psychologists Wilhelm Wundt and William James, he claims that we need a philosophy based on 'pure experience': 'In pure experience, our thinking, feeling, and willing are still undivided; there is a single activity, with no opposition between subject and object' (p. 48). Contrary, then, to the view that subject and object are realities that can exist independently of each other and that phenomena of consciousness arise through their interaction, Nishida tries to show that there are not two realities, mind and matter, but only one. Subject and object must then be understood as abstractions from pure experience, and it is failure to realise this that leads to pervasive errors in our thinking: 'Taking the distinction between subject and object as fundamental, some think that objective elements are included only in knowledge and that idiosyncratic, subjective events constitute feeling and volition. This view is mistaken in its basic assumptions' (p. 50). Any belief that there must be a realm of hard empirical fact rests upon dichotomisations that are not inherent in the fact itself: 'As a concrete fact, a flower is not at all like the purely material flower of scientists; it is pleasing, with a beauty of color, shape, and scent. Heine gazed at the stars in a quiet night sky and called them golden tacks in the azure. Though astronomers would laugh at his words as the folly of a poet, the true nature of stars may well be expressed in his phrase' (p. 49).

In the above quotation it was said that thinking, feeling, and willing are one. The reason for this is that experience is always in a state of activity, even in its apparently more passive forms. That is to say that it is always motivated by some interest in which the will is operative. Hence, there is always an activity of will through which both the subject of consciousness and its object come into being, and this will is not a purely personal thing. This tells us something about the self too. When I think of myself as something to question (Who am I? What kind of person am I?), the thing that we think of as the self is in fact false. The reflective self is not the true self because the reflective self does not act. By contrast the self that matters is what is realised in pure experience. The will is the activity that most clearly expresses the self, and it is in the action of the will that we are most clearly conscious of ourselves (p. 91), but, if I have understood this right, this is not a *self*-consciousness in the familiar sense: it is more like an absorption in what we are doing.

## Philosophy as Usual?

It is important that this is understood not just in terms of epistemology (of how we come to know things) but as an account of reality itself, for this is Nishida's sustained purpose. But up to this point, I want to suggest, the argument has taken place at a level that is more or less exclusively intellectual, in the familiar terms of Western (especially Anglophone) philosophy. This may constrain our sense of the scope of his project. Perhaps the reference to will and feeling above lead beyond these terms, to something different in the name of philosophy. To turn in this direction then is to try to see how the influence of Buddhism – which surely must be thought of not just as a set of ideas but as a practice, a way of life – leads beyond these intellectualist confines.

I do not mean to exaggerate this intellectualism in the Western philosophical tradition, for plainly there are thinkers whose work escapes its bounds. Even in so austere a work as the *Tractatus Logico-Philosophicus*, we find Wittgenstein saying that 'The world of the happy man is a different one from that of the happy man' (Wittgenstein 1961, 6.43), a thought that closely matches Nishida's reminder to us that 'Buddhist thought holds that according to one's mood the world becomes either heaven or hell' (Nishida 1990, 6.43). And there is a robust tradition that, since classical Greece at least, has understood philosophy as a way of life. But there is a narrowing, professionalization of philosophy in the modern period, supported by the growth of universities, that inhibits this broader development. (Perhaps this is particularly an English disease.) It may be significant in this respect that, during the latter part of the Meiji era, interest in Japan moved away from English philosophers such as John Stuart Mill and towards their contemporaries in Germany.

The influence on Nishida in this respect is more evident still where he speaks of nature's relation to spirit (*seishin*, *Geist*, spirit/mind/psyche). Nature cannot be objectively independent of spirit but must involve a union of our senses of sight, touch, and so forth. And – as if following Schopenhauer – nature cannot be understood independently of the will. The basis of the infinite activity that is spirit and nature is what Nishida calls 'God'. He has no time either for 'infantile' conceptions of a god who stands outside and somehow controls the world, or for hard-headed materialists who take material force as the basis for the universe, but he identifies his thought rather with the negative theology of Nicholas of Cusa (1401–1464).

Bearing in mind the inseparability of religion and philosophy in Buddhism, it is perhaps not surprising that the religious continues to be prominent in the subsequent development of Nishida's thought. In the paragraphs that follow, which relate his work more directly to currents in twentieth century Western philosophy, I want to gesture towards the questions of transcendence, nothingness, silence, and place (in Nishida: *basho*, sometimes translated as 'locus') that run through his work, knowing that other contributors to this volume are better qualified than I am to discuss these matters directly. But before this, something should be said about his philosophy as a philosophy of nothingness.

Whereas in the West being has been taken to be the ground of reality, the East, Nishida observes, seems to have taken nothingness as its ground. What can this mean? This, no doubt, is an elusive idea – yet it is as well to remember that the idea of being as ground is itself also one that is difficult to grasp. (It is arguable that a preoccupation with ontology is pervasive, but it is foregrounded only in a particular philosophical tradition.) Nishida begins, as we have seen, by seeking to overcome (to render as nothing) the self that imagines itself to be a subject perceiving the objects of the world. Later, however, he comes to think of this in more radical terms, as something that surpasses any thought of coming to be or ceasing, as an absolute that escapes any relativisation, any defining opposition. In my remarks about place below I shall try to make this more clear. It should be said, however, as was acknowledged at the start, that Nishida's thinking here is not governed solely by ideas drawn from Zen Buddhism, however powerful its resonances may seem.

Let me turn to some connections with Western thought to try to say something more about these matters.

## Nishida and the West

The sketch of Nishida's philosophy of mind in the previous section suggested some fairly obvious lines of influence that he drew from his scholarship in Western philosophy, as well as pointing to aspects of his departure from this and to his originality. That originality can be brought out by comparison with two Western philosophers of immense influence, in whose work we find connections with the themes mentioned above: Martin Heidegger (1889–1976) and Jacques Derrida (1930–2004). Let me first say something briefly about the strong connections of Heidegger with Japan.

Nishida read *Sein und Zeit* (*Being and Time*) soon after its publication in 1927, but evidently he was critical in various ways.[1] At one level this seems surprising as both philosophers are centrally concerned with overcoming the subject-object dichotomisation that has characterised so much of Western thought, and in some respects Nishida's emphasis on pure experience seems to resonate with Heidegger's insistence that the unified structure of being-in-the-world is fundamental. The difference

---

[1] See Rigsby (2010) for a rich discussion, which includes extracts from fascinating correspondence between Nishida and other members of the Kyoto School as well as exploring important connections with the work of Karl Barth.

is in part to do with Heidegger's preoccupation with the question of being (that is, of Being rather than beings, of *Sein* rather than *Seiendes*). It is worth drawing attention, nevertheless, to the fact that Heidegger's book was generally received with understanding and enthusiasm in Japan. Yet Nishida is especially critical of Heidegger's conception of nothingness, which, insofar as it is not understood in terms of God, renders his accounts of *Angst* superficial. And he was alert to and critical of the ethnocentric (and Eurocentric) tendencies in Heidegger's thought and actions. It needs to be remembered, however, that there were six translations of *Sein und Zeit* into Japanese before the first translation into English, in 1962, and a steady stream of Japanese scholars visited Heidegger in the years that followed the book's publication. For his part, Heidegger greatly appreciated this reception, believing, it seems, that his work had found in Japan an audience capable of reading it well. Moreover, in his 'Dialogue with a Japanese', he eulogised the Japanese way of life and thought (and the Japanese language), seeing it as offering a real alternative to the degradation of the West (of the English-speaking world in particular), whose thought had been progressively colonised by technology.

It is against this backdrop that I turn first to the consideration of questions of space and place.

## Nothingness and Place

It is not until Heidegger's later writings that his ideas in this respect are most fully developed. While *Being and Time* gives a strong sense of the contextual, holistic nature of being-in-the-world, it is with the later idea of the Fourfold (*Vierung*) that this is elaborated in a more striking way. Heidegger adopts the idea of the Fourfold partly in the move away from his earlier direct enquiry into the nature of Being. The Fourfold is to be understood in terms of four forces or influences that condition our experience, whose crossing might be thought of a characteristic of the places in which we find ourselves. Places, to be sure, are not geometrical spaces, to be identified by points on a grid, but constructed rather out of meaningful relations. The Fourfold comprises *earth*, *sky*, *gods*, and *mortals*. The earth is to be understood in terms of our need for sustenance: it is where we plant our feet and lay down to rest; it is the source of our daily food and shelter. The sky refers to the changeable circumstances of human lives, including the changing seasons and the way these affect us, but extending also to our own vulnerability to moods. The gods represent not personified deities but rather those higher aspirations by which we are drawn, those things that lead us to think beyond the satisfaction of our needs. That we are mortals perhaps speaks for itself, though it is important to situate this in relation to Heidegger's earlier writings about our being-towards-death as an existential structure of our lives. We live our lives (at some level and no doubt intermittently) in the knowledge that we shall die, in a way that animals do not: animals are not mortal; they merely expire. And this awareness of our own mortality casts its shadow back across our lives as a whole. Hence, in speaking of the *crossing* of this Fourfold,

Heidegger is echoing the Christian idea that we live our lives under the sign of the cross, but he is turning this to non-Christian purposes. The Fourfold is not to be understood as referring to some special state that we occasionally reach but as applicable to each and every circumstance in which we find ourselves. Looking at your life and circumstances in this way helps, for example, to show the gods you are serving. This helps us to understand the places where we are.

Insofar as the Fourfold is a means of thinking about place, I want to contrast it with Derrida's pondering of Plato's *Timaeus* in his text entitled *Khora*, a term that recurs in the Plato dialogue. The Greek word *khora* is difficult to translate: at one level it means 'place', but it also means 'womb', and so carries a suggestion of referring not just to *this* place as against *that* place but rather to the origin of place and space themselves. Plato's dialogue is in part a cosmology in which precisely such things as the origins of place and space and world are at issue. Derrida is interested by the possibility of thinking of something that must lie behind or condition space and place as these are understood, in our common lives and in our philosophy.

While Heidegger's conception of the Fourfold might perhaps be taken to suggest an occupying of space and place without remainder, where all terms are positive, Derrida's account in *Khora* might conceivably convey something closer to the nothingness behind being that Nishida seeks to reveal. I offer this only as tentative remark, but let me support the view a little further by referring to one of Derrida's last works, his *Paper Machine* (2005), published in French in 2002. In *Paper Machine* Derrida pays much attention to the significance of documents in identifying us, especially in the light of the situation of those who are 'without papers' (such as asylum-seekers). But he presses the ideas here to deeper questions about the nature of writing, in documents, books, electronic devices. What, he asks, is the support for writing, by which he means, what is it that writing is on – the paper, the stone, the screen? This attention to what supports writing parallels, I believe, his concerns with what it is that supports or lies behind space and place, a groundless ground, a support without foundations.

If this thought seems a little strained, let us relate it to a contrast between Western and Japanese art. Whereas the Western painter tends to populate the canvass, covering it in every part, even decorating the frame, in Japanese art the image lies, as it were, floating against a paper background that has not been worked, that is nothing, but that is the support for the image. Does this begin to connect with the philosophy of place in Nishida?

## Language, Silence, and Transcendence

Let me digress here to say that, when I have been in Japan, I have often found myself defending a view to the effect that language conditions human being, in a way that has been found too 'Western'. Given the ways in which Buddhism (and perhaps Eastern thought more generally) seeks to move beyond language, this reaction is understandable. But I have not wanted to be a defender of the talkativeness of the West! The point, as far as I am concerned, is a more logical one: it is the Wittgensteinian one to the effect that initiation into language goes hand-in-hand with initiation into a community, and without this a human life is not possible (except in a merely biological sense). This is not at all to advocate talkativeness, any more than it is to disparage silence. Heidegger helps here when he says that '*Hearing* and *keeping silent* [*Schweigen*] are possibilities belonging to discursive speech' (Heidegger 1962, H. 161). This is so in the sense that animals cannot *keep* silent; they cannot refrain from speech. So my view is that *practices* of silence need to be understood as possible only for the being that has language.

As will become apparent in the following section of this discussion, a doubt that I have sometimes felt in discussions of the Kyoto School in relation to education concerns the way that the idea of pure experience, which is prominent in Nishida's earlier work, comes somehow to be associated with a notion of transcendence with connotations of purity of a rather different kind. If a purification of experience were Nishida's concern, this would surely be in tension with the more intellectually confined notion of pure experience, where this was deployed to resist the positions of the empiricist and the idealist, identified in the section 'Mind, Matter, and the Methodology of Doubt' above. There is a slipperiness about this term, I think, especially given the further associations with Pure Land Buddhism (*Jodo Shu*). Nishida moved away from the use of this term quite early on, but he develops his account of transcendence, and I think this is important for those who seek to interpret his thought for education. Transcendence is normally associated with a movement upward, toward what is higher, and this has been its dominant connotation, in religious domains of thought and in Western philosophy. I am happy to find that Nishida sometimes speaks of a *transcendence down*, which for me echoes thoughts I have found in Henri David Thoreau and in Stanley Cavell's interpretations of his work. It seems, moreover, that this might usefully be related to deconstruction in Derrida's work, where the unravelling of things simultaneously produces something new, and this continually.

## Possibilities of Becoming: The Aesthetic and the Political

In discussions of the Kyoto School in relation to education it is clear that emphasis is placed on 'becoming' over 'being', and 'transformation' over 'education', and these preferences seem important in resisting notions of fixed stages of maturation and clear teleologies. The prominence that is given by Motomori Kimura (1885–1946),[2] to the individual's loneliness and anxiety seem also a powerful antidote in this respect. Nishida identified his own conception of the human being's relation to the world in terms of *poiesis*. His logic of place (*locus*, *basho*) is especially rich in overcoming Western subject-object dichotomisations, coinciding in certain respects

---

[2] See Takuo Nishimura's discussion in Chap. 6.

with insights from phenomenology, but also providing an account of the background of nothingness that is distinctly Japanese. This, to reiterate the point, is something different from the more existential thematisation of nothingness in Heidegger, but perhaps closer to Jacques Derrida's explorations, in *Khora*, of aspects of Plato's *Timaeus*.

But there are still, in the philosophy of education derived from the Kyoto School, certain assumptions of progression or development that are in tension with possibilities of transformation. Can a theory of becoming, especially under institutional pressure towards explicit formulation, avoid sliding into claims regarding stages of development? Can it avoid losing sight of the variety of human experience. The contrast I have in mind can be illustrated by the difference between the Great Doubt, in Buddhism, which involves passing through a series of stages on the way to enlightenment, and scepticism as this is explored in the work of Stanley Cavell, which sees the human tendency *continually* to call the conditions of being into doubt as inherent to the human condition. So my question to the exponents of this philosophy of education has been whether they retain a quest for foundations.

In relation to Nishida's 'active intuition' and the kind of pure experience found in intense concentration (e.g., in a piano recital), Shoko Suzuki makes the remark: 'It is as though one were making a decision with absolute confidence in the face of abiding ambiguity. In other words, it is as though the action of intuition arises by the diffusion of knowledge through the body.'[3] This may connect in certain respects with the idea of 'flow' or of being 'in the zone', as the basketball coach puts it. Nevertheless, the formulation here is a much richer evocation of the idea.

Is such a state of being, however, something we should always aspire to? My concern is with what such moments may block? Is there not an 'impurity' of experience that is inherent in the human condition, lived as it is with others with diverse purposes, and vulnerable as it is to our own irritability? Should we really transcend the messiness of human life? Do Nishida's remarks about a transcendence that goes *downwards* offer something closer to the kind of return to the ordinary I am suggesting here?

# References

Derrida, J. (2005). *Paper machine* (R. Bowlby, Trans.). Stanford: Stanford University Press.
Heidegger, M. (1962). *Being and time* (J. Macquarrie & E. Robinson, Trans.). New York: Harper and Row.
Nishida, K. (1990) *An inquiry into the good* (M. Abe & C. Ives, Trans.). New Haven/London: Yale University Press.
Rigsby, C. A. (2010). Nishida on Heidegger. *Continental Philosophy Review, 42*(4), 511–553.
Wittgenstein, L. (1961). *Tractatus logico-philosophicus* (D. F. Pears & D. F. McGuiness, Trans.). London: Routledge/Kegan Paul.

---

[3]A remark originally made in the Kyoto School Symposium at the International Network of Philosophers of Education meeting in August 2008.

# Chapter 3
# The Philosophical Anthropology
# of the Kyoto School and Post-War Pedagogy

Satoji Yano

## The Development of Philosophical Anthropology
## in the Kyoto School

This chapter attempts to trace and clarify the development in the Kyoto School of a philosophical anthropology (*philosophische Anthropologie*), specifying in particular the conditions for its inception in the pre-war period under the influence of Kitaro Nishida and Hajime Tanabe, and its post-war maturation. This did not arise out of the reception and interpretation of current strains of philosophical anthropology that prevailed in Germany at that time, such as were led by Max Scheler and Helmut Plessner. Rather, it developed out of the critical rereading of Martin Heidegger, from the perspective of Nishida's and Tanabe's philosophies. Of course, the position vis-à-vis Marxism behind this critical reading must not be overlooked. Indeed it is characteristic of the Kyoto School simultaneously to incorporate and establish a critical position on Marxism, as Nishida and Tanabe tried to do.

This re-reading by the Kyoto School began from what was also a simultaneous sympathy and antipathy to Heidegger. This may sound strange in view of Heidegger's ambivalent remarks about philosophical anthropology in his *Being and Time* (1927) and his more overt criticism in *Kant and the Problems of Metaphysics* (1929). The move into anthropology within the Kyoto School was enabled by Kiyoshi Miki, a disciple of Nishida and a former student of Heidegger, who introduced Heidegger's fundamental ontology to Japan. Miki termed Heidegger's fundamental ontology 'anthropology' and went on to develop, in tension with Marxism, his own original ideas about anthropology. This established a direction in which the Kyoto School was subsequently to develop.

S. Yano (✉)
Graduate School of Education, Kyoto University, 5-16-27, Shimosakamoto,
Otsu-shi, 520-0105 Otsu, Japan
e-mail: s-yano@ares.eonet.ne.jp

P. Standish and N. Saito (eds.), *Education and the Kyoto School of Philosophy*,
Contemporary Philosophies and Theories in Education 1,
DOI 10.1007/978-94-007-4047-1_3, © Springer Science+Business Media Dordrecht 2012

Setting aside for the moment the matter of certain internal philosophical differences, the Kyoto School can be broadly outlined in the following manner. While relying heavily on Heidegger's ontology, it strove also to overcome the individualistic aspects in his work. In particular, the anthropological theory passed down from Nishida to his disciples was that man was not simply a self-aware being, but rather an actively self-aware being (who acts, develops and expresses himself). For Nishida, therefore, the essence of human being lay in 'active self-awareness', 'formational self-awareness' and 'expressive self-awareness'. As man was man only in the context of his society, a merely ontological analysis of the human being was not enough for anthropology as a comprehensive study of man. Accordingly, a holistic understanding of the human being must incorporate the historical and social dimensions of being. In other words, anthropology must pursue an 'ontic-ontological' understanding of human being in general. Theory should be produced through a 'dialectical' approach. The Kyoto School, then, tried to overcome Heidegger's ontology through this dialectic mode of thinking.

The Kyoto School was distinct in its development of a dialectical anthropology based on the ontic-ontological stance towards man as a historical and social agent. Specifically this took the form of 'Japanese anthropology', which focused on community, nation, culture, body, race and history, in contrast to the Western prevailing individualistic and universalising Western approach to anthropology of the time. The Kyoto School can here be divided hypothetically into three elements.

The first element, represented by the work of Miki, entailed research that was based on Heidegger's fundamental ontology but that tried to overcome it as it sought to represent concrete life itself, using 'active nature' as a reference point. This approach was common to the scholars of philosophical anthropology in the Kyoto School.

The second element can be seen in the works of Tetsuro Watsuji, Shuzo Kuki and Iwao Koyama. They called into question the Western ethnocentric framework of anthropology. They conducted a hermeneutic analysis of the specificity of Japanese culture, which they called 'studies of human being through a Japanese lens'. Emphasizing a view of man as 'a socio-historical being', the Kyoto School's attempt to define man in 'ontic-ontological terms' was also a criticism of Western ethnocentrism and Western modernism as well as that of cultural colonialism. Their research was a study of 'Eastern' self-awareness in contrast to 'Western' self-awareness, and moreover, a study of 'Japanese race' and 'Japanese culture' as particular forms of self-awareness within universal humankind. The outcome of that, however, as will be seen in the third element, was inextricably tied to an assertion of tribalism and nationalism, and this created the ideological ground for the call for a 'mission in world history'.

This third element, referred to above, was represented by Iwao Koyama, Kenji Nishitani and Masaki Kosaka, and was called 'the philosophy of world history'. In seeking this theory concerning 'world history' the Kyoto School intersected actively with history. The philosophical motif of the Kyoto School was to extricate itself from the constraints of Western modernism. Expressions such as 'commitment to world history', 'the philosophy of world history', and 'the theory of world history' were used to describe its approach. This discourse of 'world history', entailed, of course, implicit criticism of Western ethnocentrism, with its reverberations through contemporary multiculturalism. A central concern, however, was how to interpret the meaning of the series of international conflicts in which Japan was involved– e.g. the intensification of the Sino-Japanese War and Japan's entry into the Pacific War in conflict with the United States.

The second and third elements can be seen as specific, situational developments of the first element, which grasped 'man as a historical-social being' based upon the 'ontic-ontological position' and according to 'a dialectical logic'. The second element developed an analysis of man according to his lived, social existence, whereas the third element, was concerned with his historical existence.

This synopsis may be somewhat overly paradigmatic, but my intention thus far has been to provide only a basic sketch of the Kyoto School. I will turn now to consider how the Kyoto School turned its attention to the study of education. In particular I want to trace the pre- and post-war development of educational studies, its continuities and discontinuities, in relation to the Kyoto School. Roughly speaking these developments can be said to have taken two particular directions. The first was the emergence of a Japanese pedagogical anthropology (*Pädagogische Anthropologie*) based on the Kyoto School. The seminal post-war work of Akira Mori entitled *Pedagogical Anthropology* (1961) encompassed not only the ontological dimension of becoming (*sei-sei*), but also the socio-historical dimension. This approach would likely not have been possible without the accumulated research of the Kyoto School, including in particular that of Iwao Koyama (1905–1994), as well as the pioneering work on pedagogy in the pre-war period, particularly that of Motomori Kimura (1895–1946). The second direction of development in the post-war period was related to pedagogy, and was heavily influenced by Miki's theory of technique.[1] For example, Mantaro Kido's educational thought was strongly influenced by Miki's theory of technique and co-operativism, which was an attempt to make sense of Japan's involvement in the war, and was passed on as a legitimate paradigm after the war. Both developments share the influence of the Kyoto School, which enabled continuity of thought between the pre-war and post-war periods in educational studies and the development and appropriation of this thought from diverse perspectives.

## The Development of the Kyoto School's 'Pedagogical Anthropology'

### *Motomori Kimura's Pedagogical Plan*

In discussing the relationship between the Kyoto School and pedagogy, it is appropriate to begin with a reference to Motomori Kimura. Kimura's contribution to pedagogy had a profound influence on the philosophical anthropology of the

---

[1] 'Technique' for Miki means a kind of logic which involves the dynamic process of creation and transformation of forms. In this sense, 'technique' is the process of becoming (*Sei-sei*) through continuous interaction.

Kyoto School. In 1933 he was requested by Nishida to move from Hiroshima University of Literature and Science to Kyoto Imperial University to assume a post in pedagogy as a successor to Sigenao Konishi. It seems that Kimura was not altogether enthralled at the prospect of relinquishing his work in aesthetics to focus on pedagogy. However, he went on to transfer the particular intellectual orientation he had cultivated in the study of aesthetics to his new field concerned with the formation of human being.

Using the notion of *poiesis*, which was central to Kimura's research in aesthetics, he understood essential human nature as either 'formative awareness' or 'expressive awareness'. In the introduction to Kimura's work entitled *Formative Awareness* (*Keiseiteki Jikaku*) (1941), he states succinctly the task of the book to be as follows:

> What, especially, is the existence called man? It is an existence that expresses itself formatively, and by so doing acquires concrete awareness of itself. By taking this position, in this book, I endeavor to ascertain the essential and ultimate meaning of culture and education through an attempt at unearthing formative awareness and expressive awareness. (Kimura 1941, p. 1)[2]

Kimura's formative awareness/expressive awareness was nearly identical in logical structure to Miki's behavioral awareness, which punctuated his view of man in his philosophical anthropology. Miki used the term 'behavior' in the same way as Kimura used his terms 'expression' and 'formation.' The unification of 'awareness' with 'behavior-expression-formation', while holding slightly different nuances according to each researcher, can be said to constitute the core of the Kyoto School's understanding of fundamental human nature.

It is also important point to indicate the particular manner in which Kimura developed his theory. Kimura posited an anthropological question: 'Just what kind of existence is man?' and subsequently answered his own question very succinctly: 'Man is that being which expresses himself in a formative manner, and by so doing who possesses concrete awareness.' This can be viewed as Kimura's definition of man as a response to his own anthropological question. Furthermore, this definition can be divided into two parts: the first component of 'formative self-expression' and the subsequent component of 'possessing concrete awareness'. While the concepts 'expression' and 'awareness' complemented each other, they were not identical. This relation was to be comprehensively termed 'formative awareness' or, alternatively, 'expressive awareness.' From this anthropological vantage point, Kimura attempted to investigate 'culture and education'. It is important here to note the juxtaposition of the two subjects. Rather than considering education as an independent entity, Kimura tied education to culture in the course of his investigation. This approach was likely to have been influenced by German ideas of cultural pedagogy (*Kulturpädagogik*) current at that time; yet Kimura transcended this influence to establish his own particular view of education. Kimura's masterpiece *Culture and Education Within the Nation State* (*Kokka ni okeru Bunka to Kyoiku*) (1946) was

---

[2]Unless otherwise indicated, translations from the Japanese are by the Editors.

published as a book shortly after his death, although the manuscript had been published in separate parts during the war years. As the title suggests, Kimura structured the description of the relationship between 'culture' and 'education' around the central theme of the 'nation.' This mode of questioning 'culture' and 'education' as a pair paralleled the coupling of ideas (formative and expressive awareness) of *Formative Awareness*. In *Culture and Education Within the Nation State*, the relationship between 'culture' and 'education' became clear in the light of 'expressive awareness'.

> While morals and arts and other academic disciplines are the self-aware developments of fundamental principles of historical life in their respective forms, philosophy is the awareness of awareness, as reflective awareness of these self-aware developments. In this sense, philosophy is an ultimate form of awareness. Historical life, which is intrinsically an existence with formative and expressive awareness, manifests through education its function of active self formation – one which within itself cultivates the basis of objective self formation. If so then, it should be thought that education in itself means an ultimate form of formative awareness in such formative and self-aware life. Suppose the essential meaning of man's cultural activities as a self-aware individual should consist in being in the absolute life, and in shedding light on such life from within and helping and cultivating it in a self-aware way. Then, education that aims to cultivate such a self-aware individual is nothing other than an ultimate form of formative awareness, one that helps and cultivates what helps the cultivation of heaven and earth. (Kimura 1946, pp. 123–124)

The above passage requires further explanation, which in the original Japanese is a sentence of no less than 250 characters. One must first pay attention to the fact that the agent of the self-aware development of culture was neither the individual nor mankind but rather 'Absolute Life', which at the same time was also 'Historical Life' as well as the 'self-aware individual'. The 'self-aware individual' was contained within 'Absolute Life' and assisted in the self-aware formative awareness of 'Historical Life'. However, these three – 'Absolute Life', 'Historical Life' and the 'Self-aware individual' – were not considered as separate entities: they were simply different manifestations of the single movement of formative and expressive awareness. 'Culture', understood in terms of nationality and ethnicity, was the self-aware development of this three-layered agent. Furthermore, 'education' was a work of promoting self-aware development of culture by cultivating a self-aware individual. In other words, education was a thorough development of the work of culture (which is formative awareness). Kimura concluded the work of education to be that which 'helps and cultivate what helps the cultivation of heaven and earth'. This was derived from an idea in the *Doctrine of the Mean* (*Chuyo*), and yet at the same time, Kimura also sought to correspond to Nishida's essay, 'On Pedagogy', – his one and only writing on pedagogy.[3]

---

[3] In this paper, Nishida distinguished pedagogy from studies on law and norms, and identified it as an equivalent to aesthetics, that is, a study on the agency of creation and formation. Furthermore, by referring to education as 'a kind of a formative agency' (Nishida 1933, p. 87), he quoted from the 'Doctrine of the Mean', and said that the mission of an educator was 'to help to cultivate what helps the cultivation of heaven and earth' (p. 92). This article by Nishida is sometimes interpreted as one that was addressed to Kimura who was contemplating a move from aesthetics to pedagogy. In that sense, Kimura's *Culture and Education Within the Nation State* (*Kokka ni okeru Bunka to Kyoiku*) can be considered a reply to this article by Nishida.

How, then, was the connection between culture and education 'within the context of the nation state', to be evaluated? Kimura, like his Kyoto School colleagues, appraised the role of species as a mediator between genus and individual in the dialectics of nothingness (*mu*). This corresponded to the relationship between 'Absolute Life', 'Historical Life' and the 'Self-aware individual' as discussed above. The conjoining of 'mankind' and 'individual' was abstract: and it was held that the concreteness of human being was first concretized through the mediation of 'race' and 'nation', which intermediated genus and individual.

A key term in Kimura's theory of national education (*kokumin-kyoiku*) was 'world historical nationhood', with clear echoes of the idea of 'world historical position' as propounded by Koyama (1942). This can be said to correspond to the issue raised with reference to the third aspect of the Kyoto School discussed earlier. For example, in Kimura's *National Polity and Civilization* (*Kokumin to Kyoyo*), Kimura made the following statement:

> If national culture as an individualized form exists in its relation to world historical univer-
> sality as mentioned above, must it not be admitted that the way that it displays truly its
> existence in principle has two facets? The first is the enhancement of the world historical
> mediating effect of one's own national culture. But the fact that a national culture can in this
> way enhance world historical meaning must depend on the depth of individual value that is
> inherent in it. The depth of world history disclosed by national and individual value for the first
> time gives an objective basis of vitality in trans-national interaction. (Kimura 1939, p. 200)

In this way, Kimura dialectically conjoined 'national culture' as individual and 'world historical universality'. The latter part of the above passage – namely, 'the depth of world history disclosed by national and individual value' – specifically meant a descent into the nadir of tradition. As Kimura's argument was highly abstract and was tightly constructed, it may be difficult to imagine what it specifically implied for the practice of education: but upon remembering that his discourse was crafted during the war years, the meaning implied in the passage above should become more readily intelligible. Kimura's pedagogy signified the consummation of pedagogy (or pedagogical anthropology) based upon the pre-war Kyoto School. But can this educational thought deal with 'the other'? Can the world historical nation truly construct an equal relation to another nation? This is the question to be raised in connection with how to appraise the 'world historical position' that manifested itself in the third aspect of the Kyoto School.

## The Establishment of the Kyoto School and Post-War Pedagogical Anthropology

### *The Post-War Perspective of the Kyoto School as Expressed by Akira Mori's Pedagogical Anthropology*

Akira Mori is a representative figure in the post-war development of the Kyoto School from its pre-war form. Barely any consideration has been given to the influence of the Kyoto School on Mori's thought, however, as the following remark by Hiromichi Ueno suggests:

Mori's work was based upon the studies in German philosophy of education of Kant and Jaspers and upon the achievements of the empirical sciences oriented by research on Dewey's philosophy. It gave a sharp criticism to the speculative mode of studies in philosophy of education, one that was preoccupied by welcoming and exhibiting foreign theories of pedagogy. Instead it aimed to pursue the goal and essence of education by connecting itself with concrete realities in education. (Ueno 1991, p. 514)

This understanding may seem reasonable, as verified by Mori's own work. Mori, who consciously strove to construct an pedagogical anthropology, absorbed the influences of Karl Jaspers' post-war existential philosophy and John Dewey's educational thought, struggling to find their common ground. He then published a book, *The Practicality and Interiority of Education* (*Kyoiku no Jissensei to Naimensai*) (1978/1955). The fact that the main subjects of discourse in this text were Dewey, Kant, Scheler, Jaspers, Heidegger, and others, may give us the impression that Mori's study of the Kyoto School was left in the past. As one reads the text, however, it becomes evident that Mori, in addition to those thinkers mentioned above, makes wide-ranging and thorough reference to the thinkers of the Kyoto School, discussing philosophers such as Motomori Kimura, Masaaki Kousaka, Shuzo Kuki, Matao Noda, Keiji Nishitani, Iwao Koyama, Tetsuro Watsuji, Hajime Tanabe, Seiichi Hatano, Risaku Mutai, Kiyoshi Miki, among others. But more importantly, Mori did not only refer to their work: the very framework in which the book is written is structured around the Kyoto School.

So what was the nature of this triangular relationship between Dewey's philosophy, German philosophy and the Kyoto School? A key to answering that question is found in the central concept for the Kyoto School, 'awareness', which occupied a prominent position in Mori's text. Mori's establishment of 'practicality and interiority' as a subject of inquiry was itself, as seen in Kimura's idea of 'formative awareness', a subject dealt with by the pre-war Kyoto School philosophers. Furthermore, the construction of a theory – one in which nature, society, culture and personality were understood as dialectically unified in the process of human becoming (*Sei-sei*) – had already been achieved in Iwao Kouyama's (1938) *Philosophical Anthropology* written by Koyama. With these points in mind, the pre-war Kyoto School's philosophical framework was evidently underlying Mori's thinking.

Mori's *Practicality and Interiority of Education* included an appendix was included entitled 'Vision of Pedagogical Anthropology' ('Kyoiku-Ningengaku no Koso'), which began by featuring Koyama *Philosophical Anthropology* along with Dewey's and Scheler's philosophies. The book is, in short, a juxtaposition of the three schools of philosophy: Dewey's philosophy, German philosophy, and the Kyoto School. From this, it is quite evident that the formation of Mori's pedagogical anthropology took shape within the context of the rich interaction between these three schools of thought. Mori did not take up the ideas of the Kyoto School unquestioningly, however:

Japan has Iwao Koyama highly reputed book, *Philosophical Anthropology*. However, this book conducts an investigation into what might be called a genealogical structure of human being and it does not give adequate attention to the ontogenetic development of human being. Neither does it explore thoroughly the psycho-physical quality of human organs. Therefore it cannot be applied as it stands to *pedagogical* anthropology. (Mori 1978/1955, pp. 237–238, italics added)

Mori was not rejecting Koyama's *Philosophical Anthropology*. Indeed, Mori was envisioning an pedagogical anthropology along the lines of Koyama's ideas. However, the Kyoto School did not integrate the discoveries of the empirical sciences, particularly psychology and physiology, into its thought. Mori, however, supplemented the achievement of Koyama's philosophical anthropology by incorporating the latest findings of the empirical sciences of the time. And while constructing an anthropology that fully investigated the 'ontogenetic development' and 'psycho-physical quality of human organisms', instead of a genealogical account of human being, Mori tried to construct a viable theory of pedagogical anthropology. This effort materialized in the publication in 1961 of the 846-page *Pedagogical Anthropology: Education as Human Becoming (Kyoiku-Ningengaku: Ningen-Seisei toshite no Kyoiku)*.

## *Visions of Pedagogical Anthropology and* The Original Theory of Human Formation

In *Educational Anthropology: Education as Human Becoming* [*Kyoiku-Nigengaku: Ningen-seisei to shiteno Kyotiku*] (1978/1961), Mori, on the one hand, clarified the various scientific findings of that time to reveal an account of the nature of human becoming based not only upon pedagogy but also upon such empirical sciences as philosophy, sociology, psychology, and biology. He did this through an integrative observation of human education from the standpoint of human becoming. On the other hand, from the standpoint of human becoming, he dialectically integrated the currents in philosophical thought of that time, namely pragmatism, philosophy of life (*Lebensphilosophie*), existentialism and Marxism. He sought to construct a systematic theory of educational anthropology as a theory of human becoming. Mori's vision of pedagogical anthropology did not mirror the hierarchical view of human beings found in Schelerian thought: rather it based itself on a holistic perspective of anthropology. This was redolent of the vision put forth in Iwao Koyama's book, *Philosophical Anthropology*, in which various philosophical world views dynamically unfolded.

Following the systematic *Educational Anthropology*, the unfinished manuscript entitled *The Original Theory of Human Formation* (*published posthumously in 1977*) was crafted with an understanding of time from the viewpoint of the person living in the actual moment (of here and now). Unlike *Educational Anthropology*, which was a complete systematic and comprehensive account addressing diverse viewpoints, *The Original Theory of Human Formation* was incomplete, fragmentary and limited in its scope. This indicated a substantial shift and not merely a formal difference.

In *The Original Theory of Human Formation*, Mori interpreted education as the cross-generational process of 'life-fulfillment' and 'self-realization' between adult and child. He understood man in terms of three basic positive and creative ways of being: a being who opens to the world, a being who becomes aware of himself, and a being who longs for the world beyond. This being questions and deepens the meaning of his life over the course of his life, venturing into the world, and builds a 'life bridge' that stretches into the future. These views were absent in *Pedagogical Anthropology*. In *The Original Theory of Human Formation*, the notion of becoming was reconceived, from the perspective of those who become, with a focus on the process of self-formation. The principle of community came to be reinterpreted as the continuation of the lifecycles of different generations.

The difference between the two works becomes increasingly clear when a comparison of the understanding of time is made. In *Educational Anthropology*, time was divided into each spatial phase of life: infancy, childhood, adolescence and adulthood. In contrast to that, in *The Original Theory of Human Formation*, time was considered to be a living process – one through which the 'being who longed for the world beyond' was searching for the meaning of life in an active and self-aware way and by so doing was accomplishing self-formation. In other words, in *Educational Anthropology*, the author who discussed education existed outside the text, whereas in *The Original Theory of Human Formation*, the author addressed the question of self becoming and formation as his lifelong task, and attempted to find its answer. Between these two texts, a major shift in perspective took place concerning where the author stood in discussing the question of human becoming (Yano 1996).

This shift indicates a conversion from the theory of becoming written against a background of an objectified and standardized theory of development to a theory based on an understanding of time from the perspective of the living subject. In this conversion, Mori again took a step towards a theory based upon the dynamic process of becoming. But if one were to interpret what has been said thus far in connection with the context of the Kyoto School, the vision of *The Original Theory of Human Formation* can be understood as the vision of anthropology based upon 'awareness' into which the theory of the lifecycle was woven. It can also be interpreted as a recounting of the structure of his earlier essay, 'Educational Reality: The Foundation in Philosophy of Education' (1941), written in his younger days under the influence of Hajime Tanabe's philosophy. With the two later texts (*Educational Anthropology* and *The Original Theory of Human Formation*), Mori's work exemplified the pinnacle of post-war pedagogical anthropology based upon the Kyoto School.

## The Kyoto School and the Educational Concept of 'Technique' (*gijutsu*)

It is not the case, however, that the tradition of the pre-war Kyoto School was simply handed down to post-war educational anthropology, although the Kyoto School remained a significant influence on central movements in post-war pedagogy.

An example can be found in Mantaro Kido's educational thought – a leading organizer of the movement of educational science and post-war pedagogy.

Kido contributed an essay entitled 'Problems of psychology as anthropology' (*'Ningengaku to shiteno Shinrigaku no Mondai'*) in a special issue of the academic journal *Ideal* (*Riso*) in 1931 on anthropology in which Tanabe's essay, 'A position of anthropology', was also published. In his essay, Kido presented 'anthropology as educational science' from the position of unifying natural science with human science (*seishin-kagaku*). According to him, psychology as a discipline in service to vital life must no longer be separated from pedagogy and sociology.

> Psychology as anthropology in the unity of natural science and human science (*Geisteswissenschaften*) may better be called anthropology as educational science in place of such conventional terms as cultural science and social science and social science. Human beings, who are the driving force of reforming and advancing social lives, should be scientifically approached and cultivated. This is the task of anthropology as educational science. (Kido 1931, p. 953)

According to Otohiko Mikasa, Kido happened to meet Kiyoshi Miki on the ship that was carrying him to his studies abroad, and it is said that they discussed the question of 'the capacity of formation and technique in pedagogy' (Mikasa 1999, p. 119). It is clear from the title of Kido's (1935) essay, 'Images and technique: An essay on the methodology of pedagogy' (*'Keisho to Gijutsu: Kyoikugaku no Houhou nitsuite no Shiron'*), published in the journal *Education* (*Kyoiku*), that this essay shared sympathies with Miki's anthropology of technique. This eight-page monograph is short but dense in the development of its argument. This essay on the methodology of pedagogy constructed a theory of human formation based upon Kant's third *Critique of Judgment*. Kido's method of argument shows an inheritance from Miki's discussion of the unity of the subject and the object, and of *pathos* and *logos* as the matter of technique. Later, in *Technique of Life and the Culture of Education* (*Seikatsu Gijutsu to Kyoiku Bunka*) (1939), Kido defined education in the following manner.

> It must be recognized that a social institution is an organization for collaboration in technique, one that is required to solve problems in life: and that what we call the system of knowledge resides in such social institution. School in this sense is a form of social institution. It, however, is not simply a unit of collaboration in technique in which resources of life are developed: it is principally an organic union for collaboration in technique in which technique for human being is cultivated for the development of such a unit of collaboration. Therefore it can be said that education is a method to teach the way of living, that is, technique as the art of life: and that an educational system is a technical organization for the way of living. (Kido 1939, p. 72, italics added)

Furthermore, in the introduction to this text Kido writes: 'Education is a technique for teaching the technique of life to the nation [people]. When such a technique is nationally organized, it becomes the culture of education' (Kido 1939, p. 2). Of course, the definition of education as technique had existed since the ancient period. Kido's idea was distinctive, however, in that the content of teaching was also considered to be technique and that education was considered to be technique as the art of life. The definition of education given by Kido is analogous to the following one given by Kimura, though the latter at first appears to be distant from the former: 'an ultimate form of formative awareness, one that helps and cultivates what helps the cultivation of heaven and earth' (Kimura 1946, p. 124). For Kido's technique was not simply the matter of repetition, but involved creation through constructive imagination. In other words, Kido's idea of technique, with the mediation of Miki's 'behavioral awareness', was connected to Kimura's 'formative awareness'. In addition, Kido expanded the definition of education as technique to include the significance of teaching materials as tools. Thus Kido's *Technique of Life and the Culture of Education* included such topics as a view on the history of teaching materials, film education and media education. It discussed a new possibility for education in technology and media.

This pedagogy based on technique provided a rational argument against the fervor that accompanied calls for 'the clarification of the concept of our national identity' and 'enhancement of the Japanese spirit'. The opposition to this, however, did not mean resistance to the war. Rather it represented the opposition to spiritualism and ultra-nationalism, on the one hand, and the rationalism of technocrats who waged the war efficiently by designing the all-out war, on the other hand.

The definition of education as technique did not, therefore, do away with spiritualism. But the formalistic and insubstantial term, 'technique', meant that education was turned into a technical process whose contents were interchangeable. Despite the understanding of content itself as technique, the subjective aspect of this was lost to a rational, objective understanding of education. Miki's claim that technique in educational practice constituted a morality was lost in this application of the idea. In an area where natural technique is involved, and alongside a fervent belief in irrational, spiritualistic discourse, it could not convert the object into reality, and hence, was powerless as technique. Naturalistic technology crushed simply subjective ideas and formed a rational relationship with objectivity. Miki said that technique itself formed morality. Surely technique had such a formative function.

This was not the case, however, where ideational technique was involved. For example, in the case of 'the Japanese spirit' which is used as a technique to unify the will of different nations, however irrational the ideational form of that technique was, it could solve problems in its own way. It was also possible to teach efficiently and rationally such an idea as technique. That is, technical pedagogy in itself did not negate the Japanese spirit. It was the very formality of the definition of technical pedagogy that constituted the method of resistance to the nation: and at the same time, immediately after the war, that enabled itself to become the central thought of the post war pedagogy by assimilating the postwar spirit of democracy and rationalism. Looking from another perspective, it was a mechanical view on education that could serve any ideals.

Turning this technical pedagogy into a scientism detached from the humanistic basis that Miki had envisioned (although his idea of 'active nature' entailed its own dangers[4]) risked undermining a vital principle. The formalistic definition of technical

---

[4] Some of the Kyoto School philosophers contributed to the justification of the war on the strength of irrational theories of life based upon the idea of 'active nature'.

pedagogy was formulated according to the spirit of the Fundamental Law of Education,[5] and as such, postwar pedagogy was intended to be understood as an integral whole, characterised not only by a form, but also by its content. The conversion of these ideas into scientism, betraying the spirit of the Fundamental Law, turned the approach into a nihilism, a logic without any substantial thought.

## The Evaluation of the Kyoto School in the Field of Educational Studies

Considerable research on educational theory and philosophy in the prewar and postwar periods has been conducted in the field of the history of education. There has been almost no research, however, into the contribution of the Kyoto School. Also in the field of the philosophy of education, there is scarcely any research on the relationship between the Kyoto School and pedagogy, except that which is focused on an individual thinker, such as Motomori Kimura. Therefore, knowledge of the relationships between different traditions, theories and scholars is almost lost today, when previously it had been a tacitly shared knowledge up to a certain generation.

Despite obvious intellectual continuities between prewar and postwar educational thoughts, the two have been disconnected either consciously or unconsciously. It can be argued, therefore, that we have been trapped unawares in the territory of the prewar tradition. Unaware because we have not acknowledged the connection between postwar thinking and the prewar period. Only by recognizing possibilities opened up by the prewar educational thoughts and what the postwar educational thoughts have consciously and unconsciously hidden can we understand the mechanism of our own discourse, one which we initiate unconsciously when we talk about education. The difficulty of discussing Japanese pedagogy is identical to the difficulty of being self-aware of the prewar and the postwar histories that appear to be disconnected by the intervention of the war.

In my essay, 'Japanese pedagogical anthropology as conceived to be a problem: Its sketch centering on the Kyoto School' ['Mondai to shiteno Nihon no Kyoiku Ningengaku: Kyoto Gakuha no Ningengaku wo chushin to shita sketch'] (2002), I wrote as follows:

> 'Japanese pedagogical anthropology' was born from the Kyoto School as a study questioning anew the relationship between human being and education from an 'anthropological' perspective. Therefore, 'Japanese pedagogical anthropology' entails the same problem as the Kyoto School. It was based upon the Kyoto School, one which considered human being to be real as a historical and social being. Therefore once it was situated in the concrete field of 'Japan' as a place filled with historical and social forces, it is indubitable that Japanese

---

[5] This is a law that was created after World War II as the principle of post-war democratic education.

pedagogical anthropology consequentially (though perhaps beyond its intentions) justified the total assimilation of the way of being as a 'human' into the 'nation': and that it played a certain role in justifying the Emperor's education policy in Japanese colonies at that time. Therefore, the discussion of 'Japanese pedagogical anthropology' cannot be contained simply within an objectively academic discourse – the discourse of chronological studies that simply tried to clarify the characteristics of work conducted by each scholar who envisioned 'Japanese pedagogical anthropology.' We must critically examine not only the colonialism entailed by Western anthropology as reflected in 'Japanese pedagogical anthropology,' but also the development of 'Japanese pedagogical anthropology' in itself from a historical perspective. Similarly 'Japanese pedagogical anthropology' can be discussed first and foremost and only as a problem to be examined, along with the uniqueness and possibilities of its vision. (Yano 2002, p. 26)

Japanese pedagogy (pedagogical anthropology) still operates as a locus of struggle over the positive and the negative assets of the Kyoto School. Here the relation between the positive and the negative can be overturned. It cannot be estimated what possibilities the Kyoto School could have for studies in pedagogical anthropology. As Noboru Shirozuka points out, the Kyoto School started with Heidegger's foundational ontology, but used 'active nature' as a crucial key to overcoming it (Shirozuka 1969, p. 186). It was an attempt to be engaged in self-understanding in the context of our historical and social life, and contributed to a deeper self-awareness of 'Japanese' culture and its historical position. This was a demand inherent in its mode of thinking, while at the same time, an external demand made by the circumstances of that time, that is, the war. In that sense, though the Kyoto School was not necessarily connected with a nationalistic idea, it is undeniable that the notion of 'active nature' had a kinship with it. As the anthropology of education based upon the Kyoto School was involved in the actual practices of education, it supported the nationalistic spiritual movement more deeply than it engaged with philosophical endeavors. The postwar pedagogical anthropology has left much unsaid, whether consciously or unconsciously, over its continuity with the prewar and mid-war attempts by anthropology of education. As discussed in this chapter, however, the prewar and mid-war attempts have been passed down in their diverse aspects in to the studies on pedagogy in the postwar period. In a sense, in the postwar studies on pedagogy a secularized version of the Kyoto School has become mainstream.

An attempt at a pedagogy based upon the pedagogy of technicism as the secularized version of the Kyoto School could avoid the danger of being engulfed by irrational vitalism, by throwing away the dimension of vitalism (of active nature) – one which risked being assimilated into nationalism. At the same time, it needed to pay the price of giving up a dimension of thinking that could have captured the vital life of children. This did not become a great problem as long as living nature and life-and-death rituals and ceremonies continued in the neighborhood of children to such an extent that the dimension of their vital lives could be explored. When the vital power became enfeebled, however, as a result of the progress of urbanization and industrialization, the secularized version of the Kyoto School started to disclose a problem in its incapacity to deal with mounting problems in education – such as school bullying, refusal to attend school, and the behavioural problems within classrooms (*gakkyu-hokai*). Thus interpreted, we might say that it is a significant task to trace the way of interacting with this precarious 'active nature' in the stream of the Kyoto School and its related endeavors of pedagogy. If we think of this precarious 'active nature' as the potential entailed by the Kyoto School, the task ahead of us is to learn how to be reengaged with it.

# References

Kido, M. (1931). Ningengaku to shiteno Shinrigaku no Mondai [A question of psychology as anthropology]. *Ideal* [Riso], *27*. Riso-sha.

Kido, M. (1935). Keisho to Gijutsu: Kyoikugaku no Houhou nitsuite no Shiron [Images and technology: An essay on the methodology of pedagogy]. *Education* [Kyoiku], *3*(6).

Kido, M. (1939). *Seikatsu Gijutsu to Kyoiku Bunka* [Technique of life and the culture of education]. Tokyo: Keibunkan.

Kimura, M. (1939). *Kokumin to Kyoyo* [National polity and civilization]. Tokyo: Kobundo Shobo.

Kimura, M. (1941). *Keiseiteki Jikaku* [Formative self-awareness]. Tokyo: Koubundo Shobo.

Kimura, M. (1946). *Kokka ni okeru Bunka to Kyoiku* [Culture and education in the nation state]. Tokyo: Iwanami Shoten.

Koyama, I. (1938). *Philosophical anthropology*. Tokyo: Iwanami Shoten.

Koyama , I. (1942). *Sekaishi no Tetsugaku* [Philosophy of the world history]. Tokyo: Iwanami Shoten.

Mikasa, O. (1999). Kido, Mantaro [Mantaro Kido]. In History of Education Thought Society (Ed.), *Kyoiku Shiso Jiten* [Encyclopedia of the history of educational thoughts]. Tokyo: Keiso Shobo.

Mori, A. (1941). Kyoikuteki Genjitsu: Kyoiku Tetsugaku Kisoron [Educational reality: The foundation in philosophy of education]. In Kyoto Tetsugakkai (Ed.), *Tetsugaku Kenkyu* [Philosophy] (Vol. 26, pp. 298–300). Tokyo: Houbunkan

Mori, A. (1978/1955). *Kyoiku no Jissensei to Naimensei* [The practicality and interiority of education]. Nagoya: Reimei Shobo.

Mori, A. (1978/1961). *Kyoiku Ningengaku: Ningen Seisei toshite no Kyoiku, Mori, Akira Chosaku Shu Dai 4, 5 Kan* [Educational anthropology: Education as human becoming, The collected works of Akira Mori, Vols. 4–5]. Nagoya: Remimei Shobo.

Mori, A. (1977). *Ningen Kiesei Genron (Iko): Mori, Akira Chosaku Shu Dai 6 Kan* [Principles of human formation (Posthumous work): The collected works of Akira Mori, Vol. 6]. Nagoya: Remiei Shobo.

Nishida, K. (1933/1950). Kyoikugaku ni tsuite [On pedagogy]. In *Nishida, Kitaro Zenshu* [The collected works of Kitaro Hinisa] (Vol. 12). Tokyo: Iwanami Shoten.

Shirozuka, N. (1969). Ningengaku no Kanosei: Miki, Kiyoshi no Ningengaku o Megutte [Possibilities of anthropology: On Kiyoshi Miki's anthropology]. In M. Koda & K. Ikumatsu (Eds.), *Nihon no Tetsugaku* [*Japanese philosophy*] (Iwanami Koza Tetsugaku [Iwanami Lecture Series of Philosophy]). Tokyo: Iwanami Shoten.

Ueno, H. (1991). Mori, Akira [Akira Mori] In Y. Kubo, T. Yoneda, T. Komagome, & K. Komikawa (Eds.), *Gendai Kyoikushi Jiten* [Dictionary of contemporary educational history in Japan]. Tokyo: Tokyo Shoseki.

Yano, S. (1996). Seisei no Kyotiku Ningegngaku Saiko: Mori, Akira, *Kyoiku-Ningengaku: Ningen-Seisei toshite no Kyoiku no Shatei* [Reconsideration of the educational anthropology of becoming: Ranges of Akira Mori's *Educational Anthropology: Education as Human Becoming*]. In S. Wada (Ed.) *Kyoikuteki Nichijio no Sai-Kochiku* [Reconstruction of the educational ordinary]. Machida: Tamagawa Daigaku Shuppanbu.

Yano, S. (2002). Mondai to shiteno Nihon no Kyoiku-Ningengaku: Kyoto Gakuha no Ningengaku o chushin to shita sketch [Japanese pedagogical anthropology as conceived to be a problem: Its sketch centering on the Kyoto School]. *Record of clinical-philosophical pedagogy* (Vol. 4). Kyoto: Chair of Clinical-Philosophical Pedagogy, Graduate School of Education, Kyoto University.

# Chapter 4
# The Kyoto School and J.F. Herbart

**Shoko Suzuki**

## Introduction: Philosophy of Education as a Place ('Topos') for a New Discourse Between East and West

The increase in antisocial behavior at Japanese schools, such as bullying, violence, suicide, and juvenile crime, in recent years has called into question the role of pedagogy and philosophy of education as academic disciplines through which to address these pressing issues. Philosophy of education was born out of the need to understand and address fundamental issues of human development and education. To that end, the fields of neurology and biology are being called to make greater strides with regard to comprehensive human science and development. Similarly, it is increasingly clear that the traditionally divided academic disciplines of the natural and social sciences and the humanities must join hands to effectively address the multifaceted issue of the human being as an animal and social creature.

Over the last 100 years or so, Japanese society and culture have developed by adopting principles from the West. Japan's assimilation of Western values and principles has been a topic of intense ongoing study. A perfunctory, superficial examination of the dynamic interplay between Western and non-Western thought is insufficient. Since the postmodern movement of the 1970s, the traditional Western concept of universalism has been criticized for already containing the premise of ethno-logocentrism because it was developed in ancient Greece. With this context in mind, I expect that the emergence of a truly comprehensive, multicultural hybrid theory regarding philosophy of education is imminent.

S. Suzuki (✉)
Graduate School of Education, Kyoto University, Yoshida-honmachi, Sakyo-ku,
Kyoto-shi, 606-8501 Kyoto, Japan
e-mail: zxd01220@nifty.com

P. Standish and N. Saito (eds.), *Education and the Kyoto School of Philosophy*,
Contemporary Philosophies and Theories in Education 1,
DOI 10.1007/978-94-007-4047-1_4, © Springer Science+Business Media Dordrecht 2012

To contribute to this process, I have focused my essay on a comparative examination of the renowned Kyoto School of Philosophy and German education philosopher Johann Friedrich Herbart (1776–1841). The Kyoto School, and in particular its progenitor, Kitaro Nishida (1870–1945), was deeply influenced both directly and indirectly by Herbart, who is commonly known as the 'father of modern pedagogy'. In particular, I refer to Nishida's focus on Herbart's monolithic worldview of Realism and his emphasis on refinement of the sense of touch in his practice-based theory of learning. In Nishida's philosophy, this is the notion of the 'logic of place'.

While absorbing various influences from Herbart, Nishida attempts to elucidate the conceptual background of Japan's unique philosophy which stands firmly on the foundations of traditional Eastern thought. It does this by conceiving of the human being not as a static being but rather as a dynamic being that moves in the midst of an interactive and constantly changing environment. I maintain that it is within this conceptual framework that philosophy of education, which has as its purpose the comprehensive understanding of the role of education, can be grasped in its most elemental form. It is my personal hope and the premise of my professional endeavors that philosophy of education will be able to provide a critical forum for a new dialogue between East and West.

## Herbart Within Intellectual History

Herbart is well-known as the successor to Immanuel Kant as chair of philosophy at Königsberg University. It was at the time when psychology was beginning to emerge from philosophy as a separate discipline that Herbart's work was categorized as philosophical psychology. Herbart wrote *Allgemeine Pädagogik* (1806) as a self-tutorial for schoolteachers, he is known as the 'father of modern studies in education'. The theory of education which Herbart propounded was then spread by what became known as the Herbartian School. Educators from Europe and America as well as Asia visited the training center for educators established by the Herbartian School and were strongly influenced by Herbart's theories. Japanese educators continue to this day to utilize Herbart's principles when designing their curricula. Applicants for teaching credentials in Japan are required to know Herbart and his theories to the same degree that they are expected to know Pestalozzi.

In this way, Herbart has left a legacy throughout the world as a scholar of pedagogy. Interestingly, though Herbart was largely forgotten in his own country, his philosophy and psychology were highly regarded and supported by the intellectual historians in Vienna, Austria–namely, Mach, Freud, and Brentano who were responsible for restoring Leibniz's reputation. Herbart once competed with Hegel for the post of professor of philosophy at Berlin University, and, as we all know, Hegel has since become enshrined as the quintessential German idealist philosopher. The situation was much different during the mid-nineteenth century, however. It was quite a triumph for Herbart to reference his philosophy of Realism to the prevailing philosophical Idealism of the day, which was predicated upon the notion of an ideal state of Man[1] as advanced by Aristotle's philosophy of monistic existence and Leibniz's philosophy of existence within motion—all of which created an environment unfavorable to the idea of human evolution and development. Herbart died, however, during the height of the debate, which was carried on by Herbart's and Hegel's respective pupils in a sort of proxy war of words. In the end, however, public opinion was swayed by the persuasive reasoning of the Hegelian School. It would not be far off the mark, however, to assert that while philosophical Idealism established itself in Germany proper, critics of that strain of thought within the German-speaking world strongly supported the Herbartian School.

Enthusiasm for philosophical Idealism began to subside even in Germany proper starting in the 1920s, and Heidegger and other philosophers of phenomenology began advancing Herbart's ideas regarding change within movement. The Kyoto School, which is the subject of this paper, incorporated elements from German philosophical Idealism as well as from their contemporary, Heidegger, and fabricated their own unique strain of Japanese thought.

## The Logic of Place, or the Epistemology of Moving/Developing

I would like to explore Nishida's interpretation of Herbart through Nishida's concept of the logic of place. Nishida viewed Herbart's ideas as an interesting interpretation of Leibniz's theory of the monad from the position of the Real—and not just the Real, but the Real imbued with perception and sense. Nishida wrote in a late work which is a supplement to the essay 'On Descartes: 1944'

> Herbart took the viewpoint of Realism after Kant. He also highly respected Leibniz. He wrote that Leibniz was unparalleled in facilitating understanding metaphysics. (Herbart 1964, Sämtl. Werke III, 72) … Instead of using the traditional metaphysical point of view, Herbart began from the concept of the given experience. So philosophy was for him the arrangement of concepts (*Bearbeitung der Begriffe*). In relation to Kant, he emphasized that the form of experience is not the subjective, but the objectively Real. In relation to Hegel, he tried to depart from the logical paradox. This is the viewpoint of formal logic. According to him, Being is the negation of all, the absolute assessment to take away all relations (the viewpoint of Absolute Position). All sense includes the absolute assessment, which should be Being. (Nishida 2004, 139 translation by the author)

Herbart claimed that the world was an amalgamation of all that was Real. Kant considered the form of knowledge to be subjective. But Herbart understood it as the objectively Real. Man should, in theory, be able to see the world before him, which is constituted by the amalgamation of the Real. Because of his impeded vision, however, Man is not able to perceive the Real as it is. Even though he encounters the world, Man fails to truly encounter it in the deepest sense. By removing the contradiction inherent in the concept—which is itself the framework of comprehending,

---

[1] In this paper, the term 'Man' is used generically to mean the human being.

touching upon the core in Herbart's theory—Man is able to improve upon the concept; and together with arrangement of concepts, *Bearbeitung der Begriffe*, be confronted with the essence of the world. In other words, Herbart claims that confrontation with the Real is the process by which Man develops his intellect. Nishida concurred with this assertion.

Nishida tried to continue on in the philosophical line of Leibniz, Kant, Herbart, the Marburg Neo-Kantian School (for example, Cohen), and Bergson. Cohen and Bergson were interested in infinitesimal calculus and planned to build the logic of moving or developing into the foundation of mathematics. Nishida proposed that our consciousness evolves from 'tiny perceptions of Leibnizian monads' (Nishida 1987, 56). Nishida describes in his work, *Intuition and Reflection in Self-Consciousness*:

> According to the Marburg school, sensation is *given as something to be determined*, and this determination is nothing other than the limit reached by the process of determination at a given moment. A given sensation is determinate in comparison with one that is less so, and still in need of determination when compared with one that is more determined. The determination of sensation resembles a mathematical limit, to which one can come nearer at will but never attain. A given sensation is like a sum added up to a certain point. For Cohen and Natorp, what is given to thought is not imposed from outside as something alien to it (*denkfremd*), but is required by thought itself. It is given as that which is to be discovered or to be determined, like the $x$ in mathematical problems, or the data (*dedomena*) in Euclid's sense. ... Thus even the cognition of a single sensory quality demands to be founded in something universal, and this cannot be the transcendent meaning of Rickert or Husserl, but must be immanent in experience. It must be related to what it founds as $dx$ is to $x$ in mathematics: as $dx$ is the basis of a finite $x$, so a certain sensory characteristic is a determination of a continuous whole. (Nishida 1987, 50)

Nishida finds meaning in a study of Cohen's profound reflections on Kant's 'principle of the anticipations of perception' in his first critique. Cohen tried to understand Kant's *Critique of Pure Reason* as the theory of experience based on Herbart's philosophy. According to Kant, the pure intuition grasps time and space. They are extensive. 'Appearances are all magnitudes, and indeed extensive magnitudes' (Kant 1998, KdrV, B203). Then an extensive magnitude—which the presentation of the parts makes possible—is the representation of the whole (and therefore necessarily precedes the latter).

Kant claimed:

> Now the consciousness of the manifold homogeneous in intuition in general, insofar as through it the representation of an object first becomes possible, is the concept of a magnitude (*Quanti*). Thus even the perception of an object, as appearance, is only possible through the same synthetic unity of the manifold of the given sensible intuition as that whereby the unity of the composition of the manifold homogeneous is thought in the concept of a magnitude; i.e., the appearances are all magnitudes, and indeed extensive magnitudes, because as intuitions in space or time they must be represented through the same synthesis as that through which space and time in general are determined. (Kant 1998, KdrV, B203)

The object of sensation is not the same as the method of sensation. The Real object cannot be measured with extensive magnitude, but with another magnitude, *quantitas*, namely, intensive magnitude. Kant says that in all appearances the Real, which is an object of sensation, has intensive magnitude, i.e., a degree (Kant 1998, KdrV, B207), and explains:

> Apprehension, merely by means of sensation, fills only an instant (if I do not take into consideration the succession of many sensations). As something in the appearance, the apprehension of which is not a successive synthesis, proceeding from the parts to the whole representation, it therefore has no extensive magnitude; the absence of sensation in the same moment would represent this as empty, thus = 0. Now that in the empirical intuition which corresponds to the sensation is reality (*realitas phaenomenon*); that which corresponds to its absence is negation = 0. Now, however, every sensation is capable of a diminution, so that it can decrease and thus gradually disappear. Hence between reality in appearance and negation there is a continuous nexus of many possible intermediate sensations, whose difference from one another is always smaller than the difference between the given one and zero, or complete negation. That is, the real in appearance always has a magnitude, which is not, however, encountered in apprehension, as this takes place by means of the mere sensation in an instant and not through successive synthesis of many sensations, and thus does not proceed from the parts to the whole; it therefore has a magnitude, but not an extensive one. (Kant 1998, KdrV, B209–210)

The intensive magnitude of Kant owes something to Leibniz's infinitesimal method. The difference between 'possible intermediate sensations' is always smaller than the difference between any sensation and zero. It can be very small, almost zero, but cannot be zero. This is the infinitesimal $dx$. From this $dx$ as the moment sensation comes to be made the Real object, Nishida introduces the significance of Cohen's interpretation of Kant:

> All this can be greatly clarified by a study of Cohen's profound reflections on Kant's 'principle of the anticipations of perception.' Since, for Cohen, what is given to thought is what thought intrinsically demands, sensation is not yet the real, but merely the index thereof, and cannot of itself be an object for thought; it is 'one form of the relationship of consciousness to its content, with a view to the determination of this content as object.' In consciousness of what Kant calls 'the unity of the manifold,' the objectification of sensation, and the securing of its objective reality, necessarily take place according to the 'principle of intensive quantity.' In other words, it is by considering sensation as intensive quantity that we are able to move toward the 'real things' which are the objects of physics. Kant did not sufficiently clarify the idea of intensive quantity, and it is to Cohen's great credit that he disentangled it from extensive quantity, clarified its significance, and recognized its strategic epistemological function. In extensive quantity one proceeds from part to whole, from *unity* to *plurality* and to its unification as *allness*, whereas in intensive quantity one proceeds from whole to part, and its unity is not the unity of a plurality, but the determination of a unitary whole according to the category of *limitation*. Intensive quantity is the quantity of 'continuous and uniform production,' that is, it is nothing other than 'differential quantity.' (Nishida 1987, 51)

In *Logik der Reinen Erkenntniss* (The Logic of Pure Perception), Cohen tried to interpret the Real as production. The fact of production precedes and develops into Reality. Movement and development occur by the infinitesimal method. Intensive magnitude, which makes the whole of the curve, is hidden everywhere on the finite curve as the infinitesimal point of production. This point of production is not the end of the curve but the beginning. From this, the intensive Reality is produced as the origin of the Real and is developed in the intensive *spatium* (space). According to Leibniz and Kant, the space of intensive magnitude, which continues before Reality or the origin of the world, is important. Intensive magnitude is connected not with the qualitative side of the Real, but with the quantitative side. The intensive *spatium* is filled with power and is moving. Although it appears as if stopping, in fact it is the located situational balance and a little disorder appears instantly in the complicated moving-body.

Nishida introduces Cohen's idea in order to look at the relationship between the conscious and the unconscious in epistemology. His approach goes to the theory of mathematics, especially on the finite and the infinite. He writes on the end of a line from the viewpoint of Cohen:

> In antiquity a point was defined as the end of a line, but following a suggestion of Kepler, the point in a tangent has come to be determined as the productive point of the curve. The concept of direction pertains to this productive significance ... This is incompatible with the ancient definition according to which the point is the limit of the line. Now the point has another, positive significance. It is no longer only the end, but rather the beginning of the line. The curve is produced from the point it shares with the tangent. The finite segment of a curve is the integral whole of tangent points, arising from what is infinitely small, as $x$ from $dx$. May we not also think of the unconscious underlying finite consciousness as similar to $dx$ in relation to $x$? (Nishida 1987, 56–57)

For Kant, the *spatium* (space) which the pure intuition grasps is extensive magnitude. Cohen tries to recast *spatium* as the intensive magnitude, as grade, and to interpret the philosophy of Kant as the epistemology of grade. This is a great challenge (Cohen 1977, Edel 1988). Cohen's aim is based on Herbart's interpretation of Kant's theory of experience. In order to prescribe the transcendental apperception from the viewpoint of psychology, he uses the concept of transcendental apperception analogically to understand Herbart's concept of 'I' (*Ich*). According to Mayerhofer, Cohen metaphorically arranged the Herbartian concept of *Ich* in order to define *transzendentale Apperzeption* from the viewpoint of psychology (Mayerhofer 2004, 44).

This concept of I (*Ich*) is the beginning of Herbart's work in educational theory, in other words, the science of human changing or development. He criticizes the theory of German Idealism, especially Fichte, who interprets the epistemology of I (*Ich*) as self-determination. From the viewpoint of human changing and developing, Herbart proposed the development of self-consciousness based on the Real (*das Reale*). His Realism should be understood in connection with the theory of moving, changing, and developing.

Nishida acknowledged this point because he tried to build the theory of *poiesis*. He tried to understand the meaning of *poiesis* of Plato and attempted to arrange it in his philosophy of moving/developing. *Poiesis* is defined by Plato:

> By its original meaning [*poiesis*] means simply creation, and creation, as you know, can take various forms. Any action which is the cause of a thing emerging from non-existence into existence might be called [*poiesis*], and all the processes in all the crafts are kinds of [*poiesis*], and all those who are engaged in them [poets]. (Plato 2000, 205b,c, translation by the author, based on the German translation cited)

Nishida interpreted Plato's *poiesis* as the principle of the human being. He understands the human being as in the process of changing in connection with the world. For him, Leibniz, Kant, Herbart, Cohen, Bergson, and Heidegger are the chain of the epistemology of human development. Man is always moving/changing, in other words, Man has the character of process. He creates the world and the same time he is created by the world. Nishida interprets this process as *poiesis*, in the Greek sense of 'to make a poet'. Man makes his life just like an aesthetic work, a work of art. Nishida's aspect can be called a theory of the *poiesis* of life.

But Nishida was not just satisfied with the concept of the Real by Herbart, because he interpreted the world of the Real by Herbart as a still space, one not in motion. Nishida tried to understand the historical world, which not only makes itself, but also is made, as the most concrete world of the true Real. For Nishida, the Real is something which makes itself and also is made, historical action, as well as *poiesis*. So he emphasized that the logic of the real world should not be formal logic in the case of Herbart, but the logic of place, the place of the contradictory self-identity. Nishida claimed:

> The intelligible world of Herbart could be interpreted as one side of the absolute now, namely, absolute space. From the viewpoint of the logic of absolute contrary self-identity, it is something like the absolute positional—not the Real as the sensual individual, but the individual specification of self as the momentary self-specification of the absolute now. In order to inquire into the concept of space, Nishida refers to Riemann (Georg Friedrich Bernhard Riemann [1826–1866]), who as mathematician should have been greatly influenced by Herbart. Nishida tried to develop Riemann's geometry and to interpret it as the logic of place. (Nishida 2004, 178 translation by the author)

He describes it in another way:

> In contrast to Herbart's concept of the Real as a placid, empty space, I view the Real as active and concrete. It comprises both the active and the passive, and I would prefer to understand it as the most concrete, truest realm of the Real, which both creates the historical world and is created by it. Man, as the Real in this world, already expresses his self simply through his aliveness, and through this act of expression, is an existence which creates the world even as he is himself created by the world. Man in his being is *poiesis* itself. (Nishida 2004, 140 translation by the author)

In this way, Nishida, in a tweaked rendering of Herbart's thought, interprets the self-identity of absolute contraries as the logic of place.

## Judgment and *Takt*

Nishida's logic of place is woven together in his attempt to place self-consciousness in the realm of logic through the form of judgment. Nishida was skeptical of premising the epistemology upon the contentious dialectic of subjectivity and objectivity. Nishida claimed:

> Usually, it is supposed that the object of thought lies outside and beyond the subjective activity of thinking and is self-identical and invariable, and that the objectivity or truth of knowledge consists in the subject's conforming to this transcendent object. But does this not imply the contrary: that subjectivity and objectivity are separate and independent? To be able to think an objective referent independent of the subjectivity of the self, subjectivity itself would first have to be raised beyond individual subjectivity. That is why Kant, arguing that the unity

objects require is nothing other than the formal unity of consciousness, sought the objectivity of knowledge in the synthesis of pure apperception: 'It is only when we have thus produced synthetic unity in the manifold of intuition that we are in a position to say that we know the object' (B135). (Nishida 1987, 28 translation by the author)

The format in which consciousness appears most clearly is through the logical structure of judgment. In Nishida's words:

The judgment of the law of identity, '*A* is *A*,' expresses the fact that we have fixed a certain thought object, and the idea that this thought object is self-identical. ...it expresses the logical 'ought' on which our faculty of judgment rests. It spells not a repetition of the same consciousness in time, but the emergence of a new consciousness, the consciousness of an 'ought' which is of a higher order than what can be apprehended in mere temporal continuity. (Nishida 1987, 25 translation by the author)

He also explains:

The consciousness of an 'ought' is the most immediate and concrete experience we have, most immediate because it precedes and founds the distinction between thinker and what is thought, and most concrete because it includes within itself various fundamental relations. This is the Act, or *Tathandlung*, of which Fichte speaks ... (Nishida 1987, 30 translation by the author)

So for him, '*A* is *A*' includes as one of its aspects the fact that *A* exists and also as one of its aspects the 'ought' (Nishida 1987, 31). Here we can see the logic, which understands existing as becoming or acting. Nishida's self-consciousness means self-consciousness in work or in acting.

In the study of formal logic, the individual subject is subsumed within the universal predicate. In other words, the individual exists within the universal. Stating that '*S* equals *P*' generally implies that the universal *P* encompasses the individual *S*. Put in other terms, however, the universal initiates a move toward individuation, interpretable as a self-imposed limitation. For a decision to become appropriate, a limited concrete universal, which has undergone a self-imposed limitation, is necessary.

This concrete universal is exactly that place (locus) within self which projects itself—Nishida developed this in his later works with the concept the 'logic of place'. The work of projecting self within self is precisely what is called awareness. The system of human knowledge proceeds from the level of the infinite universal; and within the direction of the subject an infinitely deep intuition can be discerned, while the infinitely colossal universal envelops this in the direction of the predicate.

In Herbart's monistic realism, the Real becomes gradually more discernible by modifying the framework of understanding the world. In other words, viewed as a matter involving the process of becoming more conscious, Nishida was in full accord. Nishida wrote in his later work:

Herbart thinks that the world is the combination of the Real. Leibniz's monad is understood by Herbart as the sensual Real. In Herbart's philosophy, it is begun with the form of the given experience and logically is the concept adapted. On this point I agree with him. ... Herbart's intelligible world is for me the space of the absolute now-existing, namely, absolute space. From this viewpoint of mine, the logic of the absolute contrary self-identity is the absolute setting, not the Real as the unit of sense, but as the moment of self-specialization, where he specializes himself. (Nishida 2004, 140 translation by the author)

Nishida defined the basis of consciousness as a process in which one projects oneself within. To be conscious means to have oneself projected into the purview of self. The Real, which Herbart posits, is not a mediated self but rather a direct projection of oneself, and the situation which comprises the Real is, according to Nishida, intuiting through the act of projecting. In other words, it is the place 'at work' for actional intuition.

Within this system of self-awareness, Nishida placed particular emphasis on the function of *Takt* (Eng. 'tact'). *Takt* was a key concept within Herbartian thought, expressed as educational tact (*der pädagogische Takt*). *Takt* is the most suitable vehicle for a teacher to delegate the power of decision and judgment within the context of the pedagogical relationship with the student. Further, *Takt* is viewed as a tool of didactic education, until which time the training manifests itself in action and evolves into habit (Herbart et al. 1913–1919, Scholz 1909, Blochmann 1950, Muth 1962, Ipfling 1966, Pleines 1980).

This is obvious in the etymology of *Takt* as well. Currently, *Takt* is primarily used as a musical term with a limited meaning, but its origin, *tactus*, had three meanings: (1) contact, relationship; (2) an action or influence on emotions, tactual organs, or tactual sense; and (3) capable of contact or emotion. This precisely shows that *Takt* is a sense or an emotion relating to spatiality. It should be noted, however, that contact is also a matter that is already relevant not only to spatiality but also to temporality. Hence, *Takt*, which is contact conditioned by time and space, has assumed such meanings as 'cycle' and 'stroke' in the context of mechanical engineering and other fields of science and technology, in addition to its meaning as a musical term, such as 'beat' and 'baton'. Moreover, *Takt* has also come to be used commonly as a word meaning 'consideration, sociability, or politeness to avoid hurting the other person's feeling in personal interaction'. 'Out of *Takt*' in the musical context means 'out of tune', but in the context of human interaction, it also means 'out of tune' or 'out of control'. Furthermore, 'lack of *Takt*' means 'being thoughtless, inconsiderate, indiscreet, or rude'. Consequently, when translated into Japanese, *Takt* is sometimes matched with a Japanese word meaning 'intuition, the sixth sense, knack, or discernment an opportunity'. (Suzuki 2008)

According to Herbart, *Takt* does not merely help a person to be attentive to an object. He says that *Takt* functions with a careful and rhythmical grasping of the object. He describes the function of *Takt*, citing a childhood anecdote described in the autobiography of a chemist who was his contemporary (Herbart 1964, K XIII, 234–235). At the age of five, the boy, who later became the chemist, already had an outstanding attentiveness. He was so attentive that he was able to understand the content of a book simply by flipping through the pages. Despite his attentiveness, however, the physical movements of the boy were very clumsy. If a dustbin were in his path, he always bumped into it, although he thought he was walking with care to avoid it. It was very difficult for the boy to visually measure the distance to the dustbin and adjust his stride accordingly.

What was lacking in this attentive boy? Herbart analyzes that it was *Takt* and musical talent. He also called this *Takt* and musical talent rhythmical grasping. If humans cannot immediately get an accurate grasp of each instant in their rhythmical spatial activity, they experience various forms of disharmony in their daily, routine activities. Herbart conceptualized psychology on the basis of the analysis of sound representation, while using the function of *Takt* as a clue.

Herbart, who explored the possibility of pedagogy as a practical discipline in late eighteenth century Germany, made the following statement extremely self-consciously.

> Because of its universality, theory is very wide in breadth so that every individual thing is involved in even an infinitely small part of it during its execution. On the other hand, theory also has indeterminability that arises as a direct consequence of its universality. Therefore, it disregards every detail as well as all the individual actions, considerations, and efforts that practitioners employ in responding to the individual situations that they are constantly tackling. (Herbart 1964/1965, A, 154, translation by the author)

Theory tends to universality or generality, while practice is individual and specific. Theory obtains universality by abstracting individual situations. Therefore, theory cannot perfectly deal with the contingency of practice even if it anticipates every possible situation that may occur in practice and flexibly prepares for it in order to contribute to practice. Even if you try to apply the theoretical result gained in a vacuum in a natural atmosphere, you cannot easily predict the situational factors that will actually accompany it. This explains the meaning of the statement that theory is unable to grasp the individuality and peculiarity of practice because it has universality and indeterminability.

The validity of a theory hinges on the result of its application in practice. This is the gap between theory and practice. This gap arises because theory is established as theory and practice must be practised, and it may be regarded as an aporia resulting from the structural moment of theory and that of practice. What is ultimately held responsible in practice is nothing but the judgment of the practitioner. Any problem in practice, after all, has to be resolved through an action involving decisions and judgments made in each of the specific situations. Herbart describes the modality of *Takt* that emerges as a judgment, in particular an instantaneous judgment, as follows:

> *Takt* inevitably (*unvermeidlich*) enters the place (*Stelle*) that theory has left vacant (*leer lassen*) and directly controls practice. (Herbart 1964/1965, AI, 126, translation by the author)

*Takt* 'inevitably' fills in the void, that is, the place that theory has left vacant. Herbart, who presented *Takt* as a key to filling the gap between theory and practice, attempted to resolve the discrepancy between theory and practice by developing *Takt*. He says that you have to be skillful, perceptive, and responsive to gain *Takt* and, as such, *Takt* can be acquired only through deeds. Moreover, before trying to acquire *Takt*, you need to learn by thinking, absorbing the subject you have learned, conditioning yourself, and engraving the future impression that experience will engrave upon you.

Skill can be acquired only by using it in practice, but learning has much bearing on the preparation for using the skill. Deliberation through learning will help the teacher prepare for teaching and make the teacher more perceptive during teaching. It also prepares for *Takt*. By capturing the state of mind (*Sinnesart*) in advance through deliberation, the teacher will be more sensitive and perceptive during the experience in practice, which will enable him or her to make a vivid impression on the experience, and *Takt* is developed by the emotions inspired by the experience. As the series of impressions felt through the use of the skill are absorbed deeply into the emotions of the practitioner and make an impact on them, *Takt* will be developed more effectively.

*Takt* is gradually growing knowledge, and the growth process is enabled by the map. 'The place that theory leaves vacant', which was pointed out by Herbart himself, is a blank in the map. *Takt* is brought into that void, gives it a new rendering, and reorganizes the whole map. As *Takt* intervenes in this way, the theory itself is also transformed. The map itself contains many blank areas.

Participation (*Teilnahme*) in the world of education, holding this map in one hand—which Herbart considers to be the enjoyment of aesthetics as the involvement in the idea (philosophy) of Plato—is a process of securing one's own world of education by sharing in a part of the world. Becoming familiar with the world means to enter the world and judge the whole world in one's own way based on a fragment of the world, that is, to draw a picture of the world based on the fragment that one sees through one's own experience.

Next I intend to address the question of how to nurture tact and decision-making capability (*Urteilskraft*) from the viewpoint of Nishida who interpreted the subsumed relationship of subject/predicate as a system of awareness.

Nishida did not consider the process of habit-building to be simply a matter of mechanical repetition. He was a proponent of effort and exertion. That is to say, Nishida believed that exertion comes to fruition through *Takt*. According to Herbart, *Takt* is the borderline between consciousness and unconsciousness. Nishida thought of *Takt* as unfolding into both passivity and activity and subsuming all that lies between them. *Takt* is the borderline between time and space and between the outer and the inner. Nishida, who was greatly influenced by the psychology of William James, held that human consciousness is found in the mystical interval of what is labeled exertion, which itself abides within the middle realm of *Takt* (Nishida 2004, 288–290). Nishida claimed:

> When a judgment has been gradually refined and its unity has become strict, the judgment assumes the form of a pure experience. For example, as one matures in an art, that which at first was conscious becomes unconscious. Taking this a step farther, we are led to the conclusion that pure experience and the meanings or judgments it generates manifest the two sides of consciousness: they are different facets of one and the same thing. (Nishida 1990, 10)

Nishida focused on the metaphor of an artist falling into the premitotic state of a seed during the process of creation. For example, when a pianist plays a recital and there comes an instant in which consciousness is lost in a certain type of intense concentration and a state of heightened stimulation arises—that is what Nishida labels pure experience (Nishida 1990, 6).

Exertion based on the consciousness of doing something according to set patterns disappears. Then, as action becomes free and spontaneous, the active stance takes on an unassuming naturalness (tendency, penchant) (Nishida 2004, 290). Within this continuation and repetition, Nishida says, a certain type of unclear activity arises. By sinking subtly within, as if being in a state of passivity, it rather transforms into initiative. He states that the work of self-formation is born at such a time. That is the direct knowledge of not-yet-divided-subject-and-object (*shukyakumibun*) and real intuition (*Intuition reale*) or, in Nishida's conceptualization, active intuition. For Nishida, pure experience is the alpha and omega. I would like to interpret his idea of pure experience in the context of the circulatory structure of learning. We learn and come to know that we know and understand nothing. With the acknowledgement of incomplete knowledge, we try to know and understand more and more. The indication of 'incompleteness' helps us to turn to the starting point of learning. The process of learning in this way can be characterized as the spiral structure of learning.

We can take the case of physical training. Initially, we give no thought to how to control our body, but just try to perform the task, and we succeed in doing it just fine. But later we try to do the same task again, and we fail. Rationally thinking about how to perform the task may confuse the natural way that the body moves. Then we have to try to make the way we control our bodily movement as natural as possible. In the words of Nishida, we begin the phase of unconsciousness by doing. In the second phase, we have to repeat the task successfully with the practical knowledge we gain through trials. This time, however, while we are carrying out the task, we have to put rationally-based thought out of our mind. We must begin from the point of unconsciousness and reach the point of the 'trained unconsciousness'. If we read Nishida's theory of Zen from the viewpoint of this spiral structure of learning or training, we can gain a new dimension of learning, which is made possible by combining Western and Eastern cultures.

It is as though one makes a decision with absolute confidence in the face of abiding ambiguity. It is as though the action of intuition actually arises from the diffusion of knowledge throughout the body—what Nishida discovered through his personal training in Zen and which is a phenomenological component of traditional Eastern disciplines. It is fair to say that Nishida's goal was to expound this phenomenon theoretically. As a means of doing so, Nishida utilized the philosophical Idealism of the German School as a foundation. Assuming the human condition to be in constant flux, he added the constant motion theory from Herbart and then attempted to unify this with Eastern thought.

Nishida's goal of a unitary knowledge which encompasses human becoming and transformation, thought that combines both East and West, thought that apprehends the social sciences, the humanities as well as the natural sciences may be the basis and incubator for the maturation of philosophy of education.

# References

Blochmann, E. (1950). Der pädagogische Takt. *Die Sammlung, 5*, 712–722.

Cohen, H. (1977). *Logik der reinen Erkenntnis* (Hermann-Cohen-Archiv am philosophischen Seminar der Universität Zürich (Ed.) Hermann Cohen Werke, Vol. 6, *System der Philosophie*). Hildesheim/New York: Georg Olms Verlag.

Edel, G. (1988). *Von der Vernunftkritik zur Erkenntnislogik. Die Entwicklung der theoretische Philosophie Hermann Cohens*. Freiburg/ München: Verlag Karl Alber.

Herbart, J. F., & Asmus, W. (Eds.). (1964/1965). *Herbarts Pädagogische Schriften*. Düsseldorf/ München: Küpper (as Herbart, A).

Herbart, J. F., Kehrbach, K., Flügel, O., & Fritsch, Th. (Eds.). (1887–1912). new ed. 1964. *Johann Friedrich Herbarts Sämtliche Werkem*. Langensalza, new ed. Aalen. (as Herbart, K)

Herbart, J. F., Willmann, O., & Fritsch, Th. (Eds.). (1913–1919). Herbarts pädagogische Schriften. Osterwieck, Harz- Leipzig, 3.ed. (as Herbart, W)

Herbart, J. F. (1806). Allemeine Pädagogik, aus dem Zweck der Erziehung abgeleitet (KII1-139).

Ipfling, H.-J. (1966). Über den Takt im pädagogischen Bezug. *Pädagoische. Rundschau.*, *20*, 511–560.

Kant, I. (1998). In P. Guyer & A. W. Wood (Eds. & Trans.), *Kritik der reinen Vernunft* [Referenced the eng. translation: Critique of pure reason]. Cambridge University Press (The Cambridge edition of the works of Immanuel Kant in translation/general editors, Paul Guyer and Allen W. Wood), (as KdrV with the number of the academy version).

Mayerhofer, H. (2004). *Der philosophische Begriff der Bewegung in Hermann Cohens "Logik der reinen Erkenntinis"*. Wien: WUV Universitätverlag.

Muth, J. (1962). *Pädagogischer Takt*. Heidelberg: Quelle & Meyer Verlag.

Nishida, K. (1987). *Intuition and reflection in self-consciousness* (V. H. Viglielmo, T. Toshinori, & J. S. O'Leary, Trans.). Albany: State University of New York Press.

Nishida, K. (1990). *An inquiry into the good* (M. Abe & C. Ives, Trans.). New Haven/London: Yale University Press.

Nishida, K. (2004). Tetsugaku Ronbunnshu, Vols. 6 and 7 [Essays on philosophy, Vols. 6 and 7]. In *Nishida, Kitaro Zenshu* [Collected Works of Kitaro Nishida] (Vol. 10, pp. 3–227; 231–372) (in Japanese). Tokyo: Iwanami-Shoten.

Plato. B. Z. (Ed.). (2000). *Symposion – Gastmahl*. Hamburg: Felix Meiner Verlag.

Pleines, J.-E. (1980). Die logische Funktion des Taktes im Anschluss an das Kantische System der Philosophie betrachtet. *Kant-Studien, 71*, 469–487.

Scholz, E. (1909). Pädagogischer Takt. In V. W. Rein (Ed.), *Enzyklopädisches Handbuch der Pädagogik*. Langensalza. IX:102ff.

Suzuki, S. (2008). Takt als Medium. In *Paragrana- Internatiolanle Zeitschrift für historische Anthropologie* (16, pp. 145–167). Berlin: Akademie Verlag.

# Chapter 5
# A Genealogy of the Development of the Clinical Theory of Human Becoming

Tsunemi Tanaka

## Introdution: Towards a Clinical Theory of Human Becoming

The subject of pedagogy has traditionally focused on the theme of the adult fostering the development of the child. However, issues confronting us today in the field of pedagogy do not allow for this type of limited explanation. The clinical theory of human Becoming proceeds from this difficult point of departure (Tanaka 2003).[1]

1. Traditional theory of education has assumed that adult educators should be developed to some extent. But today such frequently-encountered topics as *the failure of education at home and at school, the aging society,,* and *death* have brought into question this traditional assumption. Nonetheless, within the traditional theoretical framework of education and development, educators have been taken for granted as external factors in the educational process. It has now become clear that the existence of educators must also be included as a variable in the traditional paradigm.

2. Some of the problems in Japanese education are common to other industrialized nations, whereas others are specific to Japan's mass educational system. Accordingly, it is inappropriate to frame the issues of today in traditional terms outside the system operating *here and now*—terms that have typically focused on the past and on other nations. A new clinical and practical perspective is needed which can grasp the autogenetic system of *the here and now* while also acknowledging the realities of the increasingly homogeneous global community. A strong clinical and practical view is required in educational theory.

---

[1] All translations are by the author, unless otherwise indicated.

T. Tanaka (✉)
School of Letters, Mukogawa Women's University, Nishinomiya, Japan
e-mail: tanaka.tsunemi.1121@gmail.com

P. Standish and N. Saito (eds.), *Education and the Kyoto School of Philosophy*,
Contemporary Philosophies and Theories in Education 1,
DOI 10.1007/978-94-007-4047-1_5, © Springer Science+Business Media Dordrecht 2012

3. In today's Japan, both the coordination of educators' efforts and cooperation among educational theorists and educators are insufficient. That is to say, wide-ranging cooperation among practitioners (the professional sphere), cooperation between educational theoreticians and educators (the educational sphere), and cooperation between generations (the generational sphere)—have all failed to yield the requisite restructuring (Tanaka 2006). A theory that supports the formation of a unified public sphere is badly needed.

4. Within the field of social interactions today, human longing for personal meaning and value has largely been omitted—Max Weber defined this situation as *unpersönlich*—and people are incorporated into various social systems controlled by technological rationality and are reified ('zu versachlichen') as if they were mere functional requisites. Under such a regime, even if one is an active entity able to exercise personal initiative in order to attain a predetermined goal, one is still not able to create one's own terms. The fundamental human power of becoming—the pathos (as human potentialities inherent in their generativity), or the radically passionate, through which human beings can react actively and spontaneously to his/her own predicament—is disparaged. By demeaning pathos, educational theory and practice lose sight of their connection with the very human potentialities which would allow for a resolution to problems in education. It is necessary to reexamine the hegemony of technological rationality and establish a theory that is compatible with pathos.

In the traditional theory of education, which deals only with the development of children and the educational activities of adults, an 'educator' has been considered as a constant/invariable entity, whose existence is supposed to be outside of the theoretical framework. If we dare to incorporate the 'educator' as a functional variable into the theoretical framework of education, then the framework is bound to be destroyed. That is because such an incorporation explodes the margins of the traditional viewpoint of child development into contact with all aspects of the human lifecycle (including aging and death), and brings the margin of the asymmetrical relationship between educator and pupil into contact with all aspects of the mutuality between generations. To be daring enough to address the four theoretical points referenced above is the charge before us as academics, a charge we can dub the clinical theory of human becoming. This new theory has emerged from a clinical encounter with the reality of our educational system today, and through, its theoretical construction of human maturation and mutuality between generations within the context of the human lifecycle, it has produced a comprehensive, fundamental theory on human becoming.

This chapter surveys the theoretical genealogy of the Clinical Theory of Human Becoming. The emergence of this new discipline came about within the pedagogy of the Kyoto School. At that time, German philosophy was advancing new ideas such as life philosophy (*Lebensphilosophie*), phenomenology, hermeneutics, existentialism, and philosophical anthropology (*Anthropologie*) and they were catching on fast. The Kyoto School was, in effect, a local branch of this German philosophy and it received the latest ideas from each new German book as it was published, with a delay of one month as shipping time. The Kyoto School accepted the new ideas in their own way in their own Japanese context, where the traditional thought of Buddhism and the social hardships of poverty and illness prevailed. The Kyoto School itself became known as a factory of philosophical study (Iwaki 1999). It also produced a pedagogy, beginning with Motomori Kimura's (1895–1946) 'Ichida no Nomi' ('One Carving of a Chisel') (1933) and culminating with Akira Mori's (1915–1976) Theory of *Seimei Tuzumihashi* (the Human Lifecycle as an Arch Bridge) (1977) (Kimura 1933; Mori 1977). The clinical theory of human becoming was conceived in the context of the unfolding and eventual dissolution of the pedagogy of the Kyoto School. This is one of the supporting beams in Japan's unique structure of educational theory—a beam which was chiseled out of native Japanese timber but lathed according to the templates of Europe and America.

## The Establishment of the Pedagogy of the Kyoto School—Motomori Kimura's *Hyogen (Expression)* Pedagogy

The pedagogy of the Kyoto School was established in the 1930s and 1940s. Incidentally, the single-track school system of today had already evolved under the general mobilization system of WWII. In other words, Japan's school system had achieved a semblance of systematic independence, and there was an effort within educational theory as well to buttress this with an independent theoretical structure. Japan's educational theory had gathered enough strength to respond to the demands of the times (Morita 2008), and the pedagogy of the Kyoto School took shape independently of the broader national effort. Its seminal works were Kitaro Nishida's *Kyoikugaku ni tsuite (Regarding Pedagogy)* (Nishida 2003) and Kimura's 'One Carving of a Chisel'.

The occasion for Nishida's monograph entitled *Regarding Pedagogy* becomes clearer when considering the period in which it was written. Nishida urged his pupil Kimura—at times resorting to more than just subtle persuasion—to move from a position of teaching aesthetics in Hiroshima to one of teaching pedagogy at Kyoto University. The central concept of Nishida's monograph was the notion of a commonality between aesthetic becoming and educational becoming, which he termed *Tennchi no Kaiku ni sannsu (*cooperating with the becoming of heaven and earth in fostering the becoming of all things in it*)*. In contrast, Kimura penned 'One Carving of a Chisel', in which he employs the term *human praxis-poiesis* as a central idea. Regarding this compound expression, borrowed from Nishida's middle period, personal *mutual interaction* and inanimate *labor* were not distinguished, and as such, no distinction was made between *carving and education*. In 'One Carving of a Chisel', the term 'creation of heaven and earth' is not used, but *praxis-poiesis* becomes an expression of man's shouldering a portion of *zettaimu no hyogenn* (the manifestation of absolute nothingness). By this surrogate expression, mankind is actively reconciled with the absolute nothingness in its self-expression (alternatively understood as heaven's creation).

By demonstrating the overlap between aesthetic and educational formation through the notion of cooperation with the becoming of heaven and earth, Nishida nudged Kimura closer to his eventual transition from aesthetics to pedagogy. In fact, Kimura had accepted Nishida's invitation through his work 'One Carving of a Chisel', which anticipates the essence of Nishida's idea of cooperation with the becoming of heaven and earth. Kimura saw Nishida's notion of cooperation in this sense as the ontological underpinning for his own pedagogy and began construction of his own distinct metaphysical approach to a theoretical system of education. The common thread in both Nishida's *Regarding Pedagogy* and Kimura's 'One Carving of a Chisel' is the generative and life-philosophical ontology, which can be seen in the ideas of self-expression of the absolute nothingness and the creation of heaven and earth.

With his work 'One Carving of a Chisel', Kimura began unfolding his educational theory based on life-philosophical ontology, interpreting the notion of *koiteki chokkann (Behavioral Intuition)*, which is one of the key concepts of Nishida's middle period works and indicates the essential configuration of human creative behavior. It was most fitting for a member of the Kyoto School to advance a theory without engaging in an internecine battle for copyright privileges. Launching out with his work 'One Carving of a Chisel', Kimura argued the currently hot topic of the relationship between a nation and its education based on the Kyoto School's theory of the *sekaishiteki kokumin (World-historical Nation)* and on Fichte's later works; and, with his book *Culture and Education in the Nation-State* (Kimura 1946), he put forth an outline of the Kyoto School's pedagogy. This systematic Pedagogy—not only its key terms and theoretical framework, but also the life-philosophical ontology itself—derives entirely from Nishida's philosophy.

Nishida's successor Hajime Tanabe (1885–1962) threw doubt on Nishida's life philosophy as to whether it was an *emanatio* theory (Tanabe 1963). This suspicion was no insignificant matter for Tanabe himself. His middle period and later works (for example, *Shu no Ronnri [Logic of Species], Zettai Baikai [Absolute Mediation]*, etc.) were the fruits of his critical investigation into Nishida's alleged unreflective and unmediated *emanatio* theory. There is a typical *emanatio* theory in Buddhism, known as *hongaku shisou*, which proposes that everything in Heaven and Earth—mountains, rivers, grasses, trees, animals and human beings, too—has the inherent power to attain *nirvana*, and this ideal is reflected in the concepts of the becoming of heaven and earth or the expression of absolute nothingness.

This literary sparring between Nishida and Tanabe aside, Tanabe remained a luminary of the Kyoto School and was therefore an influence, along with Nishida, on Kimura and his thought. For example, when considering the nation-state, if one wants to go beyond the formalistic definitions of the Kyoto School, such as the simplistic idea of the *sekaishi teki kokumin* (World-Historical Nation), one cannot disregard Tanabe's logic of species. For Kimura, however, nation-states, just as individuals, are *the expression of absolute nothingness*. In Kimura's pedagogy, in spite of his superficial borrowing of Tanabe's term, logic of species, Nishida's philosophy of human life and becoming, as expressed in the terms manifestation of absolute nothingness and cooperation with the becoming of heaven and earth, had been appropriated as a firm ontological basis.

## From *Pedagogical Anthropology* to *The Principles of Human Formation*—Akira Mori

As a successor to Tanabe, Akira Mori began seriously addressing pedagogy after the sudden death of Kimura just after the Second World War. But even as the title of his main work *Pedagogical Anthropology: Education as Human Becoming* (Mori 1978; Tanaka 1999) suggests, Nishida and Kimura's theories of life and becoming comprise the ontological foundation of his works. Not only that, but with one brief exception just after the War, Mori did not refer to either the nation-state or to dialectics. Tanabe's *Logic of Species* and *Absolute Dialectics* were quite clearly avoided. This aversion may be a product of Mori's own theoretical stance as well as a general reflection of post-war individualism in Japan. Mori accepted only Tanabe's later concepts, human death and existence–cooperative. The results of the acceptance were Mori's theory of human lifecycle as an arch bridge and his theory of *Mutuality between Generations*, the two main concepts of his posthumous work, *Principles of Human Formation*. Let us now look a little more closely at the circumstances that pertain during this period.

Mori's major work, *Pedagogical Anthropology* (1961) was based on the frequent correspondence he had with his teacher Hajime Tanabe. It outlines a system of human becoming constructed along the layered strata of biological formation, socio-cultural formation and personality-based actualization. On this framework is constructed a theory of human becoming that articulates the process of self-formation in which the self dynamically breaks through the various socio-cultural and biological levels. Tanabe, just before his death, praised highly Mori's argument referring to the dynamic contradictoriness of the biological dimension of human existence, but at the same time he also pointed out Mori's theoretical omission of politics and ideals (Mori 1964). Mori acted on one part of this criticism while disregarding the rest.

A cogent theory of human development is observable within Mori's unfinished posthumous work, entitled *Principles of Human Formation*, in which he attempted to consolidate his post-*Pedagogical Anthropology* ruminations into a systematic work. In a manner blatantly contradictory to Tanabe's request and with some sympathy for nihilism, Mori shows an awareness of the extreme difficulty structuring theory on the basis of politics and ideals (educational principles), and goes on to argue that self-formation (the building and casting of the human lifecycle as if it were an arch bridge) is a process of positively embracing embracing of nihilism as a way of verifying mutual meaning in each individual. In other words, Mori destroys the reconciliatory standpoint of the human-being as a self-aware point of expression of expressive life, which forms the premise of Kimura's theory of education.

The effect of the demolition of the Kyoto School's established framework was that the standpoint of pedagogy was compelled to transform from a reconciliatory one towards a self-reflected one, which tries to grasp the process of mutual self-formation between generations in everyday life. Mori, on the one hand, took on Tanabe's two key concepts, namely human death and existence-cooperative, from his later works. But Mori, on the other hand, rejected Tanabe's appraisal of

*Pedagogical Anthropology*, which had proposed a clarification of ideals and teleology. Mori also rejected Tanabe's dialectic theoretical structure. Mori then, through his *Principles of Human Formation*, began querying the potential of human becoming amidst the mutuality between generations and the potential of existential, isolated self-formation as cast in the mold of the human lifecycle as an arch bridge. This is also the starting point of the clinical theory of human becoming, which, as we can see, was built by Mori upon the ruins of the now-defunct Pedagogy of the Kyoto School.

## The Human Lifecycle as an Arch Bridge, Mutuality, Trust in Pathos

Mankind is unable to live outside of its experience and to achieve the ultimate goal which transcends experience. What Mori termed 'human lifecycle as the building and casting of an arch bridge' refers to mankind's transitional self-actualization (*Entwurf*) in one's own manner from the everyday here and now to the shores beyond it. The individual's self-actualization is also the process of mutual response among those with whom one has a relationship in spite of the fact that it can also be viewed as the lonely expression of pathos. The human lifecycle as an arch bridge presupposes *mutuality between generations in everyday life*. Is the theory of the human lifecycle then able to help to build, for example, an educational public sphere between the parties who have constructed educational theory and those who implement it?

During years between Nishida and Mori, the relationship between theorist and practitioners changed dramatically. As Nishida actively encouraged his pupil Kimura, who wholeheartedly answered the call, so Kimura appealed to the educators in *Shinshu (Nagano Prefecture)*. By Mori's time, this unilateral chain of transmission had begun breaking down. Mori propounded a theory under the direction of Tanabe, but ended up undermining the trust between his teacher and himself in favor of a lone search for his own trail. Similarly, Mori's relationship with the *Shinshu* educators was not the traditional one of master and disciples but rather one of facilitator aiding the inevitable-formation of an independent body (Yoshioka 1978). It can reasonably be stated, then, that in this respect, the relationship between theorists and practitioners broke free from asymmetry.

Having said that, in almost all respects, Mori did not change his theories because of his dealings with the educators' association, nor did he change much himself. As recorded in *The Principles*, in which Mori's too frequent comments recalling episodes of his own life are given, his theories are basically the self-evaluative fruit of intense self-directed studies. Mori's relationship with the educators was, at least in part, a one-way street—an unsymmetrical one. In this regard, the clinical theory of human becoming maintains that the relationship between theorist and educators should not be one of expert and novice but rather one of a mutual relatedness of their own *half*-beings. That is to say, both parties should be simply dilettantes in this field possessing their own separate occupations. Through such mutual relatedness with their own half-beings, the participants are able to accrue a collective self-awareness, which constitutes the content of the clinical theory of human becoming. This discipline proceeds to develop in all its aspects, as a cooperation between theoretician and practitioners (within the educational public sphere), which Mori in his final work referred to as *mutuality*.

Metaphorically speaking, in the vacant spaces (in other words, *nothingness, contingency, latitude of creation*) of Mori's theory, in which the task assigned by Tanabe (propounding ideals and teleology and constructing dialectical theory) was relinquished, the words of Shuzo Kuki as recorded in the final words of his dissertation entitled *Contingency* reverberate (Kuki 1980).

> In order to confer eternal meaning on contingency, which possesses a fate of extinction, in which it harbors nothingness, there is no option to give birth to the moment through the future. Nobody is likely to be able to proffer a thorough solution to Biran's asking of the question Why (*Naze*?) within the confines of the theory contained. Having transferred the question into the realm of practice, it is all one can do to answer 'When you encounter someone, don't pass him over'.

There is a premise to the answer, 'When you meet someone, don't pass him over'. Before the action of a person's self-initiated response to the myriad definitions and promptings that aggregate in an individual, there wasn't any meaning and value. Putting aside the conditions which construct in advance the *Geworfenheit* of the human being, what exists before construction of the arch bridge of lifecycle is simply vacant. In the midst of contingency, however, mankind is already being defined by various dynamics such as support, acceptance, marginalization and rejection. As one encounters these innumerable promptings and proceeds to respond, one gains the ability to respond to the call for faith in self (faith in pathos) and through that process gradually realizes one's primary self.

Mori viewed Charlotte Bueler's and E.H. Erikson's lifecycle theories as incomplete, and so expounded the three contingencies of physical sustenance, social living and life history. Mori held that each person's behavioral response to these contingencies is not the pursuit of one's duty, but rather the quest for meanings; and at the end of his *The Principles of Human Formation*, Mori attempted to reinterpret the question of human existence through the following three concepts: (1) human existence, who seeks for meaning of life over the here and now, (2) the work of contingency, and (3) the search for the transcendence within the immediate. This argument was aborted upon Mori's death, but it is not difficult to surmise the subsequent direction of this argument. It is quite possible that the content of Mori's argument as it might have unfolded would have entailed the grasping of an abundant cycle, in which there were woven together in the realm of practice (Kuki) mutuality, the arch bridge of the human lifecycle and belief in pathos.

This being said, I wonder if the unraveling of the theory of the human lifecycle as an arch bridge, which holds at its core the exhortation 'When you meet someone, don't pass him over', is not ultimately an expression of Nishida's and Kimura's original intentions. Kimura's 'One Carving of a Chisel' is focused on everyday life, in which everyone is variously stimulated, and it resolutely develops an argument about the intricate connection between the stimulus (one carving) and the response to the response of the stimulus (the succeeding carving). Not only that, even the individual's loneliness and anxiety at the moment of his response is carefully incorporated into the theory. The text containing the core thesis within 'One Carving of a Chisel'— 'Everything can attain nirvana' *(Shikkai Joubutu)*—articulates the belief that is found through loneliness and anxiety. It should probably be stated that Mori, in his final conclusion, returned to this way of thinking. This point of view is in one sense accurate, but inaccurate in another.

Mori renounced the challenge handed down to him by Tanabe of incorporating into theory political and teleological aspects. This renunciation was in effect the rejection of the theoretical foundation of a transcendental belief which pre-deterministically defines personal life and action. Kimura's belief that *everything can attain nirvana* was certainly a belief which, according to 'One Carving of a Chisel', is demanded by day-to-day mutuality. It is none other than the everyday belief in an inherited power of pathos. But Kimura subsequently affirmed the mantra that *everything can attain nirvana* as the foundation stone of his own metaphysical system of pedagogy. When viewed in light of Mori's and Kuki's theories, the shift of Kimura's standpoint toward reliance on transcendentalistic belief indicates the manifest degeneration of his theory. Belief is not an a priori support to mutuality; rather, in the midst of the mundane, the pedestrian, belief is awakened by means of existential anxiety. And through nothing less than the experience of mutuality itself, the pathos—namely the passionate responsiveness of human existence to one's own situation—which supports mutuality as the way to belief, is repeatedly discovered and realized; and with that continuous discovery the belief in pathos itself is repeatedly confirmed.

If the formative cycles—driven by the three elements of everyday mutuality, the arch bridge of the human lifecycle and pathos—are shut off, mutuality will regress into asymmetrical action. Today's environment of pervasive control by technological rationality and bureaucracy is a typical example of this process of regression. The clinical theory of human becoming cannot avoid a confrontation with this domination and regression. This is the situation confronting clinical research in the sphere of university education today. We have already amassed some research in this field, but that topic will have to be addressed on another occasion.

# References

Iwaki, K. (1999). Kaisetu [Comment]. In *Kimura, Motomori. Geijutsu-ron-shuu* [A collection of essays on art]. Kyoto: Toueisha.

Kimura, M. (1933). Ichida No Nomi [One carving of a chisel]. In *Hyogen Ai* [Expressive love 1997]. Tokyo: Kobusi-shobo.

Kimura, M. (1946). *Kokka ni okeru Bunnka to Kyoiku* [Culture and education in the nation-state]. Tokyo: Iwanami-shoten.

Kuki, S. (1980). Guuzenn-sei/hakase-ronbun [Contingency dissertation]. In *The complete works of Kuki Shuuzou* (Vol. 2). Tokyo: Iwanami-Shoten.

Mori, A. (1964). Tanabe Sensei no Shokan kara [Letters from Professor Tanabe]. In *A monthly bulletin of the complete works of Tanabe-Hajime: Vol. 8*. Tokyo: Chikuma-shobo.

Mori, A. (1977). *Ningen Keisei Genron (Iko): Mori Akira Chosaku Shu Dai 6 Kan* [Principles of human formation (Posthumous work): The collected works of Akira Mori, Vol. 6]. Nagoya: Reimei-shobo.

Mori, A. (1978). *Kyoiku Ningengaku: Ningen Seisei toshite no Kyoiku, Mori Akira Chosaku Shu Dai 4, 5 Kan* [Educational anthropology: Education as human becoming, The collected works of Akira Mori, Vols. 4–5]. Nagoya: Remimei-shobo.

Morita, H. (2008). Kindai Nihon Kyouikugakushi Shiron [An essay concerning the history of the educational theory in modern Japan]. In *Kyoiku Tetsugaku Kenkyu Dai 97 Gou* [Studies in the philosophy of education, Vol. 97] (pp. 151–157). Tokyo: The Philosophy of Education Society of Japan.

Nishida, K. (2003). *Kyoikugaku nitsuite* [On pedagogy]. In Nishida, Kitaro Zenshu Dai 7 Kan [The collected works of Kitaro Nishida, Vol. 7]. Tokyo: Iwanami Shoten.

Tanabe, H. (1963). Nishida Sensei nio Osie wo Aogu [Ask for the instruction of Professor Nishida]. In *Tanabe Hajime Zenshu Dai 4 Kan* [The collected work of Hajime Tanabe, Vol. 4]. Tokyo: Chikuma-shobo.

Tanaka, T. (1999). Mori Akira no Kyoiku Ninngenn Gaku [Mori Akira's pedagogical anthropology]. In N. Sumeragi & S. Yano (Eds.), *Nihonn no Kyoiku Ninngenn Gaku* [Pedagogical anthropology in Japan]. Tokyo: Tamagawa University Press.

Tanaka, T. (2003). *Rinshouteki Ningen Keisei Ron He* [Towards the clinical theory of human becoming]. Tokyo: Keisoshobo.

Tanaka, T. (2006). Generativity kara sedaikeishouteki koukyousei he [Generativity and generative public sphere]. In K. Suzuki et al (Eds.), *Kokyo Tetsugaku 20* [Philosophy on public sphere 20]. Tokyo: Tokyo University Press.

Yoshioka, M. (1978). Shinshuu deno Mori Akira Sennsei [Professor Mori Akira in Shinshu]. In M. Mori (Ed.), *Koubou; Mori, Akira. no Omoide* [A shaft of lightning: Memories of Mori, Akira] (a privately printed book).

# Chapter 6
# The Kyoto School and the Theory of Aesthetic Human Transformation: Examining Motomori Kimura's Interpretation of Friedrich Schiller

Takuo Nishimura

## Introduction

The task of this paper is to introduce a typical theory of human education, or rather transformation, of the Kyoto School and examine its relevance for our current philosophy of education. For this purpose I have taken up Motomori Kimura (1895–1945). He was a leading student of Nishida, began with a study of Fichte and was very interested in aesthetics, but turned to the philosophy of education when he became the chair of pedagogy at Kyoto Imperial University in 1933. He merits close attention for the purpose of this paper, not only because he led the philosophy of education in the 'intellectual network' of the Kyoto School, but also because we can find a representative example of the thought of the school in his theory of aesthetic education.

Although there is some dispute with regard to the definition of the school, I will briefly summarize its characteristics in a fashion that is pertinent to this paper (cf. Nishimura 2007):

1. It is said to be the only philosophy in the history of modern Japanese thought that is peculiar to Japan and not just an import from Western thought.
2. One of the reasons for this peculiarity is that it is grounded in Eastern religious thought, especially Zen Buddhism.
3. *Geido*, the practice and theory of Japanese performing arts, which was conceptualized under the influence of Zen, often provided a very important impetus for the philosophers of the school.
4. One of the definitions of human nature in Nishida and Kimura is as follows: 'The human being is a form of existence that expresses itself formatively and is aware

T. Nishimura (✉)
Faculty of Letters, Nara Women's University,
Kita-uoya-nishimachi, Nara-shi, 630-8506 Nara, Japan
e-mail: takuo@cc.nara-wu.ac.jp

P. Standish and N. Saito (eds.), *Education and the Kyoto School of Philosophy*,    65
Contemporary Philosophies and Theories in Education 1,
DOI 10.1007/978-94-007-4047-1_6, © Springer Science+Business Media Dordrecht 2012

of its own formative expression'.[1] The meaning of 'expression' in this context is extremely broad and is not limited to aesthetic or artistic expression. The aesthetic and the arts are important as phenomena that most straightforwardly represent essence.

5. The meaning of 'express' here refers not only to an 'individual' subject. Expression of an 'individual' subject is a point of 'self-awakening' of the absolute entity called 'absolute nothingness' (*zettai-mu* in Japanese), which is a dynamic process and a 'locus' (*basho*) where everything is generated and becomes.

6. Considering the essence of human being as 'expressive-formative existence' in this meaning, the idea of beauty in aesthetic expression is identified with the value-intentionality in general acts of human being. And the thesis of 'oneness' of *praxis* and *poiesis* is derived from such an understanding of human existence.

7. Therefore we can find therein a structure of thought that the theory of aesthetic expression quickly turned into a theory of human existence and human transformation. As such, rather than saying that a theory of aesthetic education represents part of Nishida and Kimura's philosophy, it might be more fitting to suggest that the whole of their philosophy corresponds to the theory of aesthetic human transformation.

I would like to take a simple approach in trying to carry out the task indicated at the beginning, leaving a general introduction of Kimura's thought to another paper of mine (Nishimura 2007). The approach utilizes Kimura's interpretation of Friedrich Schiller's theory of aesthetic education. There are two reasons why I am taking up Kimura's interpretation of Schiller. The first is that after becoming the chair of pedagogy at Kyoto Imperial University, Kimura held a seminar to read Schiller's 'Über die ästhetische Erziehung des Menschen in einer Reihe von Briefen' (*Aesthetic Letters*). When he discussed the significance of the arts for human life, which he characterized with the Buddhist term *moksha* (*gedatsu* in Japanese), he took up Schiller's concept of the *schöne Seele* as a representative example. Accordingly, we can assume that Schiller's thought was an important influence on Kimura when he himself took up the philosophy of education. The other reason is the fact that there are multiple possibilities for interpreting Schiller's *Aesthetic Letters*.

## Aporia in the Interpretation of *Aesthetic Letters*

Schiller's *Aesthetic Letters*, one of the most important classics to argue the relationship between beauty, fine arts and education, is also famous for being difficult to understand.[2] This text has been a topic of discussion for many thinkers and scholars

---

[1] All translations, unless otherwise indicated, are by the author.

[2] cf. 'Wer aber daraufhin eine allen Regeln der philosophischen Zukunft entsprechende Untersuchung erwartet, findet sich bald verwirrt und enttäuscht. Interpreten haben die vielen Äquivokationen und imperatorischen, aber keineswegs immer zuverlässigen Schlüsse schon zur hellen verzweiflung gebracht. Dennoch überwältigt uns die große einheitliche Vision, und der Gewinn für die Ästhetik und die gesamte idealistische Philosophie steht außer Frage. Niemand sollte sich über das alte Rätsel des Schönen mehr äußern dürfen, der Schillers ästhetische Schriften nicht kennt'. (Staiger 1967, p. 67.)

for more than 200 years. The range of interpretations is so broad that some completely oppose one another. What, one might ask, causes there to be such varying interpretations? I will here attempt to give a simple schematic explanation of the problems faced in interpreting the text.

In *Aesthetic Letters,* Schiller described three stages of development of both the individual human being and human being as a whole: 'physical state, aesthetic state, moral state'. According to this assumption, the 'aesthetic state' is significant only as the preceding stage to the 'moral stage'.[3] But near the end of the series of letters (after the 25th letter), the tone of argument changes as if to suggest the 'aesthetic stage' is a goal in and of itself. In other words, it is not a step or means to a goal, but is the actual goal of aesthetic education. [4] How to interpret this 'refraction' of his argument has been the most difficult aporia in understanding *Aesthetic Letters* (Sharpe 1995, p. 4).

The interpretation of the text itself, however, is not the purpose of this paper. The main point is that how a thinker approaches this aporia becomes a touchstone for revealing his estimation of 'the aesthetic'. This is no exception in the case of Kimura. His interpretation of this aporia is quite characteristic of the Kyoto School. Through examination of his interpretation, I would like to present the characteristics of the school. This is another reason why I take up Schiller in this context. And I would like to consider how this attempt relates to the relevance of our current philosophy of education in Chaps. 7–10.

## Kimura's Interpretation of Schiller (1): 'Purity' of 'Aesthetic Feeling'

Here I take up Kimura's argument regarding Schiller in a paper titled 'Form and Ideal' (1941) (Kimura 2000). I will confine my treatment of it to how he interpreted Schiller, omitting the context.

Kimura first summarized Schiller's argument as follows. Human being is a 'sensuous-rational, contradictory existence'. But, because beauty has the nature of 'disinterestedness' as Kant has indicated, a human being becomes free from sensuous desires in an aesthetic state, in the state where there is no hindrance for him to becoming a rational-moral existence. In this sense, beauty is a 'mediative-processive' stage that makes the transfer from a physical existence toward a rational-moral existence easy. In this way, Kimura did not deny the interpretation that views beauty as

---

[3] e.g. 'In a word, there is no other way of making sensuous man rational except by first making him aesthetic.' (23rd Letter, Schiller 1967, p. 161.)

[4] e.g. 'In the midst of the fearful kingdom of forces, and in the midst of the sacred kingdom of laws, the aesthetic impulse to form is at work, unnoticed, on the building of a third joyous kingdom of play and of semblance, in which man is relieved of the shackles of circumstance, and released from all that might be called constraint, alike in the physical and in the moral sphere.' (27th Letter, Schiller 1967, p. 215.)

a 'mediation' or 'process' according to Kantian dualism. But it is noteworthy that Kimura himself argued that it is more important that Schiller 'inquired much more deeply into the significance of the aesthetic character of human being'.

Kimura wrote, 'Schiller understood the essence of beauty in the reconciliation of the sensuous principle and the rational principle'. In other words, it is not the process of transition from sensibility toward rationality but the very 'reconciliation' that is important for Kimura. Although the phrase itself is quite common in Schiller studies, his understanding of the 'reconciliation' is peculiar to him as seen here: 'the fact that beauty consists of the reconciliation of the sensuous and the rational means that it must be the concrete and higher unity of both which are originally contradictory and repulsive'. The words 'concrete and higher unity' of the 'contradictory and repulsive' have particular meaning to the Kyoto School.

Why did Kimura consider that sensibility and rationality, which are 'contradictory and repulsive' from the viewpoint of Kantian dualism, could be reconciled in beauty? This interpretation has a precondition peculiar to the school. Following his mentor Nishida, Kimura names what is inherent in the experience, that which we call 'beauty' as opposed to 'truth' or 'good', 'pure feeling'. If among the various feelings of human being there is a feeling that can be called 'aesthetic', it must be a 'pure' feeling that never participates in either sensuous desire or rational order. Kant had already drawn attention to this fact as the 'disinterestedness' and 'non-conceptuality' of beauty. Kimura's interpretation is unique in his understanding of this concept of 'pure'.

Kimura wrote that the 'purity' of 'aesthetic feeling' is not something 'abstract' which denies and excludes knowledge (conceptuality) and will (interestedness) 'to the outer', but is 'concrete purity' which 'negates them to the inner' and 'transcends them to the bottom'. In order to comprehend the unusual phrases, 'negation to the inner' and 'transcendence to the bottom', we must examine some of Nishida's central concepts which lie at the root of Kimura's argument.


## 'Pure Feeling' and 'Locus'

According to Nishida's own recollection, when Kimura first met Nishida as a student, Nishida was examining the relationships between subject and object, mind and substance, and mind and body from 'a kind of will-centered standpoint like Fichte'. Nishida considered Fichte's 'pure self' to be un-conscious transcendent 'absolutely free will', and individual concrete acts to be 'points of self-realization' of the 'absolutely free will'. Nishida named this transcendent 'will', 'nothingness' (*mu* in Japanese), because it can never be apprehended by regular consciousness. (This is the reason why the thought of the Kyoto School is called the 'philosophy of nothingness'.) Nishida argued that 'nothingness' in this sense generates all experience. 'Pure feeling' was another name that Nishida gave to this 'nothingness'.

Nishida later shifted his view to the concept of 'locus', which he called 'a kind of intuitionism' according to his own account (Heisig 2001, pp. 299–300).

The 'absolutely free will' is 'nothingness' because it always stays behind the consciousness, which participates in anything that has form, which Nishida generally called 'being' (*u* in Japanese) as opposed to 'nothingness', and consciousness can never reach the transcendent 'will', But it is no more than 'relative nothingness' because it is 'nothing' compared to 'being'. Nishida proceeded to develop the concept of 'absolute nothingness', which is the 'locus' embracing both 'being' and 'relative nothingness', where everything is generated.

'I' am in the 'locus' as 'absolute nothingness' and embraced by it. Every consciousness and will of 'I' is an 'act' generating in the 'locus', which Nishida called the 'self-determination of locus'. In this sense 'locus' is what embraces 'I' and is at the same time 'I' itself. It has often been noted that such arguments of Nishida's refer to a certain special religious 'stage'. Others say that we usually exist as Nishida described before our understanding divides ourselves from it, and Nishida tried only to clarify our ordinary mode of existence. I cannot judge which is true, but the concept of 'locus' also has another important implication. That is to say, for Nishida, being in the 'locus' as 'absolute nothingness' means receiving and absolutely affirming every 'act' as it is generated there. Considering this momentum of 'absolute affirmation', the interpretation that Nishida was referring to a kind of religious 'stage' may be true to a certain degree.

## Kimura's Interpretation of Schiller (2); the *Schöne Seele* and 'Absolute Nothingness'

I would now like to turn back to Kimura. His interpretation of Schiller is founded on Nishida's thoughts on 'pure feeling' and 'locus'. Kimura explained the above concepts of 'negation to the inner' and 'transcendence to the bottom' as follows: 'it is embracing and receiving knowledge and will, preserving them as they are, and that deeper inner background, from their subjective bottom. At that time, while they (knowledge and will) are transcended and negated, they are also affirmed absolutely and assimilated when considered from the perspective that they are free from themselves' (Kimura 2000, p. 20).

Things that 'contradict' and 'repulse' each other remain 'contradictory-repulsive' forever, so far as they are negated 'abstractly' 'to the outer'. In the context of Schiller interpretation, physical state and moral state, and aesthetic state and moral state, cannot but negate each other antinomically. To date, we have been presented with only two ways of understanding this. One is to understand that beauty is nothing but 'mediation' and 'process' toward a moral state according to Kantian rigourism that insists on the absolute predominance of practical reason. The other is to understand that the aesthetic state itself should be a goal that goes beyond Kantian precondition, as where Hans-Georg Gadamer interprets Schiller's argument as 'a new aesthetic imperative; Live aesthetically!' (Gadamer 1975, p. 71).

However, if they are 'negated-transcended' in getting back to the 'locus' where they were originally generated, towards 'their deeper inner background, their subjective bottom' as Kimura said, they are 'unified' in a way such that they are 'embraced-transcended' by 'absolute nothingness'. That is exactly what is meant by 'concrete unity' as opposed to the 'abstraction' of negation 'to the outer'. Kimura wrote, the 'Kantian morality of *Sollen* can be said to be transcended by the Ideal of beauty in Schiller. Merely moral conduct cannot get rid of abstraction. Humanity as a whole expresses itself only in the 'beautiful conduct' deriving from the *schöne Seele*'.

Moreover, not only is this 'concrete unity' a reconciliation of things that are contradictory and repulsive to each other, but it also means the absolute affirmation of every 'act' in the 'locus' as 'absolute nothingness'. Kimura thus wrote as follows: 'when they (knowledge and will) are purified and come to the world of 'pure feeling' with disinterestedness and non-conceptuality, all knowledge and will can be embraced-transcended. In this sense, beauty is whole and absolute affirmation of all the content of life'. The above interpretation of Kimura's—that Schiller argued for the 'higher' unity of sensibility and rationality in beauty—has just such an implication.

To sum up, Kimura considered Kantian 'disinterestedness and non-conceptuality' to be purity of 'pure feeling' in Nishida's sense, 'purity' to be realized by 'negation-transcendence' towards 'the inner' or 'the bottom', and he therefore interpreted Schiller's *Spiel* and *schöne Seele* to mean being in the 'locus' as 'absolute nothingness'. And if the aesthetic state that is called 'Spiel' and 'schöne Seele' by Schiller corresponds to such 'nothingness' as 'negation-transcendence', the question of whether the aesthetic state is 'process' or 'aim' becomes meaningless because it 'embraces-transcends' and 'absolutely affirms' everything. From the Kimura-Nishida viewpoint there is no contradiction or 'refraction' in Schiller's argument.

## The Kyoto School and Postmodernism

The above interpretation of Schiller by Kimura shows a solution to the aporia of understanding the *Aesthetic Letters* from the standpoint of Kimura and Nishida. It is an interpretation quite particular to the Kyoto School that identifies the 'purity' of the *schöne Seele* with 'absolute nothingness'. It is interesting in terms of the history of Schiller studies that Kimura's interpretation seems to correspond with the lineage of interpretations seeking to discover the influence of Neo-Platonic *emanatio* theory on the *Aesthetic Letters* (e.g. Lovejoy 1936, pp. 301–303; Pugh 1991, pp. 273–295). But that is something beyond the scope of this paper. Now I would like to consider briefly the relevance of 'the thought of the Kyoto School as a theory of aesthetic human transformation'.

From the high regard for music and dance in Plato's thoughts on education, to the leading role played by art education in *Reformpädagogik*, we can find a tendency to seek opportunities for overcoming difficulties when a culture and its educational methods are faced with crisis. Regarding recent cases, in the postmodernism theories of education since the 1980s, the aesthetic has often been referred to as an important theoretical impetus (e.g. Lenzen (Hrsg.) 1990; Imai and Wulf (eds.) 2007). Why is the aesthetic important? Of course, thinkers give quite differing answers. If, however, I were to dare to summarize the common problems, it would be as follows. Education in modern society has proved to be an undertaking that steers people towards goals that they do not choose themselves, based on rational causality. Even if it is argued that it is precisely education that makes educated people autonomous, the process still inevitably involves exerting control over people. It is nothing but the control of a human being by another human being. Not even self-education can be disengaged from this relationship of the control of a human being. Therefore we must seek alternative forms of education—or, human transformation—that are free from all the controls over human beings, others and selves; in other words, something completely different from modern 'education'. One may wonder if we might be able to discover an opportunity for this in the aesthetic.

On the other hand, the most famous slogan of the Kyoto School was 'transcending and overcoming the modern'. Kimura's interpretation of Schiller is one typical example of how thinkers in the Kyoto School tried to confront modern Western philosophies, and reinterpret and transcend them based on traditional Eastern thought. It is an interesting fact that such a theory of human existence and human transformation as that of the Kyoto School had a very aesthetic disposition. We can reinterpret their definition of human nature, 'expressive-formative existence' as self-awakening of 'absolute nothingness', as showing us another alternative understanding of a subject that embraces and transcends the subjectivity of the individual self for whom the relationship between 'I' and 'the other' is contradictory, as they control one another. Such a 'subject' might be quite different from the Western modern self, but it is essential and natural for Kimura and Nishida.

Despite the arguments I have presented here, I in no way intend to insist that we can simply find an alternative to modern education in the Kyoto School and 'the aesthetic'. I think that we have now arrived at the point where we can no longer speak of human nature in a naively essentialist way, stating such things as, 'the human being is *essentially* this or that, etcetera'. But it does not mean that we need not consider an alternative. Speaking in Kimura's narrative style, 'subjects' exist, forming themselves as narrated, as 'expressed'. I accept this sort of constructionist viewpoint. From this point of view, it is still a very important task for us to 'redescribe' (cf. Løvlie and Standish 2003) and imagine an alternative understanding of the subject that is different from the modern subject and its formation as a precondition of modern society and modern education.

In Japan, postmodernism seems to have already been consumed as an ephemeral modish form of thought. But the above task which postmodernism proposed has yet to be sufficiently addressed. The task is to develop an understanding of the subject and its formation for which the relationship between 'I' and 'the other' is not contradictory, but synergistically, vigorously and mutually transforming. By indicating such as possibility, 'the thought of the Kyoto School as a theory of aesthetic human transformation' has demonstrated its actuality.

# Two Possibilities of 'The Aesthetic':
# A Reply to Paul Standish

The contents of this paper were originally reported in a special panel at the biennial conference of the International Network of Philosophers of Education in Kyoto, 2008. The commentator in the panel was Paul Standish, whose comments induced me further consideration of the relevance of the Kyoto School for our current philosophy of education. His comments were comprised of three parts. First: the question of how a philosophy of education drawing upon the Kyoto School can be incorporated into educational practice. He asked, 'What are the implications of putting the ideas into practice?' and 'How are they translated into practice?' Second: the possibility of the Kyoto School philosophy of education to overcome the Western dichotomy of subject and object, and the question of whether there still remains some hypothesis of development or progress and some claim for foundation or founding. Third: he offered a different rationale for aesthetic education that respects the 'impurity' and 'messiness' of human life and experience and a 'return to the ordinary', and intends to find a so-called non-foundational foundation for political-practical life in the aesthetic, which stands in contrast to Nishida's and Kimura's idea that seemed to give, as Standish realized, privilege to aesthetic experiences.

To begin by responding to the third part, because my contribution in the panel was mainly on the theory of aesthetic human transformation, the rationale for aesthetic education presented by Standish reminded me of Hannah Arendt's theory of politics based on aesthetic-political judgment (Arendt 1982; cf. Beiner 1983). I asked him if such an understanding was appropriate or not. He answered that his idea was not restricted to one such as Arendt's but that my understanding was not necessarily wrong. The final question in Standish's comments regarded to what degree his idea of aesthetic education was complementary to or in a state of tension with the positions offered by the discussants of the panel. My answer to that question would be that it is both: complementary and at the same time in a state of tension.

In the context of Schiller studies, Standish's idea also reminded me of Jürgen Habermas' interpretation of *Aesthetic Letters*, which placed the text in a genealogy of thought from Aristotle to Arendt that finds political significance in aesthetic judgment (Habermas 1985, p. 59). I consider that such an interpretation not only shows a typical interpretation of *Aesthetic Letters*, but also is a strong rationale for the educational and political importance of the aesthetic. At this point, I completely agree with Standish's idea.

On the other hand, however, I believe that the aesthetic has another possibility and that Kimura's interpretation of Schiller shows it. This possibility is not *Aristotelian*, as Habermas suggests, but rather *Platonic*. In my opinion, the aesthetic contains both possibilities, *Aristotelian* and *Platonic*.

I must be quick to mention, however, that Kimura's conception of 'Idea' is different from that of Platonism. For Kimura, 'Idea' is not what exists beyond, or far away from, practice and leads it from there, but what is generated, so to speak, in concrete phases of aesthetic practice, as he discussed using the metaphor, 'each stroke of the chisel' (Kimura 1968, pp.141–181). I have argued in detail about the conception of the 'self-generating Idea' according to Kimura in the other paper of mine (Nishimura 2007).

## Practice Led by the 'Self-Generating Idea'

Such a conception of a 'self-generating Idea', peculiar to Kimura and the Kyoto School, is linked with the first and second parts of Standish's comments. As I mentioned at the beginning of this paper, when Kimura said 'the human being is a form of existence that expresses itself formatively and is aware of its own formative expression', the meaning of 'expression' was not limited to aesthetic or artistic expression. The aesthetic and the arts are important simply as phenomena that most straightforwardly represent essence. I have also already argued in the other paper that such an understanding of human existence is based on the thesis of a 'oneness of praxis and poiesis'. Even educational practice, so long as it is just such 'practice', is understood as follows: that which leads educational practice is not 'theory from above', but historical-physical 'Idea' generated precisely amidst ordinary practice in each of the 'segments of our practice'. Such 'practice' does not require any 'foundation' outside of ordinary concrete practice, outside of each educational relationship and educational act. Therefore, just as artistic 'creation' cannot be reduced to method, neither can we denote an external 'method' for educational practice which is understood as such. The philosophy of education that understands educational practice as such does not have any answers to 'the questions the teachers and policy-makers would want to ask' which Standish dared to present. Or rather, it dares to give no answer to the questions. In this sense, assuming the basis of an ordinary scheme of theory-practice, this philosophy of education *dares* to be non-practical. However, if an understanding of practice such as Kimura's throws light on the essential structure of practice in general, or, avoiding such an essentialist manner of narrative, if a way such as Kimura's of narrating practice is the most relevant to educational practitioners, this philosophy of education may be said to be the most practical.

Just after the panel at the International Network of Philosophers of Education meeting, I, together with Tsunemi Tanaka, one of the discussants of the panel, took part in a symposium held by the Japanese Society of Philosophy of Education that inquired into the relationship between the philosophy of education and the reality of education. In the symposium, we asked how the philosophy of education could, or should, be involved with the reality of education as compared with other 'positive' disciplines such as the psychology or the sociology of education. Unlike such 'positive' disciplines, the philosophy of education can neither guide teachers' practice directly nor give evidence to policy makers. Such a 'useless' philosophy of education is now regarded as having no reason to exist. The Kyoto School philosophy of education may be the most typical of such 'useless' disciplines. Nevertheless, I venture to reject the need to be 'useful' in the naïve scheme of 'theory-practice' and claim that there are alternative methods of education or human transformation which have been hidden by just such naïve schemes, because nothing is as real and 'practical' for myself, as a teacher at university and a parent taking part in creating a new school, as the understanding of education and human transformation expounded by Kimura. It is precisely this personal reality as an educational practitioner that is the basis of my venture.

But I would like to add that I also have a suspicion that the Kyoto School philosophy of education contains an inherent danger. If being in the 'locus' as 'absolute nothingness' is 'absolute affirmation of every act' as Kimura said when he interpreted Schiller's *schöne Seele*, is there any room for 'ethical' judgment? Can 'ethics' exist in the 'dialectic between Eros and Agape'? Does the standpoint of 'absolute affirmation of every act' rather contain the danger of losing a critical eye for preventing the corruption of education into one in which a human being is controlled by another dominant human being? These questions are the same as the problem of *honngaku shisou* mentioned by Tsunemi Tanaka, a kind of 'Emanation' theory in Buddhism which 'believes everything in Heaven and Earth to have an inherent power to attain nirvana' (Tanaka 2008, p. 8). It is this problem that I would like to discuss together when we consider practical possibilities of the Kyoto School philosophy of education.

## 'Development' and 'Becoming' in the Living Dynamics of Practice

Now let me return to the conception of 'Idea' peculiar to Kimura. Based on this conception, a reply to the second part of Standish's comments is possible. His question was whether 'a theory of becoming, especially under institutional pressure toward explicit formulation' can 'avoid sliding into claims regarding stages of development'. I think that asking such a question, or doubting that sight of 'the variety of human experience' may be lost in certain theories of progression or development, shows that we share a basic stance. The core of the Kyoto School philosophy of education never appears in the theory of developmental stages. If the discussants' reports reminded him of a kind of Buddhist theory of stages toward spiritual awakening, it was misleading. However, for the Kyoto School philosophy of education, the development theory is not what should be 'avoided'. On the contrary, the supposition of development stages and intention for progression can be positively placed as 'historical' factors of teachers and students, or their relationship in educational practice, that are always and already conditioned historically. As I could not mention the historicity of 'the inner' and 'the outer' in the 'dialectical' structure of expression and self-generation of 'idea' because my presentation in the panel at the Kyoto conference was exclusively focused on Kimura's interpretation of Schiller, I would like to ask readers to refer to the other paper of mine about the problem of historicity of practice. What we would like to call into question is the problem that such factors of 'development' and 'progress' may be abstracted from the living dynamics of practice and negatively operate to reduce the variety and vitality of practice.

I consider it most appropriate to answer Standish's second question by referring to Satoji Yano's theory of 'development/becoming' (Yano 2000). Yano compares 'development' with 'becoming'. The former intends to complete the identity of the subject after the model of 'labor' which purposely-rationally produces something useful. The latter is the transformation of life which cannot be integrated in 'development', the experience of the ex-subject such as 'melting' and 'transcendence' contrasted with the identity of the subject. Yano attaches importance to the meaning of the latter, or rather, the meaninglessness of the latter. Though the relative emphasis in his theory is obviously on 'becoming', the significance of 'development' is sufficiently recognized and placed in the theory. I consider his theory to be the most orthodox successor of the Kyoto School philosophy of education.

That completes how I would like to reply to Standish's comments, and I anticipate those comments will encourage discussion with other Japanese colleagues who were stimulated by them. Though the translatability of thoughts is always a serious problem, it was a reckless attempt to argue in English about the philosophy of the Kyoto School, which was already thoroughly dependent on 'the magnetic field of Japanese language' (Iwaki 2000). I am now keenly feeling the difficulty and realize why many wise predecessors were so cautious about making such an attempt. But struggling to pull myself away from the 'magnetic field' was a precious opportunity for me to extend my thinking. If both 'Western-modern' and 'the traditional Japanese', which might to a certain extent also be a fiction of the modern, are factors whose historicity cannot be disregarded, an attempt should be made to talk 'in between them' despite the recklessness of the task. I hope such an attempt would contribute to meaningful dialogue in international collaborations.

# References

Arendt, H. (1982). *Lectures on Kant's political philosophy*. Chicago: University of Chicago Press.

Beiner, R. (1983). *Political judgment*. London: Methuen & Co. Ltd.

Gadamer, H.-G. (1975). *Truth and method* (J. Weinsheimer & D. G. Marshall, Trans.). London: Continuum.

Habermas, J. (1985). *Der philosophische Diskurs der Moderne: zwölf Vorlesungen*. Frankfurt am Main: Suhrkamp.

Heisig, J. W. (2001). *Philosophers of nothingness*. Honolulu: University of Hawaii Press.

Imai, Y., & Wulf, C. (Eds.). (2007). *Concepts of aesthetic education: Japanese and European perspective*. Münster: Waxmann.

Iwaki, K. (2000). Kaisetsu [Commentary]. In *Bi no Praxis* [Praxis of beauty] (pp. 255–286). Kyoto: Toeisha.

Kimura, M. (1968). *Hyogen-ai* [Expressive love]. Tokyo: Nansosha.

Kimura, M. (2000). Keishiki to Risou [Form and ideal]. In *Bi no Praxis* [Praxis of beauty]. (pp. 6–58). Kyoto: Toeisha.

Lenzen, D. (Hrsg.). (1990). *Kunst und Pädagogik: Erzirhungswissenschaft auf dem Weg zur Ästhetik?* Darmstadt: Wissenschaftliche Buchgesellschaft.

Lovejoy, A. O. (1936). *The great chain of being*. Cambridge: Harvard University Press.

Løvlie, L., & Standish, P. (2003). Introduction: Bildung and the idea of a liberal education. In L. Løvlie, K. P. Mortensen, & S. E. Nordenbo (Eds.), *Educating humanity: Bildung in postmodernity* (pp. 1–24). Malden: Blackwell.

Nishimura, T. (2007). The aesthetic and education in the Kyoto School: Motomori Kimura's theory of expression. In Y. Imai & C. Wulf (Eds.), *Concepts of aesthetic education: Japanese and European perspective* (pp. 64–76). Münster: Waxmann.

Pugh, D. (1991). Schiller as Platonist. *Colloquia Germanica, 24*, 273–295.

Schiller, F. (1967). *On the aesthetic education of man: In a series of letters* (E. M. Wilkinson & L. A. Willoughby, Trans.). Oxford: Clarendon.

Sharpe, L. (1995). *Schiller's aesthetic essays: Two centuries of criticism*. Columbia: Camden House.

Staiger, E. (1967). *Friedrich Schiller*. Zürich: Atlantis.

Tanaka, T. (2008). A synopsis on the clinical theory on human becoming–From the pedagogy of the Kyoto School to the clinical theory on human becoming. In *Proceedings of a special panel, educational thought in the Kyoto School of philosophy: Towards an East–West dialogue* 4–15. International Network of Philosophers of Education, 11th Biennial Conference, Kyoto University, Kyoto, Japan.

Yano, S. (2000). *Jikohen'yo to iu Monogatari* [Narrative of self-transformation]. Tokyo: Kanekoshobo.

# Chapter 7
# Metamorphoses of 'Pure Experience': Buddhist, Enactive and Historical Turns in Nishida

Nobuo Kazashi

## Nishida's Encounter with James

### James and Modern Japan

In 1909, the year previous to his death, William James gave a series of polemical lectures under the title of 'A Pluralistic Universe' at Oxford University, then the center in England for German idealism with Francis Bradley as its leader. When it was published in book form, there was attached an appendix entitled 'On the Notion of Reality as Changing'. Arguing, from the viewpoint of what he calls 'synechistic pluralism', against the possibility of tracing a straight line of causation through a series of events in historical reality, James illustrated his point as follows:

> Commodore Perry was in a sense the cause of the new regime in Japan, and the new regime was the cause of the Russian Douma (the Imperial Parliament under Tzarism); but it would hardly profit us to insist on holding to Perry as the cause of the Douma: the terms have grown too remote to have any real or practical relation to each other (James 1912a: 347–348).

Indeed, the outcome of the Russo-Japanese war in 1904 appears to have struck James with a considerable impact. At the end of a letter written to Bergson after reading *L'Evolution creatrice*, the following passage is found:

> I say nothing more now – this is just my first reaction; but I am so enthusiastic as to have said only two days ago, 'I thank heaven that I have lived to this date – that I have witnessed the Russo-Japanese war, and seen Bergson's new book appear – the two great modern turning-points of history and of thought!' (James 1920: 294).

N. Kazashi (✉)
Graduate School of Humanities, Kobe University, 1-1 Rokkodai-cho, Nada-ku,
657-8501 Kobe, Japan
e-mail: nkazashi@gmail.com

P. Standish and N. Saito (eds.), *Education and the Kyoto School of Philosophy*,
Contemporary Philosophies and Theories in Education 1,
DOI 10.1007/978-94-007-4047-1_7, © Springer Science+Business Media Dordrecht 2012

The demonstrative firings of the cannons of Commodore Perry's four 'Black Battleships' in 1853 did cause feudal Japan to awaken and forced her out of some 250 years of seclusion from the external world. In 1868 the long reign of the Tokugawa Shogunate finally came to a collapse, and Japan plunged into its well-known process of modernization qua 'Westernization'. Originally launched under the imminently felt threat of colonization, Japan's national policy to catch up with the Western powers entailed the frantic endeavors to learn and assimilate the best fruits of Western civilization in almost every field of human activity; from sciences and arts to even clothes and cuisine.

In this regard, Western philosophy was, needless to say, far from being an exception. However, no sooner had the Japanese intellectuals realized the essential need to tackle Western philosophy from the ground up as the deepest roots of the Western civilization than they came to sense the, so to speak, schizogenetic dilemma lurking in the philosophical implications of her national enterprise to carry out the top-down modernization under the slogan of '*Wakon-Yosai*', that is to say, 'Japanese Spirit: Western Technique'.

## Buddhism and 'Pure Experience'

Kitaro Nishida, born in 1870, 2 years after the launching of the new regime, belongs to the second generation of Japanese intellectuals who struggled to steer somehow an autonomous course in the face of the overwhelming influx of Western thought and culture. Nishida, the end of whose life coincided with the end of the World War II in 1945, is generally regarded as the most significant philosopher of modern Japan. However, what is to be noted first is the fact that it was in none other than James's idea of 'pure experience' that Nishida came to believe to find a philosophical stand, not only congenial to some of the core-features of the traditional Buddhist thought, but also radical enough to ground an entire, new philosophical system on.[1]

Thus, Nishida's maiden work, *An Inquiry into the Good*, published in 1911, a year after James's death, starts with a chapter simply entitled 'Pure Experience'. And the collected works of Nishida, comprising 15 volumes of philosophical work, are, broadly speaking, considered to be the products of his persistent and strenuous endeavors, spanning more than three decades, to transform and overcome the psychologistic shortcomings of his initial stand of 'pure experience' by providing it with 'logical' or judgmental forms as well as socio-historical dimensions.

No doubt James would have been greatly surprised and delighted as well to know what a far-reaching resonance his idea of 'pure experience' was to arouse at the opposite side of the Pacific, yet it only confirms James's own understanding of the essentially unforeseeable nature of significance which a historical event, Commodore Perry's visit to Japan in this case, might take on in the future.

---

[1] In this regard, refer to Loy (1988). Loy relates the Jamesian idea of 'Pure Experience' to the Eastern tradition of thought in terms of 'neutral monism'.

However, seen from the perspective of modern Japan on her hardly autonomous way toward modernization qua Westernization, the elective affinity that came to be established between the Jamesian idea and the deepest concerns of a modern Japanese philosopher would begin to appear far from being an accidental one. The major tenet of the Jamesian philosophy of 'pure experience' was the negation of the ontological dualism of subject-object, which entailed such consequential corollaries as the 'functional' re-interpretation of the notion of consciousness, the discovery of the ambiguous body as the center for the field of lived experience, the thematization of the phenomenon of 'fringes' or 'horizon-structure' as essential to any type of experience, and the restitution of affective values as originally pre-given in the ambiguity of pure experience.

These now stock-in-trade ideas in phenomenology were propounded in James's *Essays in Radical Empiricism* in such a clearly focused manner that Whitehead once considered James's work comparable to Descartes's *Discourse on Method* in terms of the 'inauguration of a new stage in philosophy'. Whitehead wrote in *Science and the Modern World*: 'James clears the stage of the old paraphernalia; or rather he entirely alters its lighting' (Whitehead 1925: 143). In view of Nishida's responses to James's philosophy of pure experience, however, we might be tempted to expand on Whitehead's evaluation of James by an addition of the following sort: 'At the same time James transforms the very design of the theater of modern Western philosophy in such a way, without knowing it, as to strike the back stage open to the opposite side of the audience, namely, the Eastern philosophical tradition'.[2]

## *Dogen: To Learn the Way with the Body*

As is well known, the Eastern tradition of thought, particularly that of Buddhism, is characterized, roughly speaking, by the ontological anti-substantialism and the anti-dualistic view of the body-mind relationship. The former view is epitomized in such terms as '*Engi*', meaning the 'dependent co-origination of beings', and '*Jijimugé*', meaning the 'unhindered mutual interpenetration of phenomena and phenomena'; the latter in such term as '*Shinjin-Ichinyo*', meaning the 'oneness of mind and body'. As most lucid crystallizations of such views, let us refer ourselves to some of the well-known passages in *Shobogenzo*, the major work of Dogen (1200–1253), medieval Japanese Zen monk; the following translations are taken from *Dogen Kigen: Mystical Realist*, a classic work by Hee-Jin Kim (Kim 1982: 99–100).

*Realization of Enlightenment*
To exert and verify myriad things by carrying out the self is illusion; to exert and verify the self while myriad things come forth is enlightenment.

---

[2] As for an overall introduction to Nishida's life and thought, see Nishitani (1991), and as for James's, see Perry (1935). Especially regarding the significance of James's radical empiricism for the phenomenological tradition, see Wild (1969).

To study the Way is to study the self. To study the self is to forget the self. To forget the self is to be enlightened by all things of the universe. To be enlightened by all things of the universe is to cast off the body and mind of the self as well as those of others. Even the traces of enlightenment are wiped out, and life with traceless enlightenment goes on forever and ever.

*Body-Mind's Study of the Way*
*Shingakudo* [the body's study of the Way] is to learn the Way with the body – study on the part of the naked bodily whole. The body comes forth from study of the Way, and what originates from investigation of the Way is likewise the body. The entire universe is precisely this very human body; birth-and-death, coming-and-going are the genuine human body.

*Being-Time*
Do not think only that time flies away; You should not regard time's flying as its sole activity. If time were exclusively dependent on flying, there would be an interspace (between time and the self). People do not listen to the truth of being-time, because they conceive it to be only passing away. In essence, all beings throughout the entire world, while contiguous with each other, are (one-in-all, all-in-one) time. Because it is 'being-time', it is my 'being-time'.

These passages give laconic expression to such quintessential, Zen Buddhist ideas as the realization of the authentic selfhood in the detached openness to the world, the religio-cosmological status of the body, and the spatio-temporal interpenetration of all beings in the universe.

## *'Pure Experience' and the Birth of Modern Japanese Philosophy*

Now, set against the above background, it should come as little surprise that Nishida wrote in a letter to one of his friends in 1910 as follows:

These days I have been reading the recently published articles of James. I find them interesting. They seem to bear clear resemblance to Zen… (Nishida 1978e).

Nishida was reading those articles of James's which were later to be included in *Essays in Radical Empiricism*. Thus, Nishida encountered the Jamesian philosophy of pure experience under the Buddhist lighting. This is crucially important in considering the Nishida's relationship with James. It shows that a radical twist of appropriative interpretation was given to the Jamesian notion of pure experience right at the moment of its reception into Nishida.

However, in addition to a philosophical affinity, we can ascertain a more specifically historical reason for why the Jamesian notion of pure experience proved capable of providing Nishida with an initial starting-point for his attempt to establish a philosophical system; one that would draw its essential inspiration from the traditional Buddhist ideas, but would be nonetheless couched in modern philosophical expressions. As we have already seen, Japanese modernization was carried out under the national slogan of 'Japanese Spirit; Western Techniques'. What such an expedient strategy aimed at was, needless to say, to ingest the cognitive, technological achievements of Western civilization without compromising the traditional Japanese values in moral or spiritual spheres.

As Thomas Kasulis has clearly pointed out, what is implicitly presupposed in this manner of coping with the influx of Western thought is the philosophical legitimacy as well as the possibility of bifurcating 'fact' and 'value' into the two separate domains regulated by two different modes of reasoning as exemplified, for example, in Kantian philosophy (Preface to Carter 1989: xii). However, such Kantian bifurcation of human experience into the two disparate domains of 'scientific cognition' and 'value judgment' could not be considered, in the final analysis, to be compatible with a pre-eminent thrust of the Oriental, Buddhist tradition. Therefore, in Kasulis's expression, the philosophical problem which modern Japan faced was the dilemma that 'only a foreign way of thinking could justify preserving Japanese values'.[3]

Of course, popular discourses on the 'Japanese' or 'Oriental' values as sharply contrasted to 'foreign' ideas are not only philosophically futile, but also can be practically deleterious as it was demonstrated in the irreparable tragedy of the World War II. The historical significance of this notorious slogan of 'Japanese Spirit: Western Technique' should be recognized rather in the fact that the universal problem of where to place modern science and technology in the totality of a culture became urgent for Japanese almost overnight in the form of military threats from the American battleships.

The persistent universality of this problem is confirmed, to take a recent example, by the debates surrounding Habermas who has delineated the dilemma of modernity as the 'colonization of the life-world by instrumental rationality'. The poverty of the urgent but naive expedient applied by the Japanese to this universal problem is betrayed by the facile juxtaposition of 'Spirit' and 'Technique' with no consideration for the mediation of the two.

Although, in his maiden work, *An Inquiry into the Good*, Nishida does not address philosophical issues in terms of Japan's encounter with the West, some consideration of such historical context should make it easier for us to understand more fully why it was the Jamesian philosophy of pure experience that was to play a maieutic role in the birth of modern Japanese philosophy through Nishida.[4]

As seen above, the vision of 'pure experience' was far from foreign to Nishida because of its essential similarities to some of the Zen Buddhist views, and it also could be regarded by Nishida as a promising ground-principle for a philosophy capable of embracing both scientific cognition and spiritual values within one and the same perspective because of the Jamesian characterization of affective values as originally pre-given in the ontological ambiguity of 'pure experience'.

---

[3] Although Japan had undergone, all through her long history, a series of continual influxes of 'foreign' ideas and cultural products from and through the Continent of China, it would be safe to say that the almost abrupt and wide-ranging exposure toward the West starting around the middle of the last century was a historical event of an entirely different kind and scale from the previous ones.

[4] Later in his life, in 1934 and 1940, Nishida came to write two essays on the subject of comparing Eastern and Western culture (see Nishida 1978b, d).

## *Reality and Unifying Activity*

Certainly, it is another issue whether or not Nishida's enterprise to develop critically the Jamesian stand of 'pure experience' can be considered to have seen an appreciable success in this respect. However, emphasizing the 'unifying activity' allegedly operating in all pure experience, Nishida summarized his central vision in his maiden work, *An Inquiry into the Good* as follows:

> Thus, intellectual intuition is nothing more than a further deepening and enlargement of our state of pure experience, that is, it refers to the expression of a great unity in the development of a system of consciousness. Even a scholar's acquiring of new thoughts, a moralist's acquiring of new motives, an artist's acquiring of new ideals, a sage's acquiring of new insights – all are based in the expression of this kind of unity (Nishida 1990: 33).

We could expand more fully on how the Jamesian formulation of 'pure experience' was absorbed and transformed as well at the early stage of Nishida's philosophical career. But, for now, let us restrict ourselves to taking note of only two of the features conspicuous in the Nishida's formulation of 'pure experience'.

The first point is; Whereas the moment of 'unifying activity' operative in pure experience assumes a pivotal significance in both James and Nishida, it seems that, for James the pluralist, it is kept in a critical balance owing to his acknowledgement of the 'disjunctive moments' as well as the 'externality' of some relations in the field of experience.

The second point, though related to the first, is; as it has already been pointed out by a number of scholars, the state of 'pure experience' signifies, in Nishida's version, not only the originary state of experience which is 'not yet' divided into the subjective and the objective, but also, and more importantly, the 'ideal' state of experience which is 'no longer' divided into the subjective and the objective (see Miyakawa 1962: 133–140).

This processive dynamism is far from absent in James who sees the pragmatic value of 'concepts' in their function to lead us to the inexhaustible richness of the immediate experience. However, the explicit characterization of 'pure experience' as the 'ideal' state of experience, religious or artistic, to be sought after seems to be a distinctive characteristic of Nishida's first work. And now it would be needless to confirm that what is responsible for this 'religious' transformation of the notion of 'pure experience' is the intellectual backgrounds of Nishida as an Eastern philosopher steeped in the Buddhist tradition of thought.

## Acting-Intuition and the Historical World

### *The Stand of the Acting Self*

As Nishida continued to endeavored to grasp concrete reality from the viewpoint of pure experience, a radical turn was to be made in Nishida's basic stance: Nishida began his introductory overview for *Fundamental Problems of Philosophy:*

*the World of Action*, published in 1933, with such challenging statement as follows: 'I feel that philosophy has hitherto never truly philosophized from the standpoint of the [acting] self. Consequently, it has never seen what this world of reality in which people act fundamentally is'. And he goes on to summarize diachronically a variety of 'logic' that have formed the backbone of Western philosophy ever since Aristotle and through Kant, Hegel, Marx, and up to Dilthey and Heidegger as well:

In order to view the world of the [acting] self from the standpoint of the [acting] self there must be a logic of the [acting] self. Greek logic was a logic of the subject. Aristotle considered that which is a subject and cannot ever become predicate to be true substance. The world of the Greeks was not a world of action. It was a world, not of action, but objects of sight. The same can be said for Aristotle's philosophy....

Kant's logic was a logic of empirical scientific reality. ...yet it was not a logic of a world of acting beings, for it was not a logic of social and historical reality....

What exists in the world of action must be both subjective and objective. The world of action must be both subjective and objective. The world of action must include both subject and object. The subjectivity of such world is not a mere unity of subject and object but is rather a dialectical self-determination. Dialectic can be called a logic of practice. Hegel must be cited as the originator of such a logic.

But while the logic of social and historical reality was first pioneered by Hegel, his dialectical logic was still a logic of the subject and of the *noema*. In short, it was still a variation of Greek philosophy. This is the reason why Marx's materialistic dialectic emerged to turn Hegel's dialectic on its head. However, to define dialectics materialistically, as do present-day Marxists, is ultimately to negate dialectics and to revert to physical science....

Dilthey was the first to conceive of the world of historical life as a world of expression, a world of the understanding. Therefore, he laid the foundation of modern *Lebensphilosophie*. Similarly, modern-day *Geisteswissenschaft* has been greatly influenced by Dilthey. However, Dilthey conceived of the historical world as an object of cognition rather than that which personal action. But the historical world is not simply the historical world of the understanding, for it must also determine personal action. People are born and die in history. Even Heidegger's *Existenz-philosophie* which was influenced by Dilthey does not refer to a world which determines human action, but rather a world of the understanding. Even though we suffer [infinite burdens] in it and it is 'pro-jected', it is still not the world from which we are born. It is neither the world which determines the individual, nor the world which includes the I-Thou relation. It is not the world that determines us through its own self-determination. It still is a world seen from the outside and not the world in which people exist (Nishida 1970: 93–95; The brackets show the adjustments in translation by the author. For the Japanese original, see Nishida 1988a).

As often pointed out, such panoptic criticism by Nishida tends to be one-sided and overly simplified. However, what urged him to seek a 'logic of the acting self' was his conviction that 'our selves are historical because they are embodied, and we can grasp the dialectics of historical reality by analyzing the body regarded as most direct to us'. And it was from such stand of acting self situated in the historical world that Nishida was to advance such pivotal notions as 'acting intuition' and 'historical body' for his later philosophy.

In one of his major essays, 'Logic and Life', written in 1936, Nishida propounds them as follows:

We see the world of forms to the extent that our body is formed. Therefore, we can maintain that, without the body, there would be no self. It holds true for animals, too. Therefore, the body is of the logos character (Nishida 1988c: 233).

> True intuition is not, as is usually understood, simply one's losing oneself, or things and the
> self becoming one. It means that the self becomes creative.... Therein our body becomes what
> sees as well as what works.... The world becomes the self's body (Nishida 1988c: 246–247).
>
> The very life of our selves, which are possessed of *historical bodies* and are acting-
> intuitional, is self-contradictory. Historical life itself is self-contradictory. It cannot be the
> case that what knows is what is known. Our self-awareness is self-contradictory. Our body
> is also a thing. Things are what is seen. *But our body is what sees at the same time that it is
> what works....* One recognizes a self-contradiction solely in the thinking self because he
> starts with the thinking self, separating the bodily self from it. But even the thinking self
> cannot exist apart from our *historical body*. Things are expressive, and things have names.
> We intuit things acting-intuitionally as *bodily being*; our thinking self consists in intuiting
> things acting-intuitionally as names. Apart from the historical body that intuits actingly,
> there would be neither *self-contradiction* nor *self-awareness*. Therefore, there would not be
> a starting-point for the thinking self either (Nishida 1988c:264–266, my italics).

There will be no need to dwell on the seminal significance of these meditations
by Nishida on the embodied and historical nature of human existence; naturally one
will be reminded, for example, of the later Merleau-Ponty's similar meditations
carried out under the headings of 'chiasm' and the 'flesh of the world' (Merleau-Ponty,
Maurice 1968),[5] or the so-called 'enactive approach' initiated by Francisco Varela
and others[6]. Here we would like to reconsider the philosophical and educational
implications of Nishida's own 'enactive turn' by shedding light upon its conspicuous
affinity with the 'ecological psychology' initiated by James Gibson.

## *'Action-Perception Coupling' and Self-Awakening*

As is well-known, cognitive psychologist James Gibson (1904–1979) came to advocate,
drawing inspirations partly from William James's legacy, 'ecological realism'
through his research on the mutually dependent relationships between organism and
environment; that is, he came to think that in the environment there exist 'qualities
that induce and orient organisms' activities', which he named 'affordances'. Masato
Sasaki, who has been engaged in further development of Gibson's ecological
psychology, states its core as follows:

> We are always 'directly perceiving' the 'meanings' of objects at one with possibilities of our
> own action. The distinctive characteristic of Gibson's 'ecological theory of perception' lies in
> its recognition of the essential connection between the appearance of the external world and
> perceiver's action and its emphasis of the oneness of these two factors (Sasaki 1990: 95).

It will go without saying that such 'coordination between perception and action',
which Gibsonians call 'perception-action coupling', was exactly what Nishida explored
under the heading of 'acting intuition'. One of the important theses to be derived from
such fundamental insight is the 'complementarity between environment-perception
and self-perception', or, in Gibson's own words, the thesis that 'exteroception is
accompanied by proprioception – that to perceive the world is to coperceive

---

[5] See Kazashi (1995, 1999).

[6] See Lakoff (1999), Noë (2005) and Varela et al. (1991).

oneself' (Gibson 1979:141). In order to bring into relief its affinity with Nishida's later thought, it would take only juxtaposing it with Nishida's own formulation.

> Internal perception is formed always in accordance with external perception. Our internal perceptual self always has the significance of the self's seeing the self although it can never see the self fully (Nishida 1988b: 91).

However, there are some arresting differences between the two; for one thing, while what is at the center of Gibson's inquiry is the pragmatic significance of the perception-action coupling for an organism's adaptation to its environment, in Nishida it is being called into question in the philosophical context of his meditations on *jikaku* (self-awakening). Nishida writes:

> Action has the significance of denying our intellectual self. Our self cannot know the bottom of our own action... We find our true self by working; therein obtains our true *jikaku* [self-awareness] (Nishida 1978b: 54).
>   The more we consider that we see, at the bottom of reality, what goes beyond us, what is transcendent, the more what we consider deep *jikaku* [self-awareness] can obtain. It is because of this that we can think that we see things by acting. Our getting in contact with what is transcendent does not mean to leave things, but to go deep into things (Nishida 1988b: 91).

Furthermore, Nishida's perspective is characterized by its emphatic highlighting of the historical and creative moments in the action-environment relationship. In 'Shu no seisei-hatten no mondai [Problem of the generation and development of the species]' written in 1937 Nishida writes:

> It is as continuity of discontinuity that there obtains the mutual determination of environment and *shutai* [agent-subjects] as well as the connection of past and future... Because it is a continuity of discontinuity, various futures can be built on the determined past; hence, there can be infinite destination (Nishida 1978c: 537).

For Nishida, although *shutai* [agent-subjects] are '*tsukurareta mono* [what-has-been-made]', determined as 'what exists in the environment', they have not been determined causally or mechanistically; they have absolute freedom as long as they act as '*tsukuru mono* [what-makes]' with regard to their environments. In this sense, 'continuity of discontinuity' exists between '*tsukurareta mono* [what-has-been-made]' and '*tsukuru mono* [what-makes]', and it can be said that *shutai* [agent-subjects] are '*oitearu mono* [what exists in the place of ....]' in nothing but such 'continuity of discontinuity'.

## World of Historical Reality as Pure Experience

Thus, in a new preface to the second edition of *An Inquiry into the Good* published in 1936, Nishida wrote in retrospect over the 25 years of his philosophical endeavors after the first publication of this maiden work:

> As I look at it now, the standpoint of this book is that of consciousness, which might be thought of as a kind of psychologism. Yet even if people criticize it as being too psychological, there is little I can do now. I do think, however, that what lay deep in my thought when I wrote it was not something that is merely psychological. In *Intuition and Reflection in Self-Consciousness*, through the mediation of Fichte's *Tathandlung*, I developed the standpoint of pure experience into the standpoint of absolute will. Then, in the second half of

*From the Actor to the Seer*, through the mediation of Greek philosophy, I further developed it, this time into the idea of *place* [basho]. In this way I began to lay a logical base for my ideas. I next concretized the idea of place as a *dialectical universal* and gave that standpoint a direct expression in terms of *action-intuition*. That which I called in the present book the world of direct or pure experience I have now come to think of as the world of historical reality. The world of action-intuition – the world of *poiesis* – is none other than the world of pure experience (Nishida 1990: xxxi–xxxiii).

In spite of his resort to German idealism as well as Greek philosophy, which might appear incongruous with the Jamesian philosophy of pure experience, the crucial relevance of Nishida's career will have become far more evident now: the later Nishida's thinking was clearly focused on the aim of overcoming the 'psychologistic' limitations of the initial position of 'pure experience', which he initially adopted as his own central perspective, by means of establishing what he called the 'logic of *basho* (place)'.

Let us pay closer attention to some of his attempts to give shape to his stand of the 'logic of *basho*' so that we may understand it more fully in relation to his understanding of the 'true self'. The following passages are taken from a 1927 essay entitled simply '*Basho* (Place)':

The field of consciousness conceived psychologically is already something conceptualized: it is nothing but a kind of object. However, the field of consciousness that is conscious of such a field of consciousness cannot be transcended even at its limit. *Also for the field of consciousness that we take to be real, there always lies something that transcends reality at the back of it....*

The stand of cognition also must be an attitude in which experience reflects itself in itself. Cognition means nothing but experience's forming itself in itself. It is in *the place of experience* that the oppositional relationship of form and matter comes to be established. Thus, that which infinitely reflects itself in itself; that which itself is nothingness but contains infinite being, is *the true Self* in which the so-called subject-object opposition is established (Nishida 1987b: 70; my italics).

Judgment consists of the relation between a subject and a predicate. If it is to be established as judgmental knowledge at all, there must be predicative dimensions spreading at the back of it. Even concerning the so-called empirical knowledge, inasmuch as it is judgmental knowledge, there lie predicative universals at its bottom.... Ordinarily, the Self, like things, is considered to be a unity of the grammatical subject that has a variety of attributes, but *the Self must be the predicative unity instead of the (grammatical) subjective unity. It must be, not a point, but a circle: it must be, not a thing, but a place* (Nishida 1987b: 140–141; my italics).

Some of the seminal implications of the notion of the 'self as a field of experience' was brought into light by James. In Nishida, however, we witness an explicitly thematized effort to relate the structuring of self-awareness to the formation of its judgmental acts.

## The True Self and Expression

Nishida stated his central philosophical views in his last work, *The Logic of Place and the Religious Worldview*, completed in 1945, as follows:

I will repeat, therefore, that our true self cannot be found, one-sidedly, either in the direction of the grammatical subject or in the direction of the transcendental predicate. *The true self rather appears in that place in which it predicates of itself through the logic of the contradictory identity of the (grammatical) subjective direction and the predicative direction....*

The existential self discovers the self-transforming matrix of history in its own bottom-less depths. It discovers that it is born from history, is active in history, and dies to history....

In the depths of the conscious self, then, there lies always that which transcends it. And that which transcends it is not something external to the self; rather, the conscious self takes its existence from it and is conceived from it....

The true self acts from an inmost depth that is *the place of the contradictory identity, the dynamic interpenetration, of its own immanent and transcendent planes of consciousness. Intuition always has this significance of dynamic, historical expression* (Nishida 1987b: 83–84, my italics).

Transforming his former formulation of the true self as a predicative unity, Nishida now gives an undeniably 'chiasmic' twist to it *à la* Merleau-Ponty. Awakening to one's true self is now explicitly considered to come about neither by substantializing one's Self as a self-subsisting entity like other things, nor by regarding it as a transcendental nexus of universal principles.

In Nishida's view, the true self is nothing but this 'place of continual awakening' to the identity between the self-contradictory moments of our finite and incarnate existence; prominently, the identity between the moment of the invisible knower and that of the visible object known, or the identity between the moment of the self-forming activity through internal temporality and that of the formative ground of socio-historical horizon.

Before concluding, let us look at a couple of quotes from Nishida, which show how closely his key notions came to be interrelated with each other in such a way as to bring into light the internal relationships between bodily action, expression and history.

Dialectic of life means that the past and the future are simultaneously present in the present. Although the present is uniquely determined, *horizonally* it has innumerable possibilities: therein we have our body. Because the past and the future are simultaneously present in the present, *the world has fringes or horizons.* The world is through and through expressive. Expression means that the temporal is the spatial (Nishida 1988b: 72; my italics).

The fact that our body as working element of the historical world is of the Logos character implies that what is objective (*gegenständlich*) is, at the same time, what is through and through expressive. That such world forms itself as the world of historical life, this fact signifies nothing but our act of 'seeing'. For this reason, our body also is what sees (Nishida 1988b: 233–234).

In Nishida's understanding of expressivity as an essential character of socio-historical reality, it is the notion of the 'bodily field of experience' that functions in such a way as to blend the notion of the 'horizon as transcendence' with that of the 'expressive interpenetration of the internal and the external'.

We encounter here, I submit, a rendition of the notion of expression with a subdued but undoubtedly 'Jamesian' tinge; it is, as it were, a conception of the 'cross-horizonal expression' as grounded in the horizon-structurality of the bodily field of experience.[7]

---

[7] Nishida resorted to James's notion of 'fringes' at some of the crucial junctures on his way to the establishment of his 'logic of basho (place). Nishida wrote in *Fundamental Problems of Philosophy: The World of Action and The Dialectical World*: 'William James wrote of the 'fringes of consciousness'.

In concluding, let us recapitulate briefly the educational significance of the metamorphoses that the notion of pure experience underwent in Nishida's life-long philosophical career, though it would have already come out of itself quite clearly in our characterization of them given above. Firstly, Nishida's Buddhist appropriation of the notion of pure experience brought into light its liberating, or deconstructive, implications it can have for the dualistic understanding of the self, as exemplified by the famous, enthusiastic confession of Hyakuzo Kurata (Kurata 1921/2008) to the effect that reading *An Inquiry into the Good* made it possible for him to break the shackles of metaphysical solipsism. Furthermore, the moral and religious implications of the notion of pure experience were highlighted by the emphasis Nishida put on the 'unifying activity' allegedly operating in all pure experience and his characterization of pure experience as the 'ideal state to be sought after'.

However, more noteworthy will be the further metamorphoses that occurred, or had to occur, in Nishida's endeavors to build a whole philosophical system on the stand of pure experience. The enactive and historical turns taken by the later Nishida could be regarded as the necessary consequences of his further philosophical search for the true self in the face of the historical reality in which he lived. To reiterate, Nishida declared in a nutshell: 'We find our true self by working; therein obtains our true *jikaku* [self-awareness]'. Herein we can hear, it would go without saying, the straightforward, educational message coming out from the metamorphosis process the notion of pure experience underwent in Nishida's life-long thinking.[8, 9]

# References

Carter, R. E. (1989). *Nothingness beyond God: An introduction to the philosophy of Nishida Kitaro*. New York: Paragon House.
Gibson, J. (1979). *The ecological approach to visual perception*. Boston: Houghton Mifflin.
James, W. (1912a). *A pluralistic universe*. New York: Longmans, Green and Co.

---

but the world of the present has in fact infinite fringes. Therein exists the world of pure, undetermined nothingness, and the world of what Heidegger called 'man'. And therein lies the world of mere rumors as well. As long as it determines us in any sense, we feel infinite anxiety in the depths of such a world....

'Even the world of 'man' exists as a fringe of the world of the self-determination of the individual self. For this reason, the self is always individual, and yet belongs to the world of non-individual men. That things are expressive or that we objectively see a world of expression can be conceived only in this world...'. (Nishida 1970: 177)

[8] Regarding the adequacy of the later Nishida's philosophy of history as a whole, however, we would have to point out its overly idealistic or religious penchant as expressed in his later view that [t]he world of action-intuition---the world of poiesis---is none other than the world of pure experience'. (Nishida 1990: xxxi-xxxiii) See Odin (1996) and Kazashi (2009).

[9] All the references for Nishida, except Nishida (1970, 1987a and 1990), and for Sasaki (1990) are in Japanese and any quotation in the main text from these references have been translated into English by the author.

James, W. (1912b). *Essays in radical empiricism*, edited by R. B. Perry. New York: Longmans, Green and Co.

James, W. (1920). *The letters of William James*, Vol. I, edited by H. James. London: Longmans, Green and Co.

Kazashi, N. (1995). The musicality of the other: Schutz, Merleau-Ponty, and Kimura. In S. G. Crowell (Ed.), *Prism of the self* (pp. 171–188). Dordrecht: Kluwer Academic Publishers.

Kazashi, N. (1999). Bodily logos: James, Nishida, and Merleau-Ponty. In D. Olkowski & J. Morley (Eds.), *Merleau-Ponty: Interiority and exteriority, psychic life and the world* (pp. 121–134). Albany: State University of New York Press.

Kazashi, N. (2009). The passion for philosophy in a post-Hiroshima age: Rethinking Nishida's philosophy of history. In R. Bouso & J. W. Heisig (Eds.), *Frontiers of Japanese philosophy: Vol. 6. Confluences and cross-currents* (pp. 129–140). Nagoya: Nanzan Institute for Religion and Culture.

Kim, H.-J. (1982). *Dogen Kigen: Mystical realist*. Tucson: University of Arizona Press.

Kurata, H. (1921/2008). *Ai to ninshiki tono shuppatsu* [The beginning of love and understanding]. Tokyo: Iwanami Shoten.

Lakoff, G., & Johnson, M. (1999). *Philosophy in the flesh: The embodied mind and its challenge to Western thought*. New York: Basic Books.

Loy, D. (1988). *Nonduality: A study in comparative philosophy*. New Haven: Yale University Press.

Merleau-Ponty, M. (1968) *The visible and the invisible* (A. Lingis, Trans.). Evanston: Northwestern University Press.

Miyakawa, T. (1962). *Kindai-nihon no Tetsugaku* [Philosophy of modern Japan]. Tokyo: Keisô Shobô.

Nishida, K. (1970). *Fundamental problems of philosophy: The world of action and the dialectical world* (D. A. Dilworth, Trans.). Tokyo: Sophia UP. (The original Japanese edition was published in 1930.)

Nishida, K. (1978a). Keijijogakuteki-tachiba kara mita tozaikodai no bunkakeitai [Cultural forms in the classical ages of East and West seen from a metaphysical point of view, 1934]. In Y. Abe et al (Ed.), *Nishida Kitaro Zenshu* [The collected works of Kitaro Nishida] (Vol. 7, pp. 429–453). Tokyo: Iwanami Shoten.

Nishida, K. (1978b). Sekai no jiko doitsu to renzoku [The Self-identity and the continuity of the world, 1938]. In Y. Abe et al. (Ed.), *Nishida Kitaro Zenshu* [The collected works of Kitaro Nishida] (Vol. 8, pp. 7–106). Tokyo: Iwanami Shoten.

Nishida, K. (1978c). Shu no seisei-hatten no mondai [Problem of the generation and development of species, 1937]. In Y. Abe et al. (Ed.), *Nishida Kitaro Zenshu* [The collected works of Kitaro Nishida] (Vol. 8, pp. 500–540). Tokyo: Iwanami Shoten.

Nishida, K. (1978d). Nihonbunka no mondai [Problems of Japanese culture, 1940]. In Y. Abe et al. (Ed.), *Nishida Kitaro Zenshu* [The collected works of Kitaro Nishida], (Vol. 12, pp. 275–383). Tokyo: Iwanami shoten.

Nishida, K. (1978e). *Nishida Kitaro Zenshu*. [The collected works of Kitaro Nishida] (Vol. 18). Tokyo: Iwanami Shoten.

Nishida, K. (1987a). *Last writings: Nothingness and the religious worldviews* [Shukyoteki sekaikan to basho no ronri, 1945] (D. Dilworth, Trans.). Honolulu: University of Hawai'i Press.

Nishida, K. (1987b). Basho [Place, 1945]. In S. Ueda (Ed.), *Nishida Kitaro tetsugaku ronbunshu* [Essays on philosophy by Kitaro Nishida] (Vol. I, pp. 67–151). Tokyo: Iwanami Shoten.

Nishida, K. (1988a). Koiteki-jiko no tachiba [Overview: The stand of the acting self, 1933]. In S. Ueda (Ed.), *Nishida Kitaro tetsugaku ronbunshu* [Essays on philosophy by Kitaro Nishida] (Vol. II, pp. 7–36). Tokyo: Iwanami Shoten.

Nishida, K. (1988b). Benshohoteki ippansha to shiteno sekai [The world as the dialectic universal, 1934] In S. Ueda (Ed.), *Nishida Kitaro tetsugaku ronbunshu* [Essays on philosophy by Kitaro Nishida] (Vol. II, pp. 37–172). Tokyo: Iwanami Shoten.

Nishida, K. (1988c). Ronri to seimei [Logic and life, 1936]. In S. Ueda (Ed.), *Nishida Kitaro tetsugaku ronbunshu* [Essays on philosophy by Kitaro Nishida] (Vol. II, pp. 173–300). Tokyo: Iwanam Shoten.

Nishida, K. (1990). *An inquiry into the good* (M. Abe & C. Ives, Trans.). New Haven: Yale University Press. (The first English translation was made by Valdo H. Viglielmo under the title of "A study of good" and published by Printing Bureau of the Japanese Government in Tokyo in 1960.)

Nishitani, K. (1991). *Nishida Kitaro: The man and his thought* (S. Yamamoto & J. W. Heisig, Trans.). Berkeley: University of California Press.

Noë, A. (2005). *Action in perception*. Cambridge: MIT Press.

Odin, S. (1996). *The social self in Zen and American pragmatism*. Albany: State University of New York Press.

Perry, R. B. (1935). *The thought and character of William James* (Vols. 2). Boston: Little, Brown and Company.

Sasaki, M. (1990). Shisei-ga Kawaru Toki [When a posture changes]. In M. Saeki & M. Sasaki (Eds.), *Akutibu Maindo: Ningen-ha Ugoki-no-nakade Kangaeru* [Active mind: Humans think in movements]. Tokyo: University of Tokyo Press.

Varela, F., Thompson, E., & Rosch, E. (1991). *The embodied mind: Cognitive science and human experience*. Cambridge: MIT Press.

Whitehead, A. N. (1925). *Science and the modern world*. New York: The Free Press.

Wild, J. (1969). *The radical empiricism of William James*. Garden City: Doubleday.

# Chapter 8
# William James, Kitaro Nishida, and Religion

Chae Young Kim

## Introduction

In contrast to Enlightenment expectations in the West, religion has not disappeared in contemporary human life. It seemed to decline due to the influence of modern science and secularism. However, in recent times, the religious situation in the world appears to be flowing in an opposite direction. Surprisingly, religion and the experience of religious consciousness are emerging to a high and notable degree in modern human life. Especially in the wake of the tragic events associated with 9/11 and a number of contemporary world religious events, this tendency has been getting stronger. The participants belonging to traditional religious services or non-institutionalized spiritual meetings are growing in North America and around the world. This situation can also be found in the East Asia, too. For example, Christianity among many traditional religions has been rapidly growing in East Asia, China and Korea. Other traditional religions and new religions are growing also. In Japan, new religion as a kind of daily spirituality has been growing (Reader 1991: 236–237). It is also expanding its place in the West (Clark 2000: 1–2). Realistically speaking, religion continues to be an undeniable dynamic reality in any society in our world today.

In addition, the present dynamic movement of religion is changing the traditional religious geography in an increasingly more pluralistic direction. Above all the effects of globalization and immigration are rapidly contributing to build a new religious situation, especially in the West. Hence, the West is no more the place to find only Christianity. It has become religiously pluralistic. In it, one finds various religious traditions such as Judaism, Islam, Hinduism, Buddhism, Taoism and New Religions (Eck 2001). Very recently even the East is following a similar pattern.

C.Y. Kim (✉)
Department of Religious Studies, College of Humanities, Sogang University,
1, Shinsudong, Mapogu, 121-742 Seoul, South Korea
e-mail: chaekim@sogang.ac.kr

P. Standish and N. Saito (eds.), *Education and the Kyoto School of Philosophy*,
Contemporary Philosophies and Theories in Education 1,
DOI 10.1007/978-94-007-4047-1_8, © Springer Science+Business Media Dordrecht 2012

Unlike the West, historically the East has always been pluralistic although a more dynamic pluralistic contemporary scene is changing traditional religious geography in many ways.

This new situation has created a need for considering the place and role of religion within contemporary academic fields both directly and indirectly.[1] Most especially, it is inviting that a new perspective be adopted in tackling issues having to do with the dynamism that one finds in the growth and spread of religion and as this life is being expressed in today's new pluralistic religious situation (Smith 1979: 3). In considering then the kind of perspective which should be adopted, I would like to argue that, among the modern thinkers in the East and the West, one can turn to the thought of William James (1842–1910) and Kitaro Nishida (1870–1945) for direction and guidance on how an authentically proper study religion can be conducted within our new contemporary situation. Despite their cultural differences, both looked at religion and saw that it existed as an inner depth reality of human life. Both men lived as creative philosophers and thinkers in their respective countries, America and Japan. James developed a tradition of American pragmatism (Simon 1998: 284) and Nishida uniquely formed a Kyoto School (Piovensana 1968: 85–87). In addition, in their thought, they both commonly believed that religion should not be viewed as a marginal phenomenon in human life. For both James and Nishida, religion existed as a serious issue in human life. It stands more toward the center than any periphery. However, strangely enough, their religious thoughts are not been properly compared in the context of any academic discussions.

As is well known in some quarters, Nishida's early thought was related to James's thought. It is known that Nishida articulated his early thought through James's idea of pure experience. Most works about Nishida's thought emphasize repetitively this aspect of pure experience. The first Western scholar on the study of Nishida's thought, Robert Carter, clearly indicated this point in his first chapter on pure experience (Carter 1997: 1). This perception has not changed even in later research

---

[1] More concretely in our current times, if we fail to understand the currently changing condition of religion in the world, we will miss out in coming to know the world more deeply. We can no longer be illiterate about the place of religion in a global world. In this new situation of modern world religion, the understanding of religion should proceed from a pluralistic perspective. It should approach the asking of any question in a context that attends to relations which exist with other neighboring religions and distant places.

Hence recently the study of religion is changing from what it had been in earlier times. Today, it is not enough simply to focus on the origin or the birth places of each religion. One must look at the religious situation of its spread regions and countries. For instance, in the study of Buddhism, one must look at Buddhism not only in the birth and the original place, the East but also in the West. One must look also at what has been happening in terms of Buddhist immigration in a global world. Similarly, one must look at these new variables when looking at other religions. It is almost impossible to make general statements about the world of any given religion as an old or a new because of the new various different contexts which exist for each religion. In this sense, it can be argued that the present reality of religion is intra-religiously or inter-religiously a geographical pluralistic fact.

which has been done about Nishida's thought. Very recently, another Western scholar, Heisig maintains the substance of Robert Carter's thought here with respect to pure experience though he goes on to insist that Nishida's idea of pure experience differs from James' psychological idea of it (Heisig 2001: 45).

This perception of the relation between James's and Nishida's thought does not appear, however, to go beyond words about pure experience. It seems thus that Nishida's thought does not have much of a relation with James's though apart from James's idea of pure experience. Due to this bias, though Nishida had read James' religious works, especially *The Varieties of Religious Experience* in the period when he was a high school teacher in Yamaguchi (Heisig 2001: 30), the relation of James's religious thought to Nishida's has not been fully worked out yet. So, in this chapter, I would like to develop an experimental sketch which compares the religious thought of these two thinkers. I will try to show that parallels can be postulated in the work of these two thinkers. In order to do this, I will focus on their religious works as this is given in James's Gifford Lectures, *The Varieties of Religious Experience: A Study in Human Nature,* and in Nishida's the first and the last works, *An Inquiry into the Good* and *Nothingness and the Religious World.*

## New Age and Religion

Though James and Nishida lived geographically in different places, they both knew that a new age was dawning in a contemporary human culture and history. To them it was an age which differed from previous times and earlier conceptions of culture and history. In these new times, they commonly argued that familiar perceptions of the world needed to be changed and, in their later works on religion, they both argued that the main force of this new dawning age should be distinguished from what they had presupposed in their earlier works.

James identified the new age more concretely as the time of science. He believed that all books written to deal with difficult questions should be engaged in the spirit of science. In his own lifespan, in the late nineteenth and the early twentieth century, James witnessed the controversies which then raged between religion and science, especially with respect to questions about evolution and creationism as these issues were discussed in North America. However, he did not accept the kind of totalizing dogmatic perspective which one finds in scientism (James 1982: 103–104). In the first chapter of the Gifford Lectures, 'Religion and Neurology,' James identified the representative case of scientism with respect to religion as 'medical materialism' (James 1925: 10), where, by this medical materialism, all religious phenomena is related to the functioning of the human body. In strict scientism, no concern is shown about mental, psychic, or spiritual states which exist beyond or in some kind of relation to the material human body.

Likewise, Nishida recognized that a new age as that of science, especially in modern Europe, was replacing a traditional way of life (Nishida 1970: 244). In his last work, *Nothingness and the Religious Worldview*, further Nishida noted that this new age would be globally determined by scientific requirements in human thinking (Nishida 1987c: 122). In his own lifetime through two world wars he concretely experienced how great could be the impact of science and technology. Though Nishida did not deny that the contemporary human order of things in the world could be developed in a positive way under the influence of scientific thinking, he knew that science, if not sufficiently critical of itself, could create a new totalized scientific culture that would not seriously consider how a religious dimension in human life could reveal a depth dimension within it.

He critically indicated that the Renaissance of the West culturally contributed a good aspect but that, negatively, it also created a momentum which led to the loss of a sense of religious meaning within human experience. From that time on in the West, with the gradual loss of a sense of religious dimensions within human life in the West, the resulting drift of things has served to form a 'mere secular culture' (119). As Nishida argues, this secular scientific culture has fundamentally lost its ability to incarnate 'all sense of true culture' (119). It is not able to retrieve the religious meaning in human life.

However, in opposition to the negative aspects of scientism, it should not be assumed that James and Nishida did simply defended the current state of philosophical and theological discourse as it then existed in religious circles. They did not agree with the current religious discourse either. They both strongly maintained the position that the study of religion could not be fostered within a theological and philosophical context which rejected healthy forms of critical scientific reflection which did not seek to eradicate religion within human life but which had become more necessary if one was to come to a fuller understanding of human life. James and Nishida both thought that it was not helpful simply to repeat or perpetuate dogmatic philosophical and theological discourse about religious matters as it then existed since this would not lead to any understanding in depth about the religious aspiration of human beings in the coming new age. The study of religion needed to be radically changed for the articulation of the real dimension of religion within contemporary human life and culture. Though they did not accept the totalizing perspective of scientism, they maintained the necessity of an appropriate scientific perspective for the understanding of religion.

In fact, James, in his Gifford Lectures, developed a new perspective which challenged current perspectives in the study of religion. He accepted the new scientific disciplines which were current in his day. Hence, in the early part of his lectures, James clearly expressed his position as one that is based on psychology which was then emerging as a new human science (James 1925: 2). Then later on, in a chapter contained in his Lectures, 'Philosophy', on the basis of descriptions that he had collected about religious phenomena, he suggested a new direction for the study of religion as a new academic discipline: a study which would be known as a science of religion (450).

James sternly rejected focusing on speculative conceptions which would try to understand the world of religion apart from the data of concrete human experience. This point is maintained in a last work which sought to complete what James had initially left uncomplete in the text of his Gifford Lectures (James 1977). James understood the fact that religious experience is the gist or the pulse of religion. Current philosophical or theological perspectives could not point out the experiential reality which is very much a part of religion since these perspectives are plagued by an undue emphasis that is given to complexes of diverse reified words, concepts, systems, and abstractions which are articulated in a manner which is divorced from concrete human experiential reality (James 1925: 447–448). For him, conceptual approaches do not really deal with primary living facts of religion with secondary aspects.

Similarly, Nishida also rejected current discourse on religious concepts and systems which tend to exist apart from the inner experience of concrete human subjects. Beginning with his early works, he concentrated on concrete experiential aspects which belong to the human subject and which exist before any kind of conceptual discourse can possibly exist (Nishida 1987a: 3). Nishida identified this aspect in human subjects as the world of pure experience (4). In his later works, he did not reject his early position but simply expanded on it more richly. In fact, he tried to articulate this point in all his various works.

Yet, unfortunately, James's and Nishida's emphasis on the importance of the experiential dimension in religion has led to many misunderstandings about the content and import of their thought. Especially has this been the case with James and his identification of religious studies with psychology. Lamberth recently has criticized efforts to reduce James' religious experience to the dimension of psychology (Lamberth 1999). In his analysis, he has historically situated James' religious experience in the development of his religious thought. However, this has been continuously misunderstood and, as a result, his understanding has been categorized as individualistic and subjectivist. It has been seen as an approach that ignores the external world of religion. But, if one attends more precisely to the wording of his lectures, one would have to come to a different understanding. For purposes of correction thus, two things should not be forgotten. First, when James used various psychological words to speak about religious experience, the nuance or the meaning of his words should not be limited to some species of psychological reductionism or psychological behaviorism. One should also attend to meanings which transcend what seems to exist only at a conscious or narrow psychological level. Second, James did not talk about religious experience as a substantive state which exists apart from the differing contexts of this experience.

On the whole in his lectures of religion, in not emphasizing the external world of religion, James emphasizes a subject's experience in speaking about the intensity or the weakness of a subject's personal engagement in religion. In other words, James points out that the real core of religion lies not in the realm of external things nor in a conceptual abstract world which one often finds in theology but in the dynamic interiority of the human subject as this is lived out within or outside of any given religious tradition. For James, if human subjects are not personally involved in some kind of religious life, no religion can possibly evolve, endure, or communicate itself. Always, in whatever aspect, what is important is the human subject's personal engagement of religion. This is the crucial point to keep in mind in understanding what James has to say about religion. His working definition of religion clearly communicates this thesis:

> Religion, therefore, as I now ask you arbitrarily to take it, shall mean for us *feelings, acts, and experiences of individual mind in their solitude, so far as they apprehend themselves to stand in relation to whatever they consider the divine.* Since the relation may be either moral, physical, or ritual, it is evident that out of religion in the sense in which we take it, theologies, philosophies, and ecclesiastical organizations may secondarily grow (James 1925: 31).

I think thus that James's definition of religion which is given here should correct misunderstandings in respect to three points. First, James concentrated on the experiential flowing realm of religion as this exists within persons, beginning from a subject's feelings moving to a subject's acts. This spectrum not only encompasses or refers to subjective psychological states as this exists in feeling and experiences since external actions within the context of one's life are also included.

Second, James showed that religious feeling, experiences, and acts do not exist as events which belonged to an enclosed subjective inner world since all these things exist through some kind of open engagement with 'moral, physical or ritual' dimensions. Without such an engagement or relation, no religious feeling, experiences and acts can be expected. This is a key point which accordingly challenges earlier or typical interpretations of James which have tended to speak about psychological reductionism or excessive individualism in James's religious thought.

Third, James understood 'theologies, philosophies, and ecclesiastical organizations' as constituting secondary phenomena of religion. But, note that his selection of the word 'secondary' does not mean that he did not think of these things as unimportant phenomena. What it is not to be forgotten is the fact that, in his thinking about the development of religion, James is fully aware of the fact that religious persons do not grow entirely by themselves. They grow only through the subject's 'feeling, experiences and acts'. If an intellectual discourse does not consider the growth or dynamic aspects of any given religion, it will lose or forget to attend to a key aspect that is constitutive of religion. In this sense, James rejected conceptual discourses as such or to the degree that they existed apart from a subject's inner engagement with them.

James, in the later parts of his lectures, 'Philosophy' and 'Conclusions,' made more focus on feeling as the key feature of religion since, through feeling, other aspects are integrated as one finds these in experiences and in acts. According to James, the inner dimensions of human life cannot be separated from the outer dimensions of life. All is organically related (442–443). In concrete human life, the inner and the outer aspects are always intertwined. They are never parted. More so is this the case in concrete religious life. In specifying these two aspects, he selected the word 'feeling' rather than experiences or acts in his first definition of religion. By focusing so specifically on feeling, one sharply distinguishes and points out a contrast that exists between feeling and the current speculative and logical understandings of religion as these have existed. In addition, it should be noted that the realm of feeling more broadly covers or refers to the source of religion than any discussion which operates in the realm of speculative logic. In the context of speculative logic, one would apparently reveal a classification as a kind of map of the world of religion. But, this type of mapping does not deal with the deep matrix or the ongoing new emerging phenomena of religious feeling as this arises and occurs in the concrete life of human beings. As James notes:

> I do believe that feeling is the deeper source of religion, and that philosophic and theological formulas are secondary products, like translations of a text into another tongue (431).
>
> Conceptual processes can class facts, define them, interpret them; but they do not produce them, nor can they reproduce their individuality. There is always a *plus,* a *thisness,* which feeling alone can answer for. Philosophy in this sphere is thus a secondary function, unable to warrant faith's veracity, and so I revert to the thesis that I announced at the beginning of this lecture. In all sad sincerity I think we must conclude that the attempt to demonstrate by purely intellectual processes to the truth of the deliverances of direct religious experience is absolutely hopeless (455).

James' understanding about the marks of religion, especially as this exists in feeling or in the experiential dimension, can be similarly found in Nishida's expositions on the works of Goethe (Nishida 1970: 146). Later this point can be discovered in his descriptions about art, morality, and religion. He talked about these things all together in order to indicate that a general undertow similarly exists in the inner experience or feeling of a human subject in each theme. For him, the essential point of art, morality, or religion is the inner experience of a human subject. It is an experience which exists before there are any objectified expressions which speak about what is going on in the human heart. This experience exists not only in creative human subjects such as artists, moralists, or persons graced with religious genius but also in ordinary persons to observe and participate in the world which exists around them. Nishida spoke about the nature of this personal experiential interior dynamic in his different works. The following quotation is from his last book and serves as a good witness with respect to his understanding of religion:

> Not everyone is an artist. But to some extent at least everyone can appreciate art. Nor is everyone a theologian, and rare is the man who experiences a religious conversion. To some degree, however, any person can understand religion. There is probably no one who does not feel a strong resonance in the depths of his heart when he reads the fervent confessions of faith of those who have gained religious faith or the expressions of belief of the greatest figures. Moreover, upon falling into a condition of extreme unhappiness, there is probably no one who does not feel some religious sentiment welling up from the depths of his won soul (Nishida 1987c: 47).

As the above quotation indicates, Nishida commonly agreed with James's rejection of the value of abstract knowledge in religion. However, unlike James, he did not select 'feeling' exclusively as the key word in religion. He knew that religion was not related to blind feeling but, rather, to an awakening dimension which begins to stir in a subject's inner depths (Nishida 1987a: 34). His conviction here can be traced to his involvement with the Zen tradition of Japanese Buddhism. In such a context, he more specifically identified the awakening dimension as a unified, unifying intuition of life which exists in a subject although this intuition does not differ from a subject's personal inner experience because it undeniably occurs within a subject's inner heart in a sphere of being which exists beyond or outside the reach of a conceptual world that is given through words and concepts. In this sense, though Nishida used a different term rather than James' use of feeling as key word in religion, I think that his point can be interpreted as the experience or the feeling of a subject.

In his later works, Nishida went on to speak about this point in a critical way. For him, conceptually 'if religion is imprisoned in any determinate form, it is the corruption of religion' (Nishida 1987c: 90). He warned against intellectual tendencies which seemed, by their very nature, to reduce the world of religion to that which is determined by fixed words, sentences, or systems which exist as examples of dogmatism. He rejected this kind of abstract approach to the living world of religion. He believed that all conceptual views of religion lose or back away from an interior reality which exists in the real experience of a religious subjects as faith or sentiment (93).

Nishida argued that theological, ethical, or philosophical expressions about the world of religion exist only as secondary phenomena compared to the experiential dimension which exists in the active engagement of human subjects in religion as this exists in concrete life. These secondary expressions admittedly express one's religious experience or feeling either individually or communally and, simultaneously, they exist as means which can lead to similar experiences and other additional experiences which, in their way, can change a human subject. However, they do not suffice for speaking about the dynamic flow of experience as this emerges and changes within the life of any given person. The subject's experience cannot always correspond with any of these secondary expressions given certain limits which are endemic to the use of words and the use of systematic forms of expression which are wholly inadequate as carriers of meaning when one thinks about possible religious experiences or feelings which can exist in a religious human subject. Such things can come and live in a superficial manner and sometimes they can come to dwell deeply within a person's soul. It is almost impossible to identify these things as such apart from speaking about their dynamic existence as a fundament within a person's human life.

For these reasons Nishida tried to articulate the inner aspect of religion. Above all, he came to realize that the interiority which one finds in Christianity is something which exists as a key comparative point. Through interiority, one finds a link or bond which joins with Nishida's Buddhism, his Japanese Zen Buddhism most especially. In order to clarify what is meant by attending to the inner dimension of religion, as with James (1956), Nishida distinguished faith from belief dimension of religion.[2] He related various religious experiences more concretely to faith as an interior personal act and disposition rather than to belief which suggests the adoption of some kind of religious profession and proposition which exists in a creed.

> Faith is thus a unifying power that transcends knowledge. It is not that faith is supported by
> knowledge and the will, but that knowledge and the will are supported by faith. In that

---

[2] Recently this point is well articulated by a historian of comparative religion, Wilfred Cantwell Smith. Especially Smith developed this distinct point of faith and belief in *Faith and Belief*.

sense, faith is mystical. But to say that faith is mystical does not mean that it is contrary to knowledge, for faith that conflicts with knowledge cannot become the basis of life. If we exhaust our intellect and will, then we will acquire from within a faith we cannot lose (Nishida 1987a: 157).

## Self as the Locus of Religion

As has been already thus indicated, James and Nishida both attended to the reality of inner depth experiences in human life in order to understand the locus of religion as a living personal reality.

To facilitate this kind of understanding, in his lectures, James, through long quotations or through brief references, described more than 700 personal testimonies which told about religious experience in the life of human beings in his Gifford Lectures. He divided these testimonies in a manner which indicated two basic types of personality. One is the healthy-minded and the other, the sick soul (James 1925: 78–164). He dealt with them separately in two chapters given in his lectures.

With respect to the first type of personality, the healthy-minded personality type is one which has an optimistic world view (78–80). As a consequence of this general tendency, a person does not attend much to the dark realities of human life as these exist in death, sin, disease, and other human tragedies. By attending to them and by dwelling on them, one would be creating major problems for one's life. One would be creating obstacles and barriers in a way which could easily thwart the possibilities of life and healing which can come from contact with another higher world which refers to something which is transcendent. In this sense, through such an orientation, conditions are created for living a more fully human life.

In contrast, the type of the sick soul cannot live the way that the healthy – minded soul lives and breathes. It cannot be satisfied with itself unless it has solved all the many problems which attend existential human existence. In its depth of concern, it wants to be engaged with the problems of life. But, its involvement is of a kind that is not always satisfied. New demands keep appearing for new questions keep arising.

Nevertheless, the outlook remains tired and gloomy. A lack of optimism persists and the world is perceived as something that is always sick and ill. As a consequence of the limits of human existence, this type of soul longs for help which can come from a transcending dimension that can come to one in the course of one's life journey. In other words, this soul is not happy within human life as it naturally exists in its different conditions. It always demands some kind of radical conversion or a rebirth so that one can see the world in a more happy light. A second birth is needed as a supernatural relief (162). Sometimes this desire can be happily fulfilled through the mediation of a specific religious tradition but sometimes it cannot be so fulfilled. In his understanding of religious experience, James is more concerned about the sick type of soul than the healthy-minded type of soul (165).

The attention given by Nishida to the understanding of the human subject does not differ from James's. Nishida did not divide the human subject according to

James' two types but, if one reads him carefully, one finds that his talks about the human subject imply that sick souls are to be reckoned with. He was also concerned about the dramatic dynamic which exists in life in terms of the journey which all of us must take as existential persons (Nishida 1966: 199). In speaking about this, somewhat interestingly, he uses similar words to speak about the self as a struggling human subject.

For him, the existential human self cannot be described simply morally or culturally or politically. It critically questions traditional morality and culture. Inherited social systems as such are seen as problematic due to the continuing avoidance of the ultimate reality (234). More concretely, the existential human self questions human life in terms of the paradoxes that are present in it: for instance, in the pervasiveness of death, evil, and sin. In this sense, living religion does not exist as an external institutionalized affair since it is continuously evolving event with the self of a person in the context of one's human life. If the self ceases to raise any fundamental existential questions, it ceases to maintain any religion as a dynamic foundational force in human life. A religion, in its externality, would turn into some sort of social organization. Thus, for Nishida, the real concern lies not with any kind of reified religion but with the inner depths of a self. Nishida warned against a modern opposing tendency which one can find in the selves of human beings today:

> When, then, does the question of religion genuinely arise for us? Where is the religious form of life to be located? I hold that the question of religion cannot be considered a question of value. Rather, it is only when a person becomes conscious of a profound existential contradiction in the depths of his own soul – when he becomes aware of the bottomless self-contradictions of his own self – that his own existence becomes religiously problematic. The sorrows of human life and its contradictions have been constant themes since ancient times. Many people do not ponder this. And yet it is when this fact of the sorrow of human life is reflected on at a profound level that the problem of religion arises (Indeed, the problems of philosophy, in my view, arise from this same point.) (Nishida 1987c: 66).

James and Nishida both keenly grasped how a ceaseless dynamic movement or flow exists within the self of a religious subject. For both of them, the key to religion lies in the human subject's self. The self is what matters and in speaking about the self, James and Nishida both focused on three features which belong to the religious self.

First, for both James and Nishida, the religious self does not exist as one continuing self which lives in some kind of stable, fixed process. It is better understood as an ongoing complex encounter between two distinct selves. James thought that, in religious experience or feeling as this occurs within religious conversion, unification occurs between these two selves (James 1925: 175). According to James' empirical observations, in most cases of religious experience or feeling, an evolving resolution occurs through the conflict that exists between an old self and an ideal or emerging self. The distance between these two selves is bridged in a move toward unification which sometimes suddenly occurs or which sometimes gradually occurs. The result is the forming of a self. Of course, in the time that it takes to affect a new self, various types need to be pointed out. James generally spoke about two basic types of religious conversion as these are present in sudden conversion and gradual conversion (183 and 206).

Likewise, Nishida also thought all of human life is related to the self as it evolves and forms. If the self is not thus related, nothing would be happening in this world of human things as it is brought into being through human action. Nishida, in all his works, emphasized and adhered to this key element if one was to understand either the external or the internal world. As he saw it, the flowing of human consciousness needs to be unified as a self and then, for the future formation of the self, the flowing which exists in a given self becomes a condition which leads to a new evolving unified self and so on *ad infinitum* (Nishida 1987a: 65 and 125). The evolving process of self exists as a kind of constant and through which it is possible to be related to vary many other things.

Hence Nishida also thought of human life as a process where two selves are engaged in conflict situations where, within this conflict, unification occurs within human consciousness (Nishida 1987c: 66). This is a key idea in Nishida's understanding of religion. For Nishida, it is not helpful to think of religion in terms of external matters as this exists in doctrines, rituals, systems, institutionalized organizations and so on because such a thing as the reality of religion exists more in terms of inner depth encounters between two selves as a present self and the ultimate 'Self' which exists within one's inner world.

Second, James and Nishida both thought that the process of the religious self are related to shifts of psychic/spiritual energy flow. As James understood these matters, in religious experience or feeling, a shift of location occurs with respect to energy. That is, it happens as religious ideas move to the center of a person's consciousness or as they move to the periphery of a person's consciousness, depending on what is happening within the consciousness of a given person (James 1925: 196–197). Prior to religious experience, the energy which exists in a person's consciousness is located as a certain point or location as this is determined by what specific idea or belief exists at one's center. What holds one's attention? What guides one's thinking and feeling? What exists at one's center then determines where other ideas and beliefs exist and how they fit in and so, in such a situation, less or no energy can flow from a center to any spheres of consciousness which exist in a marginal fashion or to a sphere of consciousness which is being repressed or neglected in some way.

However, in the reception of religious experience or as a consequence of religious conversion, the religious subject begins to attract to ideas which had been habitually marginalized or repressed. The energy flow of the religious subject is moved. A human subject begins to attend to things which before had not been attended to. A new center of self-energy moves to a marginalized idea. In other words, prior to any religious experience, a person had felt cold about one or more religious ideas. But now, after religious experience, one feels an opposite warmth and affectionate feelings with respect to religious ideas which had once been perceived as strange and alien. A truly religious self experiences a radical change with respect to the locus of one's energy flows. In this sense, what is happening here is not or should not be seen as a purely individualistic thing since, at bottom, experiences are enjoyed which are characterized by relational and organic dimensions. In such a situation thus, one is not dealing with something that is fixed but with a dynamically moving social reality as this exists in a human subject and as this elicits a new way of living in the world. Admittedly, this point is not yet fully brought out in the study and articulation which James brings to bear in his study of religion.

Similarly, Nishida also thought that the formation of the religious self reveals that an event of dislocation as an old world to be constitutive of a given subject is brought into a new world through the application of new predicates. And so, with respect to energy flows, these are changed as the human self moves from an old familiar world into a new emerging world that replaces the old and which turns an old self into a new self. As with James, Nishida's range or sense of the self world is not something which is monotonously static. It exists as a very flexible flowing thing. It is shallow and yet deep. And it is small and yet large (Nishida 1987c: 113). Depending on the standpoint which a self has in relation to a world, the world of the self differs as it moves from one standpoint to another. In a religious conversion, the religious world of the self which can be shallow and small can be replaced by a new emerging world which is now deep and large.

Further Nishida thought that the new self could change a familiar historical world into a new foreign eschatological world. Unfortunately he elaborated this point in his discussions of Buddhism and nation in the modern Japanese history (121–123). This point exists as a continuously debated point within the scholarship which exists about Nishida's thought. Recently, Cunningham has more critically tackled Nishida's self, viewing it as a possible psychedelic in terms of how it is related to Nishida's sense of modern Japanese history (Cunningham 2007).

Third, James and Nishida both thought that the source of self is related to the dimension of depth in it. It exists not only as a complex of horizontal relationships with oneself and other selves but also as a vertical relationship with one's inner transcending self. In articulating the inner and outer transcendent dimensions of self as the source or matrix of religion, James used 'self' in a depth psychological sense. For James, 'self' existed as a psychological term with a technical meaning that was being used innovatively within current psychical research (Simon 1998: 319–320). In contrast to the current intellectuals of his day, James did not reject the paranormal human experience but rather wrote much about the possibility of its occurrence (140–141). On the basis of his personal involvement with scientific works pertaining to the value of psychical research (James 1986), he was very familiar with how "self" can be used in a very depth psychological sense. He spoke about the inner dimension of self as the realm of the 'subconscious self' (James 1925: 511). In addition, he argued that religious experience or feeling can possibly be derived from this realm of the subconscious self as the chief source of the experience.

James thought that the study of religious experience could be developed beyond current and even extreme disputes about the relation between religion and science. In James's judgment, religious experience or feeling does not exist as a simply flat form of self-experience since it also existed as a 'more' kind of self-experience (511) which exists as a fundamental with respect to the fullness of the human condition. This is an indispensable fact in the human experience which one has of one's life. Yet, James did not quickly suggest that the 'more' self dimension should be seen as proof of divine reality. He only indicated that religious experience exists as an additional aspect to the ordinary experience of self which we all have as human beings. In his day, he found that the current treatment of religious experience was not too persuasive. He observed that this additional experience is not satisfactorily described in either a traditional theological way or in a traditional philosophical way. A general tendency exists which wants to reject religious experience as something that can be investigated by legitimate scientific research. Given this limitation in science and both theology or philosophy, current research about the inner subconscious self is more helpful in developing intelligent discourse about religious experience. He movingly suggested his point in the conclusion that belongs to part of his lectures.

> Let me then propose, as an hypothesis, that whatever it may be on its *farther* side, the 'more' with which in religious experience we feel ourselves connected is on its *hither* side the subconscious continuation of our conscious life. Starting thus with a recognized psychological fact as our basis, we seem to preserve a contact with 'science' which the ordinary theologian lacks. At the same time the theologian's contention that the religious man is moved by an external power is vindicated, for it is one of the peculiarities of invasions from the subconscious region to take on objective appearances, and to suggest to the Subject an external control. In the religious life the control is felt as 'higher'; but since on our hypothesis it is primarily the higher faculties of our own hidden mind which are controlling, the sense of union with the power beyond us is a sense of something, not merely apparently, but literally true (512–513).

Likewise, Nishida also emphasized that an interconnection of self exists because of a link which it has with a world, the interconnection existing with the self functioning as a point of mediation. For him, the inner and outer world of individual, society, history, and universe cannot be experienced apart from a unity experience of self which is present to the self in its conscious life (Nishida 1987a: 62). These other worlds do not exist as fixed substances. They variously appear only through a process of ceaseless unity which exists within the human self. They can only be connected through the unity of self engagement wherever this exists and however it exists within the self. In this unity, 'there are no distinctions between subjectivity and objectivity or spirit and matter' (74). Hence, the self not only carries within it a unified experience of worlds but it also exists as the condition and source for new incidents of unified experience.

In this sense, each self does not exist as an independent substance having no reliance or connection to others. It does not exist apart from its embodied body. Its own body also exists depending upon a collection of numerous cells (139). Thus, each self or body exists not as an independent closed substance but as a mutually relational being involving a body, its cells and other selves. In addition, all these parts or elements are related to a flow which comes from prior beings and what flows from newly emerging beings as body, cell and self. Thus, the self like other beings does not exist as a self-sufficient being but as a relational, open, social, and communal being.

Ultimately, the religious self possesses a global dimension in terms of a horizontal interconnection that is joined to other persons and other things. Most especially, above all, the religious self exists as the most global form of human consciousness when one compares it to other forms of human consciousness which exist as ways of speaking about other selves as referring to specifications of consciousness which can exist within a given individual self.

Nishida also thought that the religious self is vertically rooted to the inner depth dimension which exists in human souls. In articulating his thought, Nishida developed a unique logic. It is very similar to James' open 'more' dimension. It was not a closed logic since it emphasized a 'more' realm. Something exists here which is essentially religious. In Nishida's understanding of things, the fundamental nature of self is such that it does not attempt to exist in the same, static situation or condition. Such a condition is always being negated. Thus, the self is constituted by a paradoxical nature which tries to negate or to transcend its unity ceaselessly for the sake of a new greater unity that is always being sought – a unity which ultimately moves towards an encounter with experiences of absolute nothingness.

Hence, the current present self evolves as part of a greater self and, further on, ultimately it evolves as part of an ultimate 'Self'. It is not a simple process of continuing the same world of self since, in this process, there occurs an ongoing overturning or a deluding which takes one towards a larger and deeper world which refers to absolute nothingness (Nishida 1987c: 86). What happens exists as an event which occurs within the human self as ultimate reality is encountered and confronted through absolute negation. Nishida thought that, by means only of this unique logic wherein one experiences a process of absolute negation, the inner depth foundation of world known as 'God' can be identified. In his judgment, the self exists as a journey as it seeks to negate itself and move toward a form of bottomless absolute negation which refers to the absolute affirmation of ultimate reality (91). In this sense ultimately, our self and its expressions as history, the arts, and religious traditions and various other human phenomena can be pronounced as 'a part of the personality of God' (Nishida 1987b: 107).

## Conclusion

Having then looked at the philosophy of religion as this was understood by William James and Nishida Kataro, one notices a certain commonality in their understanding of religion which bodes well as signs of a new emerging global consciousness about how religion should be perceived by different persons who live and work within different cultures and different religious traditions. James and Nishida were both interested in attending to interior conditions which exist as the subjective pole of religion wherever religion exists among different peoples living within different cultures. Both noticed that, if one were to attend to the objective pole of religion, one would find varying religious traditions: different conceptualizations about right belief and different rites of worship which indicate how transcendent sources of meaning are to be acknowledged, loved, and worshipped. Hence, in thinking about these two poles and about how these two poles are to be related to questions that ask about how religion should be spoken about in an educational context, a number of observations can be pondered and thought about.

First, all agree that religion exists as a meaningful datum of sense that is partially constitutive of the meaning of our human world. No adequate understanding of the human world can exist without some knowledge of religion in terms of particularized beliefs and practices and in terms of the kinds of consequences which can flow from the practice of a particular belief. In this sense, if one attends to any objectifications of religion which exist as an objective pole, one understands things in a certain way. A phenomenological approach leads to a phenomenological species of understanding. More bluntly speaking, a given religion would be understood as it exists in an outer way. A superficial understanding would be seen as the kind of understanding which one should have and so properly come to. Nothing more would be needed or encouraged.

Second, if religion is approached not in terms of an objective pole but as a subjective pole, it shifts from being a datum of sense to being a datum of consciousness presenting a different point of departure. A given religion or religion in general would be understood in an internal way which attends to what is happening within the lives of concrete persons and specific groups. A deeper understanding would be sought and, in order to facilitate the possibility of coming to a deeper understanding, a new approach would be needed in terms of a new kind of inquiry which should be encouraged in anyone who wants to move from partial understanding and knowledge to greater understanding and knowledge and in terms of how one might best encourage the development of this new kind of inquiry in a person through the kind of pedagogy that one would want to use.

Third, the kind of inquiry that would be needed is suggested by the religious understanding of James and Nishida. If religion is to be understood as a datum of consciousness, an understanding about the nature and structure of human consciousness becomes a necessary prerequisite. In James and Nishida, one finds a partial type of inquiry which wants to talk about religion as this is inwardly known and experienced. However, if a subjective approach to the study of religion is to be worked out, it must attend to a context that is conditioned by a comprehensive philosophy of the human subject. The subjectivism of James and Nishida elicits the need that some attention should be given to subjectivism in general and to a difference which can be postulated between the working of authentic subjectivity, on the one hand, and all other forms of subjectivity, on the other. If, in all religion a self-transcending form of relation exists between human beings and what exists for them as a transcendent source of meaning, self-transcendence needs to be understood as a general principle which exists within the subjectivity of all human beings.

Fourth, a careful and exact understanding of human subjectivity presents formidable challenges in terms of possibly reaching a common agreement that would be widely accepted by both religious persons and non-religious persons. A philosophical dialectic would be necessarily called into play since different theories of the human subject can be adverted to as one enters into the history of philosophy and as one attends to philosophical assumptions as these exist in any given philosophy of religion. Amid all these differences and to the degree that one finds them, the correctness of a theory would be determined by the degree that every known variable is acknowledged and related to each other in a scheme that omits nothing.

Without attending to such a philosophy, no pedagogy can be created which would be able to win the minds and hearts of all persons who live within different cultures and different social orders. It would also not be possible to work with religious persons to create a consensus among them which would not clash with any value that is grounded in any confessional interests and concerns. By noting how religious subjectivity is becoming a focus of interest in different religious and cultural contexts, a new general context is being created that is encouraging a global shift in consciousness which is calling for an understanding of consciousness that can join these many points of focus into one whole.

In conclusion then a bit concretely, this keen awareness of human subjectivity invites us to attend to the relation which exists between religion and education in a context which looks at how one might create a deep sense of humanity that could elicit a sense of participatory citizenship as this would exist in a global manner within our current pluralistic religious world. In this sense I think that, in the work of James' and Nishida's, one finds a pioneering achievement to attend to religion as an inner reality within the human self. A valid theoretical perspective is pointed to in a manner which reveals a common ground that exists in the nature and structure of human subjectivity. By appropriating this subjectivity, one works with and from a philosophical foundation which would allow one to mediate diverse religious meanings within a global pluralistic world.

# References

Carter, R. E. (1997). *The nothingness beyond God: An introduction to the philosophy of Nishida Kitaro*. Minnesota: Paragon House.

Clark, P. B. (2000). *Japanese new religions in global perspective*. Richmond: Curzon Press.

Cunningham, E. (2007). *Hallucinating the end of history: Nishida, Zen and the Psychedelic Eschaton*. Bethesda: Academia Press.

Eck, D. (2001). *New religious America: How a "Christian country" has now become the world's most religiously diverse nation*. San Francisco: Harper and Row.

Heisig, J. W. (2001). *Philosophers of nothingness: An essay on the Kyoto School*. Honolulu: University of Hawaii Press.

James, W. (1925). *The varieties of religious experience: A study in human nature*. New York: Longmans, Green, and Co.

James, W. (1956). *The will to believe and other essays in popular philosophy*. New York: Dover Publications.

James, W. (1977). *A pluralistic universe*. Cambridge: Harvard University Press.

James, W. (1982). *Essays in religion and morality*. Cambridge: Harvard University Press.

James, W. (1986). *Essays in psychical research*. Cambridge: Harvard University Press.

Lamberth, D. C. (1999). *William James and the metaphysics of experience*. Cambridge: Cambridge University Press.

Nishida, K. (1966). *Intelligibility and the philosophy of nothingness* (R. Schinzinger, Trans.). Honolulu: East-West Center Press.

Nishida, K. (1970). *Fundamental problems of philosophy: The world of action and the dialectical world* (D. A. Dilworth, Trans.). Tokyo: Sophia University Press.

Nishida, K. (1987a). *An inquiry into the good* (M. Abe & C. Ives, Trans.). New Haven: Yale University Press.

Nishida, K. (1987b). *Intuition and reflection in self-consciousness* (V. H. Viglielmo, Trans.). New York: State University of New York Press.

Nishida, K. (1987c). *Last writings: Nothingness and the religious worldview* (D. A. Dilworth, Trans.). Honolulu: University of Hawaii Press.

Piovensana, G. K. (1968). *Contemporary Japanese philosophical thought.* New York: St. John's University Press.

Reader, I. (1991). *Religion in contemporary Japan.* Honolulu: University of Hawaii Press.

Simon, L. (1998). *Genuine reality: A life of William James.* New York: Harcourt Brace and Company.

Smith, W. C. (1979). *Faith and belief.* Princeton: Princeton University Press.

# Chapter 9
# Ecological Imagination and Aims of Moral Education Through the Kyoto School and American Pragmatism

Steven Fesmire

Educational institutions must do a better job helping youths to see beyond simple relations of consumers to commodities if we are to respond to a global economic milieu in which expanding affluence sanctifies the innocence of consumers—an innocence purchased by ignorance of the social, environmental, and inter-species hazards posed by our 'business as usual' behaviors. Contemporary moral perception requires supplementation and expansion beyond the speck of self-interest around which most daily consumer concerns orbit. Toward this end, moral education for the globalizing twenty-first century must better enable youths to intelligently negotiate complex systems, from economic systems to ecosystems, in private choices and public policies.

Even amid rising international awareness of the unplanned systemic effects—such as global climate change—that radiate from our actions, it has ironically become increasingly difficult for ordinary citizens to give coherent and positive moral meaning to the relationships that twine us up with each other and with biotic systems.[1] Saito Naoko has argued that this lack of moral coherence reveals, at least for Japan and other techno-industrial societies, 'the state of nihilism in democracy and education'.[2] Kamata Yasuo adds that 'the narrowing of imagination, in order to bond one's interests with consumer goods, seems to be the general problem of our society'.[3]

---

[1] For American studies of this theme, see Bellah et al. (1996) and Putnam (2001).

[2] Personal communication (2007). This chapter follows Japanese naming conventions for all Japanese authors, with family name followed by given name. However, all Japanese names and words are given in Romanized characters.

[3] Personal communication (2007).

S. Fesmire (✉)
Philosophy and Environmental Studies, Green Mountain College,
One Brennan Circle, Poultney, VT 05764, USA
e-mail: FesmireS@greenmtn.edu

P. Standish and N. Saito (eds.), *Education and the Kyoto School of Philosophy*,
Contemporary Philosophies and Theories in Education 1,
DOI 10.1007/978-94-007-4047-1_9, © Springer Science+Business Media Dordrecht 2012

Clearly an education focused exclusively on technological training and transmission of discrete knowledge will do little to ameliorate this problem.

In order to clarify and develop aims for moral education that contribute to moral coherence and are relevant to the globalized effects of our choices and policies, we need global philosophical dialogue that taps intellectual resources for reinvesting our social and natural interconnections while avoiding moralistic or authoritarian instruction that impedes human becoming and freezes growth. The Kyoto School of modern Japanese philosophy and the classical pragmatist tradition in American philosophy can help us to better perceive the relational networks in which our finite lives are embedded. In the first section of this chapter I explore relational thinking in the Kyoto School and American pragmatism to help develop, in the second section, a concept of 'ecological imagination'. In the final section I draw from the foregoing to clarify some appropriate aims for contemporary moral education.

## Relational Thinking in the Kyoto School and American Pragmatism

Kyoto University is where modern Japanese philosophy began with Kitaro's Nishida (1870–1945) work reconstructing the tools and concepts of Western philosophy, such as the idea of pre-conceptual pure experience in William James (1842–1910), to contribute an Eastern standpoint to Western philosophy. Nishida built the philosophy department at Kyoto University, secured an appointment for Hajime Tanabe, launched the career of Tetsuro Watsuji, and attracted Keiji Nishitani among other students, continuing what became known as the Kyoto School (*Kyoto-gaku-ha*) tradition.

In *Philosophers of Nothingness*, James Heisig argues that the Kyoto School of Nishida, Tanabe, and Nishitani 'marks a watershed in intellectual history' (Heisig 2001, p. 3). They achieved, with varying degrees of success, a philosophy that falsifies the old essentialistic, Kipling-esque view that East is East and West is West (Heisig 2001, p. 8). These figures, Heisig argues, were much more than voices of the wisdom traditions of Japan. They wrote *for* and *about* the world, and they were among the first to bring a distinctively East Asian perspective to enlarging and challenging the philosophical tradition that began in ancient Greece (Heisig 2001, p. 8, 304). This is not to suggest that it is a mistake to speak inclusively of East Asia's wisdom traditions as philosophies, only that the Kyoto School thinkers were not using the term in this sense. For example, Nishitani wrote: 'When I say "philosophy," ... I first of all mean Western philosophy, since this is the most influential one. ... To think [the Buddhist] standpoint by way of philosophy is my basic concern' (Nishitani 1990 p. 1, 4).[4]

---

[4] Nishitani, far more than Nishida, explicitly understood his project in relation to Buddhist religion.

Nonetheless, among the minority of professional philosophers in the West who could name a twentieth century Japanese philosopher, it is common to conceive Kyoto School thinkers as relevant primarily to Japan Studies or Asian Studies. This is due in part to post-WWII blowback from their complicity in wartime nationalism,[5] but their complicity is sometimes cited as a red herring to avoid acknowledging that Western philosophers are more readily assumed to merit an audience beyond their mother tongue: imagine Heidegger introduced as a figure of mostly regional interest to scholars in Germanic Studies. Western traditions may thereby betray a more provincial countenance than is typically acknowledged, not solely due to the postmodern truism that we are limited by our culture's conceptual repertoire, but also because we have not fully taken in an emerging global philosophical culture that includes unfamiliar questions.

This highlights some difficulties for English-language writing on philosophy of education and the Kyoto School, particularly for a chapter such as this one penned by a relative newcomer to their corpus. There is a risk of orientalism, 'a kind of oriental spice to enliven certain questions on the menu' of Western philosophical traditions (Heisig 2001, p. 8). Or Kyoto School thinkers might be reduced to comparative points tethered to Western traditions that equally rebel against subject-object and theory-practice dualisms, such as phenomenology or pragmatism. If we only notice Kyoto School responses to questions currently asked in Western tongues, then we may miss what Heisig calls 'the particular constellation of their thinking' (Heisig 2001, p. 13). Acknowledging upfront that comparative projects can tend toward 'self-centered, monological, and appropriative modes of ... historical thinking' (Huang 2008, p. 156), it will nonetheless be helpful to begin, warily, with several strong affinities between the American pragmatist and Kyoto School traditions.

1. Both traditions strive to avoid fallacies of reification that privilege agents over situations, static forms over processes, substantive nouns over transitive verbs—what James dubbed the 'psychologist's fallacy', Dewey recognized as '*the* philosophical fallacy' (LW 1:27–29), and Whitehead labeled 'the fallacy of misplaced concreteness'. The term 'frog', 'pond', or 'tree' signifies not only an object one can point to at a simple location, but also 'an organized integration of complex relationships, activities, and events which incorporate a whole transactional field' (Alexander 1987, p. 109). Whitehead's 'fallacy of simple location' highlights our tendency to forget this horizonal field.

---

[5] On the Kyoto School and wartime nationalism, see Heisig and Maraldo (1994). In 'The Development of American Pragmatism', Dewey insightfully writes: 'In considering a system of philosophy in its relation to national factors it is necessary to keep in mind not only the aspects of life which are incorporated in the system, but also the aspects against which the system is a protest. There never was a philosopher who has merited the name for the simple reason that he glorified the tendencies and characteristics of his social environment; just as it is also true that there never has been a philosopher who has not seized upon certain aspects of the life of his time and idealized them' (LW 2:6).

This recognition that things exist only in relation and never wholly by them-selves informed the Buddha's teaching that all things are conditioned and imper-manent so that our thirst for fixity is the source of avoidable misery. The core Buddhist idea of dependent co-origination (Japanese: *engi*; Sanskrit: *pratitya-samutpada*) was developed in *The Heart Sutra* as the doctrine that form and emptiness (*śunyata*) are identical. In contrast with the Platonist, who conceives knowledge of form (*eidos*) as the disclosure of a thing's timeless, essential being, the Buddhist aims for immediate insight into the deep, irreducible networking of *this* or *that* concrete, transitory thing or event. The Kyoto School philosophers further developed *śunyata* into the notion of nothingness (*mu*), as in Nishida's phrase 'the field (or place) of nothingness' (*mu no basho*) and his concept of 'absolute nothingness' as the absence of any non-relational, transcendent grounding. Nishida famously contrasts the Western tendency to cognize form as timeless and placeless being with the Eastern tendency to immediately open up to *this form here* as emptiness:

> In the splendid development of Western culture in which form is regarded as being, and giving form as good, there is much to be respected and learned. But at the bottom of the Eastern culture that has nurtured our ancestors for thousands of years, isn't there something such that we see the form in the formless and hear the sound of the soundless? Our hearts long for these. (In Yuasa, 21)

Basho's most famous haiku is sufficient to clarify Nishida's point: Old pond/a frog jumps into/the sound of water. *Furu ike ya/kawazu tobikomu/mizu no oto* (Basho 2008, p. 59).[6] There is indeed a 'sound of the soundless', and it forms the auditory horizon of Basho's poem. Silence *forms* this haiku as much as the 'plop!' of the frog, and we have a greater felt awareness of the silence because it is not verbalized. That is, the form is not willfully imposed upon the material scene. The reader abstracts from the 'suchness' of the haiku's immediate visual and sonorous images, perhaps reflecting on the simplicity of truth, the transience of all awareness, or 'the sound of the soundless'. But the image suddenly, with-out commanding, recalls us from our construction of conceptual analyses and distinctions; there is just *this* concrete event, unbroken into subject and object, knower and known. There is no timeless being, nor any Western-style monistic extra-relational substratum. Nor are there separate existences. There is only this undifferentiated event that wraps itself around our awareness as the poem recep-tively invites us to enter. This is the East Asian standpoint that Nishida longs to contribute to the global philosophical dialogue. It is also an East Asian path to ecological wisdom.

Perhaps more than any other Western philosopher, James opens the way to mutu-ally transformative East-West dialogue by reprioritizing perceptual experience over conceptual experience and thereby perceiving a relational world of 'pure experience'. As John McDermott observes of James's contributions to global

---

[6] I am grateful to Thomas Alexander for an unpublished essay titled 'Form, Emptiness, and Nature' that uses Basho's poem as a way to explain Eastern and Western conceptions of form.

culture: 'James's stress on relations rather than objects … is congenial to cultures other than that of Western civilization; he espouses a congeniality far more in keeping with the contemporary reality of a truly global culture' (McDermott 2007, pp. 147–148).

2. Philosophers in each tradition articulate 'a "focus/field" or "foreground/ background" model of immediate experience which is unified by a pervasive aesthetic quality with intrinsic value' (Odin 1996, p. 381). James calls the often-obscured and forgotten relational field the horizon, penumbra, or fringe, a key James-inspired concept in Nishida's *An Inquiry into the Good (Zen no kenkyū)* (Nishida 1990, p. 4ff). James and the Kyoto School philosophers concur that the lifeworld comes in a mosaic of directly experienced natural and social continuities, and *awareness* of this horizon could fund more meaningful, value-rich, and responsive lives.[7] This is why McDermott claims we are suffering in techno-industrial societies from 'spiritual anorexia', a moral, aesthetic, and intellectual starvation for relations that make life significant (McDermott 1986, pp. 128–131). James's therapy for healing relation-starvation, his radical empiricism, aims in part to respect experience through 'the re-instatement of the vague', i.e., attentiveness to the horizon (James 1950, p. 254).[8] Following James's lead, Dewey's 'denotative method' aims at an 'intellectual piety toward experience' that liberates us from our 'will to impose' (LW 1:392). Dewey's *Experience and Nature*, in the words of one commentator, consists of 400 pages teaching you to think out of the corner of your eye.[9]

Individuals co-constitute the horizonal field. Social and natural relationships are popularly conceived as discovered, found, *given*. James, meanwhile, recognized that we create relationships as well as find them, and we thereby change reality. For James and Dewey we do not create relations from outside or above. Instead, our relational constructions are genuine possibilities of situations that we actualize through our interactions—perhaps most clearly through the arts, civilization's source of renewal and redirection.

3. Both traditions emphasize intrinsic and constitutive relations over extrinsic ones and hence criticize moral philosophies based on radical autonomy,[10] and they reject the Kantian transcendental subject—I emerge as a 'locus of activity' through interactions; I am not an antecedently existing entity.[11]

---

[7] A central thesis of William James's *Essays in Radical Empiricism* is that we also directly experience discontinuities, equally real, and we must be equally open to disjunctions as to conjunctions.

[8] Cf. James, 'The Thing and Its Relations', in *Essays in Radical Empiricism*.

[9] Thomas Alexander, personal communication.

[10] In constitutive relations, as Roger Ames explains, 'the dissolution of relationships is surgical, diminishing both parties to the degree that this particular relationship has been important to their continuing identity. …Under such circumstances, people quite literally "separate", "change each other's minds", "break up", and "divorce"' (Ames 2007, p. 55).

[11] As Heisig explains it, for Nishida I am an event, a 'locus of activity' rather than a 'preexisting entity' (Heisig 2001, pp. 73–74).

An analogy to modern physics suggests an implication for ethics of this emphasis on constitutive relations. Einstein demonstrated in the general theory of relativity that gravity is the geometric pattern of spacetime in the presence of massive bodies, and these bodies are themselves not ultimate individuals independent of velocity and time. Contrary to the common-sense Newtonian view, gravity is not a 'force' that reaches out to attract distant objects. Spacetime is a relational *event*, not a substantive thing that contains separately existing bodies in motion. This suggests as a postulate, to closely paraphrase a central thesis of James's radical empiricism, that the parts of existence are held together by relations that are themselves parts of existence. There is no need for any 'extraneous … connective support' (James 1912, p. xii). Partly under the direct influence of James's theory of relations, physicists later theorized that the same event structure holds for quantized bundles of matter and energy, a phenomenological level at which the physical universe appears to *be* statistical.[12]

Here is the 'moral': just as the 'force' of gravity is a function of relational interplay without any extraneous pressure, so no transcendent reference point is required as a connective support to bind moral agents to what is good, right, or virtuous—i.e., no divine commands, unchanging moral laws, transcendental principles, fixed teleology, or the like. The typical Western demand for a moral bedrock or ahistorical moral matrix conceals that moral life has always found guidance only from within a relational network. Unfortunately, much Western ethics continues its futile debate about the single right way to reason about morals in search of an illusory connective support, though thankfully there are positive signs that the stage of Western ethics is being redesigned.

Many Western philosophers are inclined to reject relational ethics as incompatible with transformative social criticism, due to the absence of bedrock principles. Christopher Ives, who co-translated Nishida's *An Inquiry into the Good*, criticizes what he calls Nishida's 'contemplative passivity … which provides no impetus for social criticism or transformative activism' (Ives 1994, p. 25). 'The content of our will(s)', Nishida writes, 'is given only by the self-determination of history in actuality' (In Ives 1994, p. 25). Ives argues that this fusion of is and ought is incompatible with 'morality' because it lacks a metric of transcendent 'autonomous moral principles' (Ives 1994, p. 35). Dewey develops a third way that promotes social criticism while preserving relational ethics. For Dewey things are not ultimately, even from the widest possible view, what they ought to be. Nor is there any need for transcendental principles. To say 'the act ought to be done' differs only verbally from saying 'this act will meet the situation' (EW 3:108–109).

4. For both traditions (with James's individualism as a possible exception), individual and society emerge from each other; neither is derivative of the other. Bao Zhiming compares the Confucian model of moral agency with the model of free-willing autonomy that has dominated Western ethics. He writes: 'Ultimately,

---

[12] On the influence of James's radical empiricism on Niels Bohr, see Snyder (1994).

man is social, hence relational.... Man as an individual abstracted away from the social and political relationships he is born into never enters the picture of Confucius' ethical world (In Zhiming 1990, p. 207). This East-West contrast reveals itself in linguistic usage. For example, English urges speakers to identify causal agents when interpreting events, whereas it is common in East Asian languages to avoid attribution of casual agency (Becker 1991, p. 167).

A brief sketch of themes in Dewey and Tetsuro Watsuji, Japan's premier twentieth century ethicist and a philosopher in the general orbit of the Kyoto School, reveals rich possibilities for East-West dialogue on this theme of social selfhood. Watsuji and Dewey oppose individualistic philosophies that, Watsuji writes, 'remove (or abstract) the human being from social groups, and deal with him as a self-sustaining being' (Watsuji 1996, p. 13). In his *Rinrigaku*, Watsuji defines ethics as 'the pattern through which the communal existence of human beings is rendered possible. In other words, ethics consists of the laws of social existence' (Watsuji 1996, p. 11).[13]

Dewey shares the communal and non-dualistic orientation of Watsuji's ethics, in which identity is inextricably linked to place and temporality. Both are nuanced observers of the mutualism between concrete particulars and spatio-temporal relational horizons. They each probe the aesthetics of moral understanding, recognize that there is freedom in structure, and steer between the Scylla of nihilistic drift and the Charybdis of inflexibility. And each reconstructs *res* as situational, so that ethical inquiry begins in problematic situations. 'The locus of ethical problems', Watsuji asserts, 'lies not in the consciousness of the isolated individual, but precisely in the in-betweeness of person and person (*Hito to hito to no aida*)' (Watsuji 1996, p. 10).[14]

5. In *Neglected Themes & Hidden Variations*, Bret Davis highlights another important affinity between the Kyoto School and American pragmatism: anti-zealotry and a rejection of absolute moral bedrocks. Davis discusses the rich, pragmatic anti-zealotry of Ueda Shizutera's Nishida-influenced interpretation of Zen. Davis explains Ueda: 'The zealous moralist who does not pass through this radical experience of letting go [of one's cherished distinctions between good and evil] would remain driven by the three poisons of desirous attachment to whatever has been posited as categorically good, hate of whatever has been posited as categorically bad, and delusion with respect to' the possibility of an epistemological bedrock for passing absolutistic ethical judgments (Davis 2008, pp. 242–243). Nishida translator Christopher Ives adds that for Zen ethical conceptions are 'pragmatically useful distinctions rather than unchanging, metaphysically grounded essences' (Davis 2008, p. 243). No matter how socially concerned or eco-friendly she may be, the moral zealot, fearful of moral

---

[13] Revealingly, *Habits of the Heart* author Robert Bellah published in the 1960s 'the first essay about Watsuji in a Western language'. William LeFleur, forward to Watsuji (1996, p. viii).

[14] *Hito to hito to no aida*. In *Fūdo*, Watsuji makes clear that his ethics extends to the in-betweeness of persons and nature, offering at least implicitly a resource for environmental ethics. Odin (1996, p. 397) defends this position.

ambiguity, clings to received moral codes as fixed compass points and becomes, to use a well-worn comment by Mark Twain, good 'in the worst sense of the word'.
6. Nishimura Takuo's chapter (Chap. 6, this volume) highlights the role of the aesthetic in Kyoto School theories of human transformation (education), and indeed the aesthetic is central to Nishida's and Watsuji's perspectives. Dialogue with the American philosophical tradition may be helpful for drawing out some pedagogical implications. For example, university professors East and West are aware that students too often conceive education as something that orbits the strong gravity of their self-interest. Yet the exemplary student sympathetically approaches fields of knowledge in the same way they engage other people and nature: not simply as material for their own egoistic preferences, but as immersion in a current wider and deeper than themselves. Most of the beauty and vitality of liberal learning reveals itself only after such sympathy, while concealing itself before it. The student's aesthetic receptiveness, indeed her care, is the necessary ingredient for her learning. Whatever learning takes place without what early American philosopher Jonathan Edwards would call this 'sense of heart' is pale and anemic by comparison.

There are also deep tonal and conceptual differences between the Kyoto School and classical pragmatism, differences as dramatic as that between classical pragmatism and the 'pragmatism' of Realpolitik. For example, Watsuji's *Rinrigaku* challenges any form of universalizing in moral philosophy, and Dewey's own conception of a universal human nature—which underlies his moral, educational, social, and political thought—warrants careful rethinking in light of Watsuji's critique. Watsuji, meanwhile, retains controversial elements of feudal communitarianism by subordinating individuals to the emperor as the symbol of communal life. The state, according to his famous student Yuasa Yasuo, thus becomes for Watsuji 'the ultimate standard of value'.[15] Meanwhile, Dewey conceives a democratic way of life as 'the way' of communal existence and prioritizes communicative interaction that secures 'flexible readjustment' of social institutions.[16] Watsuji's ethical and political theories tend toward centralization and unification, while Dewey's are pluralistic and democratically de-centralized.[17]

The individualism of James, inspired in part by Emerson, is more distinctively American, while the annihilated ego of Nishida is more distinctively East Asian.

---

[15] Yuasa Yasuo, Appendix to Watsuji (1996, p. 315).

[16] See Dewey, *Democracy and Education*, Chapter 7.

[17] This is not to suggest that Dewey's political stances were unproblematic. Biographically, both Dewey and Watsuji at least tacitly supported disastrous wars for the sake of a national ideal: America making the world safe for democracy (WWI, for Dewey), and Japan liberating Asia from Western colonial hegemony (WWII, for Watsuji). Dewey, while sharing none of the three myths he found prevalent in Japanese culture during his 1920 visit (see 'Liberalism in Japan', MW 11:156–73), believed in the late 1930s that American culture was unique in its liberation from European bickering, and at that time he urged isolationism on this basis. Watsuji, meanwhile, upheld the uniqueness of the Imperial system that he believed essential to unify and preserve Japan's traditional culture. The three Japanese myths Dewey criticized were (1) 'racial homogeneity', (2) 'continuity of the imperial dynasty', and (3) indebtedness to 'the original virtues of the divine founders and to those of their divine descendents' (MW 11:172).

This is not limited to East-West comparisons. American environmental philosopher J. Baird Callicott expresses a view common among some 'ecocentric' philosophers when he frames relational fields as ontologically 'more real' than focal individuals. Dewey and James would recoil, as this can underemphasize the creative contribution of individuals and downplay the need for a full, felt response to the pulse of individual organisms. Tanabe, for example, exhibits this tendency in his nationalistic writings of the late 1930s and early 1940s, though Tanabe's view differs from Western ontologizing in that he conceives 'the true self as a goal to be striven for rather than as a reality to be awakened to' (Heisig, 168). Tanabe writes:

> The act of self-denial in which individuals sacrifice themselves for the sake of the nation turns out to be an affirmation of existence. Because the nation to which the individual has been sacrificed bears within itself the source of life of the individual, it is not merely a matter of sacrificing oneself for the other. Quite the contrary, *it is a restoration of the self to the true self*. (In Heisig, p. 169)

In *Philosophy as Metanoetics*, Tanabe (1986) writes in what Heisig calls a 'spirit of repentance' for such excesses (Heisig 2001, p. 169). In 'Time and Individuality', Dewey argues that if relegation of the individual is widespread, a culture's developmental potential will go unrealized (LW 14:98–114). Nonetheless, Dewey urged a point that parallels Tanabe: social habits are temporally antecedent to individual habits (see MW 14). The relational field in which we live is temporally prior to individuation, and hence, as Yuasa observes, 'the modern European idea of seeing the world from the standpoint of self-consciousness' is deeply flawed (Yuasa 1987, p. 23). A language of 'betweeness' is an appropriate antidote to what Raymond Boisvert calls Europe's cephalocentrism. But Dewey did not value the phenomenological level of encompassing wholes *over* that of the particular, as Tanabe did in his wartime writings. Relations between things, James urges, are *as* real as, not *more* real than, the individuals they reflexively constitute. This again parallels modern physics: to give a physical description of light, James Clerk Maxwell recognized in the 1860s that electromagnetic fields *between* particles are as real as, not more real than, the particles.

In addition to the contrast between Dewey's democratic ideal and Tanabe's and Nishitani's imperialism, the Kyoto School thinkers are more concerned with ideals of religious self-awareness than with ideals to guide practical conduct. They exhibit a 'passion for inwardness', according to Tanabe's leading disciple Takeuchi Yoshinori (In Heisig 2001, p. 14). The Kyoto School's divorce of 'religious consciousness from social conscience' (Heisig 2001, p. 15), religion from morality, contrasts sharply with Dewey's notion in *A Common Faith* of religious experience as a psychological adjustment directed toward 'the doings and sufferings of the continuous human community in which we are a link' (LW 9:57).

## Ecological Imagination

Like the terms space, time, and mass to the modern physicist, the terms individual and system signify to the ecologist things and the relationships that synergistically constitute them rather than ultimate existences. Kyoto School and classical pragmatist philosophers were among those skilled in a form of imaginative inquiry discussed today as ecological, and many of the metaphors of interconnectedness used in the ecologies today are found scattered throughout their works. But they seldom framed relational connections explicitly in terms of ecosystems, and it is historically careless to refer to all thinking about interrelatedness as ecological.

Conditions demand that we extend perception deeper into the socio-cultural, natural, and interpersonal relationships in which we are embedded. Ecological literacy has become essential to this. But even the most thorough knowledge about complex systems will overwhelm rather than enhance moral intelligence if that knowledge is not framed by *imagination*—here understood not as a faculty but as a function—in a way that relates one's individual biography to one's encompassing environment and history. In Wallace Stegner's words in *Angle of Repose*, imagination is our means for shaping definite contours, lines, and forms 'out of the fog of consequences' that is our future.

Ecological thinking, at least as it enters into our deliberations about private choices and public policies, is a function of this sort of imagination. Before turning to a discussion of ecological imagination, it is essential to better understand (or at least to stipulate) what imagination *is* and *does*, particularly given dramatic variability among Western theories of imagination.

What *is* imagination from a cognitive standpoint? Cognitive scientists studying the neural synaptic connections we call imagination define it helpfully as a form of 'mental simulation' shaped by our embodied interactions with the social and physical world and structured by projective mental habits like metaphors, images, semantic frames, symbols, and narratives (Lakoff 2008, p. 241).[18] Mental simulation is the most accurate technical description of imagination from a cognitive standpoint because neuroscience reveals that imaginative cognitive processes piggyback on the same neural connections involved in physical interactions. There is no localized 'imaginative' region of the brain, nor any distinct faculty of imagination. Seeing a birch tree activates the same neural region as dreaming about it, walking on Nishida's namesake 'Philosopher's Path' in Kyoto activates the same neural region as rehearsing or remembering the walk.[19] Imagining a landscape simulates a physical encounter and strengthens synaptic connections in the same neural region that would be involved in a direct sensorial encounter (see Lakoff 2008, pp. 240–241).

Because imaginative experience is of the same stuff as physical interactions, the way imaginative habits develop along definite lines through our embodied interactions is no more (or less) mysterious than any other neural function. However, this does not imply that the way imaginative experience simulates sensorial encounters is everywhere the same or that the capacity for fine-grained mental simulation is simply a universal 'given' rather than an individual achievement. Kyoto School thinkers offer a clue beyond this tendency to universalize human transformation. In work on

---

[18] For a bibliography of research on imagination in cognitive science, see Lakoff and Johnson (1998) and Johnson (2007).

[19] For a general survey on the embodied basis of meaning, see Gibbs (2005).

mental-physical unity, they argue that body-mind integration is as much or more an achievement as an established fact. For example, Thomas Kasulis observes of Yuasa Yasuo's influential book *The Body*: 'Eastern philosophies generally treat mind-body unity as an *achievement*, rather than an essential [ontological] relation' (In Yuasa 1987, p. 1). Western philosophers neglect the meditative achievements of exemplary individuals and assume, Kasulis continues, 'that the connection between the mind and body must be constant (not developed) and universal (not variable among different people). ... [T]he emphasis falls on the universal human condition instead off on the perfected state' (In Yuasa 1987, p. 3). Such insights help to steer theories of imagination away from Piaget-style universal developmental schemes, in accord with critical concerns voiced by the INPE panelists in this volume.

What does imagination *do*? Despite eulogizing of imagination by Adam Smith and David Hume, Enlightenment faculty psychology followed the lead of Plato's low estimation of imagination in the *Republic* and *Ion*. Faculty psychology is responsible for imagination's being mostly ignored even by those who urge that moral theories must be psychologically plausible. It is conceived as a limited capacity prone to frivolous fantasy and opposed to reason, and hence of little relevance to practical issues. So it is relegated to a subsidiary role in cognitive life or, transfigured by Romanticism, admired on a pedestal. In John Searle's philosophy of mind, our flickering imaginations are thought at best merely to form a pre-intentional 'background' for thought.[20]

John Dewey's work offers a powerful resource for framing a theory of imagination that is compatible both with contemporary cognitive research and with Kyoto School insights on human becoming. Perhaps Dewey should have jettisoned the term imagination as hopelessly entangled in Enlightenment mistakes, but he chose instead to reconstruct its meaning to accord with a functional psychology. More than a capacity to reproduce mental images, Dewey highlights imagination's active and constitutive role in cognitive life. 'Only imaginative vision', Dewey urges in *Art as Experience*, 'elicits the possibilities that are interwoven within the texture of the actual' (LW 10:348). Only through imagination do we see actual conditions in light of what is possible, so it is fundamental to all genuine thinking—scientific, aesthetic, or moral. To think involves more than data storage and retrieval. Dewey observes: 'To fill our heads like a scrapbook, with this and that item as a finished and done-for thing, is not to think. It is to turn ourselves into a piece of registering apparatus. To consider the bearing of the occurrence upon what may be, but is not yet, is to think' (MW 9:153).

Imagination is essential to the emergence of meaning, a necessary condition for which is to note relationships between things. For example, many migratory songbirds I enjoy in summer over a cup of coffee in my home state of Vermont are

---

[20] See Searle (1983, ch. 5), 'The Background'. For a critique of Searle's account of imagination, see Johnson (1987, pp. 178–191).

declining in numbers in part because trees in their winter nesting grounds in Central America are bulldozed to plant coffee plantations. This awareness amplifies the meaning of my cup of coffee. 'To grasp the meaning of a thing, an event, or a situation', Dewey notes in *How We Think*, 'is to see it in its relations to other things' (LW 8:225). Or as Mark Johnson recently put it, 'The meaning of something is its relations, actual or potential, to other qualities, things, events, and experiences' (Johnson 2007, p. 265). Meaning is amplified as new connections and relationships are identified and discriminated. Such meaning enables intelligent and inclusive foresight of the consequences of alternative choices and policies.

All active intellectual life is imaginative, according to Dewey, *to the degree* that it 'supplements and deepens observation' by affording 'clear insight into the remote, the absent, the obscure' (LW 8:251). Imaginative reflection of this sort is as ordinary for humans as nest-building is for birds. Never placeless or timeless, imagination, amplified by art and science, extends perception deep into the place (*basho*, for Nishida) and time in which we live. Indeed a geographical coordinate in space becomes an inhabited place, rich in stories, only through the mediation of imagination. This fundamental role for imagination in reflective life extends beyond the conventional dualism, echoed uncritically by Stuart Hampshire in *Innocence and Experience*, that imagination 'leaps and swerves' while rational intellect advances 'by rule-guided steps' (Hampshire 1989, p. 126).

Before exploring imagination in an ecological context, consider the nature and moral import of our more general imaginative 'capacity to foresee and forestall'.[21] In *Human Nature and Conduct* and other writings by Dewey on the psychology of moral reflection, deliberation is (descriptively) an indirect mode of action that substitutes for direct action by placing before us 'objects which are not directly or sensibly present, so that we may then react directly to these objects, ... precisely as we would to the same objects if they were physically present' (MW 14:139). There is an obvious evolutionary benefit of a neural adaptation that enables experimental simulation: 'An act tried out in imagination is not final or fatal. It is retrievable' (MW 14:132–133). By means of such simulations, actual and potential relations (including past lessons and as-yet-unrealized potentialities) 'come home to us and have power to stir us' (LW 9:30). When alternatives for dealing with problematic situations contend with one another as we forecast the consequences of acting on them, the ensuing suspense sustains deliberation (LW 8:200). Such deliberation, Dewey says, is 'a kind of dramatic rehearsal' in imagination (see Fesmire 2003).[22]

In sum, dramatic rehearsal is a capacity for crystallizing possibilities for thinking and acting and transforming them into directive hypotheses. Whatever else may or should be involved in moral deliberation, an adequate theory of moral reflection and by implication of moral education must at least be compatible with

---

[21] For a book-length treatment of Dewey's theory of imagination in a contemporary context, see Fesmire (2003).

[22] Dramatic rehearsal is one phase or function of the deliberative process. But this function is so essential for Dewey that it lends its name to the whole process.

these psychological operations. Unfortunately, philosophers working on moral education have given too little attention to imagination. As Ronald Hepburn cautions, 'When a set of human experiences is ignored in a theory relevant to them, they tend to be rendered less readily available as experiences. ... the experiences are felt ... as off-the-map; and, since off the map, seldom visited' (Hepburn 2004, p. 45).

What is *ecological* imagination?[23] Because human choices and policies are themselves part of a transactional field of complex relationships and events, deliberation will tend toward irresponsibility—in the rich sense of a failure to perceive and respond, not in the more limited Western sense of a failure to be accountable (see Ames 2007)—whenever imagination fails to shuttle back and forth between things and their relations. Or more to the point, we tend toward irresponsibility whenever our imaginative rehearsals fail to shuttle between things and the contextual relationships that are relevant to intelligently mediating the situation at hand.

Environmental examples in the U.S. abound—the soda (corn syrup) or cheese (corn-fed cows) hitched to the eutrophied 'dead zone' in the Gulf of Mexico, the iceberg lettuce linked to California's Imperial Valley border farms drawing off the last trickles of the Colorado River, the light switch twined up with West Virginia's coal industry. The sort of imaginative stretching required by these examples holds relationships before attention as we reflect. It confers significance upon otherwise mechanical and surficial experiences, and it opens the way for critical assessment and redirection of individual and institutional practices.

It is a general truth that we *cannot* respond to what we do not perceive, and we *will* not respond to perceptions unless they are immediately felt. This suggests an aesthetic dimension to environmental ethics and concomitantly to environmentally responsive moral education. In the vocabulary of Dewey's aesthetic theory, all active *artistry* in life (scientific, aesthetic, or moral) is funded by *aesthetic* perceptiveness. Or in Nishida's own artistic-aesthetic vocabulary of 'active intuition' (his mature development of the Jamesian concept of 'pure experience'[24]) both moral action and artistic creativity (as examples of *poiesis*), are simultaneously active and intuitive, transformative and receptive. Along these lines, by situating us within relational fields of dizzying complexity, the ecologies dilate aesthetic perception and open us to enjoyment and bereavement on a wider scale. These relationships are immediately felt as we simulate them in imagination, and the resulting qualitative field marks an experience with its distinctive character.

This immediately felt qualitative field gives an experience its identity and meaning and funds concerted moral action—'concerted' because our wisest doings and

---

[23] The adjective ecological is preferred here because, like the Japanese word kankyo, 'environmental' dualistically connotes external surroundings. The term ecological accommodates the concept of a live creature stretching to notice the very relationships that synergistically constitute it.

[24] In 1936, Nishida wrote in the Preface to an edition of *An Inquiry into the Good*: 'That which I called in the present book the world of direct or pure experience I have now come to think of as the world of historical reality. The world of action-intuition—the world of *poiesis*—is none other than the world of pure experience' (Nishida 1990, p. xxxiii).

undergoings are seldom the works of isolated individuals. As Watsuji implies of the Japanese tradition of *renga* 'linked' poetry and we may observe of jazz improvisation, we must respond empathetically to each other instead of imposing insular designs, and we must rigorously imagine how others will respond to our actions (see Fesmire 2003). Watsuji explains: '[I]f there are self-centered persons in the company, a certain "distortion" will be felt and group spirit itself will not be produced. When there are people, who, lacking individuality, are influenced only by others' suggestions, a certain "lack of power" will be felt, and a creative enthusiasm will not appear'. We must, says Watsuji, attain to Nothingness while remaining fully individual if we are to wisely negotiate relational networks (In Carter 2004, p. 10).

A culture's understanding of ecosystems is an in-road for revealing how they conceive their place in a matrix of relations.[25] Empirical tools from cognitive science can disclose some of the rich—albeit often incoherent—ways we conceive natural systems. What we learn is that the contours and horizon of ecological imagination are marked out by metaphors.[26] There are many conventional metaphors by which English-speakers make sense of ecosystemic relationships (e.g., web, network, community, superorganism, economic system) and trophic relations (e.g., energy flows, chains/links, pyramids). Image-schematic structures such as containment, verticality, force, balance, and the like also play a vital role. These metaphors structure the logic of much of the debate clustering around Eastern and Western folk metaphysical models: what Roger Ames contrasts as the 'object ontology' implicit in the folk metaphysics of most modern Western cultures (compatible with a mechanistic, linear-sequential, and reductive philosophy) and the 'field ontology' of Confucian, Taoist, and Buddhist thinking (see Ames 2007).

An adequate account of ecological imagination would need to build a case for three interrelated theses. Space will not permit full development, but I list the theses here in order to clarify terminology. (1) Moral deliberation is fundamentally imaginative in the sense that it involves mental simulations shaped in part by metaphors and related cognitive structures. (2) One practical role of imagination is that it enables our moral deliberations to zoom in on things, events, concepts, and persons without losing sight of their relational context—a child in relation to family, a sunrise in relation to the solar system, a statement in relation to its interpersonal, sociocultural, or literary context. Many remediable moral failures stem from mal-development of our capacity for double-barreled focus on things and their

---

[25] Ecology has become more than the science of the relationships between organisms and their environments. The meaning far exceeds what Ernst Haeckel had in mind when he coined the word ecology in 1866 (a word that had been casually tossed off by Thoreau earlier) or Arthur Tansley when he coined the word ecosystem in 1935 (to substitute quantifiable energy fields for fuzzy, quasi-mystical eulogies to universal connectedness (see Callicott 1989).

[26] On Lakoff and Johnson's (1998) view, metaphors are not limited to elliptical similes for illustrating concepts that, for sharper minds, could be replaced with a precise literal rendering. Our sense of who we are, how we understand situations, how we relate to others and to nonhuman nature, and what we see as possible courses of action and mediation all depend significantly on the stable metaphors and models we inherit, share, and live by.

relations. (3) This imaginative capacity is particularly important for dealing with complex social and natural systems, from economic systems to ecosystems. Our deliberations enlist imagination of a specifically ecological sort when the metaphors we use to make sense of ecosystemic relations—some of recent origin and some millennia old—shape our mental simulations. This is ecological imagination. This conceptual approach to ecological imagination differs from the Kyoto School emphasis on immediate perception and insight. Still, the shaping of ecological imagination by blended metaphors is a valuable resource for any grappling with complex systems, and it is indispensable for direct dealings with ecosystems.

How tight, slack, localized, or stable physical relationships may be is an empirical issue. Superempirical speculation about butterflies in China very likely exaggerates the case as much as atomism minimizes it. Settling these empirical issues is, happily, beyond the scope of this chapter. Nonetheless, a theory of ecological imagination in moral education is as relevant to James Lovelock-style biosphere-as-superorganism theorists as to his detractors, who are as at ease with disjunctions between things as with conjunctions.

## Aims of Ecologically Responsive Moral Education

An adequate account of the aims of moral education must try to incorporate the best interdisciplinary and cross-cultural reflections from the sciences and humanities on the sort of people we are becoming and the world that we are helping to make. Such reflection must compensate for at least four mistakes in contemporary moral education, taking 'moral education' here to include formal and informal efforts to selectively encourage moral dispositions.

1. Moral education is confused with moralistic lessons. This style of instruction is inherently undemocratic, ethically misguided, and pedagogically bankrupt. It does not take human or social transformation seriously, but seeks only to perpetuate established mores.
2. Western education is too often conceived narrowly as content-mastery in a formal classroom while the classroom is conceived as a value-free space, aside from rudimentary manners. Moral education, in that case, is at best an oxymoron, at worst a bad idea. These narrow conceptions would nullify the social values of liberal education, where the explicit aim is to liberate human energies from enslavement to mechanized habits toward lives of critical inquiry, social responsiveness, emotional engagement, and artful consummations.
3. Most Western cultures conceive moral maturation primarily as progressive sophistication in applying moral rules and principles, either heteronomously or autonomously conceived. This ignores cultivation of imagination. As a result, much work in philosophical ethics is too cut-and-dried to mediate the relational muddles of moral life.

4. The fourth mistake is that citizens of techno-industrial societies tend to see themselves in detachment instead of in relation. We must aim to awaken dormant imaginative capacities in youths to be more context-responsive, yet *not* simply to minimize jostling of societal norms, meet group expectations, or maximize interpersonal comfort.

I claimed at the outset that moral education should aim to help youths intelligently negotiate complex natural and social systems. This may sound like a simple plea for including ecological literacy as a curricular aim. That plea is warranted, but it lacks philosophical import. The foregoing reflections on American pragmatism and the Kyoto School support several interrelated, general inferences about some appropriate experimental aims to guide moral education toward ecological responsibility.[27]

1. There is rarely a single right thing to do. Moral education should help to cultivate tolerance for ambiguity.
2. We can rarely if ever do a single thing. Insofar as actions affect any complex system, wise moral deliberations forecast overlapping shock waves that will spread invisibly and irrevocably. For example, although above-ground we see trees as individuals, they form network communities in which individuals are root-grafted to each other and share energy through mycorrhizal fungi, so logging often kills non-targeted trees. Due to relational continuities of this sort, as Garrett Hardin observes, no action has a singular result.

   In a chapter on 'The Standpoint of Śunyata' in *Religion and Nothingness*, Nishitani uses this image of a tree root as a metaphor for conceiving inter-being from the standpoint of nothingness: 'To say that *a thing is not itself* means that, while continuing to be itself, it is in the home-ground of everything else. Figuratively speaking, its roots reach across into the ground of all other things and help to hold them up and keep them standing. It serves as a constitutive element of their being' (Nishitani 1982, p. 149). Any focal object is simultaneously, David Jardine observes, 'on the periphery of ... others, proximal to some, distant to others' (Jardine 1998, p. 71). From the standpoint of classical pragmatism, a vague sort of religious awareness of *general* interconnectedness is insufficient on its own. We must attend to *specific* relationships that are relevant to our dramatic rehearsals if we are to practically mediate troubled situations. The consequences of past decisions should be our guide. 'With James', McDermott observes, 'we hold that all events, all decisions are pregnant with connections, many of which show themselves only subsequent to the human plan enacted' (McDermott 2007, p. 152). Moral education should aim to cultivate the habit of forecasting (in imagination) the way *this* act *here* will tug at proximal and distant others.
3. The prototypical Western—and particularly American—concept of harm as immediate, localized, intentional, and directed toward individuals is out of step

---

[27] 'Aims' are here understood in Dewey's sense in *Democracy and Education*: 'The educational process has no end beyond itself; it is its own end; the educational process is one of continual reorganizing, reconstructing, transforming' (MW 9:54).

with the actual conditions of our lives in complex systems. The concomitant concept of responsibility for these harms is likewise inadequate. Take global climate change as an example. We are increasingly aware that the simple acts of heating or cooling a home, fueling a car, or turning on a light switch cause harm. The Intergovernmental Panel on Climate Change and international relief organizations project that the harm will be worst for future generations, impoverished citizens of developing nations, poor and disenfranchised citizens of industrialized nations, other species, and non-human nature more generally. That is, the greatest harm caused by local greenhouse gas emissions is long-term, widely distributed, unintentional, and not directed toward individuals.[28] Yet the harm is real, we are causing it, so moral education should help youths to perceive and respond to a wider range of harms.

In tandem with expanding the perception of harm, moral education should help youths understand that the causes of harms are frequently systemic rather than individual. Yet it is easier to think atomistically than systemically. With more refined relational imaginations, the coming generation will be better equipped to make individual choices and systemic policies to squeeze through the social and ecological bottlenecks they are inheriting.

4. Moral principles and rules must be analyzed and justified without recourse to the Enlightenment assumption of an autonomous, detached, dispassionate individual consciousness that reduces ethical decision-making to applying rational principles to concrete cases. Of course we need all the help we can get to ameliorate troubling circumstances, and principles and rules can help us to feel and think our way through tangles of our relational web. Moral education should help youths to become aware of themselves in relation, from the standpoint of being situated or placed. This should be the primary standpoint rather than standpoints steeped in Platonic conceptions of form as timeless being, such as divine commands, universal laws of reason, timeless moral intuitions, natural laws, or universal maxims.

The foremost need in moral life is for what Ames, in an essay on Chinese philosophical themes, calls 'relational virtuosity'. Youths should also learn to use and develop principles and rules, which in Confucian-influenced societies of East Asia may compensate for the partiality exhibited in family or group-based relational moralities. Greater skill in principled deliberation could also potentially help to compensate for anthropocentric tendencies in Confucianism.[29] But these principles should be conceived as tools to be evaluated by the work they do, not as ahistorical, a-contextual, and placeless verities. Contrary to centuries of Western moral philosophy, principles and procedures cannot on their own tell us what we should do. They make people *confident* that that they are acting within precise moral limits, but no matter how much we 'magnify the signs of rigorous thought and rigid demonstration' (MW 12:91) confidence does not entail responsibility.

---

[28] Cf. Dale Jamieson's (2007) analysis of harm and global climate change.

[29] On this theme, see Hall and Ames (1999).

5. We cannot respond to everything that makes a legitimate demand upon us. Hence, moral experience is irreducibly tragic, in the classical sense: in any moral situation there are more things to which we *ought* to respond than we *can* respond. That is, there are circumstances in which, contrary to Kantian rationalism, ought does not imply can. Moral education should help youths beyond the usual attitudes we learn to cope with the burden of inexhaustible oughts: resignation, guilt (especially in Western cultures), or shame (especially in Eastern cultures). Instead, moral education should cultivate the courage to respond to moral problems without cowering from the truth in James's defense of pluralism, the pragmatic upshot of his theory of a relational world: 'The word "and" trails after every sentence. Something always escapes. "Ever not quite" has to be said of the best attempts made anywhere in the universe at attaining all-inclusiveness' (James 1977, p. 145).

6. We must nonetheless believe and act with patience and courage amid ambiguity, and ethical reflection is born of this need. Unfortunately moral theorizing has quested for a certainty of conviction even greater than the moral convictions of the majority who parrot the reactive mores that philosophers rightly distrust. Most Western ethicists still want three things from a theory: a right way to reason about morals based on principle-driven moral agency, a clear procedure for definitely resolving moral quandaries, and a single right thing to do. This would be fine if moral problems could be solved by hitting upon a coherent and compelling arrangement of ideas, but the locus of moral problems is situational.

As with many of the moral images and conceptual models we construct to organize our moral experiences, traditional Western ethical theories can help us to be more perceptive and responsive. Philosophical ethics can proffer hypotheses that, in Dewey's words, enlarge perceptions and 'render men's minds more sensitive to life about them' (MW 12:91–92). It is valuable only insofar as it renders this service, so the quest for finality and completeness has been a distraction save as it has unconsciously enlarged perceptions. There is always a remainder, expanses of the relational network that legitimately press for our consideration yet are not spotlighted by our moral framework or conceptual schema. As McDermott writes of James's philosophy of relations: 'Everything we perceive teems with relational leads, many of them novel, and therefore often blocked from our experience by the narrowness and self-defining, circular character of our inherited conceptual schema' (McDermott 2007, p. 147). Thus James's pluralism, as Dewey explains it in 'The Development of American Pragmatism', 'accepts unity where it finds it, but it does not attempt to force the vast diversity of events and things into a single rational mold' (LW 2:9).

There is a Chinese idiomatic phrase for tunnel-vision: 'like looking at the sky from the bottom of a well'. The emphasis in the Kyoto School and classical pragmatism on immediately experienced relations and connections, to draw from McDermott, 'provides us with the metaphysical subtlety necessary as an antidote to the single vision which dominates so many of our endeavors' (McDermott 2007, p. 154). Moral education should aim to help youths to be patient with the suspense of moral inquiry, distrustful of ego attachments that breed moral zealotry, aware of the fallibility and incompleteness of any moral deliberation, and imaginative in pursuing 'relational leads'. There is need for fallibilistic confidence without sanctimoniousness and puritanical fervor, boldness and courage in mediating troubled situations without need or expectation of certainty, and ameliorative action without fatalistic resignation or paralyzing guilt and shame. As an aim for moral education, this is perhaps the most difficult. As McDermott observes: 'it would take a major change of heart for the present human community to take seriously even the possible plausibility of positions, claims, and attitudes to be inevitably pluralistic' (McDermott 2007, pp. 150–151).

7. When in pain, near death, Einstein was asked 'Is everything all right?' 'Everything is all right', he replied, 'but I am not' (In Isaacson 2007, p. 541). Most people believe, with Einstein, that there must be a relational attunement that can ultimately be affirmed as good and beautiful and worthy of our greatest contemplative moments. This is not a faith Dewey shared, nor is it needed in a robust, defensible account of ecological imagination and ecological citizenship. One of course has a right to believe this, but neither the right nor the need to insist that others believe this. Most philosophers prior to the twentieth century, and most people today (East and West), assume such a congenial universe as a condition for the possibility of the best-lived human life. Perhaps the relational fabric(s) is ultimately congenial to being grasped as a unity by our minds and warmly appraised by our judgments, but moral education must proceed independent of such faith.

8. Finally, moral education should aim to cultivate ecological imagination, both to help youths deal intelligently with the global scene of human impact on the natural environment *and* to help them become aesthetically (perhaps religiously, Nishitani urges) reconnected with encompassing natural and social relationships. Ecological imagination is both a tool of awareness-through-mental cultivation, as Kyoto School thinkers would emphasize, and simultaneously a tool of responsibility-through-action, as classical pragmatists would highlight. Through active exercise of ecological imagination we are already healing ourselves and our environments. Naming this capacity simply discloses its contours so we can avoid a situation that is both hopeless and meaningless.

A fine-tuned ecological imagination is not a panacea for aesthetic insensitivity. But married to virtues of patience, courage, and responsibility, and framed in the context of respect for human becoming, a finely aware ecological imagination can make the deliberations of the coming generation more trustworthy than that of their forebears as they appraise possible avenues for acting with an eye to systemic effects.

The presenters at the INPE session that occasioned this book were inspired by the Kyoto School philosophers to critique the theory-*praxis* split as an impediment to human becoming. This is perhaps the most notable parallel between the Kyoto School philosophers and Dewey with regard to their philosophies of education. The INPE presenters did not, however, engage the actual practice of education. I close with a very brief practical test case for cultivating ecological imagination in moral education.

The disconnection most of us have from our modern industrialized food system exemplifies a paucity of ecological imagination, yet it also signals a way for educators to cultivate this vital cognitive capacity in formal and informal settings. Dewey observed that people, whether children or adults, learn in concentric circles of increasing abstraction. Children in his 'laboratory school' at the University of Chicago at the turn of the last century learned mathematics and economics through a carefully designed curriculum that included cooking in the school kitchen. Today, children at the Martin Luther King, Jr. Middle School in Berkeley, California plant, nurture, and harvest food in a schoolyard garden, cook it in the school kitchen, and consume it in the dining hall. This is not superadded onto the 'real' curricular work at the school; it is thoroughly interwoven into the curriculum. Through an ongoing rhythm of doing and reflection they learn, for example, about the recycling loop of growth, maturity, decline, death, and decay.[30]

As mentioned, imaginative simulations activate the same neural regions as physical interactions, so these children are continuously developing their capacity for ecological simulation in the garden, in the kitchen, in the dining hall, and in the brick-and-mortar classroom. They explore, for example, how food cycles in the garden intersect with larger natural systems: the water cycle, the cycle of seasons, and the like. In this way these children learn that every action has systemic consequences, and they are more likely to become the kinds of people who habitually take a measure of responsibility for these consequences.[31]

This accords well with the work of progressive educators in the sustainability movement, who have for some decades been experimenting with pedagogies that are more rooted (place-based, bioregional, etc.), contextualized and relationship-based (vs. mechanical and disconnected), interdisciplinary/integrative (vs. isolated), and pluralistic (for diversity rather than mere efficiency and uniformity). Such educators strive to refine aesthetic sensibility and disclose relations (rather than obscuring them); they regard teachers and students as co-inquirers (vs. a pedagogy of content-delivery and data storage/retrieval); and they prepare students for success in their ability to perceive and respond to complex relationships rather than preparing students for success in their ability to out-consume others.

## Conclusion

Earth's 7 billion people, and the billions still to join us, will determine much of the future of terrestrial life. We will simultaneously determine the extent to which we will share dwindling natural resources, or continue through military means to

---

[30] In 2006 and 2008 presentations at the Terra Madre international Slow Food gathering in Turin, Italy, representatives of Green Mountain College in Vermont presented on a college-scale version of Berkeley's edible schoolyard.

[31] Cf. Capra (2005). On the Edible Schoolyard Project, see: http://www.edibleschoolyard.org/cla_eco.html. A free packet titled *Getting Started: A Guide to Creating School Gardens as Outdoor Classrooms* can be obtained at: http://www.ecoliteracy.org/publications/getting-started.html. On ecological education, cf. Orr (1992).

enforce a disproportionate distribution of environmental burdens and benefits. The Kyoto School and classical American pragmatism can help us along the path of ecological wisdom. Infinite relationships between ourselves and our 'fellows and with nature *already* exist', Dewey observed (MW 14:226). The chief end of moral education is to attend and respond to these relationships, ideally with wise ecological perception of the complex nature of problems, cultivated empathy for those affected by our choices, imaginative probings for technical and communal solutions, sensitivity to cultural traditions, and rich aesthetic responses to natural and cultural landscapes.

**Acknowledgements** This research was supported in part by a Fulbright lecturing-research grant which allowed me to teach and conduct research at Kyoto University and Kobe University from March through August 2009. I am grateful to David Satterwhite, Mizuho Iwata, and their colleagues at the Japan-United States Educational Commission in Tokyo for their generous support. James Heisig at the Nanzan Institute for Religion and Culture generously hosted a brief yet productive visit to Nagoya. I am also grateful to Tomida Yasuhiko (Kyoto University), Kazashi Nobuo (Kobe University), Abe Hiroshi (Kyoto University), Carl Becker (Kyoto University), and many others for their unfailing support and friendship. Any scholarly errors in this chapter are of course entirely my own.

**Note on Abbreviations** All references to Dewey are to 1969–1991. The Collected Works of John Dewey, ed. Jo Ann Boydston, 37 vols. Carbondale: Southern Illinois University Press. Citations are to EW, MW, or LW (Early Works, Middle Works, or Later Works), followed by volume number, followed by page number.

# References

Alexander, T. (1987). *John Dewey's theory of art, experience, and nature: The horizons of feeling*. Albany: SUNY Press.

Ames, R. (2007). 'The way is made in the walking': Responsibility as relational virtuosity: Chapter 3. In B. Darling-Smith (Ed.), *Responsibility*. Lanham: Lexington Books.

Basho, M. (2008). *Basho: The complete haiku* (J. Reichhold, Trans.). Tokyo: Kodansha International.

Becker, C. (1991). Language and logic in modern Japan. *Communication & Cognition, 24*(2), 167–177.

Bellah, R., et al. (1996). *Habits of the heart: Individualism and commitment in American life* (2nd ed.). Berkeley: University of California Press.

Callicott, J. B. (1989). The metaphysical implications of ecology. In J. B. Callicott & R. Ames (Eds.), *Nature in Asian traditions of thought: Essays in environmental philosophy*. Albany: State University of New York Press.

Capra, F. (2005). Speaking nature's language: Principles for sustainability. In M. K. Stone & Z. Barlow (Eds.), *Ecological literacy*. San Francisco: Sierra Club Books.

Carter, R. (2004). Watsuji Tetsuro. In *Stanford encyclopedia of philosophy*. http://plato.stanford.edu/entries/watsuji-tetsuro/. Accessed 1 July 2007.

Davis, B. (2008). Letting go of god for nothing: Ueda Shizuteru's non-mysticism and the question of ethics in Zen Buddhism. In V. Hori & M. Curley (Eds.), *Neglected themes & hidden variations*. Nagoya: Nanzan Institute for Religion and Culture.

Dewey, J. (1969–1991). In J. A. Boydston (Ed.), *The collected works of John Dewey* (37 volumes). Carbondale: Southern Illinois University Press.

Fesmire, S. (2003). *John Dewey and moral imagination: Pragmatism in ethics*. Bloomington: Indiana University Press.

Gibbs, R. (2005). *Embodiment in cognitive science*. New York: Cambridge University Press.

Hampshire, S. (1989). *Innocence and experience*. Cambridge: Harvard University Press.

Hall, D., & Ames, R. (1999). *The democracy of the dead: Dewey, Confucius, and the hope for democracy in China*. Chicago: Open Court.

Heisig, J. (2001). *Philosophers of nothingness*. Honolulu: University of Hawai'i Press.

Heisig, J., & Maraldo, J. C. (Eds.). (1994). *Rude awakenings: Zen, the Kyoto School, and the question of nationalism*. Honolulu: University of Hawai'i Press.

Hepburn, R. (2004). Contemporary aesthetics and the neglect of natural beauty. In A. Carlson & A. Berleant (Eds.), *The aesthetics of natural environments*. Toronto: Broadview Press.

Huang, Y. (2008). *Transpacific imaginations: History, literature, counterpoetics*. Cambridge, MA: Harvard University Press.

Isaacson, W. (2007). *Einstein*. New York: Simon & Schuster.

Ives, C. (1994). Ethical pitfalls in imperial Zen and Nishida philosophy: Ichikawa Hakugen's critique. In J. Heisig & J. Maraldo (Eds.), *Rude awakenings* (pp. 16–39). Honolulu: University of Hawai'i Press.

James, W. (1912). *Essays in radical empiricism*. New York: Henry Holt.

James, W. (1950). *The principles of psychology* (Vol. I). New York: Dover.

James, W. (1977). *A pluralistic universe*. Cambridge, MA: Harvard University Press.

Jamieson, D. (2007). The moral and political challenges of climate change. In S. Moser & L. Dilling (Eds.), *Creating a climate for change* (pp. 475–482). Cambridge: Cambridge University Press.

Jardine, D. (1998). *To dwell with a boundless heart: Essays in curriculum theory, hermeneutics, and the ecological imagination*. New York: Peter Lang.

Johnson, M. (1987). *The body in the mind*. Chicago: University of Chicago Press.

Johnson, M. (2007). *The meaning of the body*. Chicago: University of Chicago Press.

Lakoff, G. (2008). *The political mind*. New York: Viking.

Lakoff, G., & Johnson, M. (1998). *Philosophy in the flesh*. New York: Basic Books.

McDermott, J. (1986). *Streams of experience*. Amherst: University of Massachusetts Press.

McDermott, J. (2007). *The drama of possibility: Experience as philosophy of culture*. New York: Fordham University Press.

Nishida, K. (1990). *An inquiry into the good* (M. Abe & C. Ives, Trans.). New Haven: Yale University Press.

Nishitani, K. (1982). *Religion and nothingness* (J. Van Bragt, Trans.). Berkeley: University of California Press.

Nishitani, K. (1990). Encounter with emptiness: A message from Nishitani Keiji. In *The religious philosophy of Nishitani Keiji*. Berkeley: Asian Humanities Press.

Odin, S. (1996). *The social self in Zen and American pragmatism*. Albany: State University of New York Press.

Orr, D. (1992). *Ecological literacy*. Albany: State University of New York Press.

Putnam, R. (2001). *Bowling alone*. New York: Touchstone Books.

Searle, J. (1983). *Intentionality*. Cambridge: Cambridge University Press.

Snyder, D. (1994). On complementarity and William James. *American Psychologist, 49*(10), 891–892.

Tanabe, H. (1986). *Philosophy as metanoetics* (T. Yoshinori, Trans.). Berkeley: University of California Press.

Watsuji, T. (1996). *Watsuji Tetsuro's Rinrigaku: Ethics in Japan* (Y. Seisaku & R. E. Carter, Trans.). Albany: State University of New York Press.

Yuasa, Y. (1987). *The body: Toward an eastern mind-body theory* (N. Shigenori & T. Kasulis, Trans.). Albany: State University of New York Press.

Zhiming, B. (1990). Language and world view in ancient China. *Philosophy East and West, 40*, 207.

# Part II
# Thinking of Education around the Kyoto School of Philosophy

# Chapter 10
# Martinus Jan Langeveld: Modern Educationalist of Everyday Upbringing

**Bas Levering**

The educationalist Martinus Jan Langeveld (1905–1989) was often mistakenly thought to be German and it is easy to understand why. Langeveld had very close contact with Eduard Spranger, Theodor Litt, Hermann Nohl, Erich Weiniger, Joseph Dolch, Fritz Blättner and Otto Friedrich Bollnow. Urged on by Litt, he even translated his theoretical magnum opus *Beknopte theoretische pedagogiek (Concise theoretical pedagogy)* (Langeveld 1945) into German himself in 1951. He wrote a number of his books, such as *Studien zur Anthropologie des Kindes* (1956) and *Die Schule als wegs des Kindes (The School as the Road of the Child)* (1957) in German, and he was a member of the editorial boards of the most prestigious German educational journals. Pontgraz's four-part compilation of autobiographical portraits of renowned German educationalists (1978) includes a portrait of Langeveld.

Langeveld was not German though; he was the Dutch educationalist who laid the foundation for pedagogy as a course of study at university in the Netherlands after the Second World War. He was at the birth of the Utrecht School, an international group of influential psychologists, psychiatrists, sociologists and criminologists, who championed a human science approach. The Utrecht School is associated with names such as Frederik J.J. Buytendijk, Jan Hendrik van den Berg, Jan Linschoten and Willem Pompe. Through these associations the social sciences as a whole in Utrecht became steeped in the pedagogic project. Langeveld's practical outlook on scholarship was hugely inspired by his clinical practice. For him, even when he was addressing the theory, it was about this child, in this situation, at this moment in time.

After he was accorded emeritus status in 1972, he made a number of visits to Japan, where he worked closely with Professor Shuji Wada, one of his former students from Utrecht in the 1960s. It was Wada who saw to it that Langeveld's *Beknopte theoretische pedagogiek* was translated into Japanese.

B. Levering (✉)
Faculty of Social Sciences, Utrecht University, P.O. Box 80.140, 3508 TC Utrecht,
The Netherlands
e-mail: B.Levering@uu.nl

P. Standish and N. Saito (eds.), *Education and the Kyoto School of Philosophy*,
Contemporary Philosophies and Theories in Education 1,
DOI 10.1007/978-94-007-4047-1_10, © Springer Science+Business Media Dordrecht 2012

This chapter focuses on Langeveld's theoretical work. After a brief introduction to his life and work, Langeveld's outlook on his subject is explained: pedagogy as practical science. Then his pedagogic theory and how it links in with anthropology and developmental psychology are explained. His particular use of the phenomenological method is examined next, showing how this connects with situation analysis: the analysis of what those who are responsible for bringing up children are to do. Finally Langeveld's relevance today is considered.

## Life and Work

After secondary school in Amsterdam, Langeveld went to that city's municipal university to study Dutch and history in 1925, where from the very beginning he also showed a great deal of interest in pedagogy. His tutor, Philip Kohnstamm, put him in touch with the philosopher H. J. Pos who had studied under Husserl. It was Pos who encouraged Langeveld to study abroad. During his student years in Amsterdam, from 1925 to 1931, Langeveld also spent time studying in Hamburg under psychologists William Stern and Martha Muchow and the philosopher Ernst Casirer. In Leipzig he studied philosophy and pedagogy under Litt. He attended lectures given by Edmund Husserl and Martin Heidegger. At the beginning of his studies Langeveld was Kohnstamm's research assistant and after he graduated he taught Dutch, history and philosophy at the Lyceum in Baarn. He obtained his doctorate in 1934 with a thesis on the 'language and thinking' of 12- to 14-year-olds (Langeveld 1934). Immediately after he got his Ph.D., Langeveld went into private practice as an education and child-rearing consultant, laying the foundation for the clinical pedagogy, diagnostics and treatment practice that he was to develop later at his pedagogic institute in Utrecht. He was offering a service to parents of normal children who were having child-rearing problems.

A teaching post in child psychology at the *Nutsseminarium* in Amsterdam followed in 1935 and an unsalaried teaching post in adolescent psychology at Amsterdam University in 1937. In 1939 Langeveld became Professor of Pedagogy by special appointment at Utrecht University and head of the Cultural Statistics Department of the Central Statistical Office (CBS) in The Hague. During the Second World War Langeveld took over the responsibilities of Kohnstamm, who was forced to go into hiding. He finished his *Beknopte theoretische pedagogiek* in the later years of the war, a work that has been studied not only by generations of students in pedagogy at universities, but also by students at teacher education colleges, and it remained on university book lists right up to the 1980s.

In 1946 Langeveld was appointed Professor of Pedagogy, Developmental Psychology and Didactics at Utrecht University. He was actually the sole survivor after the war. A number of his colleagues did not survive the war and one or two were not permitted to come back to the university because they had shown too much sympathy with the occupiers. After the War Langeveld not only began to develop the discipline of pedagogy, but he played a major part in determining the course of the social sciences as a whole. He recruited the physiologist and physician Frederik J. Buytendijk, for instance, as well as Van Lennep who later was to gain an undisputed reputation in psychologist circles. Even more decisive for the character of psychology in Utrecht was that he managed to prevent the appointment of A.D. de Groot, a vehement critic of the human science approach.

Post-war development of education and research was still mainly dominated by teacher training and secondary education as it had been in the pre-war years. Interest in primary education was soon added to that and the 1950s saw the emergence of social-educational research and the development of special education. Separate chairs were established in these fields in these years, so that Langeveld was able to concentrate on clinical pedagogy: case work in theory and practice. The 1960s were the age of expansion and consolidation. His international influence was growing but in the Netherlands the typical Utrecht approach was coming under pressure due to the rise of empirical-analytical research. The late-1960s also saw the arrival of critical pedagogy, which was especially popular among students, which saw Langeveld's pedagogy as bourgeois and middle class. However, by the time that movement had radically changed the complexion of the university, Langeveld had already left. When he was awarded his emeritus professorship in 1972, his one-man band of 1946 had grown into a fully fledged subfaculty with a staff of around 130 and a rapidly increasing number of students.

## Pedagogy as Practical Science

It is not easy to convey an idea of Langeveld's academic work within the scope of a short chapter. He occupies a unique position in Dutch pedagogy. He published many tens of books and more than 400 articles. There does not seem to be much left for present-day educationalists to do other than to modify and refine themes introduced or discussed by Langeveld. Because of the extensive specialization in the field, comparisons cannot be other than to the detriment of contemporary practitioners. Langeveld practised pedagogy 'across the full range'. This does not take away the fact that all the modern subspecialisms can still learn a lot from his contributions even today. Though this chapter concentrates on Langeveld's theoretical work, and therefore largely ignores his clinical work, it is important to stress the unity of his work. Langeveld was no system builder; his theory is too open to change for that. All the same it is coherent; the different elements fit together well; and it is precisely that clinical interest, that concern for the individual child and his or her parents, on which that coherence is based.

It may seem odd to begin an overview of Langeveld's theory with an explanation of his idea of science. The early editions of his *Beknopte theoretische pedagogiek* did not contain any such account. Only after 10 years, in 1955, did he rather ungraciously add a chapter on 'The scientific nature of pedagogy': 'Better than opening a theoretical pedagogy with a plea or a theoretical discourse or suchlike, these belong at the end and in the umpteenth edition (the fifth, B.L.) of a book, that has proved meanwhile that it can stand on its own two feet without having studied the theory of balance' (Langeveld 1979a, p. 167). He does not shy away from the fact that for him this kind of discussion of the foundations of pedagogy is of secondary importance. From the very beginning he characterized pedagogy as a '(…) discipline which not only wants to know its object in order to know how things *are,* it wants to learn about – what it is studying – in order to know how to act' (Langeveld 1955, p. 11). (By characterizing pedagogy as a practical discipline, Langeveld was leaning heavily on the work of Litt (cf. Bijl and Levering 1979)). The significance of his pursuing academic prestige for pedagogy at this late stage should not be underestimated as a motive. Right through to the present day things related to children have not always been taken seriously as a matter of course. Langeveld spoke of 'The disdain for education' (cf. Langeveld 1950). He classified pedagogy as '(…) an empirical discipline, and one of the humanities, and a normative discipline, that is practised with practical intentions in mind' (Langeveld 1979a, p. 178). He was contrasting empirical with 'pure' science that is not based on experience. Humanities are the opposite of the natural sciences, a distinction made by the nineteenth century German philosopher Wilhelm Dilthey, who classified the sciences by the nature of the object studied. The attribute 'normative' here means that the definition of the object is dependent on value judgments. To find out what upbringing is, in contrast to the definition of what language is, for instance, you need to make value judgments, according to Langeveld. Theoretical science is about knowing how things are. A practical discipline, as we saw earlier, is about knowing how to act. Practical science is therefore fundamentally different from applied theoretical science.

To understand the precise significance of the practical intent of pedagogy, it is important to remember that clinical practice is at the heart of it. '(…) what it is in fact about is *helping this* child in the concrete circumstances in which s/he is living (…) to achieve *his/her* best potential' (Langeveld 1979a, p. 174). This makes clear that pedagogy is not only about rational (theoretical) responsibility, it is also about moral responsibility (cf. Langeveld 1979a, p. 23). What that moral responsibility means is easy to understand when you read how certain things are dealt with in clinical case work. The descriptions of how it turned out to be impossible to deny the requested help in a number of serious cases are not devoid of emotion – but how else could such situations be described? When in a number of concrete cases Langeveld describes how he had to get involved 'there was no turning back', as he put it, it is clear that it was impossible to look the other way (cf. Langeveld 1974, pp. 96–98). This sense of personal responsibility for the individual child in need and his/her parents forms the basis of the researcher's moral responsibility. 'From a pedagogic perspective, therefore, *those* methods that lead to *individualizing* (earlier he had 'individual', B.L.) knowledge are absolutely fundamental' (Langeveld 1979a, p. 174). After all it is not about a '(…) mechanical combining of forces, but insightful formulation of pictures and policies for the benefit of this specific human child (…)'.

There is no question, therefore, of unilateral application of a method (cf. Langeveld 1972, p. 93), but care for the individual child remains the constant theme. Pedagogy also has a very special relationship with psychology and sociology. Pedagogy is autonomous in the sense that it determines the significance of psychological and sociological knowledge in its own context. Psychology and sociology, according to Langeveld, are essentially situation-free disciplines. They aim at generalization and so are impractical. Moreover psychology and sociology ignore the basic fact that the child is a child that is being brought up. 'Much developmental psychology operates on the basis of the fiction of biomechanical autonomous developmental events' (Langeveld 1979a, p. 172). Were such events to occur, then they could only be observed in a derivative form in children, according to Langeveld. This means that pedagogy needs its own pedagogic psychology and pedagogic sociology. Langeveld himself paid far and away the most attention to the former. If psychology aims to come up with valuable facts that can be applied to education and child-rearing, then its basic structure would have to be determined by pedagogic axiomatics. In other words, it would have to be based on the fundamental fact that people start their lives as small children and cannot constitute themselves into human beings without being brought up by other human beings (cf. Langeveld 1956, p. 8).

## Pedagogy, Anthropology and Developmental Psychology

Now that we have established the practical nature of his pedagogy, it will come as no surprise that, in his definition of what upbringing is, Langeveld arrives at the actions of parents and educators. Upbringing is what happens in the interactions between adults and children, and influence is exercised in the course of those interactions. When it comes to upbringing, the direction of influence is from adult to child. The influence is purposeful, that is to say the adults take deliberate actions to achieve the goal of upbringing.

This is not merely a statement of fact: given its full meaning the term 'bring up' incorporates a value judgment. If one of the defining features mentioned above is absent, then we are not dealing with a poor form of upbringing or anything of that nature, we are simply not dealing with upbringing at all. This is not to deny that children exercise an influence upon adults; what is being denied is that this influence has anything to do with upbringing. Equally it cannot be denied that adults exercise influence upon children unintentionally and it is impossible to determine the ratio of intentional and unintentional influence, but the term 'bring up' is reserved for conscious purposeful influence.

The essence of the relationship between the upbringer and the child being brought up is that it is a relationship of authority. This authority is defined as a moral responsibility and liability for the benefit of the minor. Clearly parental authority aims to gradually phase itself out: the child's growing independence is its complement. That is what defines the upper limit of upbringing: when the child being brought up becomes an adult. The authority is technically necessary in upbringing. That is what defines the lower limit of upbringing: it is only possible from the moment that the child is able to recognize authority, roughly speaking from the development of language. The relationship of authority is embedded in a relationship of trust.

We will round off this description of the form of the parenting relationship by mentioning two characteristics which that relationship has to meet if it can be said to be a relationship of authority. In the first place, the authority has to be acceptable, both with respect to form and substance. The exercise of authority is an activity of the adult, who can be expected to have appropriate expectations. In the second place the authority has to be accepted in one way or another. Acceptance is an activity of the child, without whose agreement there can be no question of authority. It is these two characteristics in particular that link the characterization of the parenting relationship to its anthropological foundation, and it was Langeveld's view of the child, in particular, that sent pedagogy off in a new direction.

The first condition, that of the acceptability of authority, is tied up with the view of the human being as 'animal educandum', as able to be brought up (educable) and as dependent on upbringing (cf. Langeveld 1979a, p. 182). The second condition, that of the acceptance of authority by the child being brought up, is tied up with the characterization of the child as a being that itself wants to become something – this is known as the emancipation principle (cf. Langeveld 1979a, pp. 38–39). These anthropological assumptions about children correspond to certain principles in developmental psychology. Being dependent on upbringing, for instance, has features of the biological moment and the principle of helplessness. The emancipation principle is linked to the exploration principle (cf. Langeveld 1969, pp. 41–45). There is also a great deal of overlap between what Langeveld calls pedagogic 'trust' and what he classifies a 'security' in developmental psychology terms. 'Security' and 'exploration' are the categories that form the basis of the Columbus test, a pedagogic diagnostic test developed by Langeveld (Langeveld 1968).

There is a substantial risk of dependence on upbringing being conceived in an extremely limited way. Obviously upbringing is more than just taking care of a child, it involves testing against a goal; but 'self-responsible self-determination', the words that Langeveld chose for the goal of upbringing, seems to guarantee huge scope for individual interpretation. He did not leave it there though and so a more detailed definition that yesterday was self-evident cannot be taken for granted at all today. Langeveld, for instance, pointed to a further characteristic of adulthood that in his eyes is one of the most essential acts of the adult: the choice of a life partner. 'After all, through that choice a person takes responsibility for new life or at least takes upon him or herself joint responsibility for a spouse'(Langeveld 1979a, p. 51). Formal marriage has a much less prominent place in Western European societies than it had 60 years ago, and voluntary childlessness is now fully accepted in the Netherlands as it is in other countries.

The fact that Langeveld's theorizing and analysis are coloured by the times in which he was working is also apparent elsewhere. The way he distinguishes between 'upbringing' and 'humanization', for instance, chimes clearly the concern about 'the social degeneration of youth' which so preoccupied him and which was the focus of his large-scale research in the early 1950s. After the Second World War the Dutch government was trying to bring the young people that had gone astray during the war back into line and they called on educationalists to help them in this task. Langeveld wrote the final report (Langeveld 1952a, b). The distinction he developed between 'upbringing' and 'humanization' (= assimilation into the species) (Langeveld 1979a, p. 182) shows that his proposed goal was still much more strictly bound to a specific way of life. Humanization unlike upbringing is not tested against the demands of adulthood. All it means is to grow up among other humans just as animals grow up with other animals. Humanization can be taken for granted, it is not intended but it is always accomplished. When children are left with only this minimum provision, when they are not brought up, then they are being neglected (Langeveld 1957, pp. 158–159). The outcome when humanization is all that is on offer takes the form he referred to by terms such as 'polished mass youth' and 'social degeneration'. It would be better perhaps to turn the narrative on its head: 'social degeneration' is seen as an inhuman (infrahuman) form of human life and the reason why such lives occur is sought in the absence of upbringing. In this specific sense human children depend on upbringing to become people. What though does that social degeneration entail? What is the phenomenon that is being condemned?

Let us reproduce Langeveld's picture of neglected children in full: 'They are likely to become toilet-trained late; they hardly discriminate in their reactions to different people, they are indifferent to other people, unless these people are either a threat to them or offer them some advantage; they are aggressive to those who appear weaker than themselves or a threat, etc. They have little structure to their day, nothing to do and no proper work structure. They do not work and are not willing to work, nor do they play, except in a rudimentary sensopathic way. They seek food, they seek gratification and do not concern themselves with those who help them to get it; others are there to be used. Their faces express little, though they do betray fear or greed or hate. Their physical development manifests itself in the need to grow, in using their strength and a vague searching for an object on which they can exercise that strength. They have a limited range of expressions which are not adapted to a general audience: they come across to observers as 'unintelligible' or 'too loud' for the place they are in. They are unengaged, that is to say they do not operate from a personal core to engage with objects around them. One would be more likely to say 'something is getting them to do something' than 'they are involved in something', unless in their ego-affective world they are rushing headlong toward gratification, or pursuing or attacking an enemy, etc …' (Langeveld 1957, p. 158).

## Situation Analysis and Phenomenology

The pivotal role of action in Langeveld's pedagogy is evident from the fact that for him it was essentially about situation analysis. He defines 'situation', in line with the work of Anton Reichling, as ' the entirety of opportunities for experience in which people act' (Langeveld 1979a, p. 117). In simple terms, what it comes down to is that Langeveld defines situation subjectively, so it is not about all the 'objective' factors with which people are surrounded, but the factors with which subjects are involved in their actions. He uses different formulations to define the concept of 'situation'. Elsewhere, for instance, he emphasizes the normative aspect of situation as ' ... the entirety of information with respect to which action has to be taken' (Langeveld 1979a, p. 169). At first sight, therefore, the pedagogic situation would seem to be about the parent. After all, it is the parent who acts, s/he is responsible. However, there are many occasions where the activity of the child seems to be included as part of the pedagogic situation. (Upbringing as a situation involving action with respect to the child and action by the child him/herself (cf. Langeveld 1972, p. 93). All the same the relationship between the upbringer and the child being brought up is still ambiguous in the sense that only in the last revised edition of his *Beknopte theoretische pedagogiek* did Langeveld allow that 'the active participation of the child in his/her own upbringing' is part of the whole phenomenon of upbringing (Langeveld 1979a, p. 45). The interpretation of Langeveld's theory that this pushes him back into the territory of the intentional, which accuses him of neglecting all manner of unintentional influences on the child's development is a misinterpretation. In his own words: 'And even though upbringing entails far more than just the actions of a parent or educator – as there is so much that we call 'environment', 'circumstances' etc – all the same upbringing assumes responsibility for this whole complex as the pedagogic situation, makes use of it or struggles against it' (Langeveld 1979a, p. 19).

Now this is typical of Langeveld's way of analysing things. The concepts he developed derive their meaning from events that happen in the upbringing process itself and not from a general concept. There is, for instance, no question of a general concept of agogy from which pedagogy and andragogy are derived as particular subtypes, as is sometimes assumed, just as upbringing cannot be considered to be a special form of the general phenomenon of influence or as *'Anwendung philosophischer Einsicht auf eine besondere Situation des menschlichen Lebens'* (Applying philosophical insight to a specifying situation of human life) (Langeveld 1979a, p. 27). Upbringing has a character all of its own that is based on the fundamental helplessness of the child and the anthropological given of the responsibility of the adult. Pedagogy's claims to be an autonomous discipline are based on the unique nature of the pedagogic relationship.

It is impossible, for instance, to say anything worthwhile about responsibility in the context of education and upbringing based on general philosophical analyses of the concept. Such analyses tend to be based on the premise that responsibility presumes freedom, in the sense that we only hold people responsible for acts that they performed when they were free to do otherwise. While such an analysis is very important to a legal definition, it says nothing about the responsibilities of the parent or educator. '(...). And the first explanation that should be given after pointing out his *personal* responsibility, is that of his joint liability for what he personally has not done or was powerless to prevent; (...)' (Langeveld 1979a, p. 192). The fact is that it is a specific characteristic of pedagogic responsibility that freedom is *not* presumed.

'Parental authority', to give another example, is not derived from power in general but has a strict meaning of its own. It is not possible to explain authority in a general sense by demarcating it from 'power' and pointing to a freely chosen hierarchy. Parental authority is not based on free choice but on the dependent way of being of the child. To give a final example to illustrate that pedagogy has its own conceptual framework, which results from analysis of the pedagogic situation, and which cannot be understood to be a particularization of general scientific concepts, we refer to the relationship between interaction and upbringing. When Langeveld tries to establish what 'upbringing' is and when he places 'upbringing' in the interactions between adults and children, it should be clear that upbringing is not construed as a particularization of interaction in general. Indeed without further specifying what interaction in general is, he specifies the characteristics of interaction in the field of upbringing. (In the last revised edition of *BTP* a confusing paragraph has been added with respect to this. Compare Langeveld (1971, pp. 29–30) with Langeveld (1979, p. 35).)

Up to now we have been discussing pedagogic theory and related matters but have said nothing about the method of acquiring knowledge. Langeveld's phenomenology has often been misunderstood, and the fact that he rarely had anything to say himself about his method is partly to blame for this (Langeveld 1972, pp. 105–110, 1973/1974, 1979a). It should also be remembered that phenomenology was not Langeveld's only method. All knowledge that could make a contribution to children becoming morally independent human beings was worthwhile from a pedagogic perspective, notwithstanding the fact that it was Langeveld who reignited the debate about the phenomenological method even in Germany.

If there is one thing that is clear in Langeveld's outlook on phenomenology, then it is how far he distances himself from the father of phenomenology, Husserl. There are no philosophical intentions behind Langeveld's phenomenology. He does not admit transcendental subjectivity. If phenomenology were indeed to turn away from the concrete world and the concrete subject, it would not produce any knowledge of scientific relevance. It is just about making the immediate relationship between the human being and his world visible. It is about shining a light into the human world, it is about the relations of meanings in which being human in fact comes about. Langeveld replaces Husserl's phenomenological or transcendental reduction by what he calls immanent reduction. Immanent reduction means that what he calls 'coaccidental information' is abandoned in three areas. The three areas are subjectivity, prior theoretical knowledge and tradition. In this way Langeveld takes up Husserl's method without its philosophical pretentions.

Husserl's eidetic reduction, where incidental characteristics are systematically eliminated, can also be found in Langeveld. Langeveld calls the eidetic reduction 'the abstraction directed at the essential (…)' (Langeveld 1972, p. 107). Certain issues remain sketchy in Langeveld's work, but when he gives an example it does become clear which type of knowledge is at issue and on what foundations this knowledge has been built. There is intuition, but not the kind of intuition that we mean when, for instance, we say that we know intuitively that we are dealing with a swindler. In that case it is induction based on insufficient facts which would normally serve us very well in everyday practical situations. Intuition in phenomenological knowing is an immediate experience that produces knowledge of a strictly general nature. This is how we know that regret always relates to the past, while hope always relates to the future. There is no question of induction here: I will never come across any form of regret that is not retrospective and forms of hope that do not look forward are not actually forms of hope. These characteristics can be neither confirmed nor denied by the experiences of others. Phenomenological knowledge is knowledge gained from experience, but it is nevertheless knowledge a priori.

This is the point on which many misunderstandings about phenomenology in general and therefore also about a phenomenology à la Langeveld come together. The obvious question is which subjects allow themselves to be understood in phenomenological terms. We need to ask ourselves, for instance, whether the analysis of fundamental pedagogic concepts in the *Beknopte theoretische pedagogiek* really is a phenomenological analysis. It is presented as phenomenological and the line of reasoning is eidetically varied, but the outcomes allow a great deal of scope for convincing criticism and objections, even within the boundaries of historico-cultural legitimacy. Without doubt though it is phenomenology where the experience of the immediate human response to the world is being revealed, as in the analysis of *De verborgen plaats in het leven van het kind* (The hidden place in the life of the child) (1953) or in the analysis of *Das Ding in die Welt des Kindes* (The thing in the world of the child) (1956) or *Phaenomenologie van het leren* (Phenomenology of learning) (1952). Even these analyses are characterized by local colour, some of the experiences analyzed describe concrete things that are no longer of this era, but that does not affect the essence of the experiences described which were only amenable to description in their involvement with the concrete. And it is precisely that involvement with the concrete that gives the outcomes of phenomenological analyses their practical strength. To sum up: those who let fly at successful phenomenological analysis as a failed form of induction are missing the point. The immediate experience is the decisive factor. It is no contradiction that Langeveld recommended a sound philosophical education for educationalists in that context, '(…) who would through that intensified form of rational thinking learn to recognize *potential relationships* and fundamental structures, which may in fact never have occurred in the reality of upbringing in *that* form but which have been consistently thought through and which as an *idea* underpin that which *does* occur unsystematically and without much thought being given to it in the real world of upbringing' (Langeveld 1979a, p. 177).


## Conclusion: Langeveld's Relevance Today

Compared with his influence in the German-speaking world, Langeveld did not have much influence in English-speaking academic circles (see Rang and Rang 1991). He had much closer contacts with the French academic community and enjoyed a very fruitful collaboration with educationalists in South Africa. Langeveld never managed to fulfil the bridging role to the Anglo-Saxon world that his German academic friends assigned to him (cf. Hohmann 1971, p. 6). He was familiar with the work of the younger British philosophers of education, Richard Peters and Paul Hirst, and he also knew them personally, but he himself was emphatically not a philosopher of education, nor did he want to be. Langeveld's pedagogy was an empirical discipline in the broad sense of the word. His whole life long he argued against the distorting reductionism of the empirical-analytical approach to science, which offered no serious scope at all for other research methods to be used. That attitude does partially explain why his contacts with American scholars did not go that well. His pedagogy was philosophical in so far as upbringing as a phenomenon itself generates philosophical questions. The normative questions that have to be asked in connection with the goal of upbringing and the anthropological questions that require answers in connection with the foundations of the pedagogic relationships are examples of such philosophical questions. Langeveld's pedagogy was not a subcategory of philosophy, therefore, but it belonged with the social sciences. However, just as pedagogy could not be reduced to the status of applied philosophy, equally it could not be considered to be applied psychology or applied sociology. This view did indeed place him firmly in the camp of German pedagogy (cf. Süssmuth 1968; Hohmann 1971; Warsewa 1971; Lippitz 1980, 1997).

Pedagogy is also not confined to what goes on in school (education in the narrow sense), but covers everything that is relevant and important for a child on the path to adulthood. Education, in that broad sense of upbringing encompasses what happens within and outside the home too. On the one hand, therefore, Langeveld's pedagogy has a broad purpose and can present itself as a multidisciplinary subject in its ideal form; on the other hand, it specializes in the study of the personal relationship between parents and children. The relationship between teacher and pupil is also seen primarily as a pedagogic relationship, as convincingly expounded in the work of the Canadian educationalist Max van Manen for instance (cf. e.g. Van Manen 1991). It was Van Manen who brought Langeveld's ideas to the attention of North American educationalists. He made a number of Langeveld's older articles available to them by publishing them in English translation in the journal he founded *Phenomenology and Pedagogy*.

One of Langeveld's most exceptional contributions must be his introduction of the idea of 'the worth of the child'. It had been recognized for almost 200 years that children were a different kind of creature from adult human beings. That discovery is generally attributed to Jean Jacques Rousseau. But the insight that being a child should be considered a fully fledged mode of human life and not merely a temporary clearing house on the path to adulthood, that insight belongs to Langeveld. According to Langeveld, what typifies children is that they want to grow up at the same time as they want to be children, and with that assertion he creates an image that is as impossible as it is striking. Respecting children therefore means both giving them the opportunity to grow up and the opportunity to be children.

Langeveld's work was continued in the 1970s and 1980s by two of his students at his own subfaculty of pedagogy at Utrecht University. Ton Beekman took on theoretical pedagogy and Rob Lubbers took up the chair in clinical pedagogy. In his Ph.D. thesis Beekman developed the practical science concept for modern times but later, under the influence of the work of Paul Feyerabend, his theories developed in an increasingly anarchistic direction. He also democratized Langeveld's phenomenological method. Where phenomenology in Langeveld's time was still mainly a subject for erudite, literary, highly gifted intellectuals, Beekman started from the idea that actually anyone should be able to apply the phenomenological method as an empirical method (cf. Beekman and Mulderij 1977; Barritt et al. 1985). This found its best expression in the life-world research of Beekman's students Hans Bleeker and Karel Mulderij. Their research into the conditions for child-friendly living environments and their research into the perceptions of children with motor disabilities, elevated Langeveld's idea of the worth of the child to the highest norm (cf. Mulderij and Bleeker 1982; Bleeker and Mulderij 1986). Lubbers' clinical pedagogy assigned an important role to image communication in diagnostics and treatment. Lubbers emphasized the hermeneutic aspects of Langeveld's work rather than the phenomenological. Thirteen years after his retirement Langeveld contributed to a volume on hermeneutic diagnostics of Lubbers in 1985 (cf. Langeveld 1985). However, because his students lost their battle against the dominance of empirical-analytical methods as time went by, Langeveld's work faded into obscurity.

The concrete picture that Langeveld had of the goal of upbringing, adulthood, was, as we have seen, undeniably of its own era. The concrete social manifestations of adulthood that Langeveld described strike us now as old-fashioned, but the psychological traits that he ascribed to adults are also outdated in a way. The stable character traits that Langeveld observed young people developing around the age of 21, are not attained in our times before the age of 30. Only then do people accept responsibility for another life. The average age at which Dutch women have their first child is now 32. Viewed from the perspective of its pretentions to universal scientific truths, it is perhaps problematic that the findings produced by concrete phenomenological life-world research are certainly products of their own times. However, it is precisely that datedness that gives the knowledge much of its practicality, that is what makes it a practical discipline. In that case therefore it is much easier simply to distance oneself from those universal pretentions. The postmodernist critique that emerged as a philosophical movement in the period when Langeveld stopped publishing strike at the heart of the potential universal pretentions of Langeveld's theoretical concepts. Sticking with the goal of upbringing: Langeveld's open formulation 'self-responsible self-determination' can no longer be seen as a description of a state that can really be reached, at best it has to be conceived as an indispensible ideal for the upbringing process. Postmodernism has shown us that people are not able to become anything like as autonomous as Langeveld assumed based on the old Kantian ideal of autonomy (cf. Levering 1991).

Not only the upper limit of upbringing, the goal of upbringing, was a problem, the lower limit of upbringing as formulated by Langeveld has also come under attack. Since the 1960s there has been ever increasing interest in very early mother-child interaction in developmental psychology. The old assumption that early childhood learning comes down to imitation has been found in a particular way to be false. It is not the child that imitates the mother, it is the mother who imitates the child. The child does not babble away in imitation of its mother, it is the mother who 'answers' the child. The parent-child relationship is a two-way relationship from the very beginning, not just from when the child starts to talk (the moment that the child can accept, and so can also reject, parental authority). The Amsterdam educationalist Ben Spiecker redefined the concept of the 'pedagogic relationship' because the original lower limit had lost its meaning (Spiecker 1984). According to Spiecker, the parent manages to draw the child into the human community by treating the child as a developing person from the very beginning, and the parent believes in that from the moment the child is born. Anyway Langeveld's lower limit to upbringing had been criticized before, because it had long been clear that young children have other ways to show that they refuse to cooperate than simply spoken language.

As a modern educationalist in the socio-politically compartmentalized country that the Netherlands was in the post-war years, Langeveld developed a pedagogy that was acceptable to both the Christian and humanist sectors of the Dutch population. He established the subject at university level – in research and teaching – across the full range, concentrating himself mainly on theoretical pedagogy and clinical pedagogy. In Germany only his theoretical work attracted attention, but there too he is seen as one of the most important educationalists of his time. Postmodernist criticism of modern scholarship's optimism about what governments can achieve does not apply to Langeveld's pedagogy. He was more convinced than anyone of the fact that a normal upbringing has nothing to do with 'making' a person, and he always tried to prevent too many social demands being put upon pedagogy.

# References

Barritt, L. S., Beekman, A. J., Bleeker, H., & Mulderij, K. J. (1985). *Researching educational practice*. Grand Forks: University of North Dakota Press.

Beekman, A. J., & Mulderij, K. J. (1977). *Beleving en ervaring, werkboek fenomenologie voor de sociale wetenschappen*. Meppel: Boom.

Bijl, J., & Levering, B. (1979). Theodor Litt, cultuurfilosoof en pedagoog. In J. D. Imelman (Ed.), *Filosofie van opvoeding en onderwijs* (pp. 49–69). Groningen: Wolters Noordhoff.

Bleeker, H., & Mulderij, K. J. (1986). What did you do to your feet? I put my shoes on them! On the experiential value of the home-environment of physically handicapped children. *Children's Environment Quarterly, 3*, 4.

Hohmann, M. (1971). Die Pädagogik M. J. Langevelds: Untersuchungen. Zu seinem Wissenschaftsverstandnis. In: *Neue Folge der Erziehungshefte zur Vierteljahrschrift fur wissenschaftliche Pädagogik*, Heft 14. Bochum: Verlag F.Kamp.

Langeveld, M. J. (1934). *Taal en Denken*. Groningen: Wolters.

Langeveld, M. J. (1950). Educatio despecta [The disdain of education]. In *Verkenning en Verdieping. Een bundel herdrukken en nieuwe studien op pedagogisch en psychologisch gebied* (pp. 301–313). Purmerend: Muusses.

Langeveld, M. J. (1952a). Phaenomenologie van het leren. *Pedagogische Studien, 29*, 265–273.

Langeveld, M. J. (1952b). *Maatschappelijke verwildering der jeugd. Rapport betreffende de geestesgesteldheid van de massajeugd*. Den Haag: Staatsuitgeverij.

Langeveld, M. J. (1953). De 'verborgen plaats' in het leven van het kind. In J. H. van den Berg & J. Linschoten (Eds.), *Persoon en Wereld* (pp. 11–32). Utrecht: Bijleveld.

Langeveld, M. J. (1956). *Studien zur Anthropologie des Kindes*. Tübingen: Niemeyer.

Langeveld, M. J. (1957). 'Humanisering' mede in verband met 'opvoeding' – 'Kultuur'. In: *Gedenkboek voor Prof. Dr. Ph. Kohnstamm* (pp. 153–162). Groningen: Wolters.

Langeveld, M. J. (1968). *Columbus: Picture analysis of growth towards maturity: a series of 24 pictures and a manual*. Basel/New York: Karger.

Langeveld, M. J. (1969). *Ontwikkelingspsychologie (1953)*. Groningen: Wolters Noordhoff.

Langeveld, M. J. (1972). *Capita uit de algemene methodologie der opvoedingswetenschap (1959)*. Groningen: Wolters Noordhoff.

Langeveld, M. J. (1973/1974). De grenzen der vruchtbaarheid van Husserls fenomenologie voor de opvoedingswetenschap. *Tijdschrift voor Opvoedkunde, 19*(2), 151–154.

Langeveld, M. J. (1974). *Elk kind is er een, Meedenken en meehelp en bij groot worden en opvoed en*. Nijkerk: Callenbach.

Langeveld, M. J. (1978). Martinus Jan Langeveld. In L. J. Pongratz (Ed.), *Padagogik in Selbstdarstellungen III* (pp. I09–I149). Hamburg: Felix Meiner Verlag.

Langeveld, M. J. (1979a). Fenomenologie en Pedagogiek. In A. J. Smit (Ed.), *Die Agein Perenne. Studies in die Pedagogiek en die Wijsbegeerte opgedra aan Prof. dr. C. K. Oberholzer as Gedenkskrif b. g. v. sy 75ste verjaardag 17 dec. 1979* (pp. 46–56). Pretoria: Van Schaik.

Langeveld, M. J. (1985). De Babylonische spraakverwarring om het kind. In R. Lubbers (Ed.), *Hermeneutische diagnostiek en probleem oplossen*. Nijmegen: Dekker & Van de Vegt.

Langeveld, M. J. (1945¹, 1955⁵, 1971 1ᵉ herz., 1979 2ᵉ herz.). *Beknopte Theoretische Pedagogiek*. Groningen: Wolters (Noordhoff).

Levering, B. (1991). Zelfverantwoordelijke zelfbepaling kan echt niet meer. In F. Heyting et al. (Eds.), *Individuatie en socialisatie in tijden van modernisering. Bijdragen aan de Pedagogendag 1991* (pp. 169–177). Amsterdam: SISWO.

Levering, B., Bleeker, H., & Mulderij, K. J. (1986). On the beginning of qualitative research in pedagogy in the Netherlands. *Phenomenology and Pedagogy, 4*(3), 3–11.

Lippitz, W. (1980). Möglichkeiten eines lebesweltlichen Erfahrungsbegriffs im pädagogisch a-anthropologischen Denken – dargestellt an Langevelds Pädagogik. *Pädagogische Rundschau, 34*, 695–721.

Lippitz, W. (1997). Martinus J. Langeveld (1905–1989): "Integrale Pädagogik" im Zeichen ihrer Pluralisierung. Die phänomenologisch orientierte Pädagogik auf dem Weg zur lebensweltlichen pädagogischen Forschung. In W. Brinkmann & W. Harth-Peter (Eds.), *Freiheit. Geschichte. Vernunft. – Grundlinien geisteswissenschaftlicher Pädagogik – Festschrift f. W. Böhm* (pp. 374–390). Würzburg: Echter.

Mulderij, K. J., & Bleeker, H. (1982). *Kinderen wonen ook, suggesties ter verbetering van een kindvergeten woonomgeving*. Deventer: Van Loghum Slaterus.

Rang, A., & Rang, B. (1991). Een bekende onbekende. Over de receptie van Langevelds werk in Duitsland. *Pedagogisch tijdschrift, 16*, 178–192.

Spiecker, B. (1984). The pedagogical relationship. *Oxford Review of Education, 10*(2), 203–209.

Süssmuth, R. S. (1968). *Zur Anthropologie des Kindes. Untersuchungen und Interpretationen*. München: Kösel Verlag.

Van Manen, M. (1991). *The tact of teaching. The meaning of pedagogical thoughtfulness*. New York: SUNY Press.

Warsewa, E. (1971). *Die Welt des Kindes als menschliche Lebensform: Eine Einfuhrung in Langevelds anthropologisches Denken*. Dissertation Universität Tübingen.

# Chapter 11
# Zeami's Philosophy of Exercise and Expertise

Tadashi Nishihira

## Introduction

So-called postmodern philosophy is often considered to be the philosophy of deconstruction. The ontological basis of modern human sciences has been disrupted. The identity of the 'Ego' has been displaced. The allegedly substantial entity 'Reality' has been destroyed. And, of course, the value of 'Progress' has been completely undermined.[1]

After the experience of such deconstruction in the postmodern age, we must look for a different understanding of (human) 'development'.[2] As such the concept of expertise also requires a new framework of thought. This does not mean the introduction of new methods for the master and the expert. We need to ask not how to be a master or expert, but 'what does it mean to be a master or expert?' We must seek a different philosophical framework with which to reorient our thinking.

With this in mind, this chapter introduces an insight from traditional Japanese art, the theoretical work of the progenitor of the Noh play, Zeami Motokiyo (1363–1443). Zeami, as I will refer to him, is one of Japan's most celebrated actors and a playwright

---

[1] Toshihiko Izutsu who is considered to be one of the most remarkable Eastern philosophers of the twentieth century examines this post-modern situation from the perspective of Eastern Philosophy (Izutsu 2008).

[2] Nakagawa (2000) discusses this problem. See also Nishihira (2003) for a short comment on his discussion and a very brief introduction to this topic (Nishihira 2003).

T. Nishihira(✉)
Graduate School of Education, Kyoto University, Yoshida-honmachi, Sakyo-ku,
Kyoto-shi, 606-8501 Kyoto, Japan
e-mail: nishi@educ.kyoto-u.ac.jp

P. Standish and N. Saito (eds.), *Education and the Kyoto School of Philosophy*,      147
Contemporary Philosophies and Theories in Education 1,
DOI 10.1007/978-94-007-4047-1_11, © Springer Science+Business Media Dordrecht 2012

who composed more than 30 of the finest plays of Noh drama.[3] He also wrote a variety of theoretical texts on theatre and performance, and in particular, offered a profound insight into 'Keiko', meaning expertise in the sense of lesson, practice, exercise, or discipline. It is this sense of expertise that I will elucidate in the outline of his conceptual schema here.

His theoretical texts called 'Performance Notes' were originally written as secret 'letters' only for authorized followers.[4] His work was not accessible to general readers for nearly 500 years, until in 1909, the first substantial body of the text was discovered. Further parts continued to emerge until as recently as 1955. Since these texts came to light, Zeami has become popular as a representative intellectual of the so-called Middle Ages.[5]

This chapter is a brief introduction to Zeami's profound insight into exercise and expertise intended to indicate the different perspective it offers on the development of expertise, particularly in the transfiguration that his idea entails (Nishihira 2009).

## The Main Features of Zeami's Thought

### *'The State of Non-precaution': Beyond Precautions*

As an actor and director, Zeami emphasizes the significance of 'precautions' in the performance. This refers not only to the need to be aware of one's own actions but also to be mindful that one cannot always notice one's own behavior. This refers, then, in his words, to 'the precautions regarding what is right and what is wrong that are beyond perception' (Zeami 2008, p. 184). Noh-performers must have such precautions (mindfulness or self-awareness). But these precautions alone are not enough to be a great and virtuous performer. For this, Zeami says, one needs 'Non-precaution beyond precautions'.

In his schema 'the rank of non-precaution' is higher than 'the rank of precautions'. Noh-performers should forget, or transcend, the state of being conscious of precautions informing their performance. The rank of non-precautions is, he writes:

> the rank of performance from which any such hazard regarding precautions is gone, and whatever the character of the performance, it is of great virtuosity, while it may strike one as a truly unusual display, it nonetheless is interesting and empty of right and wrong or good and bad. If both right and wrong are interesting, then there can be no judgment as to right or wrong. (ibid.)

---

[3] Noh drama is a stage art that has been passed down from master to disciple, in an apparently unbroken line for over 650 years. Noh performers were traditionally male. Noh has been designated a 'Masterpiece of the Oral and Intangible Heritage of Humanity' by UNESCO (http://www.unesco.emb-japan.go.jp/htm/nogaku.htm).

[4] I refer throughout to the English translation of Zeami's texts, 'Performance Notes', by Tom Hare (Hare 2008). There are many other translations in different languages (Zeami 1960, 1961, 1984).

[5] There are a number of discussions on this topic. For example, see Hare (1986) and Shelley Fenno Quinn (2005).

The performance given in the state of non-precaution is so natural that the audience and critic must also transcend the normal criteria by which they appreciate the performance.

For Zeami, then, the performance given in the rank of non-precautions appears to be superior to the performance given with precautions. What, then, is the distinction between 'non-precaution *beyond* precautions' and the earlier stage of 'non-precaution *before* precautions'? This distinction and the form of expertise it entails will become clearer as the outline of Zeami's schema is elaborated. At this stage I provide a diagram of the first distinction, discussed above:

Precautions

Non-precaution *before* precautions          Non-precaution *beyond* precautions

I turn now to the second distinction, 'Without-skills'.

## *'Without-Skills': Beyond Skills or Before Skills*

Zeami's discussion of the context of the appeal of and expression in singing in Noh provides a further distinction in his schema, With-skills and Without-skills, as well as further indicating the distinction between 'Non-precaution before precaution' and 'Non-precaution beyond precaution'.

Zeami differentiates between two types of attractive performance in singing: on the one hand, 'With-skills', or U-MON, meaning with figure, brilliant texture, and on the other hand, 'Without-skills', or MU-MON, meaning without-figure, unobtrusive texture.

While a Noh actor 'With-skills' sings 'plenty of passages to display a brilliant musical texture of voice', the actor 'Without-skills' sings with 'unobtrusive vocal texture and no melodies that draw particular attention to himself, but merely an overall beauty and fullness of body in his vocal expression' (ibid., p. 179).

Zeami, however, further distinguishes between two different types of 'unobtrusive texture'. One is the *refined* 'unobtrusiveness' that transcends brilliant texture, and the other is the *unrefined* 'unobtrusiveness' that comes simply from his lack of practice. The former type, Zeami writes, is 'a type of excitement that sounds like no melodic articulation and has a patternlessness that comes only from the long experience of the performer'; it is a 'patternlessness that has transcended brilliant texture' (ibid., p. 179).

By contrast, the latter type describes 'someone who is patternless out of his pure obtuseness, who in fact doesn't know anything about melody, who has not been taught about accentuation, whose patternlessness is simply vacancy of mind' (ibid.).

We may now make the following diagram:

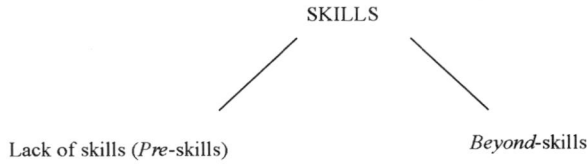

SKILLS

Lack of skills (*Pre*-skills)                     *Beyond*-skills

Here, the term '*Pre*-skills' means 'without discipline' or 'non-skills before mastery of skills' and 'non-precautions because of inattention'. The term '*Beyond*-skills' means 'non-skills beyond mastery of skills', 'impressive with no special melodic skills' and 'patternlessness which transcends brilliant texture' (ibid.). The idea here of 'Beyond skills' as without melodic skills does not mean a lack or loss of skills. I will now elaborate further on the nature of the expertise Zeami refers to in the idea of 'Beyond skills'.

## '*Beyond Skills*' Contains '*A New Kind of Skill*' Inside

Zeami explains that 'beyond-skills' does not simply mean 'without-skills'. Here he explains the difference in ranking between skills and 'Beyond-skills'. A performance that displays 'Beyond skills' he writes,

> sounds like patternlessness, but the excitement you should recognize to be the patternlessness that has transcended brilliant texture. This is the rank of the wondrous voice in its greatest achievement. That being the case, this unobtrusive musical texture is to be considered the best, because it *contains* the brilliantly textured. Since it has yet to reach that unsurpassed level, a brilliant musical texture alone is counted second to this. (ibid., pp. 179–180)

He suggests here that the state of 'beyond-skills' contains a new kind of skill. Being 'Beyond-skills' is not a lack of skills, but harbors a new kind of skill within the performance.

To picture this relationship more clearly, let us add a new rank to the diagram.

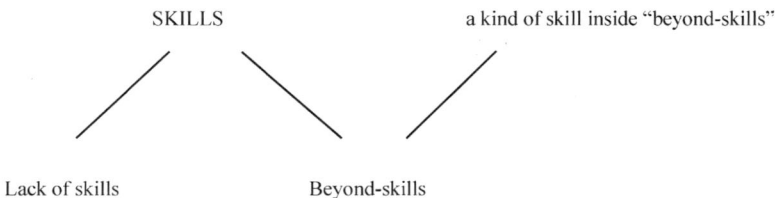

SKILLS                                        a kind of skill inside "beyond-skills"

Lack of skills                    Beyond-skills

## A Tentative Framework for the Discussion

I will now recapitulate and further elaborate the aspects of the schema described and depicted so far:

1. 'Lack of skills' means the state of being inexperienced and unskilled. This is termed the stage of the 'IMMATURE'. This stage also contains pure potentialities. The paradoxical relationship between the negative state of the immature and the positive state with potentialities will be discussed later.
2. The notion of 'SKILLS' means techniques conducted with self-awareness. The action produced by self-conscious reflection means this is understood as artificial play/performance.
3. 'Beyond-skills' transcends the rank of SKILLS. There is no intention at this stage. No artificial technique, no self-conscious control of one's own movement, no reflective awareness. Zeami names this stage 'MU-SHIN', which means literally 'non-mind' (from 'MU' meaning no, nothing, emptiness, or naught and SHIN meaning mind, heart, or intention). In the context of Zeami's texts this term is translated as 'being without intent', 'excitement without intent', 'the kind of excitement that transcends the mind', or 'a selfless level of art' (ibid., p. 115).
4. The rank of 'a kind of skill inside beyond-skills' can be seen as an example of what is termed 'DOUBLE-EYES'. The idea of DOUBLE-EYES expresses a new kind of skill and a new kind of intention emerging from the rank of MU-SHIN (i.e., no skills or no intentions). Skill or intention in the rank of 'SKILLS' is transformed by MU-SHIN.

A person with DOUBLE-EYES can accept two moments that are ordinarily assumed to be mutually exclusive: he can perceive autonomous events in a fluid dynamic process. This state will be examined later in connection with the idea of 'beyond dichotomy' or the 'unity of opposites'.

I will now elaborate the diagram further in line with the above.

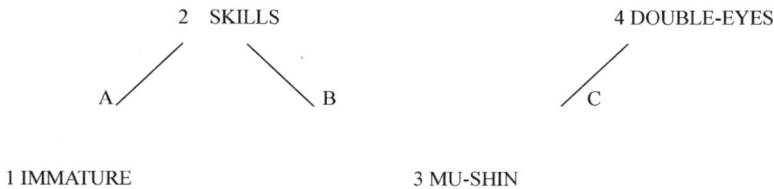

On this diagram, Process A (from 1 to 2) may be understood as that of *construction*, Process B (from 2 to 3) may be understood as that of *deconstruction*, and Process C, that of *reconstruction*.

## Deconstruction and Reconstruction: Casting Off the Old Self and Putting on the New Self

### *Process of Deconstruction: Self-emptying, Self-denial and 'Abnegation'*

Zeami's 'Performance Notes' does not begin with Process A, but instead with Process B. He did not leave the 'Notes' for those followers in the state of the 'IMMATURE' but for those with SKILLS. The main focus of his teaching is on the surrender of SKILLS, which happens in Process B, the passage from the stage of SKILLS to that of MU-SHIN.[6] Skills and techniques are, of course, important to the actor. What Zeami wishes to express, however, is that if the actor is clinging to these artificial skills, his performance continues to be intentional. There is the danger of being captivated by self-awareness and thus of impeding a natural fluid movement.

Through his own performance, Zeami is able to convey to the audience the state of 'no intention' and 'no artificiality', and that of 'not paying attention to one's own movement'. It is important for Noh performers to move according to the natural movement of one's body, that is, to move just as his body dictates in the situation of the drama. In order to fulfill his roles in the play, the Noh-performer has to release not only all the skills he has acquired, but also all of his intentions, motivations and self-awareness.

The process of deconstruction can be depicted thus:

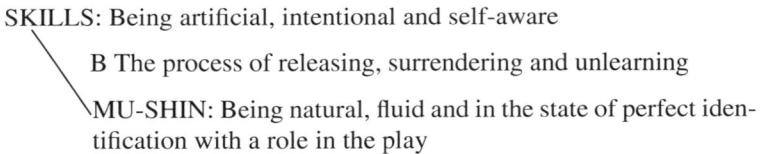

SKILLS: Being artificial, intentional and self-aware

  B The process of releasing, surrendering and unlearning

 MU-SHIN: Being natural, fluid and in the state of perfect identification with a role in the play

### *Process of Reconstruction: Rebirth with New Awareness*

Process C is the process of reconstruction and rebirth with new awareness.[7] It is important to avoid the misunderstanding that the intention entailed by the state of SKILLS is preserved behind the state of MU-SHIN and then re-appears again in Process C. Rather it is the case that intention and awareness will pass away in Process B. In the process of deconstruction, performers should seek the perfect

---

[6] Process B is similar to the idea of 'via negations' in Catholic mysticism and the idea of St. Paul of 'kenosis' (Philippians 2–7).

[7] In Buddhist thought, the way of deconstruction is 'the way of going forth to spiritual enlightenment' (Oh-so), and the way of Re-construction is 'the way of returning back to the daily life (with new enlightenment)' (Gen-so). Japanese-English Buddhist Dictionary.

abnegation of their intentionality. And a new kind of intention will emerge from within the state of no-intention.

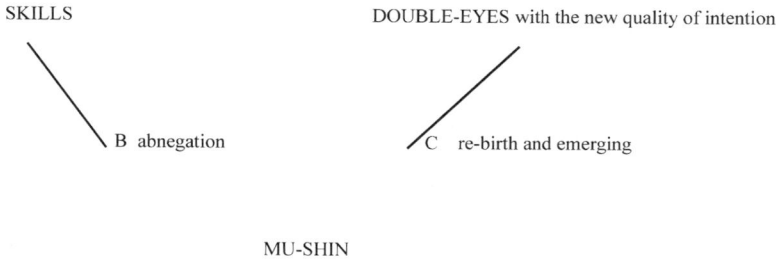

SKILLS                                    DOUBLE-EYES with the new quality of intention

        B  abnegation                          C   re-birth and emerging

MU-SHIN

In the way the schema has been described and depicted so far, the development between processes seems linear. We might understand Process C as taking place consecutively after Process B. This is not the case, however. Rather, as in Zen-Buddhism, Processes B and C are said to begin 'immediately' and 'simultaneously'. Two different processes are united into one. Deconstruction and reconstruction have to be understood as simultaneous events. The way to MU-SHIN and the way from MU-SHIN are united into one (Izutsu 1982, 1984). Zen-Buddhism has a special category called 'SOKU' (literally, at once) to describe 'the state in which two things that seem to be different outside are one inside' (Japanese-English Buddhist Dictionary). This is the provocative state of dichotomy, or in other words, the 'unity of opposites'. As we shall go on to discuss, the state or perspective of DOUBLE-EYES realizes this 'unity of opposites' (Izutsu 1980, 1983, 1984).

This stage of DOUBLE-EYES is exemplified in what is termed 'writing Zeami'. A special emphasis should be put on this point. 'Writing Zeami' refers to the conscious level on which Zeami has written, self-referentially, the theoretical texts, the 'Performance Notes'. We can differentiate the conscious level of 'writing Zeami' from that of 'dancing Zeami'. The latter plays on the stage in the state of MU-SHIN, without any intention. 'Writing Zeami', however, transcends that state and examines his own performance with DOUBLE-EYES, that is, with no original intention and yet with renewed intention. The perspective of DOUBLE-EYES casts off the old consciousness and immediately acquires new consciousness.

## Process A from the Viewpoint of DOUBLE-EYES

Let us now come back to Process A, which can be understood as a process of construction. The follower who is still unskilled, inexperienced, and immature must practice skills in order to control his body and mind consciously. Exercise and discipline for children are an example of this process of construction. The status of the child is not straightforward in relation to immaturity and expertise in Zeami's text, however.

Roughly speaking, according to Young, or early, Zeami, children must practice because they are unskilled. For Old, or later, Zeami, however, this is not the case.

He does not wish to imply a linear development from unskilled to expertise. Rather, he finds a kind of analogy between children's movements and a performance by an expert. They both dance naturally without paying any attention to their own movement. In Zeami's later work, he finds that children's performances are perfect and ideal. At the same time, he demands that children acquire basic skills.

```
        SKILLS                                    DOUBLE-EYES

           /        \                                    /
  A       /          \                                  /
         /            \                                /

  IMMATURE:   children's movements          MU-SHIN
```

## Lack of Skills vs. Ideal Fluidity

According to the later Zeami, while the performances of children are ideal, in the sense of coming from a spontaneous, unselfconscious state, children also have to learn skills and precautions. These do not come spontaneously from the children's natural movement. Children have to learn skills that lie outside their instructor's and their own traditions.

Is there any danger that children's ideal performances might be damaged by seeking to develop their skills and precautions? For Zeami, the answer is complicated. His philosophy of discipline is highly complex and nuanced and contains many apparent paradoxes. On the one hand, we have to teach and train children so that they can acquire basic skills. On the other hand, children's ideal pure movements should be conserved within their skills. We must respect and nurture both children's natural movements and formal skills. As skills should be accompanied by children's natural fluid movements, the acquisition of the rank of SKILLS cannot be the final goal. It is dangerous for children to be constrained by skills. Zeami, however, emphasizes the significance of basic skills to be practiced repeatedly by children. He prohibits them from simply imitating the natural fluid movement of their masters. Only after having mastered certain skills will children be able or permitted to cast off these skills.[8]

The wisdom of Zeami's DOUBLE-EYES may then appear to us (those with a single eye) to contain diverse paradoxes. For him, however, the idea of DOUBLE-EYES is never a paradox.

---

[8] Instructors in the rank of SKILLS sometimes overlook this dynamic and paradoxical relationship. On the one hand, they tend to consider the mastery of skills to be the ultimate goal of practice and try to initiate children into their skills. On the other hand, they tend to consider children's movements to be ideal and leave them alone, and therefore, prevent them from conducting a regular practice. It is important to acknowledge this paradox.

# Conclusion

Unlike skills or techniques, the essence of Noh (Zeami called it the 'flower of Noh') cannot be taught directly: like heat or fragrance it is transmitted naturally.

Zeami tells us, however, that we should never try to transmit this 'flower' directly to children. We should initiate children deliberately into skills and techniques in the initial phase of teaching (or discipline). After the mastery of skills there comes the stage of self-learning – learning that can never be taught. Skills and techniques should dissolve into 'flower' fragrance. We should not, however, remain even at this level. We should go further and keep discovering more sophisticated or more advanced states of DOUBLE-EYES.

DOUBLE-EYES make us notice the subtle danger in the relationship between master and child. On the one hand, the master must teach skills to children, while on the other hand he must also know that these skills may constrain the spontaneous performance or movement of the child, the movement which is the essence of the 'flower of Noh'. Nevertheless the master must teach and train children so that they acquire basic skills. DOUBLE-EYES make us notice the subtle proposition of self-awareness. On the one hand, actors must acquire the awareness of their own performance, while also knowing the danger of being in the captivity of self-awareness. On the other hand, actors must acquire the state of MU-SHIN (no awareness, nor intentions), while also seeking to acquire a new kind of awareness.

The perspective of DOUBLE-EYES is the wisdom of Zeami's theoretical text and is also a representative idea of Eastern Philosophy.[9]

# References

## Zeami's Texts

Benl, O. (1961). *Die geheime Überlieferung des No: aufgezeichnet von Meister Seami.* Frankfurt am Main: Insel Verlag (German).

Hare, T. (2008). *Performance notes.* New York: Columbia University Press (English).

Rimer, T., & Yamazaki, M. (1984). *On the art of the no drama: The major treatises of Zeami.* Princeton: Princeton University Press.

Sieffert, R. (1960). *Zeami La tradition secrete du No suivie de Une journée de No.* Paris: Gallimard (French).

---

[9] In Eastern Philosophy, the perspective of DOUBLE-EYES means an insight of 'a mode of generation in an event' or 'a mode of becoming in process'. It is from this perspective that Eastern Philosophy asserted all beings are fundamentally unified. All beings are nothing but 'a self-manifestation of the Metaphysical Unarticulated'. The 'Non-Being' is the 'Ur-grund (pre-phenomenal foundation)' for every phenomenal world (Izutsu 2008).

## *Secondary Texts*

Hare, T. (1986). *Zeami's style: The Noh plays of Zeami Motokiyo*. Stanford: Stanford University Press.

Hare, T. (2008). *Performance notes*. New York: Columbia University Press.

Izutsu, T. (1980). The nexus of ontological events: A Buddhist view of reality. *Eranos-Jahrbuch, 49*, 357–392.

Izutsu, T. (1982). *Toward a philosophy of Zen Buddhism* (2nd ed.). Boulder: Prajna Press.

Izutsu, T. (1983). *Sufism and Taoism: A comparative study of key philosophical concepts*. Berkeley: University of California Press.

Izutsu, T. (1984). Die Entdinglichung und Wiederverdinglichung der 'Dinge' im Zen-Buddhismus. In herausgegeben von Nitta, Yoshihiro (Ed.), *Japanische Beitaege zur Phaenomenologie*. Freiburg: Verlag Alber.

Izutsu, T. (2008). *The structure of oriental philosophy: Collected papers of Eranos conference* (Vol. 1 and Vol. 2). Tokyo: Keio University Press.

Nakagawa, Y. (2000). *Education for awakening: An eastern approach to holistic education*. Brandon: Foundation for Educational Renewal.

Nishihira, T. (2003, September). Child development from the perspective of eastern philosophy. *Encounter; Education for Meaning and Social Justice, 16*(3), 24–26. Brandon: Holistic Education Press.

Nishihira, T. (2009). *Seami no Keiko Tetsugaku* [*A Philosophical investigation into Zeami's teaching of exercise and expertise*]. Tokyo: University of Tokyo Press.

Quinn, S. F. (2005). *Developing Zeami: The Noh actor's attunement in practice*. Honolulu: University of Hawaii Press.

Zeami. (1960). *Zeami: La tradition secréte du No :suivie de Une journée de No* (R. Sieffert, Trans.). Paris: Gallimard (French).

Zeami. (1961). *Die geheime Uberlieferung des No: aufgezeichnet von Meister Seami* (O. Benl, Trans.). Frankfurt am Main: Insel Verlag (German).

Zeami. (1984). *On the art of the no drama: The major treatises of Zeami* (J. T. Rimer & M. Yamazaki, Trans.). Princeton: Princeton University Press (English).

Zeami. (2008). *Performance notes* (T. Hare, Trans.). New York: Columbia University Press (English).

## *Dictionary*

*Japanese-English Buddhist Dictionary* (Rev. ed.). (1999). Tokyo: Daito Shuppansha.

# Chapter 12
# 'We Are Alone, and We Are Never Alone': American Transcendentalism and the Political Education of Human Nature

Naoko Saito

## Introduction: Reconsidering the Politics of Environmentalism

Henry David Thoreau, the nineteenth century American transcendentalist, is known as a nature writer. The work by which he is best known, *Walden* (1854), is a record of his living in the woods at Walden Pond for nearly two years. It is interpreted typically as a book in the tradition of 'American pastoralism' (Leo Marx 1992, p. 379) and is understood as the revelation of a possible ecology or environmentalism that would resist the plundering and destructive consequences of booming industry and commerce – in other words, of capitalism (Standish and Saito 2005, p. 222). Lawrence Buell, in his *The Environmental Imagination: Thoreau, Nature Writings, and the Formation of American Culture* (1995) presents Thoreau's view on nature from the perspective of environmentalism and in the light of its implications for nature politics. He points out the historical fact that Thoreau loved to read Darwin's *Journal of Researches into the Natural History and Geology of the Countries Visited During the Voyage of HMS Beagle* (1839) (Buell 1995, p. 117) and shared with Darwin the idea of the 'conflation of natural and human phenomena' (p. 417). Nevertheless, unlike Darwin, Thoreau 'undermines the hierarchies of civilization/barbarity' (p. 418). Buell raises three distinctive features of Thoreau's view on nature. First is his 'empirical' approach to nature. Second, Thoreau sustains 'a deeply personal love and reverence for the nonhuman' (p. 137). Third is the political implication of Thoreau's environmentalism. Thoreau dissented from 'nineteenth-century norms' and propounded a 'self-conscious politics of environmentalism: a defense of nature against the human invader' (p. 135). In sum, Buell concludes, Thoreau took a 'path from *homocentrism* toward *biocentrism*' (p. 138, italics added).

N. Saito (✉)
Graduate School of Education, Kyoto University, Yoshida-honmachi, Sakyo-ku,
Kyoto-shi, 606-8501 Kyoto, Japan
e-mail: saitona@educ.kyoto-u.ac.jp

P. Standish and N. Saito (eds.), *Education and the Kyoto School of Philosophy*,
Contemporary Philosophies and Theories in Education 1,
DOI 10.1007/978-94-007-4047-1_12, © Springer Science+Business Media Dordrecht 2012

Buell's environmentalist reading of *Walden* may show something of its worth today, in the predicament of the post-modern globalized world – one in which the apparent advances of science and technology have risked the destruction of nature and the alienation of human beings from nature. The politics of environmentalism raises the question of how to (re)connect human beings with nature in such a way as to achieve a harmonious coexistence. Its underlying assumption is of a dichotomous picture between, on the one hand, the natural and the biological, and, on the other, the social, the cultural, and the conventional. As Rousseau's *Emile* illustrates, the former is a purer, more aboriginal state of human nature, the latter, a state that has degenerated from its original purity. Hence, a shift from homocentrism to biocentrism is called for.

This chapter questions this Buellian politics of the environment and tries to destabilize its assumptions of coexistence between man and nature. In order to show why this is problematic and to present an alternative vision of environmentalism and political education, I shall discuss Stanley Cavell's reading of Thoreau, a reading conditioned by ordinary language philosophy. Centering on Thoreau's idea of transcendence in the ordinary with the mediation of language, I shall try to show that the natural is always already cultural and that a reengagement with nature in itself is the very process of becoming political. Cavell's Thoreau will redirect us from biocentrism to humanism and provocatively turn political education away from anodyne aspirations for coexistence and towards a qualified isolation. Political education is learning how to be a 'neighbor', with nature and other people, bridging the private and the public – a political education for the perfection of human nature. To be a neighbor in this sense, I shall argue, is something other than mere coexistence. Through my discussion of the theme of transcendence in the ordinary within American transcendentalism, its common ground with, and difference from, the Kyoto School of Philosophy with regard to human transformation should become apparent.

## From Biocentrism to Humanism: Cavell's Reading of Thoreau's *Walden*

Buell says that 'Thoreau's environmental perception remained energized throughout his life by a sense of natural piety' (p. 129). In this regards he indicates some common traits between Thoreau and Ralph Waldo Emerson. Emerson's view on nature, according to Buell, is characterized by a relation of unity, intimacy and sympathy between man and nature (p. 209). To use Emerson's own expressions, the relation is typified by 'unison' (Emerson 1957, p. 29), 'il più nell' uno' (the many in the one) (p. 30), and 'Unity' (p. 40). Buell says that 'the Emersonian correspondence project continued to affect Thoreau's work' (p. 131). While Thoreau, however, took a 'scientific', 'empirical' and 'detranscendentalized' approach to nature, especially after 1850 (pp. 117, 134), Buell demonstrates Thoreau's multiple identities by quoting the following phrase from his journal: 'I am a mystic, a transcendentalist, and a natural philosopher to boot' (Thoreau quoted by Buell 1995, p. 117). In Thoreau 'pastoral aesthetics and romanticist natural piety [are found] interacting with empirical study and scientific interests' (Buell 1995, p. 138).

It is the notion of continuity that underlies Buell's environmentalism. There is the quest for a 'continuum or a monism' beyond any 'binary schism' (p. 211). Thoreau's interest in Native American culture is read as a manifestation of his idea of 'kinship between human and nonhuman realms' (ibid.), with nature a 'common habitat' (p. 264). Politically it implies 'organizing the environment in terms of its points of non-human interest instead of in terms of the directions and markers that most human beings depend on' (p. 135). This, Buell claims, epitomizes Thoreau's 'ecocentric thinking' (p. 143). By 'political' Buell does not mean 'the political process as such', but rather an 'interest in provoking social reflection and change' (ibid.). In this bio-centric picture of a unified relationship between the human and the nonhuman, the human and the civilized are opposed to the natural and the biological, and priority is given to the latter. The political is an overarching realm in the unity of the two.

There are two initial, intuitive questions to be raised concerning Buell's reading of Thoreau and, more generally, his idea of the politics of environmentalism. First, as a way of achieving the unity of two realms, Buell presents us with a structure in which the human being is absorbed into the totality of nature: the self is relinquished in nature (p. 171) and the 'persona' fades into the natural scenery (p. 476), which he refers to as an 'aesthetics of relinquishment' (p. 143). Thoreau's view on nature is seen as a kind of vitalism based upon coexistence between man and nature (or the human and the nonhuman). If this is the structure of man's relation to his environment, and if this is what is at the heart of what Buell takes Thoreau to mean by being political, is it not the fate of an individual human being eventually to be assimilated into the totality of nature? A second question is related to the internal structure and the way *Walden* is written. If Thoreau is an anti-homocentric, biocentric/ecocentric environmentalist, why is it that this book is not just about nature but about nature *and language*. The fact that there is a chapter actually called 'Reading' is by no means the only reason for saying that *Walden* is a book about reading and writing. These are factors that are seriously underexamined in Buell's account.

In helping us find whether these intuitive questions are adequate or not, Cavell's alternative interpretation, presented in *The Senses of Walden* (1992), sheds light not only on Thoreau's *Walden*, but also on what can be meant by environmentalism and, more broadly, the political. But we need to tread carefully with the terms here. Cavell rereads *Walden* as a book not on nonhuman transcendentalism, but on *transcendence in the ordinary* as the crucial momentum for becoming political – a theme that is of undoubted relevance to the Kyoto School of Philosophy.

Thoreau's view on nature, like Emerson's, is based upon the analogy between man and nature. *Walden* is filled with detailed observations and descriptions of nature and of living creatures as 'neighbors' to man. He writes:

> . . . if we take the ages into our account, may there not be a civilization going on among brutes as well as men? They seemed to me to be rudimental, burrowing men, still standing on their defence, awaiting their transformation (Thoreau 1992, p. 182).

This suggests a correspondence between man and nature, and yet at the same time, as Buell points out, it implies the overturning of any received hierarchical relationship between man and nature.

Cavell's reading, however, disturbs interpretations of Thoreau as a proponent of sheer continuity between man and nature.

> 'Our moulting season, like that of the fowls, must be a crisis in our lives. The loon retires to solitary ponds to spend it (I, 36)'. This use of 'must be' is a key to his position. What the imperative means is that our moulting season, unlike that of the fowls, is not a *natural* crisis… So at the heart of this apparent return to nature, it is not haphazard for him to say, 'Nature is hard to be overcome, but she must be overcome (XI, 12)'. Our nature is to be overcome (Cavell 1992, p. 43).[1]

The word 'must' connotes both the sense of inference and of obligation. The analogy between men and fowls is shown by the former sense, but the latter sense indicates the distinction or, say, discontinuity between them. The double meaning of this 'must' signifies that man is both a natural being and a trans-natural being. Cavell's statement that a crisis is not a 'natural' accomplishment means that man, as human being, is obligated to undergo a crisis (Saito 2005, p. 197). As Cavell says, 'nature is not my habitat, but my exemplar, my dream of habitation' (Cavell 1992, p. 43). Here see a slight but significant difference from Buell's interpretation of nature as a place, a 'common habitat'. Man must overcome nature, though not necessarily by an aggressive invasion of it. Cavell's distinction between a habitat and a habitation implies that nature is for sure a place for human beings *to live*, and yet to live does not automatically mean to find one's home in nature. In fact, the descriptions of place in *Walden* are suggestive of rather of transitivity and sojourning than of settling and owning. Yet still at the same time, Thoreau says, 'There is a solid bottom everywhere' (Thoreau 1992, p. 220), for the places you pass through can provide foundation enough in every act of finding. Hence, place is *displaced* in his writing. This is a paradoxical and dual relationship between man and nature, to live in intimacy and yet astride a rift.

How, according to Thoreau, can human beings rebuild such a relationship with nature? In response Cavell highlights Thoreau's idea of 'neighboring' as our relation to nature 'at its best' – 'knowing the grandest laws it is executing, while nevertheless "not wholly involved" in them' (Cavell 1992, p. 105). The relation of neighboring is neither man's invasion of nature nor his complete immersion in it; not even 'a mutual absorption' but 'a perpetual nextness, as an act of neighboring or befriending' (p. 108). This is not a relationship of unity, but one of 'doubleness', with the dual sense of nearness and distance (or say, continuity and discontinuity). This, Cavell says, is Thoreau's response to the Kantian project of answering skepticism (p. 64): '*Walden*, in effect, provides a transcendental deduction for the concepts of the-thing-in-itself and for determination – something Kant ought, so to speak, to have done' (p. 95), that is, '[t]he externality of the world is articulated by Thoreau as its nextness to me' (p. 107).

Thoreau's act of living in the woods at Walden Pond is an experiment in displacing and rebuilding the relationship between man and nature: that is, it is a 'continuous *activity*' of '*placing* ourselves in the world' (p. 53). In Cavell's reading of Thoreau, language plays a crucial role in this experiment. *Walden* is a book about 'the creation

---

[1] Cavell's references to *Walden* give chapter and paragraph.

of a world by a word' (p. 112). It is only through words (relearned) that we can release nature from the bondage created by human beings, and recover for ourselves the things of this world (p. 64). The writer of *Walden* stands 'on tiptoe' (Thoreau 1992, p. 71), on the border between man and nature. And as Cavell remarks, 'Heaven is under our feet as well as over our heads' (p. 188; Cavell 1992, p. 112). Walden Pond is the point of contact at which heaven and earth meet: Thoreau as a human being locates himself between heaven and animal, representing the position of achieving transcendence from within nature, to become human again.

The relationship of neighboring between human beings and nature represented by Cavell's Thoreau contrasts with the picture one gains from Buell, with its emphasis on unity, continuity, and, as we saw, the conflation of natural and human phenomena. Though Buell acknowledges Cavell's idea of 'nextness', he fails to pick up the ways that this is different from (or say, more complicated than) the coexistence and 'sympathetic intimacy' implied in his own account (Buell 1995, p. 364). It is this critical juncture at which language plays its crucial role in Cavell's reading. If *Walden* is the record of the recreation of the world by the word, it cannot be the case that the human being immerses himself in nature as the 'nonhuman', hence, as *dehumanized*. Such labor is rather, as Cavell says, the 'work of humanization' (Cavell 1992, p. 76).

## Transcendence, the Ordinary, and Language

Cavell says that Thoreau's transcendentalism underwrites *ordinary language* philosophy (and, by implication, that language plays a crucial role in transcendence) (Cavell 1984, p. 32). The unique features of language are elucidated not only by Thoreau's direct reference to the role of language in *Walden*, but also by the trace of language that Thoreau, writing on the border between heaven and earth, between the human and nature, has left us: that is, the book of *Walden* as the record of his experiment in living. Let us note three points about this.

First, language not only serves as a bridge between man and nature, but also constitutes a rift: it demands not only sharing and continuity, but also separation. This is captured by Thoreau's and Cavell's idea of the father tongue – 'a reserved and select expression, too significant to be heard by the ear, which we must be born again in order to speak' (Thoreau 1992, p. 69; Cavell 1992, p. 15). In his theory of communication John Dewey says that language is 'the cherishing mother of all significance' (Dewey 1981, p, 146). Thoreau and Cavell, by contrast, while not negating the role of the 'mother tongue', say that the human being needs connection with the father tongue, in order to 'be born again'. If the mother tongue is characterized by the immediacy typically represented by spoken language, the father tongue is represented by written language as 'the maturity and experience' of the mother tongue (Thoreau 1992, p. 68; Cavell 1992, p. 15). We are as humans fated to this dual relation to language. The experience of rebirth is inevitably associated with death, with the image of ourselves being divided by 'a line of words so matured and experienced', divided as if by a sword (Thoreau 1992, p. 66; Cavell 1992, p. 17). The image of death and the undergoing of rebirth symbolizes the moment of crisis brought by this heightened, more exacting relation to language. From this perspective, Cavell reads *Walden* as a book an attempt to 'free us and our language of one another, to discover the autonomy of each' (Cavell 1992, p. 63).

Second, language in Thoreau's transcendentalism serves not to solidify the object or meaning, but to confront and acknowledge the gap that lies between the occurrence of words and of objects: word and object (via the human being) do not stand in a relationship of correspondence. The gap between soul and body, and of mind and world, is underwritten by the nature of language. The sense of the rift entailed by language betrays our expectation of correspondence. In *The Claim of Reason*, Cavell expresses this mismatch in such expressions as: 'I found that words were not failing me (not, anyway, in the sense that they were abandoning me); they were overwhelming me' (Cavell 1979, p. 61); and 'words have not failed me, but I have gladly left them behind' (p. 63). Thoreau expresses this with the phrasing: 'the volatile truth of our words should continually betray the inadequacy of the residual statement' (Thoreau 1992, p. 217; Cavell 1992, p. 27). Truth refuses to be finally fixed: it is 'instantly *translated*' (ibid.). This might be said to be Thoreau's anti-representationalist view of language. He sees language as characterized by transitivity and volatility.

Third, with the mediation of language, man is engaged in the task of temporal dislocation and relocation. The following passage symbolizes this:

> In any weather, at any hour of the day or night, I have been anxious to improve the nick of time and notch it on my stick too; to stand on the meeting of two eternities, the past and the future, which is precisely the present moment; to toe that line (Thoreau 1992, p. 11; Cavell 1992, p. 9).

The act of 'notching' the nick of time, standing in this moment, requires a certain exactness, as well as the acceptance of precariousness and uncertainty, captured by the image of standing on a tightrope. 'We should live quite laxly and undefined in front, our outlines dim and misty on that side' (Thoreau 1992, p. 216). Language is prophetic here. The temporal nextness, going beyond what is, invites the self to go beyond itself. As Thoreau declares: 'I desire to speak somewhere *without* bounds; like a man in a waking moment, to men in their waking moments' (ibid.). Awakening and rebirth, or say, transcendence, are not simply natural bestowals or accidental events: rather they are the work of humanization through language.

Man is a natural being all the way through, while at the same time fated to live as a trans-natural being. And yet, the 'natural' here does not mean the biological as opposed to the cultural. Human nature is already involved in linguistic activity, and hence there is no such thing as the purity of a child's natural impulse existing before language. *Human nature is already and always cultural and social.* For Thoreau, the process of socialization is accompanied by phenomenological and temporal displacement and relocation, with the moment of crisis and rebirth as the critical juncture and disjuncture between the human being and nature, and within human beings themselves. Thoreau's father's tongue serves to undergo such a disjunctive moment. This implies that language does not serve to solve or absorb a tension between natural instinct and culture, but to sustain the rift.

A parallel difference here is observed between Buell's and Cavell's interpretations of Thoreau. Buell appreciates Cavell's representation of *Walden* as a 'post-Kantian recovery of the thing-in-itself by apprehending nature's "nextness to me"' (Buell 1995, p. 364). From here Buell draws his own interpretation that '[n]ature remains other but connected, meaningful albeit not fully known: not terrain, but place' (p. 268). It follows that human beings undergo a 'process of conversion' in nature (i.e., at Walden), to be enlightened by nature to nonhuman interests, and to reenter 'civilized life' again as human beings but with a different (allegedly broader) perspective on social life. In this scheme, 'conversion' and rebirth are represented as if they were purified and spiritual moments in nature, outside society: the inner (the private) is juxtaposed against the outer (the public). By contrast, Cavell represents Thoreau's placing himself 'one mile from any neighbor' not as a romantic 'literary withdrawal', but as an act of manifesting himself as a 'visible saint' (Cavell 1992, p. 11). Acting as an example to his neighbors, he symbolically stands at the intersection between the natural and the social.

In contrast to Buell, Cavell considers 'being alone' and 'separateness' to be conditions of neighboring (p. 54). Still this is not a matter of choice between being alone or being with others. With the tone of paradox, Cavell says that the drift of *Walden* is that 'we *are* alone, *and* that we are never alone' (p. 80): the realization of our kinships is 'an endless realization of our separateness' (p. 54). This directs us to a dimension of social relationships that exceeds the state of coexistence. Cavell's philosophy of ordinary language is not merely a linguistic analysis: it has social implications. It is demonstrated in the emphasis on the 'we' in the language community and the 'I' as the voice of dissent. Engagement with 'criteria' is the discovery of who your neighbor is: you cannot know a priori who your neighbor is (Cavell 1979, p. 22).

> The philosophical appeal to what we say, and the search for our criteria on the basis of which we say what we say, are claims to community. And the claim to community is always a search for the basis upon which it can or has been established (p. 20).

Participation in the language community has political implications. First, human beings as linguistic beings are already involved in a social contract. 'What I consent to, in consenting to the contract, is not mere obedience, but membership in polis… [C]itizenship… is the same as my autonomy; the polis is the field within which I work out my personal identity and it is the creation of (political) freedom' (p. 23). Second, the political is reconsidered in such a way as to form an extension of one's self-examination and discovery of others. A Cavellian approach bridges the psychological (or psychoanalytic) with the political. 'Political' here means the process of discovering one's neighbor while discovering one's contributing of one's own voice to the community. Third, in Thoreau's experiment in living, at Walden and in the writing of *Walden*, this political relationship already manifests itself within nature. Through ongoing moments of conversion through language, as it were, from the inner to the outer, we learn to be good neighbors, '*to get our living together*' (Thoreau 1992, p. 49; Cavell 1992, p. 79).

In the dynamics of the 'we' and the 'I', of aloneness and togetherness, Thoreau's and Cavell's views on language shed light on what might be called an alternative space for 'privacy' or the inner – one that is distinguished from egocentrism and monologue. There is nothing inward, no 'ghost in the machine', which is the essence of the self, or the original mold of the self. This alternative innerness is crucial for the sake of and in the process of realizing outwardness (or becoming public) from within. It is different from Buell's reading of Thoreau because of its combination of the fading of the persona in nature *and* the retaining of a 'coherent figure' and 'responsible agent' in society (Buell 1995, pp. 477, 549). Cavell's reading of Thoreau's idea of the self does not fall into this dichotomous scheme. The Thoreauvian self dissolves, and yet at the same time, there is an 'intimation of the wholeness of the self. . . out of a present sense of incoherence or division or incompleteness' (Cavell 1992, p. 103). The partiality of the self remains throughout, while the self is dissolved constantly, sustaining the space for the strange and the unknown both within and without the self (i.e., the natural fact confronted by the 'I'). The relationship of neighborhood, then, is built not only outwards towards others, but also within oneself. This, as we have seen, Cavell and Thoreau call the state of the 'double' – 'consciousness of self, and of the self's standing, beyond self-consciousness', or 'being beside oneself' (pp. 102, 104). This dual relation can never be reduced to 'mutual absorption' but continues to a 'perpetual next-ness' (p. 108). Thoreau's and Cavell's idea of individual separation, with its prophetic force, cannot be fully realized in a confluence with nature.

## Conclusion: Political Education for Isolation

[T]hose capable of the deepest personal confession (Augustine, Luther, Rousseau, Thoreau, Kierkegaard, Tolstoy, Freud) were most convinced they were speaking from the most hidden knowledge of others (Cavell 1979, p. 109).

In philosophizing, I have to bring my own language and life into imagination. What I require is a convening of my culture's criteria, in order to confront them with my words and life as I pursue them and as I may imagine them; and at the same time to confront my words and life as I pursue them with the life my culture's words may imagine for me: to confront the culture with itself, along the lines in which it meets in me (p. 125).

The discussion of this chapter started with initial and intuitive questions concerning Buell's environmental politics, a politics based on the ideas of coexistence and of a dichotomization of the human and the nonhuman. Buell speaks of a conflation, but ironically his understanding of this depends upon an initial dichotomization, one that on Thoreau's view is, I have tried to show, unwarranted. Cavell's rereading of Thoreau has shown what is missing from Buell's approach, and it offers an alternative possibility for our engagement with the environment, an alternative way of becoming political.

In considering our way of being with and in the environment, Cavell's philosophy of ordinary language transcends the dichotomy of the natural (impulse of the child or instinct) and the conventional (the norms and normality of adults or culture), and brings into the picture the idea of 'a natural fact' (p. 125) as a 'new (human) nature' (p. 121). The natural here cannot simply be biological (as juxtaposed against the social or conventional). Rather it is already a part of our civilization and culture, and so is broader than what we consider to be conventional in our social lives. The gap between natural instinct and culture is not a dichotomy between abnormality (as unconventional) or dissent (as nonconformist), on the one hand, and normality or conventionality, on the other. Cavell says that the skeptic's doubt that there are other minds is tantamount to denial of, or failure to confront, the natural fact of shared forms of life (p. 109), for these inevitably include elements of dissonance and the abnormal (p. 112). The presence of a 'lunatic child' in Cavell symbolizes the natural fact of the asymmetry between teaching and learning (ibid.). The 'I' is the locus in which the natural and the cultural meet each other in the language community, in which the gap (with the sense of the unknown) must always remain. The unknown, however, is not to be mystified. Rather it is the starting point of our rethinking and rebuilding our conventions from within, and hence reconstructing our political lives.

Cavell claims, that *Walden* is 'a tract of political education', with the provocative thesis that 'education for citizenship is education for isolation' (Cavell 1992, pp. 85–86). 'Self-examination' is at the heart of Cavellian and Thoreauvian political education (Cavell 1979, p. 25). Its implications are diverse. It resists the contemporary communal politics, which is often based upon the natural home as a place to return. It reminds us that we are always at the border of acceding to the closure of politics, in the shadow of inclusion. This is legitimized by the idea that the natural is cultural because it disturbs the romantic purification of nature in spiritual education, or naïve realism (with its concomitant illusion of being in direct commerce with nature). By resisting the taming of voice and aesthetic judgment by the sloganizing of environmental politics, it protects the space of the dissident 'I' as member of the polis. Thoreau's philosophy of language, with its idea of the father tongue, characterized by doubleness, nextness, and transitivity, provides us with the mechanism in which the singularity of an individual is never dissipated in publicity and sharing, and yet at the same time, without falling into the 'interiorisation of the spiritual' (Standish 2011). One's reengagement with the father tongue is a way of sustaining the space of the inner and the sense of rift – what Cavell calls 'the daily, insistent split in the self that being human cannot… escape' (Cavell 2004, p. 5) – the only means through which transcendence (the moment of converting crisis into hope) takes place: it is through this that the public is energized from within.

Thus the political (the most outward) needs the natural (as the cultural), and the natural awaits transcendence (the most inward): to become political from the inmost, we need education. There is no society before individuation: singularity and eccentricity of the self needs to be acknowledged before and throughout the process of socialization. It is this component of separation and isolation that is missing from the discourse of coexistence. The idea of participation in the language community implies that each self is responsible to *her* own voice, to be contributed to *her* society (which is a democratic aspect of American transcendentalism.) Hence, the perspective of dissent in Cavell's philosophy of ordinary language is never a proposal for anarchism; nor is returning language to the ordinary simply as an endorsement of a common society with its averaged, everyday, mundane use of language. Rather it means to rethink our familiar relation to our words, to *re*turn ourselves to the ordinary, while *re*turning the ordinary itself. Such returning is the very meaning of transcendence in the ordinary. Transcendence here does not mean some quasi-religious or mystical experience, or dramatic moment of conversion which takes place in exceptional (say, *extra*ordinary) moments. It does not mean some purified movement upward, but rather, 'transcendence downward' (Standish 2008), to keep finding a solid bottom. It is the continuous activity of undergoing the moment of rebirth from within the ordinary, through language.

The following passage from *The Claim of Reason* captures the sense of transcendence that is at the heart of Cavell's idea of the education of human nature:

> The anxiety in teaching, in serious communication, is that I myself require education. And for grownups this is not natural growth, but *change*. Conversion is a turning of our natural reactions; so it is symbolized as rebirth (Cavell 1979, p. 125).

Philosophy as the education of grownups here points to the very moment when I stand on tiptoe, at the limits of language, when I am thrown back upon my own nature, to reexamine my relation to my culture. At such critical junctures, it is not that normal adults accept the abnormal child. Neither is this a matter of the celebration of the diverse talents of unique individuals. Philosophy as education begins when we lose our way.

When we think about how the experience of transcendence can find its place in the tide of globalization today, we realize that it must be geared neither towards biocentrism nor spiritualism in any dichotomous scheme of nature and civilization. Instead transcendence in the ordinary seeks to return humans to *human* nature (with the mediation of language, that is, through thinking). Linguistic activity itself is the work of humanization. Hence, political education is in a broad sense language education. Philosophy as the education of grownups is a call for education to regain humanity, for us to become human again, to become more humane. This, I believe, is particularly relevant to the idea of human transformation in the Kyoto School of Philosophy.

# References

Buell, L. (1995). *The environmental imagination: Thoreau, nature writing and the formation of American culture*. Cambridge, MA: The Belknap Press of Harvard University Press.

Cavell, S. (1979). *The claim of reason: Wittgenstein, skepticism, morality, and tragedy*. Oxford: Oxford University Press.

Cavell, S. (1984). The politics of interpretation (Politics as opposed to what?). In *Themes out of school: Effects and causes*. Chicago: University of Chicago Press.

Cavell, S. (1992). *The senses of Walden*. Chicago: University of Chicago Press.

Cavell, S. (2004). *Cities of words: Pedagogical letters on a register of the moral life*. Cambridge, MA: The Belknap Press of Harvard University Press.

Dewey, J. (1981). *Experience and nature*. In J. A. Boydston (Ed.), *The later works of John Dewey* (Vol. 1). Carbondale: Southern Illinois University Press.

Emerson, R. W. (1957). Nature. In S. E. Whicher (Ed.), *Selections from Ralph Waldo Emerson: An organic anthology*. Boston: Houghton Mifflin Company.

Marx, L. (1992) *Walden* as transcendental pastoral design. In W. Rossi (Ed.), *Walden and resistance to civil government*. New York: W. W. Norton & Company.

Saito, N. (2005). Chu-shaku [Endnotes to the Japanese translation]. In Stanley Cavell, *Sensu obu Woruden* [The senses of Walden], (N. Saito, Trans.) (pp. 191–212). Tokyo: Hosei University Press.

Standish, P. (2008). Educational thoughts in the Kyoto School of Philosophy: Towards an East-West dialogue – A response. In *Proceedings for the special panel, educational thoughts in the Kyoto School of Philosophy: Towards an East-West dialogue* (at the 11th Biennial Meeting of the International Network of Philosophers of Education) (pp. 64–66). Kyoto: Kyoto University.

Standish, P. (2011). Education's outside. *European Educational Research Journal, 10*(3), 322–330.

Standish, P., & Saito, N. (2005). Stanley Cavell to *Waruden* no sekai: Nihon no dokusha heno izanai [Stanley Cavell's *Walden*: An introduction for the Japanese reader]. In Stanley Cavell, *Sensu obu Woruden* [The senses of Walden] (N. Saito, Trans.) (pp. 213–240). Tokyo: Hosei University Press.

Thoreau, H. D. (1992). *Walden* (1854). In R. William (Ed.), *Walden and resistance to civil government*. New York: W. W. Norton & Company.

# Chapter 13
# Whitehead on the 'Rhythm of Education' and Kitaro Nishida's 'Pure Experience' as a Developing Whole

Steve Odin

## Introductory Remarks

In this essay I will use Alfred North Whitehead's pedagogical theory of mental cultivation through a 'rhythm of education' in three periodic stages, to elucidate the modern Japanese philosopher Kitaro's Nishida idea of 'pure experience' as a threefold developing system of consciousness.

## Whitehead on the Rhythm of Education

Chapter two of A. N. Whitehead's *Aims of Education,* itself termed 'The Rhythm of Education', describes the rhythmic character of the educational process governing mental growth.

> Lack of attention to the rhythm and character of mental growth is a main source of wooden futility in education. I think that Hegel was right when he analysed progress into three stages, which he called Thesis, Antithesis, and Synthesis; though for the purpose of the application of his ideas to educational theory I do not think that the names he gave are very happily suggestive. In relation to intellectual progress I would term them, the stages of romance, the stage of precision, and the stage of generalisation. (Whitehead 1957, p. 17)

As stated above, for Whitehead there is a rhythmic, cyclic and periodic character of mental progress. Also, he agrees with Hegel that the progressive development of consciousness takes place by means of three dialectical moments: (i) thesis,

S. Odin (✉)
Department of Philosophy, University of Hawai'i at Manoa,
2530 Dole Street, Sakamaki Hall D301, Honolulu, HI 96822, USA
e-mail: Steveo@hawaii.edu

P. Standish and N. Saito (eds.), *Education and the Kyoto School of Philosophy*,
Contemporary Philosophies and Theories in Education 1,
DOI 10.1007/978-94-007-4047-1_13, © Springer Science+Business Media Dordrecht 2012

(ii) antithesis, and (iii) synthesis. Furthermore, Whitehead names these three dialectical moments in the rhythm of progressive education: (i) romance, (ii) precision, and (iii) generalisation.

In Chapter three entitled 'The Rhythmic Claims of Freedom and Discipline', Whitehead goes on to further explicate this developmental process of rhythmic education by three phases in terms of a threefold Hegelian dialectic of freedom, discipline and freedom:

> I am convinced that much disappointing failure in the past has been due to neglect of attention to the importance of this rhythm. My main position is that the dominant note of education at its beginning and at its end is freedom, that there is an intermediate stage of discipline with freedom in subordination. I call the first period of freedom the 'stage of Romance', the intermediate period of discipline I call the 'stage of Precision', and the final period of freedom is the 'stage of Generalisation'. (p. 31)

Whitehead clarifies how this threefold developmental rhythm in the educational process corresponds to the ages of students within a school system:

> In a general way the whole period of education is dominated by this threefold rhythm. Till the age of thirteen there is the romantic stage, from fourteen to eighteen the stage of precision, and from eighteen to two and twenty the stage of generalization. (pp. 37–38)

Moreover, for Whitehead this threefold educational process of romance, precision and generalization, or freedom, discipline and freedom, is itself unified, directed and normatively governed throughout its various stages by a single pervasive quality:

> I mean through a distinction of emphasis, of pervasive quality—romance, precision, generalisation, are all present throughout. But there is an alternation of dominance, and it is this alternation which constitutes the cycles. (p. 28)

Whitehead then asserts: 'Education should consist in a continual repetition of such cycles' (p. 19).

(i) *Romance.* The stage of romance involves 'chance flashes of insight' (p. 36) into 'immediate experience' (p. 37), characterized by 'vividness of novelty' (p. 17), 'unexplored connexions with possibilities' (p. 17), 'Romantic emotion' (p. 18), 'vivid freshness' (p. 22), 'imagination' (p. 21), 'freedom' (p. 31), 'the creative impulse to create something' (p. 119), 'aesthetic appreciation' (p. 50), and so forth. This romantic stage initiates the cyclic educational process through the wonder, curiosity, and excitement of learning. Whitehead describes the romantic stage as an 'initial awakening' (p. 36). Again, 'An infant's first romance is in awakening to the apprehension of objects and to the appreciation of their connexions' (p. 19). Thus, he characterizes the three moments in the rhythm of education as follows: 'We are analysing the general law of rhythmic progress ... embodying the initial awakening, the discipline, and the fruition on the higher plane' (p. 39). One can further understand Whitehead's idea of the romantic stage of development from his chapter 'The Romantic Reaction' in *Science and the Modern World* (Whitehead 1967). Here Whitehead critically undermines the abstract mechanistic paradigm of nature held by scientific materialism based on the fallacy of misplaced concreteness, by making reference to romantic nature poets such as Wordsworth, who returns to pre-reflective immediate experience directly grasped by feeling, thereby to provide empirical testimony for a concrete organismic model of living nature as an aesthetic continuum funded with beauty.

For Whitehead the failure of most systems of childhood education is that they neglect the romantic stage of development However, 'The success of the Montessori system is due to its development of the dominance of romance at this period of growth' (Whitehead 1957, p. 22). Although Whitehead praises the Montessori system of childhood education for its emphasis on the first period of romance, at the same time it is criticized in that 'it lacks the restraint which is necessary for the great stages of precision' (p. 22).

(ii) *Precision*. The second dialectical moment in the rhythmic growth of consciousness through progressive education is termed the stage of precision, which cultivates precise detailed knowledge of science, logic, mathematics, language, and the literary classics through rigorous discipline: 'This is the stage of precision. This is the sole stage of learning in the traditional scheme of education, either at school or university' (p. 34). Although Whitehead underscores the importance of this second moment in the rhythm of education, at the same time he points out that the stage of precision is the *only* stage of learning in most conventional schools: 'In our conception of education, we tend to confine it to the second stage of the cycle; namely, to the stage of precision' (p. 18). Furthermore, he criticizes the mistake of rushing the child into the stage of precision before completion of the stage of romance:

> My point is that a block in the assimilation of ideas inevitably arises when a discipline of precision is imposed before a stage of romance has run its course in the growing mind. There is no comprehension apart from romance. It is my strong belief that the cause of so much failure [of education] in the past has been due to the lack of careful study of the due place of romance. Without the adventure of romance at the best you get inert knowledge ... (p. 33).

Yet even during the stage of precision, 'a skillful teacher will keep romance alive in his pupils', for instance, by discussing 'the beauty of a mathematical argument', or 'the beauty of a passage from Virgil' (p. 35). Since the rhythmic developmental process of education is unified throughout by a pervasive quality, he adds: 'During the stage of precision, romance is in the background' (p. 34).

(iii) *Generalisation*. The third dialectical moment of progressive education is termed generalisation: 'The final stage of generalisation is Hegel's synthesis. It is a return to romanticism with added advantage of classified ideas and relevant technique' (p. 19). For Whitehead, this third moment in the rhythm of education termed the stage of generalisation should dominate the student's University period:

> The whole period of growth from infancy to manhood forms one grand cycle. Its stage of romance stretches across the first dozen years of life, its stage of precision comprises the whole school period of secondary education, and its stage of generalisation is the period of entrance into manhood. For those whose formal education is prolonged beyond the school age, the University course or its equivalent is the great period of generalisation. The spirit of generalisation should dominate a University. (p. 25)

One can see this third moment in the rhythm of education termed the stage of generalisation, in terms of Whitehead's own view of speculative philosophy. As Whitehead argues in *Process and Reality,* speculative philosophy, or metaphysics, is a systematic effort to formulate the most generic categories of events through imaginative generalisation, thereby to articulate the ultimate notions of the highest generality at the base of actuality. The stage of generalisation is thus of a generic philosophical description of nature based on a cyclical return to the pre-reflective immediate experience of romantic feeling, now enriched by the intermediate stage of precision through the discipline of mental reflection.

## Nishida on Pure Experience as a Developing Whole

Kitaro Nishida (1870–1945) is founder of the Kyoto School of modern Japanese philosophy. Like Whitehead, Nishida was deeply influenced by the phenomenological concept of pure, direct, or immediate experience as qualitative flow articulated in William James' method of radical empiricism. Nishida's first book titled *An Inquiry into the Good* (*Zen no kenkyu* 1911) (Nishida 1965, 1984), sets forth a Zen-tinged notion of 'pure experience' (J. *junsui keiken*), as 'immediate experience' or 'direct experience' (J. *chokusetsu keiken*), emerging prior to subject-object bifurcation and anterior to cognition. In Nishida's words:

> To experience means to know facts just as they are … What we usually refer to as experience is adulterated with some sort of thought, so by *pure* I am referring to the state of experience just as it is without the least addition of deliberative discrimination. … In this regard, pure experience is identical with direct experience. When one directly experiences one's own state of consciousness, there is not yet a subject or an object, and knowing and its objects are completely unified. This is the most refined type of experience. (Nishida 1990, p. 3; 1965, p. 9)

Here it should be noted that for Nishida, in pure or direct experience 'there is not yet a subject or an object' (J. *mada shu mo kyaku mo nai*: Nishida 1965, p. 9). This initial stage of pure experience in its concrete immediacy thus emerges *prior* to the subject-object distinction.

Nishida's initial concept of pure experience further describes it as empty of thought and void of cognitive meaning. However, making reference to William James' idea of pure or immediate experience as an ever-flowing 'stream of thought', Nishida goes on to point out that 'the activity of thinking constitutes a kind of pure experience' (Nishida 1990, p. 13). Then, citing the views of Hegel, Nishida continues: 'If in line with Hegel's emphasis on the power of thinking we assume the essence of thinking is not abstract but concrete, then thinking is nearly identical to pure experience … pure experience is none other than thinking' (p. 17). He concludes: 'In summary, thinking and experience are identical' (p. 19).

Students of Nishida usually find a problematic contradiction, ambiguity, or confusion to arise between his initial formulation of pure experience as devoid of thinking, and his subsequent formulations of pure experience as not only containing thought, but even being identical to thinking. However, this apparent contradiction is resolved by Nishida's idea of pure experience as a Hegelian dialectical process of developing consciousness that unfolds in three moments. As emphasized by the Kyoto School philosopher Takeuchi Yoshinori: 'But James was not the only philosopher who influenced Nishida in his initial stage. The impact of Hegel's philosophy was likewise conspicuous' (Takeuchi 1982, p. 182). Here Takeuchi cites the words of Professor Noda Matao:

> Thus, pure experience comes to cover actually the whole range of knowledge, physical, mathematical and metaphysical. ... Here Nishida's thought is akin to the dialectic of Hegel. Nishida's pure experience proves to be a spontaneously developing totality which includes even reflective thinking as its negative phase and in the end pure experience is identified with ultimate reality. (Noda 1955, 347; cited by Takeuchi 1982, 182)

Takeuchi hence concludes that for Nishida, pure experience is 'a self-developing whole, similar to Hegel's Notion (*Begriff*)' (Takeuchi 1982, 183).

In his book *An Inquiry into the Good*, Nishida himself clearly describes pure experience as a developing process of consciousness that unfolds in three stages:

> [T]he whole first appears implicitly, and from it the content develops through differentiation; when that development ends, the whole of reality is actualized and completed—one entity has developed and completed itself. We can most clearly see this mode of development in our own consciousness. (Nishida 1990, 52)

Here it should be emphasized that for Nishida, as for both Hegel and Whitehead, this threefold developmental process by which consciousness unfolds is directed not just toward realization of wholeness, but also freedom: 'As our knowledge advances, we become freer people' (p. 99).

In his treatise *Experience and Language in Nishida,* the Kyoto School philosopher Ueda Shizuteru, develops the threefold stages of development in Nishida's dynamic notion of pure experience.

> It seems to me that the characteristic of *An Inquiry into the Good* as a philosophy lies precisely in the fact that at the base of Nishida's discussion is the movement between three qualitatively different levels A, B, and C and that all of these levels are undiscriminatingly folded within level C. (Ueda 1991, 115)

Ueda holds that the levels of A, B, and C characterizing the three moments of pure experience, are ever-deepening stages of Nishida own Zen-influenced notion of 'self-awakening' (J. *jikaku*). For Ueda, level A is the pre-linguistic stage as an initial awakening to the primordial fact of pure experience, level B is the linguistic stage as self-awakening to mental distinctions within pure experience, and level C is the trans-linguistic stage of self-awakening to pure experience, which now includes within its unity the previous levels, thereby representing the standpoint of a generalised philosophy which interprets everything from the standpoint of pure experience (p. 115).

Kosaka Kunitsugu has most explicitly and systematically articulated Nishida's pure experience as a Hegelian process of developing wholeness progressing by three dialectical moments. He describes the three moments of pure experience as follows: (i) the primal direct contact with phenomena in original implicit unity; (ii) the development of mental distinctions of various phenomena, and (iii) the ideal unification of consciousness as a whole enriched by the moment of cognitive differentiations (Kosaka 1987, 45–46, 1991, 26). Kosaka's clarification of Nishida's pure experience as a developing system of consciousness that unfolds in three stages functions to solve the apparent contradictions in Nishida's account. (i) The first stage as the primal fact of pure experience is before subject-object differentiation and anterior to mental distinctions; (ii) the second stage is separation of subject-object differentiation and development of mental distinctions; (iii) while the third stage is transcendence of subject-object differentiation and inclusive of mental distinctions within an ideal whole apprehended by 'intellectual intuition'. Kosaka thus clarifies that Nishida's idea of pure experience operates as a threefold developing process of consciousness that moves from the pre-conceptual stage of the first moment, to the conceptual stage of the second moment, to the trans-conceptual stage of the third moment, whereupon the unifying act of intellectual intuition grasps the enveloping wholeness underlying all cognitive judgments in the background of experiential immediacy.

The eminent Kyoto School philosopher Keiji Nishitani (1900–1990) sums up Nishida's idea of pure experience as a threefold process revealed through the very structure of Nishida's *An Inquiry into the Good*:

> The form of pure experience is developed from an explanation of its seminal form in the first chapter through an elucidation of its systematic development in terms of 'thinking' and 'willing' in the next two chapters. Finally, in a chapter entitled 'Intellectual Intuition', it is given its consummate expression as the basic form that it is. In short, the structure of book reveals a threefold approach to pure experience. (Nishitani 1991, p. 94)

Nishitani thus clarifies how for Nishida, pure experience is a threefold process of development, and that while all three stages are forms of pure experience, the unity of them all at the third stage is grasped only by a unifying act of intellectual intuition.

For Nishida, the third moment of pure experience as an ideal whole grasped by intellectual intuition, is itself a return to the first moment of pre-reflective pure experience, now enriched by the second intermediary moment of mental reflection. In consonance with the Zen doctrine of 'ordinary mind' (J. *heijoshin*), Nishida holds that while the content of an intellectual intuition of the wholeness of pure experience is richer and deeper than normal experience, in its form as a unifying activity, it is at base identical to the natural functioning of ordinary perception in everyday life (Nishida 1990, pp. 30–32). According to Nishida, the third moment of pure experience directly grasped by intellectual intuition, is illustrated especially by 'the aesthetic spirit' (p. 32). As an example he cites Mozart's ability to picture a whole symphony while composing each and every note in long musical compositions (p. 31), further citing examples from painting, sculpture and other arts. Finally he sees the intellectual intuition of pure experience as a developing whole that culminates in religious awakening: 'True religious awakening is neither an abstract knowledge based in thinking nor a blind feeling. ... It is a kind of intellectual intuition, a deep grasp of life' (p. 14). It is this notion of 'intellectual intuition' (J. *chiteki chokkan*; G. *intellektuelle Anschauung*) operating at the third stage of trans-rational or post-reflective awareness, which itself provides the key to Nishida's Zen-tinged notion of pure experience (pp. 30–34). Although James himself sees pure experience as being a limit-point approached in the buzzing confusion of infancy, or in a semi-comatose state induced by sleep, drugs or blows to the head, he otherwise seems unsure as to whether a fully conscious pure experience is possible. By contrast, Nishida holds that this third moment of self-awakening to immediate or pure experience as the unity of subject and object is directly grasped through a shift of attention by a unifying act of intellectual intuition.

## Aims of Education in Whitehead and Nishida

### Wisdom as Useful Knowledge

To begin with, it should be pointed out that similar to Confucian, neo-Confucian and Zen doctrines of learning as 'self-cultivation', Whitehead views rhythmic education as a dynamic process of 'mental cultivation' (Whitehead 1957, pp. 26–27). For Whitehead, a problem with conventional education is 'the aimless accumulation of precise knowledge, inert and unutilised' (p. 37). As a remedy to the standard idea of education as an accumulation of inert knowledge, he holds that rhythmic education as mental cultivation is to be governed by an aim toward 'active wisdom' (p. 37). Whitehead here sets forth a pragmatic doctrine of education whereby ideas are to be used and tested by experimentation in the ordinary experience of everyday life. He asserts: 'The importance of knowledge lies in its use, in our active mastery of it, that is to say, it lies in wisdom' (p. 32). Again, he states that 'education should be useful' (p. 2). Moreover, 'Education is the acquisition of the art of the utilisation of knowledge' (p. 4). Whitehead thus stands in accord with the experimentalist philosophy of education articulated by John Dewey and others in American pragmatism, whereby ideas should be useful in daily life as tools or instruments enabling an organism to adapt to the environment in a problematic situation, so that there is *a continuity of knowledge and action,* whereupon each moment is both instrumental and consummatory in an ends-means continuum funded by pervasive value quality.

Likewise, Nishida cites the neo-Confucian philosopher Wang Yang-ming's pragmatically oriented educational doctrine based on the cultivation of wisdom as *the unity of knowledge and action,* stating: 'As in Wang Yang-ming's emphasis on the identity of knowledge and action, true knowledge is always accompanied by the performance of the will' (Nishida 1990, pp. 90–91). Wang Yang-ming (1472–1528) sets forth a pragmatic neo-Confucian educational doctrine of mental cultivation whereby knowledge is the beginning of action, and action is the completion of knowledge. Hence, like the pedagogical ideas of Whitehead and American pragmatism, Nishida underscores the pragmatic view that knowledge should be *useful* in everyday life, so that knowledge is continuous with action through practical active wisdom.

## *Wisdom as Realization of Values*

According to Whitehead, the aim of education toward practical active wisdom is mental cultivation of what he calls 'the sense of values' (Whitehead 1957, p. 39). He states: 'Education is a discipline for the adventure of life … It is the function of the teacher to evoke into life wisdom and beauty' (p. 98). Just as his metaphysics, cosmology and vision of nature aims to overcome the nihilistic worldview of scientific materialism based on the fallacy of vacuous actuality, or the erroneous belief in material substance devoid of beauty, meaning and value, Whitehead's philosophy of education is likewise directed toward practical realization of values through mental cultivation. He states,

> Education is the guidance of the individual towards a comprehension of the art of life … Science, art, religion, morality, take their rise from this sense of values within the structure of being. Each individual embodies an adventure of existence. The art of life is the guidance of this adventure. (p. 39)

Here Whitehead expresses one of his signature notions, that education is an experimental adventure of ideas. Moreover, he underscores the function of aesthetic education (p. 40–1). Whitehead now explicates how education aims toward practical realization of wisdom as an 'artistic sense' (p. 39), including the 'sense of value', the 'sense of importance', the 'aesthetic sense', and the 'sense of beauty' (p. 40). He adds: 'This thought leads me to ask whether in our modern education we emphasise sufficiently the functions of art. … You cannot, without loss, ignore in the life of the spirit so great a factor as art. Our aesthetic emotions provide us with vivid apprehensions of value' (p. 40). Hence for Whitehead, a primary aim of education is cultivation of practical active wisdom through enhancement of ordinary, everyday life by heightened pervasive value quality, including scientific-technological, as well as religious, moral, and artistic values.

In his speculative metaphysics and scientific cosmology, Whitehead analyzes the mechanistic paradigm of nature described by the Newtonian-Cartesian paradigm of scientific materialism as being rooted in the 'fallacy of misplaced concreteness', whereby frozen abstractions are mistaken for the concrete aesthetic events of qualitative immediate experience from which they were derived, thereby to arrive at an abstract picture of nature as composed of material substances without purpose, value or beauty. As a corrective to this abstract mechanistic view of nature, Whitehead proposes a return to the concrete aesthetic field of immediate experience as given empirical testimony by the romantic nature poets. Similarly, in his pedagogical theory, Whitehead argues that our standard educational system has become restricted to the study of reified abstractions: 'At present our education combines a thorough study of a few abstractions, with a slighter study of a larger number of abstractions' (Whitehead 1967, p. 198). As a remedy Whitehead calls for a return to the romantic stage of concrete aesthetically immediate experience. He thus advises that the school curriculum should include a study of 'art and aesthetic education' (p. 199). The rhythm of education should cultivate 'habits of aesthetic appreciation' (ibid.). Again, aesthetic education must aim to 'strengthen habits of concrete appreciation of the individual facts in their full interplay of emergent values' (p. 198). Elsewhere, he writes that education should cultivate habits of appreciating values, including scientific as well as aesthetic, moral and religious values: 'The ultimate motive power, alike in science, in morality, and in religion, is the sense of value, the sense of importance. ... The most penetrating exhibition of this force is the sense of beauty, the aesthetic sense of realised perfection' (Whitehead 1957, p. 40). Further underscoring the importance of cultivating religious and moral value through aesthetic education, he asserts: 'The essence of education is that it be religious. A religious education is an education which inculcates duty and reverence' (p. 14).

Likewise, Nishida's idea of pure experience as a spontaneously developing whole aims toward practical realization of values. In his essay on Nishida's concept of pure experience, Dilworth misinterprets Nishida when he claims that the aim of Nishida's pure experience is 'to find such [pure] experience "empty", prior to the superimpositions of intellectual meanings' (Dilworth 1969, p. 96). Moreover, Dilworth asserts: 'Nishida's position may again suggest a kind of Zen phenomenalism which finds experience richest in its own subjective immediacy, after it has been "emptied" of the noise of meanings ...' (p. 98). Dilworth views Nishida as giving a Zen-colored notion of pure experience 'emptied' of meaning, or devoid of all mental content, similar to Zen nothingness, emptiness, or voidness. However, if Dilworth's nihilistic interpretation is valid, then it cannot account for Nishida's own view that pure experience is the source of cognitive meanings, as well as aesthetic, ethical and religious values. For Nishida pure experience is the 'unification of truth, goodness and beauty' (J. *shinzenbi no goitsu*). Nishida thus characterizes pure experience as 'the union of subject and object, which is the ultimate meaning of religion, morality, and art' (Nishida 1990, p. 145). Nishida goes on to analyze realization of nondual pure experience, now described as the ultimate meaning of religion, morality and art, in terms of the achievement of Zen enlightenment or religious self-awakening through *kensho* as direct insight into Buddha-nature (ibid.).

It seems Dilworth, like various other scholars of Nishida, have committed what transpersonal psychologist Ken Wilber has termed the *pre/trans fallacy* (Wilber 1983, pp. 201–202). The 'pre/trans fallacy' is the conflation between precognitive and trans-cognitive phases in the spectrum of consciousness, so that either the trans-cognitive stage is reduced to the romantic pre-reflective stage, or the romantic pre-cognitive stage is elevated to the trans-cognitive stage (ibid.). To further clarify this pre/trans fallacy, I would like to cite Robert Wargo's discussion of Shimomura Torataro's similar critique of Nishida's concept of pure experience, as failing to adequately clarify the distinction between the *before* and *after* stages of subject-object differentiation.

> Shimomura Torataro raises a more serious question when he states that *An Inquiry into the Good* does not distinguish clearly enough between 'not yet differentiated' and 'no longer differentiated'. ... Nishida has not, Shimomura insists, clarified the relation between one who has attained this level of intellectual intuition and one who has yet to make the subject-object distinction. (Wargo 2005, 53–54)

| | Hegel's dialectic of consciousness | Whitehead's rhythm of education | Nishida's developing whole of pure experience |
|---|---|---|---|
| 1 | Thesis | Romance | *Pre*-reflective pure experience |
| 2 | Antithesis | Precision | Reflective pure experience |
| 3 | Synthesis | Generalisation | *Trans*-reflective pure experience |

Shimomura holds that Nishida has not clearly distinguished between the 'not yet differentiated' level of pure experience such as a child at play, and the 'no longer differentiated' level such as a musician grasping the unity of pure experience through intellectual intuition (Wargo 2005, 54). However, as I have pointed out earlier, in his initial formulation Nishida asserts that in pure experience 'there is not yet a subject or an object' (J. *mada shu mo kyaku mo nai:* Nishida 1965, p. 9). Next, he explains pure experience as an organic system of consciousness that 'differentiates and develops' (J. *bunka hatten*). Nishida then discusses pure experience in the completion phase as the 'unity of subject and object' (J. *shukyaku no goitsu*). But this unity of subject and object entails that there was a moment of pure experience before the differentiation of subject and object, a subsequent phase positing the differentiation of subject and object, followed by a stage where subject and object are restored to unity now enriched by difference. It is the unifying act of intellectual intuition which directly grasps this unity of subject and object at the third stage of pure experience. At the same time, I would agree with Shimomura that Nishida has not distinguished clearly enough between 'not yet' and 'no longer' stages of subject-object differentiation within the developing whole of pure experience, thereby resulting in the pre/trans fallacy. By committing the pre/trans fallacy, one erroneously reduces the higher *trans*-reflective stage of pure experience that is full of meaning and value as apprehended by an artist, poet or musician, to the sheer immediacy of the *pre*-reflective, regressive and romantic stage of infancy that is empty of cognitive meaning and devoid of mental content. Hence, when one does not commit the pre/trans fallacy, it becomes clear that for Nishida this third moment at the trans-reflective stage of pure experience grasped by intellectual intuition, is itself the unifying source of all meaning and value.

## Conclusion

The present essay has been an exploration of Whitehead's idea that learning as mental cultivation advances through a rhythmic cycle of education that develops in three phases unified by pervasive quality, termed romance-precision-generalization, or freedom-discipline-freedom. For Whitehead, this periodic rhythm of education stands in accord with Hegel's threefold dialectical evolution of consciousness by the three moments of thesis, antithesis and synthesis. Furthermore, I have used Whitehead's idea of mental progress cultivated by a threefold rhythm of education, to clarify Nishida's Zen-tinged concept of pure experience as a spontaneously developing system of consciousness that unfolds in three stages: (i) the pre-rational stage of aboriginal pure experience as an implicit unity; (ii) the rational stage of pure experience that emerges by development of mental distinctions; and (iii) the trans-rational stage of pure experience as a unified enveloping whole underlying cognitive judgments grasped by a unifying act of intellectual intuition. Moreover, I have emphasized how for both Whitehead and Nishida, the development of consciousness in three moments itself culminates in practical wisdom as the *use* of knowledge in everyday life, thereby establishing a *continuity of action and knowledge*. Finally, I have criticized Nishida scholars who commit the *pre/trans fallacy*, whereby the higher *trans*-reflective or *post*-cognitive stage of pure experience that is full of meaning and value, is mistakenly reduced to the romantic *pre*-reflective stage of pure experience that is empty of meaning and devoid of value. In this context, it has been underscored how for both Whitehead and Nishida, mental cultivation is aimed toward practical wisdom as an awakening to the vivid qualitative flow of pure or immediate experience, itself functioning as the unifying source of all value-realization in ordinary experience of everyday life, including all cognitive as well as aesthetic, moral and religious values.

## Glossary

| | |
|---|---|
| Bunka hatten | 分化発展 |
| Chiteki chokkan | 知的直感 |
| Chokusetsu keiken | 直接経験 |
| Heijoshin | 平常心 |
| Jikaku | 自覚 |
| Junsui keiken | 純粋経験 |
| Kensho | 見性 |
| Mada shu mo kyaku mo nai | まだ主も客もない |
| Nishida, Kitaro | 西田幾多郎 |
| Shinzenbi no goitsu | 真善美の合一 |
| Shukyaku no goitsu | 主客の合一 |
| Zen no kenkyū | 善の研究 |

## References

Dilworth, D. A. (1969). The initial formations of 'pure experience' in Nishida Kitaro and William James. *Monumenta Nipponica*, 24(1–2), 93–111.

Kosaka, K. (1987). Shoki Nishida Tetsugaku ni Okeru Junsui Keiken no Gainen to Shoso [Concept and varieties of 'pure experience' in Nishida's early philosophy]. *Nihon Daigagku Keizaigaku Kenkyukai Kenkyu*, 6, 45–98.

Kosaka, K. (1991). *Nishida Tetsugaku no Kenkyū* [A study of Nishida's philosophy]. Kyoto: Mineruva Shobo.

Nishida, K. (1965). *Nishida Kitaro Zenshu* [The collected works of Kitaro Nishida] (2nd ed., Vol. 1). Tokyo: Iwanami Shoten.

Nisida, K. (1984). *Zen no Kenkyu* [An Inquiry into the good]. Tokyo: Iwanami Shoten.

Nishida, K. (1990). *An inquiry into the good* (A. Masao & C. Ives, Trans.). New Haven: Yale University Press.

Nishitani, K. (1991). *Nishida Kitaro* (Y. Seisaku & J. Heisig, Trans.). Berkeley: University of California Press.

Noda, M. (1955). East-West synthesis in Kitaro Nishida. *Philosophy East and West*, 4(4), 345–359.

Takeuchi, Y. (1982). The philosophy of Nishida. In F. Franck (Ed.), *The Buddha eye: An anthology of the Kyoto School* (pp. 179–202). New York: Crossroads.

Ueda, S. (1991, May). *Experience and language in Nishida* (N. Tokiyuki, Trans.). Annual report from The Institute for Zen Studies, No. XVII.

Wargo, R. J. J. (2005). *The logic of nothingness: A study of Nishida Kitaro*. Honolulu: University of Hawaii Press.

Whitehead, A. N. (1957). *Aims of education*. New York: Free Press.

Whitehead, A. N. (1967). *Science and the modern world*. New York: Free Press.

Whitehead, A. N. (1978) Speculative philosophy. In D. R. Griffin & D. W. Sherburne (Eds.), *Process and reality* (Corrected ed.) (pp. 3–17). New York: Free Press.

Wilber, K. (1983). *Eye to eye: The quest for the new paradigm*. New York: Anchor/Doubleday.

# Chapter 14
# A Different Road: The Life and Writings of Soseki Natsume as a Struggle for Modern Accommodation

Lynda Stone

## Introduction

Created by Un'ichi Hiratsuka, the woodblock reprinted in this chapter is symbolic of the process of modern accommodation in Meiji Japan. Change, Western incursion and influence took place that led not only to the appearance of the Kyoto School of Philosophy as both modern and Japanese but ultimately to the Japan of today. Rather than philosophy and the Kyoto School, the principal focus of this chapter is Japan's great novelist, Soseki Natsume, his life and writings and what they reveal about the themes of initial accommodation.

The purpose of the chapter is to complement others in this volume on the Kyoto School. A penultimate section undertakes a brief comparison of Soseki with Kitaro Nishida, the school's founder. To begin, for the Japanese and scholars of Japanese culture, Soseki is universally known. He is not well recognized by typical readers of English or those in philosophy of education. He is most significant, however, not only in order to understand Japanese life and culture of his time, but also because his life is one representation of worldwide change that subsequently results from the particular 'meeting of East and West' of which he was a part. That his novels written about 100 years ago have retained their popularity and that his face appears on Japanese currency today are two manifestations of his enduring acclaim. Here are the chapter sections: Initial Situating, Soseki, Meiji Japan, Three Stories of Teachers, with several subsections, Modern Accommodation, Comparing Nishida, and Conclusion. Education figures throughout the chapter: First is attention to Soseki's own education and his later teaching; second is evidence of his views on bad and good teaching, implicit and explicit; third is his novelistic teacher figures,

L. Stone (✉)
School of Education, University of North Carolina at Chapel Hill,
CB#3500, Peabody Hall, Chapel Hill, NC 27599-3500, USA
e-mail: lstone@email.unc.edu

P. Standish and N. Saito (eds.), *Education and the Kyoto School of Philosophy*,
Contemporary Philosophies and Theories in Education 1,
DOI 10.1007/978-94-007-4047-1_14, © Springer Science+Business Media Dordrecht 2012

their personal and institutional travails and what these say about education; and fourth, finally, is comment for philosophy of education today.

## Initial Situating

Published contemporary to the writings of Soseki and Nishida, the print below, *Lake Kizaki,* shows a road through a village at lakeside.[1] What is especially significant is the suggestion that it combines Eastern and Western artistic perspectives, in the use of unfilled space and the direction of the road. In its whole, a particular artistic accommodation has been accomplished by Hiratsuka. This interpretation need not have been that of the artist, of course, but it might well have been.

This print is an early example of the movement known as *sosaku hanga* or creative prints. It is one tradition that contrasts in method and style with a second one, *shin hanga*. The main difference is that prints in the first are done entirely by the artist— a new method—and in the second are undertaken in a team that includes the artist, the engraver, the printer, and sometimes the publisher—a return to, perhaps maintenance of, tradition. In their own ways, both processes entail East and West, pre-modern and modern art subjects and techniques.

---

[1] I am grateful to the artist's granddaughter, Penelope Moore, for permission to reprint *Lake Kizaki*. Thanks also to Reiko Matsui of the Floating World Gallery in Chicago for assistance to obtain this right. Information about Hiratsuka and photographs of prints is available from the US website at: http://www.unichihiratsuka.com/home

Hiratsuka's life is similarly symbolic. He was born mid-Meiji in 1895 and died early-Heisei in 1997, his life spanning several historic eras.[2] Over 30 years were spent living in Washington, DC, where he had first traveled to visit a daughter. Many of his later prints are of US sites. In her introduction to *Hiratsuka: Modern Master*, a catalogue for a 2001 exhibition at the Art Institute of Chicago, art historian Helen Merritt names him as the 'best-trained block carver' of *sosaku hanga* (Merritt 2001, p. 13) and as its 'practical teacher, mentor, and grass-roots leader' (Ibid., p. 14). Not only did he influence many artists through his teaching but also across his career he developed a unique 'modern' style. Merritt summarizes thus,

> While Hiratsuka focused on strong and jagged strokes and the richness of black ink, it was sensitivity to traditional Japanese pattern and design that provided the essential structure and cohesion in his prints. He returned occasionally to fine lines or color, but his basic vocabulary was built around rugged strokes and the contrast between black and white. (p. 16)[3]

Today Japanese prints are known worldwide and surely have influenced Western art. Best known are *shin hanga*, the 'tradition' described above. Beyond this chapter, research is needed to explain this dominance: what opportunities for production and commerce existed, what was seen as exotic or desirable. Suffice, while much is usually made of the impact of Western art on that Japanese, the other influence must surely be acknowledged. Two Western artists who exhibit this influence are the American Mary Cassat and the Australian Ethel Spowers. In art and in all matters of cultural life, two way accommodation of East and West has occurred. Any visitor to contemporary Tokyo or Los Angeles seems to see a modern marriage but then marriages always entail tensions too.

While not the aim of this chapter, detailed study of the lives of Hiratsuka, Soseki, and Nishida would reveal individual variation on a number of topics. First each has a personal biography, a set of circumstances that helps determine who each is and becomes: artist, novelist, philosopher. Second the work of each occurs in a specific historic and cultural context that helps define directions, emphases, and accomplishments. Third the reception of their work is also so situated. Finally because the specific era that they share begins in Meiji, each has to traverse the logics of East and West and does so uniquely. In what follows, the frame from Hiratsuka remains as background to the fore-grounded study of Soseki. Near the conclusion, his 'story' receives brief comparison to that of Nishida in order to help locate the chapter within the present volume.

One last introductory comment is personal. Since the late 1960s, I have visited Japan six times and have a modest art and artifact collection begun by my late mother, a flower arranger by avocation from California, USA. I grew up around

---

[2]Continuing a tradition from the sixth century, emperors of Japan established auspicious names for their periods of reign. After Meiji is Taisho (1912–1926), Showa (1926–1989), and Heisei (1989 to present). Emperor Akihito has given the phrase 'peace everywhere' to the present reign. Information retrieved February 2010 from http://www.albany.edu/eas/205/205%20historical%20eras.pdf and http://en.wikipedia.org/wiki/Heisei_period

[3]See the Van Zelst Family Collection and the Art Institute of Chicago (2001) and Doizaki Gallery (1985).

'things Japanese' as well as Asian-roots people. While at one time I gave workshops for teachers on Japan, this is my first academic writing on Japan and on Japanese literature. As someone who can only be Western, I offer apology for its possible immaturity or misunderstanding and am especially apologetic about my first look at and treatment of Nishida.

## Soseki

Beloved as he and his novels are by the Japanese and as Eastern literature has become 'open' to the West in the English language, a substantial cross cultural field of Soseki Studies exists today.[4] Therein biographers and commentators have made much of his personal life and its relationship to novelistic themes. This is even as he denied strong autobiographical presence except in one novel—one of three presented below. In this section, a brief life sketch is followed by attention to his education and academic career. In his writings overall it seems clear that the author was uneasy, and therefore resistant to, a Westernization of Japan and all that this threatened to what became a specific Eastern culture's evident move to modernization.

Natsume Kinnosuke was born in 1867, the year before Admiral William Perry's black ships succeeded in breeching a relatively, although not entirely, isolated Japan. His life crossed the Meiji period; Taisho was 2 years old—and he was 50 when in 1916 he died of an illness that plagued his adulthood. Historian Marius Jansen has named Soseki a 'non-conformist', capturing his life story in this term (Jansen 2000, p. 480).[5] It appears that he was an unwanted child, passed back and forth through three families in early age. While adoption of a youngest son was not unusual, he was ignored at some times, petted at others, had almost no relationship with his natural father but later a warm one with his mother who died when he was 14. Yet he emerged as a student able to acquire a highly regarded education. Following higher education and study in England, he taught school and university. Then came the momentous decision to abandon academic life in traditional form and at all levels to become a writer for popular tastes. Various reasons in his personal and professional life have been put forward. Not least is Soseki's own statement of realizing a lifelong stance toward Japan's modernization and then finding a kind of inner peace through his writing. By the way, part of this professional move—and probably partly a result of his childhood—was adoption of Soseki Natsume, his pen name.[6]

---

[4] Angela Yiu overviews Soseki studies (Yiu 1998, beginning p. 6). In addition to sources cited as biographic or historical, see McCellan (1959, 1969); also 'reflections' from Soseki interpreted recently by Marvin Marcus (2009).

[5] Jansen's history of the emergence of modern Japan appears definitive today. Historian at Princeton, the late Jansen studied under Reischauer at Harvard and took military sponsored Japanese language lessons in late WWII directed by Elisséeff. In his book's preface, his is a source for the connection between the latter and Soseki and the indirect connection to Nishida described below.

[6] Gessel writes that 'soseki' means eccentric or obstinate. See Gessel (1993), p. 21.

In writing about Soseki posthumously, Western biographers emphasize personal struggle and the psychology of 14 novels, and say little about inner peace. Instead labels such as unloved and unloving, lonely, mentally unstable, anguished and melancholic, are typically applied to him and most of his novelistic characters. In the 1970s, in an interesting interconnecting of West and East, the latter have even been psychoanalyzed by the famous Japanese psychiatrist, Takeo Doi.[7] One Asian writer disagrees with the more standard view: Beongheon Yu poses that the influence of domestic unhappiness on his writings is a matter of speculation. And he adds that Soseki's spirit was not crippled, that he had 'an abundant zest for life' (Yu 1969, p. 22). Across interpretations, biographic facts include a largely unsatisfactory marriage, a need for money to support his family, adult reminders of childhood difficulties in complex family relations, and perhaps most of all, unfulfillment and disillusion in his career. This is before he became a celebrated novelist but continued, sources indicate, as a perpetual insecurity. While a personal statement late in life, turned to below, suggests self realization and contentment, characters in late novels still belie happiness. As literary biographer Van Gessel puts the dominant theme,

> Much of the struggle that comes through in Soseki's fiction is the battle between the old and the new, the Asian and the Western. These struggles are not waged in the abstract, however. Soseki reduces them to a level of the individual, who is often confused or frightened. (Gessel 1993, p. 13)

Non-conforming that Soseki was, perhaps many other Meiji intellectuals also were not happy due to societal struggles over modernization, results and manifestations of tensions East and West, over which they had little control.

In turning to Soseki's life and writings, and especially to teacher figures, it seems relevant to consider his own education; carving out his own road, he was still a product of an era. By the time he entered middle school, two curricula were available, one main and traditional that included an emphasis in Chinese classics and one progressive that focused on English study. Soseki initially chose the first and from accounts this sparked an early interest in writing. However he was soon persuaded to turn to English in order to contribute to the new society. This led in time to attendance at the college of and then Tokyo Imperial University and there a first occupational interest in architecture. At this time, he began to write *Haiku*, traditional Japanese poetry but more importantly *Kanshi*, poetry in classical Chinese—for which he is still highly regarded. Simultaneously in his studies he also turned to English literature. He was unhappy with his university teaching but as scholar/translator Edward McCellan and others report, he 'attained a surprising mastery of the English language … was able to read English with ease, and could write with a fluency that must have been far beyond the ability of the average student' (McCellan 1969, p. 6). He was the second student to graduate in English literature in the history of the top university in Japan. Following graduation, however, he did not receive the faculty appointment at the university college he desired but was hired at Tokyo Normal College instead.

---

[7] See Doi (1976).

Two years later he quit this post and took one of two subsequent positions as high school and college teacher, leaving the capital city for rural Japan.

One last significance in his education remains; this is his time in London on a fellowship ordered by the government to study English. Several factors are important. He went without letters of introduction to Cambridge or Oxford. He had a small and inadequate stipend to live abroad. Health problems begun at university continued and developed into a 'nervous breakdown'. By all accounts, he was miserable; in *Michikusa*, his autobiographical novel, the strain of two years strongly appears. However elsewhere, McCellan identifies the one positive outcome, that 'in the future he would find his *raison d'ĕtre*, not as a student of another country's literature, but as a pioneer within his own culture, whose opinions and standards, whether original or not, were at least the result of honest and independent inquiry' (Ibid., p. 12). Upon return home and in a period Yu names as 'the frustrated years' (Yu 1969, beg. p. 29), Soseki assumed a top academic post at Tokyo University, began to write on English literature, attempted to earn extra money to support his family through teaching and other endeavors, all of this contributing to great personal and interpersonal struggle.[8] His university appointment, by the way, was the first for a Japanese, as replacement for the eloquent and popular Greek born, American, Lafacadio Hearn.[9]

## Meiji Japan

Soseki's personal story reveals that, for some Japanese at least, accommodation to modernization was a struggle. In this section, the Meiji era is introduced and commentary on change and struggle for accommodation is presented, largely as a clash of values of East and West, old and new, to which there were various responses. A significant lecture/essay from Soseki in turned to at the close that begins to 'define' his viewpoint.

The Meiji era, or Restoration as it is known, is named for the time period 1868–1912, when the government of Japan reverted to the emperor after more than two and a half centuries of Shogunate rule.[10] The traditional Western story is that this ended centuries of feudal isolation in Japan opening it up to 'much needed and desirable' Western ways of living and modernity. As mentioned above, precipitating this change was the arrival of American Commodore Matthew Perry's armada

---

[8]The theory of literature developed from work in London and which might be called a philosophy is collected in Soseki (2009b).

[9]Hearn was a journalist, writer and later professor of English studies who spent the happiest years of his life in Japan. His writings were among the first to 'open' the country to the West. One important book is *Japan: An Attempt at Interpretation*, 1904, 1955. See http://en.wikipedia.org/wiki/Lafcadio_Hearn, retrieved February 2010.

[10]Shoguns, usually meaning general, were warlords of pre-modern Japan. Tokugawa Ieyasu united the shogunates and the last period before Meiji begins with his rule.

(a quarter of the nation's Navy) in 1853 to compel the opening of ports to American trade. Preferring the term 'seclusion' to isolation, Hidemi Suganami's (1998) relatively recent account provides a longer view beginning from the early seventeenth century. Across several hundred years, Japan had had contact with Europeans beginning with sailors and then 'trade and government interest' from Portugal and Spain. Over the period only the Dutch remained in Japan but under strict restriction and confinement. As Suganami reports, there were also complex relations with China, Korea, the Ryuku islands (Okinawa, incorporated into Japan in the 1970s) as well as 'approaches' by American and Russian ships. Amending the traditional Western story, two aspects are herein important as precursors to Meiji: there was no isolation as seclusion proved impossible to implement and, contra the traditional story, the extant feudal society was itself not barbaric.

Whether traditional or amended, history seems clear that the Meiji era was one of Western importation and rapid change. In his brief account for a popular audience, *The Japanese*, American historian and ambassador Edwin Reischauer (1977, 1978) names categories of widespread change that included the system of land ownership, and modeled on various European systems, reorganization of the nation's political, legal, financial, military, and as indicated, educational institutions. These were accompanied by rapid industrialization: lighthouses, railroads and telegraph lines were built; new manufacturing was begun such as an internationally successful cotton fabric industry. From Reischauer's list, military preparedness was especially important with strategic development of weaponry and ammunition. As the Sino-Japanese and Russo-Japanese Wars around the turn of the century and later events were to demonstrate, the point of modern change was that Japan need not be subservient nor subdued by the West in any regard. Jansen points out a significant political slogan for the entire era: 'civilization and enlightenment … [along with] rich country, strong army' (Jansen 2000, p. 457).

Japan thus wanted to remain 'Japan' whether changes were or were not welcomed. Arguably three political sides vied for control of change. First of all, conservatives supported Meiji and its emperor. As American anthropologist Ruth Benedict explains in the classic work *The Chrysanthemum and the Sword*, developed from interviews with Japanese people following World War II, the initial slogan of political victory was 'Restore the Emperor and expel the Barbarian' (Benedict 1946, p. 76). She writes,

> It was a slogan that sought to keep Japan uncontaminated by the outside world and to restore a golden age of the tenth century before there had been a 'dual rule'…. It meant reinstatement of traditional ways of life in Japan. It meant that 'reformers' would have no voice in affairs. (Ibid.)

Two aspects are significant. Largely ignored in history, the first is that restoration meant freedom from Chinese encumbrances (Jansen 2000, p. 457) and the other is that 'from the first the regime followed the opposite course' (Benedict 1946, p. 77), that is, an Emperor-redefined nation meant becoming modern. Ironically in agreement was a second group committed to very strong support for reform and modernization. A young set of intellectuals constituted this group and for them '[it] was, in some ways, the best of times' (Pyle 1969, p. 6). Thoughtful and progressive, they were not those to whom Soseki directed his criticism. A third, from the latter's age group, seemed to favor change with caution. This is arguably because of the 'extraordinary mental agonies... [endured by] the generation that was growing up amidst ... revolutionary social and cultural change' (Ibid., 1969, p. 3).[11]

Adding to background understanding, Suganami, from above and in hindsight, identifies several factors that indeed 'favored' Japan's struggle with Westernization. These included a millennial sense of national superiority, the Emperor's leadership, an administrative organization that strategically sought beneficial technology, the historical mistakes of China as a negative example, and, against isolation, a desire to learn from abroad. Here is Suganami: 'Although few in number, the so-called Dutch scholars, especially after the middle of the eighteenth century ... [, illustrate] readiness to seek any new form of knowledge regardless of its cultural or ethnic origins' (Suganami 1998, p. 13). Not developed further by this author, one other factor is very significant. This is that precipitating struggle yet providing continuity, traditional values remained central in a deep social psychology of personal relationships among the Japanese people (Ibid., 1998, p. 14).

Insight for this section on Meiji Japan comes in an important lecture and essay from Soseki. From 1911, *The Civilization of Modern–Day Japan*, his personal view of modern accommodation is exemplified. He begins defining 'civilization' with a caution not to be too determinate. It is, he writes, 'the process, the manifestation of man's vital forces' (Soskei 1911/1992, p. 262). These are both positive and negative, the latter that refer to duties composed from without and the former composed from desires to do what one wants. The latter have led to developments to conserve energy such as the train and the telephone; the former have led to pleasures such as literature, science, and philosophy (Ibid., 1911/1992, pp. 265, 264). These energies serve as an analogy to the civilization of Japan, where developments are in principle externally and internally motivated. External motivation, of course, has come from the West. He writes, 'Western civilization flows along as naturally as clouds or a river, which is not all what we see in the case of Japan since the restoration and the opening of relations with the West' (Ibid., p. 272). For him, at this time the result is a pitiful nation, with people feeling empty, dissatisfied, and anxious. He concludes, however, that there is no choice but to proceed in the present way until the nation reaches a point of 'self-centeredness', of internal motivation. His view of Japan's future, as novels will illustrate, is largely pessimistic.

## Three Stories of Teachers

Soseki's lecture/essay from above is published 6 years after his first novel, *Wagahai wa neko de aru, I Am a Cat*, is serialized beginning in 1905 (Soseki 1905–1907, 1911/1972, 2002). Also in this time period, among the 14 novels, *Botchan* is

---

[11] Ironically what also came from the emperor-led nation was the militaristic, ultra-nationalist Japan beginning in the early twentieth century decades, that continued through the century and even is present but without connection to the emperor today.

published, with *Kokoro* and *Michikusa* to follow before his untimely death. Teachers, perhaps better teacher figures, from the three latter novels help exemplify the struggle for modern accommodation. These novels share characteristics of what becomes the early modern novel in Japan: often referred to as 'psychological', narrators tell the stories, human introspection and frailty abound. 'Heroes', if they can be called such, are men caught in the Meiji era, each of whom attempts to 'be his own person' and with difficulty. More specifically, each of the 'teachers' is a life-and-professional-failure of sorts but, of course, lessons are learned in their stories. In this section, there are three subsections: Stories, Teachers and Teaching, and On Individualism.

## *Stories*

*Botchan*,[12] a comic tale compared to *The Adventures of Huckleberry Finn* and *Catcher in the Rye*, recounts a brief season of a Tokyo-bred, young teacher of mathematics in a rural boys school. The story is one of personal betrayal, of witnessing dishonesty and pitting of persons against each other for individual gain, and of taking advantage of goodness and weakness. Moreover, Botchan is not greatly successful as a teacher. By the conclusion the hero escapes back to the city, honor intact and no longer youthfully naïve. The most humorous incident concerns a student prank when grasshoppers are let lose in his bed as he serves night duty for the boarders. Even as he is bested at times by students and peers, his own form of personal 'accommodation' is scorn and disdain and later retribution for wrong done to another.

While *Botchan* is light and in the end positive, *Kokoro*, best translated 'the heart of things',[13] is a contrasting story of mystery and ultimately darkness. The narrator is a student rather than the teacher figure, the latter named Sensei.[14] There is no actual teacher. Again there are important life lessons, as a young person 'grows up'. The story has three parts, one of a mentor relationship formed between the student and Sensi, another of the student's relationship with his parents and the death of his father, and the important third part in which the mystery of Sensei's life—and the confession of his own terrible failing—leads to a youthful suicide of a friend and then his own. As in most of Soseki's novels, a central theme, relating to modern accommodation, is personal loneliness and the consequences of 'going life as one desires', even as Sensei had wished for one different.

*Michikusa*, translated as *Grass by the Wayside*,[15] is Soseki's only autobiographical novel—no matter coincidences with his life in other texts. The narrator is the author

---

[12] Botchan means 'Little Master', referring to an over-protected child, as he is by the family maid. See Doi (1976), p. 12.

[13] McCellan writes that this translation from Hearn best captures the meaning of the title. See McCellan (1959), p. vi.

[14] While I know that the Japanese meaning of sensi is complex, its general understanding in English as something like 'honored teacher' is assumed.

[15] McCellan suggests that the title refers to Soseki's life as an outsider, 'like a weed growing beside the main road' (McCellan 1969, p. xi).

who recounts the time when he returned to Tokyo from London, started his university academic career, but had not yet quit to write his novels. The tale is very self-revealing, in the person of Kenzo, manifesting a miserable life but one in which little is done at this time to change it. Soseki is unlovely; his wife and their combined relatives are also unlovely. Continuing the theme, there is no easy accommodation to modern life. The principal plot concerns Kenzo's adoptive father who needs money and of husband and wife unable to communicate over this and other matters of their lives. In the account, he describes himself as a failed and very unhappy teacher, while in actuality he was a dedicated mentor to other scholars and writers.

## Teachers and Teaching

In the novels, the portrayals of teachers and teaching help frame the broad picture of accommodation that so worries Soseki. Each hero, as the nation, responds in his own way to Westernization and indeed does and must modernize. As persons and as a society, convention and ritual, duty and obligation, and perhaps honor and pride above all, clash with change and produce struggle between the old and the new. None of the teacher figures in the three novels, in terms of being happy with occupation—teaching as life's work—and working well with 'students', succeeds. Ironically, in *Botchan* and *Kokoro*, the heroes make a statement, in action, about honor, however one might evaluate their choice of actions today. In *Michikusa*, perhaps there is redemption in facing oneself. In addition to that cited above on Japan and civilization, a lecture and essay from 1914, *My Individualism*, is significant in revealing Soseki's views; insights from it start this subsection.

In the lecture/essay Soseki overviews his career choices and its steps to a group of elite, male secondary students. He focuses at the outset on his failure as a teacher both right after university and later returning from England. He says, 'I felt not the slightest interest in my work as a teacher. I had known from the start that I was no educator' (Soseki 1914/2009a, p. 249). At university, here in *Michikusa*, is his image as told by the narrator (himself):

> He saw his own pathetic figure standing on the podium before all those young men. They would look up and stare intently at … [him and] then solemnly write down all of the half-baked comments. He felt he was letting them down badly and was ashamed…. [At] this moment there was not a trace of self-confidence. (Soseki 1915/1969, p. 82)

Returning to the essay, he tells of one of his professors of English literature whose pedagogy consisted of reading aloud and providing dates (Soseki 1914/2009a, p. 248). Seeing himself similarly, perhaps this is one reason why he later gave up on his own teaching.

While Soseki is critical of poor teaching he also values a good teacher, 'even' a Westerner. A chapter in a recent book, *Japan's Love-Hate Relationship with the West* by Sukehiro Hirakawa, recounts Soskeki's relationship with Scotsman, James Murdock. Details provide elaboration and make more complex the novelist's struggle. Murdock was his teacher at the First Higher School prior to his university days.

Based in Soseki's reflections, a relationship of 'very warm and genuine affection' existed between the two (Hirakawa 1981, 1984/2005, p. 255). Murdock's 'best student' sat in the front row almost daily for classes in history and English, and as well, 'went to his home to listen to him talk' (Ibid., 1981, 1984/2005, p. 252). After a few years of a peripatetic life, Murdock settled in rural Japan, taught school, and wrote a very significant three volume, *History of Japan*.[16] From above, foreshadowing Suganami's general position many decades later, one contribution is to suggest that many positive characteristics of the Tokugawa era contributed to Japan's modernization. Here is Hirakawa's list from Murdock: 'the Japanese capacity for organization, the social stability, a strong sense of honour shared by the people, … [and] a high degree of literacy and numeracy' (Ibid., p. 267). Even though Soseki does not share Murdock's optimism, 20 odd years after their teacher-student relationship, the now famous 'student' pens a commentary in volume one's introduction that compliments the historian Murdock even as he disagrees with him. This commentary becomes the basis for the lecture on 'civilization' and Japan overviewed above.

## *On Individualism*

Before taking up broad novelistic themes of accommodation, from the essay above attention to Soskei's view of individualism is significant since it is this theme upon which his own life and life's work ultimately holds meaning and value. A similar preoccupation, both as consciousness and the place of the person in society, appears to be predominant among intellectuals of the Meiji and Taisho eras—it seems to tie Soseki to Nishida and the Kyoto School and is taken up in comparison below.

Individualism for Soseki is comprised of three aspects of personal consciousness and choice. The first is 'self-centeredness', the initial recognition in one's life of a need for and a path toward a 'true calling' (Soseki 1914/2009a, b, p. 249). With this comes, he claims, confidence and some sense of peace of mind. He writes,

> I confess that self-centeredness became for me a new beginning…. I resolved to write books to tell people that they need not imitate Westerners, that running blindly after others as they were doing would only cause them great anxiety. If I could spell this out … it would give me pleasure and make them happy as well. (Ibid., 1914/2009a, b, p. 253)

This recognition is integral to one's individuality, one's personality, the unique character of a person found in the place where one belongs, one's life work (Ibid., p. 255). However, individualism is not realized until a third aspect is integrated: From the freedom of one's own individuality one must grant the same freedom to others. He says, '[It] would seem to me that we must keep for ourselves and grant to others a degree of liberty such that I can turn left while you turn right, each of us equally unhindered so long as what we do has no effect on others' (Ibid., p. 259). Further, and this is important, his 'ethical individualism' replaces from the Feudal era,

---

[16]The historian George Sansom paid tribute to Murdock's history even as his own project differed. See Hirakawa (1981, 1984/2005), p. 278. Murdock wrote his history as a school teacher.

the 'cliquism' that traditionally characterized Japan. By early Taisho, Soseki sees himself as 'modern'—but of course still Japanese. Two concluding comments about his view. A first is that for the person it entails loneliness as choices based on this individualism in his day often come into conflict with those of the group. A second concerns the nation. In pursing this view, Soseki sees no conflict for the nation and understands that if there were danger of annihilation, one will restrict one's personal liberty. However, with emphasis he asserts, '[the] nation may well be important, but we cannot possibly concern ourselves with the nation from morning to night, as though possessed by it.... [To] pretend ... [to do so] is simply a lie' (Ibid., p. 262).

## Modern Accommodation

In this section, the focus turns to what Soseki's teacher figures and the novels illustrate about modern accommodation. Several themes have been suggested throughout the chapter.[17] The most general is the tension between East and West and the results of societal and social upheaval for individuals, families, institutions, conventions and values. In transition new political, economic and educational realities emerge even while old ways persist. While there is some agreement that 'most' people are better off, it is clear that the former upper classes, the samurai and their counterparts especially, experience alteration of their positions and fortunes. Importantly, and including intellectuals and artists, this is the class about which Soseki largely writes. Three topics follow that introduce but ultimately do little justice to the complexity of accommodation: These are appearance of elements of Western lifestyle, generational shift especially in terms of social and family values, and tensions between urban and rural life. A central topic of individual psychological adjustment already should be apparent in the chapter.

The first, 'things Western', appear in the novels in various forms and are treated in complex and sometimes contradictory ways. One form is foreign references. The young Botchan, Tokyo bred, picks fun at his arch enemy, Redshirt,[18] the university graduate but teacher in a rural town. A reverse snobbery is evident. Botchan says,

> Redshirt just loved dropping foreign names, making it sound like he was pronouncing them in a foreign alphabet ... A totally obnoxious habit.... If he was going to throw around this foreign stuff at all, he should have struck with things that even people like me have heard of, like Benjamin Franklin's autobiography. (Soseki 1906/2005, p. 66)

Botchan's pal, Porcupine, tells him that this is all affectation and that what Redshirt knows comes solely from an 'unimportant' literary magazine.

Another form of Westernization is adoption of elements of lifestyle. In *Michikusa*, Kenzo recalls better days for his father-in-law, a government official who does well during transition but later falls on hard times. Kenzo says, 'What a proud figure he

---

[17] I had determined the categories of this section before I came upon a similar treatment. See Takehisa Iijima (1987), that primarily uses *I am a Cat*.

[18] One of the delightful elements in *Botchan* is the hero's use of characteristic nicknames.

used to cut in the mornings ... as he marched out of his Western-style official residence with its imposing stone gate, in his frock coat and silk hat' (Soseki 1915/1969, p. 116). The house, it should be said, also had a separate, impressive Japanese style wing, such was the first accommodation of the old rich. A third form, one surely of which Soseki ironically did approve—as scholar and student of English literature—was of a blending of the West with the East (that for some continues today), utilizing that which works best for particular elements of daily life. Here is the student in *Kokoro*:

> Sensei's wife bade me sit down on a cushion by the brazier.... [I was in Sensei's study] furnished partly in western style with a desk and some chairs. A great number of books, bound beautifully in leather, gleamed through the glass panes of the book cases (Soseki 1914/1957, [2000], p. 33).[19]

For the young, unsophisticated student (even from Tokyo), accommodation is not yet accomplished as she serves him black tea in a Western teacup. She says, 'How many? One lump? Two lumps?' 'She had picked up a lump of sugar with a strange instrument', he recalls. In *Michikusa*, Soskei's ambivalence about Western things becomes even more manifest. He possesses a desk and clothes for university teaching. And, at his most miserable and miserly he takes what little outside money he has earned and has a spree, buying Japanese pottery for the living room alcove and silk for a kimono and haori for himself.[20] Self-revelatory, '[during] the shopping spree Kenzo had given no thought to others—not even to the baby that was about to be born' (Ibid., 1915/1969, p. 141).

One divide, East and West, need not but sometimes did align with another divide, that between generations transiting the old and new nation. At first glance, it appears as if older Japanese held on to Eastern-inspired life while those younger favored Western change. Soseki's characters reveal the limitation of this stereotype and the complexity of generation and modernization. Indeed across generations, in the novels people use the modern to support changing social relations—and to bolster one's own place in the new order. On the one hand, the student has this to say about Sensei:

> [Sometimes] I was inclined to regard his reserve unfavorably. I liked then to think that his reluctance to discuss such a matter ... [as the tragic circumstances of his marriage] was due to timidity born of the conventions of a generation ago. I thought of myself as more free ... and more open-minded ... than either Sensei or his wife. (Soseki 1914/1957, [2000], p. 24)

On the other hand, while the student believes his father does not understand present difficult conditions for employment, the new Japan 'frees' the latter from obligation that change of circumstances cannot support. Here is the student again:

> Secretly I felt that there was little chance of my finding a decent position.... [even as a university graduate]. But my father ... believed otherwise.... He said, 'You must become independent as soon as you find employment. It really isn't right that one should, immediately

---

[19]While copyrighted in 1957, this text is a reprint from 2000. One notes that Soseki's treatment of women in often unflattering to say the least. See for example, Soseki (1914/2009a, b), p. 258.

[20]Kimono is familiar to English readers; a hoari is a coat worn over a kimono.

after graduating, live on others. It would seem that the younger generation today knows
only how to spend money. It doesn't seem to occur to them that money has to be made too'.
(Ibid., 1914/1957, [2000], p. 98)

One other indication of change is that the student's parents expect Sensei to obtain
a position for him. Readers know that this is 'impossible' for the reclusive Sensei,
but it may also have become more difficult in new times.

Conflict of values is manifest in the central 'plot' of Soseki's life story: Kenzo's
actions above are indicative of selfishness but much more. He is torn between 'true'
feelings for adoptive parents who smothered him and made him feel guilty for their
sacrifices in his childhood and a duty in adulthood that results from adoption.
Moreover, as the 'success' in the family, he also has a duty to siblings and other
family relations including those of his wife. All of this, in modern Japan of the early
twentieth century, becomes financial. At the end of the autobiography, Kenzo pur-
chases his adoption document thus severing ties. His wife believes that this ends
obligation but Kenzo, caught between old and new, recognizes the ambiguity that
remains in modern accommodation.

Since this section takes up themes in three novels, treatment of generation in
Botchan deserves mention; here is a third form, one of the seeming accommodation
of and by youth. Overall, this early novel from Soseki is much more positive and
hopeful than those later. Does Botchan have it both ways, new and old? Out of a
youthful death of parents and brother betrayal, the young man retains a very positive
relationship with a family retainer, an older maid Kiyo. She is his anchor to family
and to a sense of self-worth because of her unfailing belief in him.

Many themes of accommodation are located within Soseki's novels and no
attempt is intended either to encapsulate nor to represent them all. In addition to
Western incursion and generational change, a third and final theme for the chapter
concerns lifestyles and attitudes that 'contrast' between urban and rural life in the
changing Japan. A first point is that both through humor and irony, the Tokyoite
Soseki privileges urban life, its practices and values, and its people even as early in
his own life, he fled the city for provincial teaching assignments.

Botchan's prejudice is evident right from his own arrival to teach in a rural city.
He exclaims, 'From the look of it the place was a fishing town about the size of the
neighborhood of Omori in Tokyo. Who the hell did they think they were, sending
me to a place like this? How was I supposed to stand it?' (Soseki 1906/2005, p. 26).
Throughout the novel, city amenities that Botchan is use to are either not available
or forbidden by local custom. These include his favorite foods. Teased by his
students for indulging in tempura at a small restaurant, he says this:

> I guess if you live in a town so small that once you've walked around it for an hour there's
> nothing more to see, the sight of somebody eating some tempura seems like a big deal,
> right up there with the War with Russia.... Absolutely pathetic! Considering the way
> they've been brought up, it's no wonder they turn into such small-minded twerps. (Ibid.,
> 1906/2005, p. 44)

In Kokoro, the student recognizes his father's parochialism. He explains, 'The
little community, of which my father had been a part for so many years, was his
world, and he could not think beyond it' (Soskei 1914/1957, [2000], p. 93). Yet

when the latter is gravely ill, the student offers the lure of Tokyo as an inducement to get well:

> Remember, you are coming to Tokyo to enjoy yourself when you are better. And mother will be coming with you. You will really be amazed to see how much Tokyo has changed since your last visit. For example, the tram lines have become numerous, and you know how they affect the appearance of streets. There's been a rearrangement of the boroughs too. Why, one can say that in Tokyo today, there's not a moment of quiet, day or night. (Soseki 1914/1957, [2000], p. 104)

The point, of course, is that the modern city lures the student and not the father.

Tokyo also lures the novelist; as biographical commentary and *Michikusa* attests, London may have been 'alien' for Soseki but the modern capital of Japan (Kyoto had been the feudal capital) is his home. In the years of the novel it gives him little pleasure. However, while the city home does not offer domestic bliss, it does contain his study and his books, and it is at least in the decade before his death, the locale of his own mentoring.

## Comparing Nishida

Elsewhere in this volume, particular attention has been paid to Kitaro Nishida and his contribution to the Kyoto School.[21] For this chapter, three aspects of comparison with Soseki are important—especially as the purpose is to point to and broaden understanding of Meiji change and the meeting of East and West in Japan. First, they were intellectual contemporaries, each with great accomplishment. Second, they have similar significant stature in Japanese culture both in their time and since and as it turns out relatively similar personal biographies. Third, they demonstrate specific, differently formed but complementary relationships of modern accommodation. These comparisons are considered in this section that largely but all too briefly incorporates information on and ideas from Nishida's philosophical writings.

As Meiji men and scholars with overlapping lives, one would have thought that Nishida and Soseki would be friends—and little seems to be made of comparing them. One source does offer a direct connection and there are other sources of ones indirect. First biographies: Born in 1870, Nishida was 3 years younger than Soseki. From middle class backgrounds each endured family difficulties that influenced their education paths and their early professional lives. Both ultimately attended and graduated from Tokyo Imperial University. With a degree in philosophy, Nishida graduated in 1894, 1 year later than Soseki whose degree was in English studies. At early points both taught secondary school away from the urban centers of Tokyo or Kyoto. Additionally both seem not to have enjoyed secondary school level teaching and as indicated above, Soskei even quit the university.

---

[21] Although I have read some of Nishida's writings; as a non-scholar of Japanese thought I have had to rely to a great extent on English language commentaries for this section.

At some times in their lives—at least, Nishida across his career—both read Western thought avidly.

Nishida published his first major book, *Zen no kenkyu, An Inquiry into the Good*, in 1911. By this time, Soseki's prolific career as a novelist was well underway beginning in 1905; he wrote until his death in 1916. Nishida taught and wrote until retirement from Kyoto Imperial University in 1927 where he had been professor of philosophy since 1910. He then continued to lecture and publish until his own death in 1945 at the age of 75. One final comparative mention concerns their respective attachment to religion. Both practiced Zen meditation and gave it up. Influenced by his friend, the Zen scholar D. T. Suzuki, Nishida's writings are full of religious references and his last essay specifically focuses on religious thought. Ironically even as he desired to maintain Japanese culture in the face of Westernization, Soseki does not appear to have lead a particularly religious life.

Above, a question of connection between Nishida and Soseki was raised. One source details direct contact. Here is a statement from Valdo Vigliemo, the respected translator and commentator, quoted at length:

> [In an essay on Tokyo University life, Nishida reports that one] year ahead of him … was Soseki…. [Writes Vigliemo, he] gives us a tantalizing bit of information that he and Soseki were actually in the same class in German literature, reading … under Florenz, the renowned literary historian. Thus, for a brief moment in their youth the eminent philosopher and novelist, perhaps the two most creative minds of modern Japan, were actually classmates. (Vigliemo 1971, p. 524)

Their association did not further develop although in his diary Nishida names Soseki as one of his favorite Japanese writers and notes his death (Knauth 1965; Vigliemo 1971, Ibid.). Vigliemo comments, 'Perhaps Nishida was aware that both he and Soseki were really attempting to achieve the same thing by different means: namely, to probe the nature of reality and define man's place in the cosmos' (Ibid.).

Indirectly the following is known about a network association. In 1960, Nishida's first English translator of *Inquiry* was actually Vigliemo whose Harvard University dissertation completed in 1955 was on Soseki. Just cited, in 1971 Vigliemo contributed a biography of Nishida's early life that is still one of few sources in English (Heisig 2001, p. 284). Vigliemo's mentor was a Russian émigré, Serge Elisséeff, now mentioned in the notes, one of the founders of Japanese studies in North America. He attended Soseki's student salon in Tokyo beginning in 1909 and was befriended by him.[22]

Nishida was himself prolific. Over 30 years he produced writings that have been collected and published together in 19 volumes. Commentator David Dillworth asserts this in the late 1980s: 'Nishida's works reflect a level of serious intercivilizational encounter in the twentieth century … [along with] his contemporaries—notably, such literary giants as Natsume Soseki … [and Mori Ogai] which still … [has] no counterpart in our own occidental culture' (Dillworth 1987a, p. 1). In terms of Western

---

[22]Elisseéeff went on to teach at Harvard and the Sorbonne.

thought, Dillworth favorably compares Nishida with Husserl, Whitehead, Heidegger, and Wiitgenstein (p. 2). Nishida's project has been called a 'continuing dialogue' between the two civilizations, cultures, and logics.

In furthering this explication, Masao Abe, citing Nishida expert, Torataro Shimomura, asserts that Nishida had to 'include but go beyond the demonstrative thinking that is characteristic of the west and both arrive at an unobjectifiable ultimate reality and give it a logical articulation by conceptually expressing the inexpressible' (Abe 1990, p. x). Logical articulation is especially important as by his death, Nishida claimed to develop a new logic. It comes to found a religious worldview based in what James Heisig names as his 'metaphysical principle proper ... of absolute nothingness' (Heisig 2001, p. 63). The roots of this principle are located in *Inquiry* and are reworked across Nishida's career. His last essay, *Nothingness and the Religious Worldview* (Nishida 1949, 1966/1987), was written just before his death.

In *Inquiry*, Nishida is initially influenced by reading among others William James, Ernst Mach, and Henri Bergson. Abe focuses his 1990 introduction to the book on central concepts of pure experience and ultimate reality. Here is Nishida's opening statement from the book's Preface:

> Over time I came to realize that it is not that experience exists because there is an individual, but that an individual exists because there is experience. I thus arrived at the idea that experience is more fundamental than individual differences. (Nishida 1921, 1987/1990, p. xiv)

For him, experience is both a priori and active. As Abe explains, 'In actual experience it is not that *the self experiences* something but that *the self as well is experienced*' (Abe 1990, p. xvi, emphasis in original). He continues that in Western terms, 'the knower and known are not two but one ... systematically self-developing and self-unfolding' (pp. xvi, xvii). At this early writing, Nishida claims that ultimate reality is neither consciousness nor matter but 'from the perspective of pure experience ... is an independent self-sufficient, pure activity.... A unifying power ... of all realities' (p. xix).

In his very useful overview, Heisig's concluding judgement is that Nishida's *oeuvre* expands in 'ever wider circles' that cannot be either 'molded' into Western, linear stages nor significantly accommodated into Eastern philosophy (Heisig 2001, p. 104, my interpretation). Nishida's synthesis, developed in greater detail by disciples in the Kyoto School, does surely reflect his genius. Several general ideas organize the synthesis. First, to see the circles as discrete does their evolving character a disservice. Second, in overlapping, the initial concept of pure experience takes on more in-depth conception as a series of changing terms. Third, ever 'approximating' the absolute for Nishida, these include will, self-awareness, active intuition, becoming and absolute nothingness. For emphasis, it is vital to recall that Nishida is working, arguably, on the basic modern, Western philosophical problem, the relationship of person to world.

For this section, a brief look at absolute nothingness and the final logic must be sufficient, taken largely from Heisig and Dillworth, respectively. First, this synthetic move is to locate nothingness along with being, contributions of Eastern and Western thought, but to go a step further. Here is Heisig:

> [Absolute] nothingness ... is to say that it is beyond encompassing by any phenomenon, individual event, or relationship in the world.... [This] means that it is not defined by an opposite to anything in the world of being.... Nothingness opposes the world as absolute to relative.... [It is the principle that] true negation is a negation of negation]. (Heisig 2001, pp. 62–63)[23]

Second, it seems significant that Nishida turned to and wrote about religious consciousness just before his death. This move, also interestingly, is to a non-sectarian form of spiritual consciousness arising, writes Dillworth, from Nishida's life-long reading of both Buddhist and Christian texts. The commentator explains thus, 'The religious "act" of self-awareness is the place of realization of the coincidence of eternal life and death in one's own life and death.... The dynamics ... [of conversion] entail the reciprocal, but nondual, intentionality of God and the individual soul' (Dillworth 1987a, p. 35). One final idea is that such consciousness is to constitute a 'world philosophy'.

To close this section, it is also instructive to note a political contrast between the two men: Nishida largely paid no attention to Japan's militaristic role in the East until nearly the end of his life while Soseki early on used his novel, *Shumi no iden*, *The Heredity of Taste* (Soseki 1906, 2004) to be highly critical. In defense of Nishida, Heisig suggests this: 'Nishida ... [was] convinced that Japan could gather other nations into its spirit to the advantage of all. What keeps this process "moral" is that it is the self-expression of a wider historical life and not just the self-expression of national interests' (Heisig 2001, p. 98).

## Conclusion

While the conclusion emphasizes Soseki and his own struggle with modern accommodation, if Vigliemo is accurate about the similarity of their life projects, a final comparative comment on Soseki and Nishida is in order. This can be phrased in terms of overcoming dualisms of East vs. West of their day. Nishida wrote to overcome the basic, Western philosophical duality of the subjective and objective in order to pose intellectual parity. His evolving concept of absolute nothingness does this by resolving oppositions, by offering a metaphysical foundation, an essence, that cannot itself be conceived in either Eastern or Western terms but that requires his synthesis. In novelistic rather than philosophical form, Soseki sought to transcend the cultural dualisms that in his day he saw as a dominating Westernization. An important point to remember is that he did not hate the West but worried that modernization was being adopted in Japan by many people without careful thought.

---

[23] In his epilogue, Dillworth compares Nishida's logic to the work of Jacques Derrida. See Dillworth (1987b).

Now to close: as a complement to other chapters in this volume on the Kyoto School of Philosophy and education, this chapter has focused on the life and writings of Japan's great modern novelist, Soseki Natsume. The purpose has been to underscore the society and the lives of people in the eras around which the indigenous philosophy emerged. It is clear from Soseki's novels and other sources that the nation 'had' to become modern, that accommodation occurred. Accommodation meant dealing with Western incursion and influence, meant altering ways of living and concomitant values. There might well be stories of dealing with change in which there was little struggle. Soseki's life and his stories tell a different tale. As he said explicitly, his novels were a warning against Japan losing to the West its culture, its tradition, its sense of itself.

Hiratsuka's woodblock prefacing the chapter intimates that accommodation of East and West surely was and has been possible; Japan is modern and remains Japan. History has demonstrated two things: one is that at times in the nearly 150 years since Perry's ships arrived, the nation has struggled with a conservative jingoism that ultimately led to military defeat and subsequently a commitment to peace. The other is that 'a different road' for the nation has resulted in Japan's prosperity and global influence. The nation is entirely 'first world' but visitors are treated to 'things Japanese'[24] if they want to get a feel for the nation's essence: sleeping on the floor in a futon, enjoying sashimi in a neighborhood restaurant with stools for ten, browsing in a local antique shop filled with dusty treasure-filled kogo.[25] That these same pleasures are to be found across the modern globe, in my town and my home and those of many others, attests in part to influence. That the economy and politics of Japan, each and everyday, affects nations and peoples around the world is another indicator of modernization and importance.

The focus of this chapter, novelist Soseki Natsume died in 1916 at the age of 50 of stomach ulcers that plagued his adulthood. Not feeling well coupled with the problems of his life, it might be claimed, contributed to the largely pessimistic view of his era that the novels portray. His teachers, teacher figures, did struggle in their lives—their modern accommodation was not easy. It is ironic that even as his warning went largely unheeded, the novelist did not live to see the positive rise of modern Japan that remains Japanese. Perhaps the value and popularity of his novels have contributed to this.

A final matter concerns philosophy of education and education itself. The lesson for the latter seems apparent: living in a global village means that 'students' in any culture must search out, learn about, and be generous to any other culture. The lesson from the former is that a philosophy and philosophy of education arises within a context that must be explored for understanding. Insights from the times and lives of

---

[24] I have used this phrase a couple of times in the chapter. It pays tribute to a very early volume for Western travelers to Japan from Basil Hall Chamberlain who was a professor of Japanese and philology at the Imperial University of Tokyo. See Chamberlain (1905, 1927).

[25] Kogo is a box; for antiques these are wooden boxes with calligraphy identifying their valued contents. The other terms—given the two way road of the chapter—are familiar.

those in Meiji Japan, as exemplified in the life and writings of Soseki, contribute to the purpose of this volume, as background and complement to a scholarly understanding of the Kyoto School of Philosophy and its applications for education. This philosophical school engendered its own modern accommodation that continues to today.[26]

# References

Abe, M. (1990). Introduction. In K. Nishida (Ed.), *An inquiry into the good* (pp. vii–xxvi). New Haven/London: Yale University Press.

Benedict, R. (1946). *The chrysanthemum and the sword: Patterns of Japanese culture*. Boston: Houghton Mifflin.

Chamberlain, B. (1905, 1927). *Things Japanese: Being notes on various subjects connected with Japan*. London: Kegan Paul, Trench, Trubner.

Dillworth, D. (1987a). Introduction: Nishida's critique of the religious consciousness. In K. Nishida (Ed.), *Last writings: Nothingness and the religious worldview* (pp. 1–45). Honolulu: University of Hawaii Press.

Dillworth, D. (1987b). Postscript: Nishida's logic of the East. In K. Nishida (Ed.), *Last writings: Nothingness and the religious worldview* (pp. 127–149). Honolulu: University of Hawaii Press.

Doi, T. (1976). *The psychological world of Natusme Soseki* (W. Tyler, Trans.). Cambridge: East Asian Research Center, Harvard University.

Gallery, D. (1985). *Un'ichi Hiratsuka: A retrospective exhibition of woodblock prints in celebration of the artist's 90th birthday*. Los Angeles: Japanese American Cultural & Community Center.

Gessel, V. (1993). The anguish of modernity: Natsume Soseki. In *Three modern novelists: Soseki, Tanizaki Kawabata* (pp. 11–67). Tokyo: Kodansha International.

Hearn, L. (1904, 1955). *Japan: An attempt at interpretation*. Rutland: Charles E. Tuttle.

Heisig, J. (2001). *Philosophers of nothingness: An essay on the Kyoto School*. Honolulu: University of Hawai'i Press.

Hirakawa, S. (1981, 1984/2005). Natsume Soseki and his teacher James Murdock: Their opposite views of modernization of Japan. In *Japan's love-hate relationship with the west* (pp. 249–279). Folkstone: Global Oriental.

Iijima, T. (1987). Criticism of twentieth century civilization in *Wagahai wa neko de aru*. In T. Iijima & J. Vardaman (Eds.), *The world of Natsume Soseki* (pp. 125–150). Tokyo: Kinseido.

Jansen, M. (2000). *The making of modern Japan*. Cambridge, MA: Belknap of Harvard University Press.

Knauth, L. (1965). Life is tragic: The diary of Nishida Kitaro. *Monumenta Nipponica, 20*(3–4), 334–358.

Marcus, M. (2009). *Reflections in a glass door: Memory and melancholy in the personal writings of Natsume Soseki*. Honolulu: University of Hawai'i Press.

McCellan, E. (1959). An introduction to Soseki. *Harvard Journal of Asiatic Studies, 22*, 150–208.

McCellan, E. (1969). Introduction. In *Two Japanese novelists: Soseki and Toson* (pp. vii–xi). Chicago: The University of Chicago Press.

Merritt, H. (2001). Hiratsuka: The artist and his prints. In *Hiratsuka: Modern master* (pp. 9–19). Chicago/Seattle: The Art Institute of Chicago and the University of Washington Press.

---

[26]This chapter is dedicated to my mother, Margaret Duncan Stone, and to James Marshall for support. Thank you to Naoko Saito and Paul Standish for their invitation, infinite patience, and faith.

Nishida, K. (1921, 1987/1990). *An inquiry into the good* (M. Abe & C. Ives, Trans.). New Haven/London: Yale University Press. (Originally published, 1911)

Nishida, K. (1949, 1966/1987). *Last writings: Nothingness and the religious worldview* (D. Dillworth, Trans.). Honolulu: University of Hawaii Press.

Pyle, K. (1969). *The new generation in Meiji Japan: Problems of cultural identity, 1885–1895.* Stanford: Stanford University Press.

Reischauer, E. (1977, 1978). *The Japanese*. Cambridge, MA: Belknap of Harvard University Press.

Soseki, N. (1957) [2000 printing]. *Kokoro: A novel* (E. McCellan, Trans.). Washington, DC: Regnery/UNESCO. (Originally published, *Asahi Shimbun* , 1914.)

Soseki, N. (1969). *Grass by the wayside.* (E. McCellan, Trans.). Chicago: The University of Chicago Press. (Originally published, *Michikusa, Asahi Shimbun*, 1915.)

Soseki, N. (1972, 2002). *I am a cat* (A. Ito & G. Wilson, Trans.). Tokyo: Tuttle. (Originally published, *Wagahai wa neko de aru, Asahi Shimbun*, 1905–1907, 1911.)

Soskei, N. (1992). The civilization of modern day Japan. In *Kokoro: A novel and selected essays* (J. Rubin, Trans., pp. 257–283). Lanham: Madison. (Originally published, 1911.)

Soseki, N. (2004). *The heredity of taste* (S. Tsunematsu, Trans.). Boston: Tuttle. (Originally published, *Shumi no iden*, 1906.)

Soseki, N. (2005). *Botchan* (J. Cohn, Trans.). Tokyo: Kodansha. (Originally published, *Asahi Shimbun*, 1906.)

Soseki, N. (2009a). *My individualism* (J. Rubin, Trans). In M. Bourdaghs, A. Ueda, & J. Murphy (Eds.), *Theory of literature and other critical writings* (pp. 242–264). New York: Columbia University Press. (Originally published, *Watakushi no Kojinshugi*, 1914, 1918.)

Soseki, N. (2009b). In M. Bourdaghs, A. Ueda, & J. Murphy (Eds.), *Theory of literature and other critical writings*. New York: Columbia University Press.

Suganami, H. (1998). Japan's entry into international society. In *Meiji Japan: Political, economic and social history, 1868–1912* (The emergence of the Meiji State, Vol. 1, pp. 3–15). London: Routledge.

Van Zelst Family Collection and The Art Institute of Chicago. (2001). *Hiratsuka: Modern master*. Chicago/Seattle: The Art Institute of Chicago and the University of Washington Press.

Vigliemo, V. (1971). Nishida Kitaro: The early years. In D. Shively (Ed.), *Tradition and modernization in Japanese culture* (pp. 507–562). Princeton: Princeton University Press.

Yiu, A. (1998). *Chaos and order in the works of Natsume Soseki*. Honolulu: University of Hawai'i Press.

Yu, B. (1969). *Natsume Soseki*. New York: Twayne.

# Chapter 15
# Negativity, Experience and Transformation: Educational Possibilities at the Margins of Experience — Insights from the German Traditions of Philosophy of Education

**Andrea English**

> Die Fremdheit, die schon bei uns selbst, also auch in der Heimat beginnt, findet ihrem prägnanten Ausdruck in einem Haiku des Dichters Basho:
> 'In Kyoto wohnend sehne ich mich, beim Schrei des Kuckucks, nach Kyoto'.
> Der Schrei des Kuckucks mag noch so bekannt sein, er kann uns immer wieder aus dem Gewohnten herausreissen, solange wir bereit sind, uns überraschen zu lassen.
>
> The Otherness, which begins within ourselves, at home, finds its laconic expression in a haiku of the poet Basho:
> 'Living in Kyoto, upon the sound of the cuckoo, I long for Kyoto'
> The cry of the cuckoo, though so familiar, can tear us from habit again and again, as long as we are prepared to let ourselves be surprised.
>
> —Bernhard Waldenfels[1]

The Japanese art of *Haiku* proves a fruitful starting point for inquiring into the elusive meanings of negativity. According to the theory of Haiku, there are many ideas of negativity working together in the Haiku poem: the negativity of the creative attitude of the poet as 'with no mind' (*mu-shin*); the negativity of the poetic

---

[1] Waldenfels (1998), translation AE. Many of the German texts cited below were not available in English translation. In these cases, I have provided my own translation of the texts. In cases where a standard translation was available, I cite both the German and English versions of the texts and note when I have modified the original English translation. In certain instances, for longer citations, I have provided an English version in the body of the paper with the original German text in footnotes.

A. English (✉)
Faculty of Education, Mount Saint Vincent University, 166 Bedford Highway, Halifax, NS B3M 2J6, Canada
e-mail: andrea.english@msvu.ca

P. Standish and N. Saito (eds.), *Education and the Kyoto School of Philosophy*, Contemporary Philosophies and Theories in Education 1, DOI 10.1007/978-94-007-4047-1_15, © Springer Science+Business Media Dordrecht 2012

field of expression as a blank space or void (*yo haka*); and the negativity within the dialectic encounter between the poet as creative subject and the otherness of the external world.[2] This third moment, which addresses the encounter between self and other, is particularly productive when thinking about the meaning of *negativity* in education. The negativity of experience arises in our encounters with difference and otherness, and locates the moments in which we begin to learn from disillusionment, struggle and suffering.

## Preface: Why Do We Need the Term Negativity?

To use the terms *negative* and *negativity* to describe experience might bring a bad taste to the English speaker's palate. In everyday language, these terms commonly describe something bad, such as a tragic event or an undesirable experience. Although these and related terms have now been incorporated into Anglo-American philosophy, it was primarily with reference to the German philosophical tradition, such as Hegel, Heiddeger or Gadamer that the terms were given meaning in English-language philosophical discourse. Despite this, with the translations of these philosopher's works using terminology such as 'the negation of negation' (for Hegel's *'Negation der Negation'*) or 'the nothing noths' (for Heiddeger's *'Das Nichts nichtet'*), the concepts of negativity in English-language contexts have maintained a distinctly foreign quality to their tone.

In educational philosophy, the concept of negativity is vital for inquiring into the limits of human experience, knowledge and understanding in ways that harken back to the paradoxical and aporetic aspects of experience and learning discussed since the Socratic tradition. These moments cannot be avoided. They occur in our experiences of otherness and difference, in which the world defies our expectations and are often coupled with perplexity, frustration, fear or resistance. Plato's *Meno* provides an illustrative example of this experience. In the *Meno*, the learning slave boy, who attempts to answer Socrates' questions, becomes disillusioned and perplexed about his own knowledge until he is led to eventually proclaim 'I do not know'. This admission of ignorance is a pre-condition for the boy's search for knowledge (Plato 1961).

In modern Anglo-American educational philosophy, in particular that which is aligned with the tradition of Pragmatism, the paradoxical and aporetic moments of experience and thinking are more commonly referred to using philosophical terms such as *doubt*, *uncertainty*, or *perplexity*. These notions are important for educational thought and relate to the negativity of experience (see Benner 2003; Benner and English 2004; English 2005a, b, 2008). However, such concepts as doubt and perplexity tend to emphasize the cognitive dimension of negative experience, without addressing deeper existential aspects of the human condition. The concept of negativity provides the philosophical basis to examine and describe phenomena at the margins of experience in ways that get lost or can be easily overlooked without this terminology.

---

[2] See Toshihiko and Izutsu's (1981) analysis of the theory of Haiku, Chapter 4.

The Kyoto School has drawn upon the German tradition of philosophical thinking about negativity, using terms such as *negation*, *self-negation* and *not-I*, or even *non-I*. This terminology has been taken up for example in Kitaro's Nishida concept of 'active intuition' (see Nishida 1987; see also Heisig 2001), in Tanabe's 'dialectics of the species' (Tanabe 1946/1969; see also Heisig 2001) or in Motomori Kimura's idea of 'expressive-formative existence' (see Nishimura 2007) to describe the dialectical confrontation of the self with the world.[3] Beyond this, these thinkers of the Kyoto School have developed the idea of 'absolute nothingness' (*zettai-mu*), placing a uniquely Japanese stamp on the tradition of discourse surrounding negativity and the human condition.

In recent literature on the Kyoto School, it has been noted that its early thinkers tended to focus on the relation between the self and the world in order to understand the subject-object relation within reflective consciousness, and in doing so failed to pay special attention to the relation between subjects. In other words, the focus has been on the *intra*personal not the *inter*personal relationship. James Heisig emphasizes for example, that in Nishida's theory of active intuition 'the problem of other selves is left out' of the discussion of the self-world encounter (Heisig 2001, p. 79). He adds that even in Nishida's 1932 book, *I and You*, the I-you relation proves to be 'no more than a secondary or derivative function of self-reflection on the field of absolute nothingness [...] The encounter of the I and the you is simply one instance of the "I" en route to its own negation in self-awareness of nothingness' (Heisig 2001, p. 83). Additionally, Takau Nishimura, commenting on Kimura's theory of expressive-formation, remarks that 'communication with the concrete other personality' encountered in *praxis* 'is not adequately clarified in the theory' (Nishimura 2007, p. 74).

At the 2008 *International Network of Philosophers of Education* conference, authors took a critical stance towards this aspect of the tradition. They emphasized the need to capture the self-other relation between human beings, in particular as it relates to educational contexts. This comes through, for example, in Tsunemi Tanaka's idea of the need for 'mutuality' and responsiveness to the other between generations, in Takuo Nishimura's call to develop an understanding of the otherness of the learner, and Shoko Suzuki's discussion of the implications of 'pedagogical tact' and 'active intuition' for the teacher-learner relation.[4]

The questions that I ask in this paper relate to the difficulties and possibilities surrounding the relationship between self and other in education. How does the learner experience the world and learn to interact with other human beings? What is the teacher's role in the learner's process of experiencing and learning about the world? Can and should the teacher guide or even *interrupt* this process?

Of course, these questions are very broad and can be examined from many angles. Here, I seek to answer these questions by examining the educational meaning

---

[3] I am relying on English translations of Nishida's and Tanabe's works, and in the case of Kimura's text, which is only available in Japanese, I am only citing Nishimura's account of Kimura.

[4] See Tanake (2008), Nishimura (2008), and Suzuki (2008b) and also the articles by these authors in this volume.

of *negativity* as it plays a constitutive role in transformational encounters between the self and the other. To do this, I turn to the German traditions of philosophy of education. As I will seek to show, the discourse in German educational philosophy in the nineteenth and twentieth centuries and in its more recent developments provides fruitful grounds for furthering the conversation around cross-cultural concerns about education.

In this chapter, I focus on three interrelated aspects of negativity that are central to understanding what makes the teacher-learner relation educational. In the first section, I address the meaning of negativity as the *unknown* of human nature by examining the concept of *Bildsamkeit* or educability. I explicate the concept in its connection to *Bildung* and distinguish it from notions of the mind as a blank slate, of the human being as deficient or as having a pre-determined endpoint. In the second section, I examine negativity of experience as constitutive of the process of learning. Here, I focus on the concept of *Umlernen* as a notion of transformative learning. I argue that our encounters with the otherness of the unfamiliar and new in learning necessarily involve interruptions that occur when we reach the limits of our knowledge and experience. In these moments we break with ourselves and become open to difference. In the third section, I examine the concept of *pedagogical tact* as a way of addressing the need for risk and improvisation in teaching to deal with the unexpected in teachers' experiences.

In closing, I address some of the specific challenges faced by philosophers and educators when dealing with negativity as it arises in experience and the current trends in school reform that ignore these challenges. In looking to the future of cross-cultural dialogue on this topic, I discuss the indispensable need for inquiry into how we might continue to theoretically and practically approach negativity as a permanent blind spot which marks the human experience.

## *Bildsamkeit*—On the Human Being as a Learning Being

The concept of *Bildsamkeit,* which can be translated as educability, plasticity or perfectibility, addresses the very possibility of one person learning from another. *Bildsamkeit* describes an aspect of the human condition that educators have to pre-suppose, namely, that the individual is capable of being formed through his interaction with the world *and* of forming himself within that interaction. The idea of *Bildsamkeit* as an indispensable educational concept was put forth by the philosopher Johann Friedrich Herbart who proclaimed in his 1835 *Outlines of Educational Doctrine* that the 'educability [*Bildsamkeit*] of the individual learner' is the first and 'founding principle of education' (Herbart 1977, 1835, translation modified AE). The idea may seem tautological, as Otto Friedrich Bollnow points out, since the concept says that in order to educate we have to assume education is possible (Bollnow 1965, p. 16). Herbart's point was not to state the obvious. Rather, it was to underscore that without making explicit the assumption that educators can have an influence on another person there is no basis for theoretical discussion about the limits or possibilities of pedagogical interaction. Thus, without such a concept neither a science [*Wissenschaft*] of education nor the practice of education would be possible (Benner and Schmied-Kowarzik 1967, p. 95ff.). Herbart's statement underscores the idea that pedagogical interaction is grounded in the human capacity for learning through encounters with difference and otherness. In defining Herbart's concept of *educability* more closely we can look at two other concepts that inform it, namely Jean-Jacques Rousseau's notion of *perfectibilité* and Wilhelm von Humboldt's notion of *Bildung*.

Rousseau's concept of *perfectibilité* expresses the idea that the human being is capable of learning in all areas of his life (Rousseau 1764/1979, p. 61). In his *Discourse on the Origin of Inequality*, Rousseau (1755/1999) highlights the term *perfectibility* as a way of making a distinction between the human being and other animals. This distinction lies in the fact that human beings, unlike other animals, have the potential *not* to follow their instincts, but to move past these with reason and understanding (Rousseau 1755/1999, pp. 33 and 34). Thus we can say that Rousseau's concept locates the basis for human self-transformation and learning, which lies in the human ability to go against inclinations, to break with oneself and, in doing so, change direction of thought and action.

Herbart's notion of *Bildsamkeit* draws upon the idea of perfectibility and empha-sizes that this human ability to break with oneself and go against self-interested inclinations is the basis for the human capacity to become moral (Herbart 1835, 1977; see also Herbart 1804/1964). This break with oneself which we can call a form of self-alienation relates to how we learn through encounters with things in the world that are unfamiliar, unexpected and strange. This type of interaction with otherness as a basis for learning about the world and about oneself is expressed in the idea of *Bildung*, which is most often translated as education or formation. Both terms, *Bildung* and *Bildsamkeit*, stem from the root word *bild* which means *form*, and the term *bildsam* can be connected to the Latin *formabilis* or *docilis*, meaning formable or teachable, respectively. Herbart's use of the term *Bildsamkeit* reflects this meaning in two senses. It captures the individual's capacity *to form* and *to be formed* and thereby connects to the notion of *Bildung*, which expresses the active and receptive self-other relation implicit in education.

In Humboldt's fragment, Theory of Bildung (1793), he draws out the understanding of education as *Bildung* by explicating that in order to learn and grow the human being relies on a world being something other than himself, something outside himself, that is, '*NichtMensch*' (Humboldt 1969a, p. 235; Humboldt 2001) In encounters with the world, the human being meets difference and learns through the process of active *and* receptive interplay with that world (Humboldt 1969a). The process of *Bildung* is transformative in that it is mediated by the self-alienation involved in distancing ourselves from habitual understandings and forms of action and allowing new self-understandings, abilities, thoughts and aims to take shape.[5]

---

[5] Compare Humboldt (1969a, b); on this concept see also Klafki (2001), Reichenbach (2002); on the connection to *Bildsamkeit* see Benner and Brüggen (2004); see also English (2009).

Herbart's term educability refers to the process of change through *Bildung*, of which all human beings are capable, without making claims about a blank starting point or a pre-determined final destination point to this process. It differs fundamentally from concepts of the human being as deficient from the start or as a being that follows a path to completion. On the latter point, Herbart was in agreement with Rousseau, when Rousseau stated, 'we do not know what our nature permits us to be' (Rousseau 1764/1979).[6] For Herbart, we can say *Bildsamkeit* expresses an understanding of the human being as a 'changeable being', a fact which all forms of education must address:

> The object [*Gegenstand*] upon which all education [*Erziehung*] must orient itself is without doubt none other than man himself, namely, man as a changeable being, as a being, who can transition from one state to another, and at the same time maintain something of himself in the new situation.[7]

The notion of *Bildsamkeit* thus expresses the idea of the human being as a *learning being*. The capacity for change common to all human beings relates to both their organic being, and their will or ability to make choices (Herbart 1835, 1977). However, this capacity for change and formation through the teacher-learner relation and through encounters with the world is not limitless, and should not be seen as such to the educator. Herbart defined two limits to the individual's capacity for change that are equally limits for the educator: the circumstances of the situation and 'the individuality' or uniqueness of the human being expressed in his capacity to make choices based in his own unique history (Herbart 1835, p. 2; Herbart 1977, p. 2; see also Benner and Schmied-Kowarzik 1967; Benner 2001).

The recognition of the human being as a *learning being* is indispensable for understanding the limits and possibilities of educative interactions between teachers and learners. Specifically, to recognize the human being as a learning being has three significant consequences for the teacher. First, it means that the teacher must recognize his or her ability to have an influence on the learner, and therefore take responsibility to make conscious choices about how he or she will influence the learner. In this sense, *Bildsamkeit* has a prescriptive quality for the teacher (see Benner and Schmied-Kowarzik 1967). Second, it implies that the learner is unique and can always choose differently than the teacher. Thus, the teacher must recognize that the otherness of the learner represents a certain blind spot, a reminder to teachers that despite their best intentions there is always a chance they could get it wrong. In all teacher-learner interaction there must remain this space for difference and surprise, for something the teacher had not thought of and could not

---

[6] See also Herbart (1806/1956, 1902); on this point see Buck (1985); Herbart criticizes doctrines of fatalism and transcendental freedom on account of the fact that they cannot be consistent with the idea of *Bildsamkeit*, because they do not allow for an understanding of the historicity of the individual and therefore do not allow for discussion of how education influences the individual's choices (1835, p. 2 and 1977, p. 2). On Herbart's critique of Kant and its limits see Benner and Schmied-Kowarzik (1967) and Müssener (1986). Also, Saito examines Emersonian moral perfectionism as an ateleological concept in a way that I find connected to the idea of perfectibility I am discussing in this chapter (see Saito 2004).

[7] Herbart (1802/1965, p. 131) and Herbart (1896, p. 27f), translation modified AE.

possibly foresee. Thirdly, the human as a learning being expresses the idea that neither the educator nor society at large can determine an individual's future. *Bildsamkeit* is an a-teleological notion that says it is up to each learner to decide for him or herself in particular cases, and in life as a whole, what to think and do. Thus, to describe the human being as *bildsam*, *perfectible* or *capable of learning*—the latter of which I find to be the most accurate translation—reminds us that there always remains something unknown and unknowable, and in Herbart's words 'indeterminate' about human nature. As Dietrich Benner and Friedhelm Brüggen emphasize, *Bildsamkeit* is 'that unknown something' ['*das unbekannte etwas*'] of human nature (Benner and Brüggen 2004, p. 195).

## Learning as *Umlernen*—On Negativity of Experience and Its Connection to Learning

How is it that one opens oneself up to something new, something different and unfamiliar? To answer this question we have to analyze learning as a process, not simply as a product. Only by inquiring into learning as a process can we understand how the interaction between the self and other becomes educative, an interaction that we no longer see in the final product. For educators, it is tempting to grasp learning solely as a product, because we can see when a child learns, that is, learning reveals itself as an observable event in the world (Prange 2008). In other words, teachers, parents and educators see learning happen when the learner knows an answer to a math problem or is able to do something such as play scales on a piano, that he or she was not able to do before. So the attempt to examine learning processes proves difficult in practice, because when we observe the learning processes of others, we do not know if learning is taking place until it is done and reveals itself in some, at least tentative, positive result. Similarly, it seems that one cannot witness one's own learning processes, because there is something about learning that involves being *in the moment* and not knowing you are learning prior to coming to that moment, in which you realize you have grasped something new. But what is that experience of learning like for the one experiencing it? By turning to contemporary German philosophical inquiries, in particular those taking a phenomenological approach, we can show that philosophical examination of the connection between experience and learning can reveal something otherwise hidden about the structure of learning. Namely, it can reveal the negativity of experience that is constitutive of all learning processes.

In his influential work *Lernen und Erfahrung* [*Learning and Experience*], the German philosopher Günther Buck draws upon Aristotle, Kant and Herbart, but also twentieth century traditions of phenomenology and hermeneutics to uncover the vital discontinuity in experience and its relation learning. In analyzing the connection between learning and experience, he first points to some common understandings of experience that begin to illuminate the meaning of negativity in experience. He points out, for example, that the experiences we tend to call 'instructive' or 'learning experiences' are the ones we were resistant to and happened to us in ways contrary to expectations (Buck 1969, p. 16). He argues, however, that this connection alone is too simplistic because it only allows us to see learning as a 'possible consequence' of experience, and not as an 'immanent consequence' of experience (Buck 1969, p. 17). Buck explains, the deeper connection between learning and experience can be grasped when we think about those experiences we call 'life experiences' ['*Lebenserfahrung*'] (Buck 1969, p. 18). We consider something a life experience at that point when we draw out the consequences of the experience and realize we learned something. In this sense, seeing the consequences of an experience is what makes it *an experience*, such that 'an experience, without consequences, from which one learned nothing, is not an experience' (Buck 1969, p. 18). As Buck writes, actual experiences appear to be both 'negative' and 'positive': they are 'negative' because we 'learned the hard way [*Lehrgeld bezahlt*]'; they are 'positive' because 'we learned' (Buck 1969, p. 18, translation AE).

Learning that is connected to experience in this way is what Buck refers to as *Umlernen* (a term formed from the German verb *lernen*, meaning to learn). Buck's use of the terms *negative* and *positive* above plays on the pejorative meanings of the terms as they are commonly used colloquially, but this usage proves a way into the deeper educative meaning of negativity in learning. The term *Umlernen* implies that all genuine learning involves struggle, disillusionment or suffering, because it involves encounters with something new, such as a new concept, a different perspective, or an unfamiliar activity that we are trying to get to know and understand. Experiences of the new and unfamiliar, and therefore, unexpected, are part of everyday life. They are part of the contingency with which we live that allows us—and often forces us—to experience our own limitations. No amount of planning can take into consideration all possible unexpected circumstances. When the world defies our expectations, we experience an *interruption*, a disruption, an opposition or resistance from things or other human beings that counteracts our attempts and implicitly tells us that what we thought, did, or said does not suffice to deal with the situation at hand. However, this experience is not an immediate feeling of lacking something or of making a mistake that is quantifiable, such as getting a wrong answer on a test. Since it is not immediately felt as a lack, it doesn't immediately indicate to us a step forward in the form of a simple acquisition of knowledge that could fill the void. Rather, the experience of one's own limitations is an experience of opposition and resistance that Käte Meyer-Drawe calls *Widerfahrnis*, or 'a counter-happening', in which the human being breaks with himself and opens himself up to new ways of being in the world (Meyer-Drawe 2005, p. 31, translation AE). The term *Umlernen* is necessary because it takes account of the fact that the experience of receptivity, of something happening to us, of suffering and undergoing, of becoming disoriented, is an indispensable part of the process of learning. The fact that we are receptive and not just active as human beings makes our experiences unavoidably discontinuous and in this sense *negative*.

Using the term *Umlernen* we can differentiate *transformative* learning processes as forms of *Umlernen* from *additive* learning processes as forms of *Dazulernen*. The former recognize the educative meaning of negativity and discontinuity in learning, whereas the latter assume learning is a continuous process of steps on the path of the accumulation of knowledge:

> Umlernen [...] is not simply the correction of this or that idea, that one had about something; it means also an alteration of one's 'disposition', that is, of one's entire horizon of experience. He who learns 'um' is confronted with himself; he becomes conscious of himself. Not only certain ideas change, rather the learner himself changes. On account of this essential negativity, the process of learning is the history of the learner himself.[8]

When learning brings about true change in the sense of a transformation, as Meyer-Drawe points out, it is experienced as a 'painful turn-around' ['*schmerzhaften Umkehr*'], in which one breaks with one's prior knowledge, but also with oneself as a person (Meyer-Drawe 2003, p. 511; see also Meyer-Drawe 1996, p. 89f.). Meyer-Drawe calls this experience of one's limits a 'confrontation with one's own experiential history' (Meyer-Drawe 1982, 520f., translation AE). When our experience breaks with itself, then we can learn in a way that is not just a matter of adding on or correcting the content of our thought, or exchanging one aspect of knowledge for another. Rather, this negativity and discontinuity makes a different type of learning possible; learning becomes *Umlernen*, a transformative restructuring of one's entire horizon of foregoing and possible experience (Meyer-Drawe 1982, p. 522; see also Meyer-Drawe 1984).[9]

The beginnings of learning cannot be consciously self-initiated, rather they are *felt* in the pre-reflective experience of negativity, that is, of a break with ourselves, our habitual modes of being, our assumptions and our own learning history. These breaks or gaps in experience cannot simply be closed by attaining new knowledge, but they can be productively dealt with through reflection and inquiry.[10] Learning begins in the breaks and gaps in experience and 'come forth as a response to the call of the other' (Meyer-Drawe 2003, see also Meyer-Drawe 2005). Something or someone takes hold of us before we become aware that something has happened. In this moment we are entangled in the situation, held in suspense, not knowing— even if, for only a split second—what happened or why it happened. Our response to the other does not begin with speaking, rather it begins 'with listening and looking'

---

[8] From the original German: 'Umlernen aber, das ist nicht nur die Korrektur dieser und jener Vorstellungen, die man sich über etwas gemacht hat; es bedeutet auch einen Wandel der 'Einstellung', d.h. des ganzen Horizontes der Erfahrung. Wer umlernt, wird mit sich selbst konfrontiert; er kommt zur Besinnung. Nicht nur gewisse Vorstellungen wandeln sich, sondern der Lernende selbst wandelt sich. Kraft dieser prinzipiellen Negativität ist das Geschehen des Lernens die Geschichte des Lernenden selbst' (Buck 1969, p. 44, translation AE). Buck recognizes Dewey had a place for negativity as doubt and uncertainty in his concept of experience, but he criticizes Dewey for not fully grasping the transformative significance of negativity as a break with oneself, see e.g. (1969, p. 70f). I analyze Dewey's notions of negativity in experience (2005a, see also 2005b) and a comparative analysis of moral meaning of negativity in Herbart and Dewey's works, (English 2007).

[9] See also Benner (2003), Benner and English (2004), Mitgutsch (2008), Rumpf (2008), and see also my discussion (English 2009) of this concept in the context of connections between the German tradition and the work of education philosopher Richard S. Peters.

[10] On this point see Waldenfels (1971, 2002). See Oser (2005) on negativity in moral learning.

(Waldenfels 1998, p. 44). This means responding to the other is initially *taking in* the other, by listening and looking for the difference between what we anticipated from another person, an object or ourselves, and what is revealed in the moment when those expectations break down. This ability to respond is indispensable for the teacher who seeks to create an educational relationship.

Before turning to examine the educative aspect of negativity in the teacher-learner relation, I would like to turn to the autobiography of the African-American author Richard Wright in order to illustrate the connection between the two aspects of negativity discussed thus far. In writing about his life, Wright takes his readers to painful moments in his childhood growing up in early 1900s in the segregated South of the United States, in which he was not given the opportunity to receive continuous formal schooling. Despite this, he explains that his curiosity for words and his desire to read began at an early age. He describes one formative experience when he received some initial encouragement of his curiosity from his mother:

> In the immediate neighborhood there were many school children who, in the afternoons, would stop and play en route to their homes; they would leave their books upon the sidewalk and I would thumb through the pages and question them about the baffling black print. When I learned to recognize certain words, I told my mother that I wanted to learn to read and she encouraged me. Soon I was able to pick my way through most of the children's books I ran across. There grew in me a consuming curiosity about what was happening around me and, when my mother came home from a hard day's work, I would question her so relentlessly about what I had heard in the street that she refused to talk to me.[11]

The text that baffled him and that confronted him with his own limit became the source of possible new ways of seeing the world, a horizon of new, unanswered questions. However, throughout his life Wright did not have an active guide or teacher to cultivate his learning process. The individuals around him and society at large discouraged him from asking questions, from inquiring into their possible answers, from transforming as a learning being. To recognize another person as a learning being means to see him or her as someone who can learn from the negativity of experiences and to provide him or her with the opportunity to do so. This is the task of the teacher in answering the call of the learner.

## Pedagogical Tact—On Improvisation, Risk and the Negativity of Experience in Teaching

In his lecture from 1810, Herbart offers a critique of schools that continues to be relevant 200 years later. His critique lies in the fact that schools do not allow for 'true teachers' [*echten Erzieher*] to be cultivated, because they don't allow for forms of pedagogical activity that 'connect to individuals' [*anschliess[en] an Individuen*] (Herbart 1810/1964, p. 149). The pedagogical activity that develops in

---

[11] Wright (1989), From Black Boy by Richard Wright. Copyright, 1937, 1942, 1944, 1945 by Richard Wright; renewed (c) 1973 by Ellen Wright. By Permission of HarperCollins Publishers, p. 29.

practice, but is guided by theory is what Herbart refers to as 'pedagogical tact' ['*pädagogischer Takt*'] (compare Herbart 1810/1964; see also Herbart 1802/1964, p. 131; Benner 2001). Herbart's notion of tact connects to what Aristotle called *phronesis*, or the art of making informed, wise decisions in the moment. When Herbart refers to tact as *pedagogical*, he means that it is a form of practical wisdom that is unique to teachers (Herbart 1802/1964).[12] For teachers, tact requires making judgments which take into account the learning beings who stand before them. The complexity and difficulty of these decisions can be easily underestimated by those outside the practice of teaching. Teachers are embedded in educational situations and lived experiences with learners. They are in the moment and they can only connect to the individual by finding out where he is at, what questions or problems he has, and, on that basis alone, decide how to bring him to somewhere new. Every act of teaching that is educative is directed towards an individual and involves being open in a way that makes teachers vulnerable to the call of the other. Pedagogical tact is a complex concept that addresses this existential experience of teachers. Here, I will examine this notion in its connection to the teacher's experience as one that necessarily involves risk and improvisation.

The nature of the educational situation is that it is 'always changing', as Max Van Manen emphasizes (Van Manen 1991, p. 187). This means first that if it is educational then the learner is learning and changing within themselves. But the changes in the learner do not happen in isolation. The teacher is observing, anticipating and, initiating changes in the learner's situation such that the teacher is also changing. It might seem that if a teacher could only learn to anticipate the learner's next step in the learning process then, he or she could plan for these changes and there would be little need for risk and improvisation in teaching. Of course, this would be to miss the point that the *change* is what makes the situation *educational*. Despite planning, teachers find themselves faced with the unexpected and unforeseeable in their practice. This may come as a child who begins to cry in class because of a death of a family member, a parent angry at her child's grade, a teenage student who expresses anxiety due to pressure by his peers to cheat on a test, a young girl who feels left out of a class activity because of her gender or the color of her skin. Students and teachers bring their lives to the classroom. The teacher is faced with the task of responding in an educative way, a task that calls for risk.

The author and teacher Frank McCourt illustrates the complexity, innovation, and risk involved in teaching in his memoir *Teacher Man*. He describes his experiences as a High School English teacher in New York in the 1970s. He illustrates a particular dilemma he faced with his students who are consistently forging parent-excuse notes for their absences from class. He realizes he cannot simply confront the students and accuse them of lying, because it would only lead to 'strained' relationships (McCourt 2005, p. 84). He also realizes that he could just simply ignore the situation since forging notes is 'just part of school life' (McCourt 2005, p. 84).

---

[12] On this point see also Müssener (1986), p. 200f.

Then, as he begins to read the notes, he suddenly sees the writing talent of his students that he had never seen before:

> Isn't it remarkable, I thought, how they resist any kind of writing assignment in class or at home. They whine and say they're busy and it's hard putting two hundred words together on any subject. But when they forge excuse notes they're brilliant. Why? I have a drawer full of excuse notes that could be turned into an anthology of Great American Excuses or Great American Lies.[13]

McCourt does confront his students, but he confronts them as learners, not simply as liars. He hands the whole class the notes with the names omitted and has the students read them. The students in his class are shocked. They are suddenly made to think about something that they took for granted, namely, that they could lie and get away with it and that they could avoid *learning* to write. McCourt then turns the situation into a creative writing assignment on the topic 'An Excuse Note from Adam [or Eve] to God' (McCourt 2005, p. 87).

The situation shows how teachers can make an unanticipated and even unwanted situation into a pedagogically fruitful experience for both learner and teacher. This requires a teacher who can judge the situation using the art of pedagogical tact, which is a form of judgment that skillfully opens up learning opportunities when and where they are lacking. The teacher can never fully plan for these situations, they are part of the discontinuity and negativity of the *teacher's* experience that arise due to the call of the other, the learner.[14] Jakob Muth describes this aspect of the educational situation as follows:

> In the continuous flow of activity a discontinuous moment breaks in. And this makes apparent, that we have to understand that tact cannot be planned in two respects: Unplanned is every discontinuous moment that breaks into and thwarts the ordinary flow of activity in school; Unplanned is also the action the teacher will take in this moment that demands quick judgment and decision.[15]

When teachers open themselves up to the new and unexpected within the teacher-learner relation, they open themselves up to the voice of the learner that breaks into and breaks open the educational situation, with an unexpected question, a frustrated look, a difficulty with a concept, or a paralyzing fear to move on. Pedagogical tact requires that teachers judge on the basis of looking, listening to, and taking in students' questions, difficulties and frustrations in engaging the material—that is, the negativity of students' learning experiences. To do this is to recognize that educational situations are never fully in the hands of the teacher, and therefore it is an essential part of the educational atmosphere that there remain a tension between

---

[13] McCourt 2005, p. 84.

[14] On the twofold negativity of teachers' experiences see Benner (2003); Benner and English (2004).

[15] From the original German, 'In einen an sich stetigen Ablauf bricht ein unstetiges Moment. Und das macht wiederum deutlich, dass die Nichtplanbarkeit des Taktes in einer doppelten Weise gesehen werden muss: Nichtplanbar ist jenes unstetige Moment, das in den Handlungsablauf der Schule einbricht und ihn durchkreuzt; nichtplanbar ist aber auch das Handeln des Lehrers in dieser Situation, die schnelles Beurteilen und Entscheiden fordert' (Muth 1967, p. 77, translation AE).

the teacher's expectations of learners and what the learners actually reveal about themselves in practice (Bollnow 2001, p. 54) The alternative to a fully controlled environment is not chaos in teaching; rather, for the teacher, it is thoughtfully planning ways to make learning happen, while at the same time remaining open to failure and having to rethink one's efforts (Prange 2007). To be open to failure as a teacher means to be open to the experiences of unease about your choices, to the fear of not knowing how to respond, to getting lost, to the frustration of balancing innovation with the requirements of the curriculum, and most significantly, to the sense of despondency in not knowing if you are reaching students.

When the voice of the learner breaks open the learning situation, teachers can feel thrown off course. Yet these moments of discontinuity in teaching present opportunities to create a new course together with the learner. Tact is the ability to create this new course so that the learner feels recognized, not because the teacher leaped onto the learner's path, but because the teacher used the learner's path to take him somewhere new and undiscovered.[16] Through pedagogical tact the teacher creates an educational environment that is dialogic and dialectical. Thus he or she not only responds to the learner, rather also creates educational situations in which a response to the learner is necessary. To do this means that teachers have to take the risk of *interrupting,* and *disrupting* student's taken-for-granted ways of seeing and being in the world by making the familiar strange. Interrupting learner's experiences is indispensable in teaching if genuine learning as *Umlernen* is to take place. When teachers interrupt the learner's experiences, learners break with themselves and only then can they as learners realize that they have a choice about who they are and who they want to become. When teachers see learning happen in a transformative way, they see students make choices in recognition of the other. For example, teachers may see a group of students change their language when they realize it is offensive, a student volunteer to work with a student who is outcast, a student who acted selfishly choose to share something with a classmate, or a student who was reclusive thrive in a group project. In these moments, the teachers also learn. They learn what is possible in teaching, and thereby they learn who they are as teachers and who they can become.

## Conclusions

In many classrooms around the world teachers are faced with reforms that stifle their ability to productively respond to the ever-changing nature of educational situations. They are pressured with testing, accountability measures, and increased efficiency in achieving learning objectives and curriculum outcomes. This technical reductionist version of the classroom situation in its most extreme form attempts to erase failure from the educational equation.[17] These attempts also *erase* the individual

---

[16] On this point, see Muth (1967); see also Van Manen (1991).

[17] On this point, see Blake et al. (2000) for a critique of Reynold's 'Highly Reliable Schools'.

learner. The learner breaks open the educational situation with his or her unexpected voice, which makes teaching personal and interpersonal. Of course in the classroom, just as in everyday life, it is not possible to account for all unexpected situations; it is not possible to erase the negativity in teachers' and learners' experiences of encountering one another as learning beings in the world. However, the danger is that school administrators, policy makers and the public will continue to choose to ignore these negative experiences and operate as if they are educationally insignificant. In doing so, they make it impossible for teachers to cultivate pedagogical tact and cultivate transformative learning in schools, because as Herbart stated so long ago, schools will not provide teachers the opportunity to 'connect to individuals'.

Herbart believed that educators could create situations that allowed for educative teacher-learner interaction to flourish. However, he presented an underlying dilemma that philosophers and educators would have to face in creating this situation in practice. He notes that for open and meaningful educational environments to exist in schools there needs to first be an 'educational spirit' [*pädagogischer Geist*] in society, that is a public state of mind that believes in and supports the rich potential of such environments (Herbart 1810/1964, p. 150). Yet, for such an *educational spirit* to come into being in society, society must first witness the fruits of these environments (Herbart 1810/1964, p. 150). This aporetic situation still faces philosophers and educators who strive to understand the conditions under which transformative education can take place.

If policy makers and those outside the lived situations of education continue to attempt to make the classroom environment controlled and controllable, they may eventually succeed in their efforts to remove the personal and interpersonal side of teaching and reduce teachers to automatons awaiting the next command. The genuine problem that faces humanity as a whole in halting and reversing these efforts is that good teaching and true pedagogical tact cannot be observed from the outside. Rather, it is something *felt* by the learner within educational teacher-learner relations. Pedagogical tact, when it hits the right tone, meets the core existential need of the learner such that the learner feels recognized in his or her being and forgets the pain of the foregoing difficulty. In this way, the *touch* of pedagogical tact is in a certain sense forgotten.[18] This connects to the fact that as adults we generally remember our bad teachers by *what they did*, the ones who yelled, threw things, were not attentive, said we were not good at a particular subject, whereas we typically remember our good teachers, not for something specific that they did, but more often for *who they were* as people. By tactfully encountering students, true caring and professional teachers who possess the art of pedagogical tact make teaching appear easy. Just as a ballet dancer is seen as a master of her art when she makes the difficult look graceful and effortless, a truly pedagogically tactful teacher makes teaching appear so effortless as if anyone could do it.

---

[18] On the connection between pedagogical tact and the latin *tactile* or touch, see Van Manen (1991) and Suzuki (2008a).

Policy makers, administrators and the public on the whole who look in and observe education happening in classrooms from an external perspective, will observe that when everything is working, it looks smooth and easy. This fact perpetuates the present problem that strategies for the measurement of teaching start from the *results,* that is, the situations where good teaching has already been learned. When these strategies fail to work, policy makers, school boards and administrators seem to continue to believe that they have simply not yet perfected their strategies and techniques, and in the meantime, in certain cases, lower standards so far such that no *failure* is recorded.[19] In reality, such reformists have a fundamentally wrong approach that no amount of superficial adjustment can rectify.

Cross-cultural dialogue about education is a starting point for creating the educational spirit in society. Such dialogue must surround questions of how to create situations in which every human being is recognized as a *learning being* and given promising opportunities to learn. A pre-condition for such a discussion is that we, as philosophers, educators and human beings establish the *Bildsamkeit* of every individual as the starting point for our inquiry into education. The darkest periods of oppression in human history were connected to the lack of recognition of human beings as learning beings based on group affiliations such as race, gender, or religion. This injustice hits us at the core of who we are. To recognize another person as a learning being means not simply to recognize that he or she is *capable of learning*, but also that he or she can be *learned from*.

We could go on with our lives indifferent to the other because of an indifference to the other within ourselves, that is, the otherness that gets drawn out in the negative experiences of everyday life. However, if we become aware of the otherness within ourselves by hearing the cry of the cuckoo, we can learn to be open to the other in ourselves *and* the other in the world around us. We have to ask ourselves would we rather have the cry of the cuckoo that disturbs our comfort or risk not hearing it at all. Which path we take as human beings becomes a question of whether we value the discomfort of negative experiences and the educational possibilities that arise therein.

**Acknowledgements**  I would like to thank *Mount Saint Vincent University* for an internal grant that has helped to support the research on this project.

# References

Benner, D. (2001). *Allgemeine Pädagogik*. Juventa: Weinheim.
Benner, D. (2003). Kritik und Negativität. Ein Versuch zur Pluralisierung von Kritik in Erziehung, Pädagogik und Erziehungswissenschaft. *Zeitschrift für Pädagogik, 46*, 96–110.

---

[19] For example, in April 2009 *The New York Times* reported that the US Secretary of Education was to give $44 billion to improve each state's schools, due to the prospect of embarrassing findings that states were lowering their testing standards to increase students' scores and teacher evaluation scores, see Dillon (2009).

Benner, D., & Brüggen, F. (2004). Bildsamkeit und Bildung. In D. B. Benner & J. Oelkers (Eds.), *Historisches Wörterbuch der Pädagogik* (pp. 174–225). Weinheim: Beltz.

Benner, D., & English, A. (2004). Critique and negativity: Toward the pluralisation of critique in educational practice, theory and research. *Journal of Philosophy of Education, 38*(3), 409–428.

Benner, D., & Schmied-Kowarzik, W. (1967). *Herbarts Praktische Philosophie und Pädagogik. Möglichkeit und Grenzen einer Erziehungsphänomenologie*. Ratingen: A. Henn.

Blake, N., Smeyers, P., Smith, R., & Standish, P. (2000). *Education in the age of nihilism*. London: Routledge.

Bollnow, O. F. (1965). *Existenzphilosophie und Pädagogik*. Stuttgart: Kohlhammer.

Bollnow, O. F. (2001). *Die pädagogische Atmosphäre*. Essen: Die blaue Eule Verlag.

Buck, G. (1969). *Lernen und Erfahrung*. Stuttgart: Kohlhammer.

Buck, G. (1985). *Herbarts Grundlegung der Pädagogik*. Heidelberg: Carl Winter.

Dillon, S. (2009). Education secretary says aid hinges on new data. *The New York Times*. http://www.nytimes.com/2009/04/02/education/02educ.html/ Accessed 7 Dec 2009

English, A. (2005a). Negativity and the new in John Dewey's theory of learning and democracy: Towards a renewed look at learning cultures. *Zeitschrift für Erziehungswissenschaft, 3*, 28–37.

English, A. (2005b). *Bildung, Negativität, Moralität: Eine systematisch-komparative Analyse der Erziehungskonzepten Herbarts und Dewey*s, Dissertation, Humboldt University Berlin, Germany, University Archives.

English, A. (2007). Die experimentelle Struktur menschliches Lehrens und Lernens: Versuche über die Rolle negativer Erfahrung in den Lehr-Lerntheorien Herbart und Dewey. In R. Bolle & G. Weigand (Eds.), *Johann Friedrich Herbart. 200 Jahre Allgemeine Paedagogik* (pp. 97–112). Berlin: Waxmann.

English, A. (2008). Wo '*doing*' aufhört und '*learning*' anfängt: John Dewey über Lernen und die Negativität im Erfahrung und Denken. In K. Mitgutsch, E. Sattler, K. Westphal, & I. M. Breinbauer (Eds.), *Dem Lernen auf der Spur* (pp. 145–158). Stuttgart: Klett-Cotta.

English, A. (2009). Transformation and education: The voice of the learner in Peters' concept of teaching. *Journal of Philosophy of Education, 43*(1), 75–95.

Heisig, J. (2001). *Philosophers of nothingness. An essay on the Kyoto School*. Honolulu: University of Hawaii Press.

Herbart, J. F. (1802/1965). Die ersten Vorlesung über Pädagogik. In W. Asmus (Ed.), *Johann Friedrich Herbart Pädagogische Texte: Vol. 1. Kleinere Pädagogische Grundschriften* (pp. 121–131). Düsseldorf: Helmut Küpper.

Herbart, J. F. (1804/1964). Ästetische Darstellung der Welt asl ds Hauptgeschäft der Erziehung. In W. Asmus (Ed.), *Johann Friedrich Herbart Pädagogische Texte: Vol. 1. Kleinere Pädagogische Grundschriften* (pp. 105–120). Düsseldorf: Helmut Küpper.

Herbart, J. F. (1806/1965). Allgemeine Pädagogik. In W. Asmus (Ed.), *Johann Friedrich Herbart Pädagogische Texte: Vol. 2. Pädagogische Grundschriften* (pp. 9–158). Düsseldorf: Helmut Küpper.

Herbart, J. F. (1810/1964). Über Erziehung unter öffentlicher Mitwirkung. In W. Asmus (Ed.), *Johann Friedrich Herbart Pädagogische Texte: Vol. 1. Kleinere Pädagogische Grundschriften* (pp. 143–151). Düsseldorf: Helmut Küpper.

Herbart, J. F. (1835). *Umriss pädagogischer Vorlesung*. Göttingen: Dieterichschen Buchhandlung.

Herbart, J. F. (1896). Introductory lecture to students in pedagogy. In *Herbart's ABC of sense-perception, and minor pedagogical works* (W. J. Eckoff, Trans., pp. 13–28). New York: D. Appleton.

Herbart, J. F. (1902). *The science of education* (H.M. Felkin & E. Felkin, Trans). Boston: D.C. Heath & Co.

Herbart, J. F. (1977). *Outlines of educational doctrine* (A. Lange, Trans.). New York: MacMillan Company.

Klafki, W. (2001). The significance of classical theories of Bildung for a contemporary concept of Allgemeinbildung. In I. Westbury, S. Hopmann, & K. Riquarts (Eds.), *Teaching as a reflective practice: The German Didaktik tradition* (R. MacPherson & W. Klafki, Trans., pp. 85–106). Mahwah: Lawrence Erlbaum Associates.

McCourt, F. (2005). *Teacher man*. New York: Scribner.
Meyer-Drawe, K. (1982). Phänomenologische Bemerkungen zum Problem des Lernens. *Vierteljahresheft für Wissenschaftliche Pädagogik, 58*(4), 510–524.
Meyer-Drawe, K. (1984). Lernen als Umlernen. Zur Negativität des Lernprozesses. In W. Lippitz & K. Meyer-Drawe (Eds.), *Lernen und seine Horizonte* (pp. 19–45). Königstein/Ts: Scriptor.
Meyer-Drawe, K. (1996). Vom anderen Lernen. Phänomenologische Betrachtungen in der Pädagogik. In M. Borrelli & J. Ruhloff (Eds.), *Deutsche Gegenwartspädagogik: Vol. II* (pp. 85–99). Hohengehren: Schneider-Verlag.
Meyer-Drawe, K. (2003). Lernen als Erfahrung. *Zeitschrift für Erziehungswissenschaft, 6*(4), 505–514.
Meyer-Drawe, K. (2005). Anfänge des Lernens. *Zeitschrift für Pädagogik, 49*, 24–37.
Mitgutsch, K. (2008). Lernen durch Erfahren: Über Bruchlinien im Vollzug des Lernens. In K. Mitgutsch, E. Sattler, K. Westphal, & I. M. Breinbauer (Eds.), *Dem Lernen auf der Spur* (pp. 263–277). Stuttgart: Klett-Cotta.
Müssener, G. (1986). *J.F. Herbarts 'Pädagogik der Mitte'. Sieben Analysen zu Inhalt und Form*. Darmstadt: Wissenschaftliche Buchgesellschaft.
Muth, J. (1967). *Pädagogischer Takt. Monographie einer aktuellen Form erzieherischen und didaktischen Handelns*. Heidelberg: Quelle und Meyer.
Nishida, K. (1987). *Intuition and reflection in self-consciousness* (V. Viglielmo, T. Yoshinori, & J. O'Leary, Trans.). Albany: SUNY.
Nishimura, T. (2007). The aesthetic and education in the Kyoto School – Motomori Kimura's theory of expression. In Y. Imai & C. Wulf (Eds.), *Concepts of aesthetic education. Japanese and European perspectives* (pp. 64–78). Berlin: Waxmann.
Nishimura, T. (2008). Schiller, Motomori Kimura and the Kyoto School. In *Educational thoughts in and around the Kyoto School of Philosophy: Towards an East West dialogue* (pp. 21–47). Conference Proceedings of the International Network of Philosophers of Education 2008 Conference.
Oser, F. (2005). Negatives wissen und moral. *Zeitschrift für Pädagogik, 49*, 171–181.
Plato. (1961). Meno. In E. Hamilton & H. Cairns (Eds.), *The collected dialogues of Plato, including the letters*. New York: Pantheon Books.
Prange, K. (2007). Die Funktion des pädagogischen Takts im Lichte des Technologie Problems der Erziehung. In B. Fuchs & C. Schönherr (Eds.), *Urteilskraft und Pädagogik* (pp. 125–132). Würzburg: Königshausen und Neumann.
Prange, K. (2008). Lernen im Kontext des Erziehens. Überlegungen zu einem pädagogischen Begriff des Lernens. In K. Mitgutsch, E. Sattler, K. Westphal, & I. M. Breinbauer (Eds.), *Dem Lernen auf der Spur* (pp. 241–248). Stuttgart: Klett-Cotta.
Reichenbach, R. (2002). On irritation and transformation: A-teleological *Bildung* and its significance for the democratic form of living. *Journal of Philosophy of Education, 36*(3), 409–419.
Rousseau, J-J. (1755/1999). *Discourse on the Origin and Foundations of Inequality Among Men*. In P. Coleman (Ed.), *Discourse on the origin and foundations of inequality* (F. Philip, Trans.). Oxford: Oxford University Press.
Rousseau, J-J. (1764/1979). *Emile or on education* (A. Bloom, Trans.). New York: Basic Books.
Rumpf, H. (2008). Lernen als Vollzug und als Erledigung – Sich einlassen auf Befremdliches oder: Über Lernvollzüge ohne Erledigungsdruck. In K. Mitgutsch, E. Sattler, K. Westphal, & I. M. Breinbauer (Eds.), *Dem Lernen auf der Spur* (pp. 21–32). Stuttgart: Klett-Cotta.
Saito, N. (2004). Awakening my voice: Learning from Cavell's perfectionist education. *Educational Philosophy and Theory, 36*(3), 79–89.
Suzuki, S. (2008a). Takt als Medium. Überlegungen zum Takt-Begriff von J.F. Herbart. *Paragrana, 17*, 145–166.
Suzuki, S. (2008b). The Kyoto School and Herbart. In *Educational thoughts in and around the Kyoto School of Philosophy: Towards an East West dialogue* (pp. 53–61). Conference Proceedings of the International Network of Philosophers of Education 2008 Conference.
Tanabe, H. (1946–1969). The logic of the species as dialectics (D. Dilworth & T. Sato, Trans.). *Monumenta Nipponica, 24*, 273–288.
Tanake, T. (2008). Towards a clinical theory of human becoming. In *Educational thoughts in and around the Kyoto School of Philosophy: Towards an East West dialogue* (pp. 3–17). Conference Proceedings of the International Network of Philosophers of Education 2008 Conference.

Toshihiko, I., & Izutsu, T. (1981). *The theory of beauty in the classical aesthetics of Japan*. London: Martinus Nihoff.

Van Manen, M. (1991). *The tact of teaching. The meaning of pedagogical thoughtfulness*. London: Althouse Press.

von Humboldt, W. (1969a). Theorie der Bildung des Menschen. In A. Flitner & K. Giel (Eds.), *Wilhelm von Humboldt, Werke in Fünf Bände: Vol. 1. Schriften zur Anthropologie und Geschichte* (pp. 234–240). Darmstadt: Wissenschaftliche Buchgesellschaft.

von Humboldt, W. (1969b). Über den Geist der Menschheit. In A. Flitner & K. Giel (Eds.), *Wilhelm von Humboldt, Werke in Fünf Bände: Vol. 1. Schriften zur Anthropologie und Geschichte* (pp. 506–518). Darmstadt: Wissenschaftliche Buchgesellschaft.

von Humboldt, W. (2001). Theory of Bildung. In I. Westbury, S. Hopmann, & K. Riquarts (Eds.), *Teaching as a reflective practice: The German Didaktik tradition* (G. Horton-Krüger, Trans., pp. 57–61). Mahwah: Lawrence Erlbaum Associates.

Waldenfels, B. (1971). *Das Zwischenreich des Dialogues*. Den Haag: Martinus Nihoff.

Waldenfels, B. (1998). Antwort auf das Fremde. Grundzüge einer responsiven Phänomenologie. In B. Waldenfels & I. Daermann (Eds.), *Der Anspruch des Anderen Perspektiven phänomenologischer Ethik* (pp. 35–50). München: Fink.

Waldenfels, B. (2002). *Bruchlinien der Erfahrung*. Frankfurt am Main: Suhrkamp.

Wright, R. (1989). *Black boy. A record of childhood and youth*. New York: Harper and Row.

# Chapter 16
# The Sense of Indebtedness to the Dead, Education as Gift Giving: Tasks and Limits of Post-War Pedagogy

Satoji Yano

## Reconsidering the Origin of Education and the Tasks of Post-war Pedagogy

In the past 10 years, I have been exploring diverse experiences that can bring us to the world outside our immediate experience, as part of the task of educational anthropology. These include such topics as pure gift giving, death, rituals, squandering, hospitality, eroticism and play. These concerns contribute to what might be called 'pedagogy towards limits' – an attempt to disclose the limits of the educational and pedagogical matrix and practices of post-war pedagogy, which have been constituted by the concepts of human being, community, labor, experience and development centering on the principle of exchange.

My project was launched by the presentation of a paper at the annual meeting of the Society of Educational Thoughts and History in 1997, entitled 'Notes on the origin of education' (hereafter cited as 'Notes') (Yano 1998). In place of the conventional idea that education originates inside a community out of necessity, I proposed the possibility of an alternative model of the origin of education: education being initiated on a border between the inside and the outside of a community by the act of pure gift giving – as an excess that is brought about from the outside of community. My attempt in the present chapter is to reconsider and revise this alternative model on the origin of education. 'Notes' was originally written with the aim of critically reconsidering the notion of development as socialization, as one of the central concepts in post-war pedagogy in Japan. In this chapter, through the reconstruction of the original model proposed in 'Notes', I would like to elucidate an alternative idea of how the power that inspires teaching and provides a driving

S. Yano (✉)
Graduate School of Education, Kyoto University,
Yoshida-honmachi, Sakyo-ku, Kyoto-shi, 606-8501, Japan
e-mail: s-yano@ares.eonet.ne.jp

P. Standish and N. Saito (eds.), *Education and the Kyoto School of Philosophy*,
Contemporary Philosophies and Theories in Education 1,
DOI 10.1007/978-94-007-4047-1_16, © Springer Science+Business Media Dordrecht 2012

force for post-war pedagogy originates, from the standpoint of the theory of the gift giving. In doing so I offer a critical examination of post-war pedagogy, and to expose the limits of this educational and pedagogical matrix. I find this to be a necessary task at a time when the Fundamental Law of Education is being reconstituted in Japan, and an emphasis has begun to be placed on the sense of indebtedness to those sacrificed in the war (the dead). Under these circumstances, it is necessary to reexamine the meaning of the 'post-war' in post-war pedagogy, and to reconsider the relationship between war and education, and between nation and education. This requires us to inquire into the foundation of education, in a way that helps us resist a form of education derived from the sense of indebtedness to the dead.

## The Origin of Community and Education
## Derived from the Sense of Indebtedness

Let us begin by reconsidering the theory that locates the origin of education inside the community. I reexamined this in 'Notes' and claimed exchange to be the fundamental mode of education. Exchange, however, does not exist in itself from the beginning. For the system of exchange to operate, a first gift giving must take place. In other words, for the community to exist as a community, the initial stroke of gift giving is essential (Asada 1983). If we pay attention to this initial act of gift giving, an explanation of the origin of education based upon exchange is not adequate: we need an account of the process of converting the initial stroke of gift giving to exchange.

As Benjamin shows in 'Critique of Violence (1920/1921)', the beginning of the law is presented as violence. Normally for the law to be recognized as the law, it requires another law to justify the law which precedes it. The very first law in itself, however, cannot be justified by any other laws. That is to say, the law has an origin in a force which is not the law. The initial law is anything but violence in that it exercises its force without relying on the law. Benjamin calls such aboriginal violence 'lawmaking violence' (Benjamin 1986, c1978 (1990/1921), p. 288). This initial law (as a code) as an enforcing violence, however, is also gift giving in the sense that it produces an order. (As could be said of a gift, it is both a poison and a present.) Seen in this way, a community has undergone 'a stroke of force' in Jacques Derrida's phrase, which is to say, a stroke of gift giving, by gods or ancestors.

As will be elaborated later, the stroke of gift giving is one that anticipates a return (and is therefore a different understanding than in pure gift giving). Viewed in this way, it becomes clear why a community revisits the date of its birth repeatedly through ceremonies and rituals. All the members of the community are given this life, this land, and this code as gifts by the initiators of the community (call them gods or ancestors). Therefore the later generation is obligated to thank these gift givers. In other words, the later generation carries a tremendous sense of indebtedness to their predecessors, and this constrains the way the later generation lives. Mauss thinks that gift giving and the act of returning takes place between the living and the dead (Mauss 1925). It is Nietzsche who makes explicit this thought in philosophy. *On the Genealogy of Morality* (1887), he says as follows:

> Within the original tribal association ... the living generation always acknowledged a legal obligation towards the earlier generation, and in particular towards the earliest, which founded the tribe.... There is a prevailing conviction that the tribe *exists* only because of the sacrifices and deeds of the forefathers, - and that these have to be *paid back* with sacrifices and deeds: people recognize an *indebtedness* [*Schuld*], which continually increases because these ancestors continue to exist as mighty spirits, giving the tribe new advantages and lending it some of their power. Do they do this for nothing, perhaps? But there is no 'for nothing' for those raw and 'spiritually impoverished' ages. What can people give them in return? Sacrifices (originally as food in the crudest sense), feasts, chapels, tributes, above all, obedience.... (Nietzsche 2007, pp. 60–61)

For the exchange of gift giving to take place in this world, a stroke of gift giving needs to be contributed from the outside of the community. It is the first generation who gave this stroke from outside. Starting with the mark of indebtedness to the dead, the exchange of gift giving begins to operate as an endless cycle. The original giver, however, is already dead, and hence, it is impossible for her offspring to reciprocate her directly. Therefore from the beginning, a way towards complete reciprocation is closed despite the fact that the offspring is given this life, this land, this law and everything else. Thus the later generation cannot escape from the mark of indebtedness left by the original giver. As is well known Nietzsche describes the morality of good and evil as an issue of debt, which is an economic principle. Here is a further passage from his *On the Genealogy of Morality:*

> How, then, did that other 'dismal thing', the consciousness of guilt, the whole 'bad conscience', come into the world? ... Have these genealogists of morality up to now ever remotely dreamt that, for example, the main moral concept '*Schuld*' ('guilt') descends from the very material concept of '*Schulden*' ('debts')? Or that punishment, as *retribution*, evolved quite independently of any assumption about freedom or lack of freedom of the will? ... And where did this primeval, deeply-rooted and perhaps now ineradicable idea gain its power, this idea of an equivalence between injury and pain? I have already let it out: in the contractual relationship between *creditor* and *debtor*, which is as old as the very conception of a 'legal subject' and itself refers back to the basic forms of buying, selling, bartering, trade and traffic. (Nietzsche 2007, pp. 39–40)

Nietzsche makes clear that such a phenomenon as 'all "bad conscience"', which has been highly regarded in Christian morality, has its origin in the contractual relationship between *creditor* and *debtor*, and attempts to overturn this value system. This, however, is not limited to Christian morality. In her *The Chrysanthemum and the Sword* (1946), the anthropologist Ruth Benedict explains the Japanese view of morality in terms of concepts relating to debt and reciprocation (Benedict 1946/1967). Like the idea of the sense of guilt, the ideas of '*On*' (the sense of obligation) and '*Giri*' (the sense of debt), which used to be the cores of the Japanese sense of morality, are related to gift giving and returning of gratitude in the relationship of gift giving. '*Giri*' is derived from equal relationships among independent individuals and, therefore, it is possible for this to be reciprocated: once it is fully reciprocated, the sense of indebtedness is gone. By contrast, '*On*' can never be fully reciprocated as, for example, in the child's relation to her parents: however much she reciprocates, the act of returning never ends (Oda 1994, p. 89). This is illustrated by the narrator, the 'I', in Soseki Natsume's novel, *Kokoro* (*The Heart*). The 'I' runs away to his teacher, leaving his father who is near death. The 'I' is to be charged not only by his relatives, but also by society, as an undutiful person who forgets the '*On*' owed to his father. Though not to the same degree as in the times depicted in Soseki Natsume's novel (1914), we might say that the sensitivity to the sense of indebtedness still continues to be ingrained in the Japanese mind.

The phenomenon of the relationship between a creditor and a debtor in morality can also be applied to the model of education that views it as originating in the inside of a community. Where does the code of community begin which is essential to it becoming a community? Like the origin of the exchange of gift giving, the code of morality is derived from the outside of the community. The stroke of gift giving is replaced by the system of exchange. From the sense of indebtedness to the ancestor (i.e. the dead), the offspring pass down the teaching to their own successors – the teaching that forces the offspring to undergo the same sacrifice and achievement as the ancestor. This is, at the same time, a transmission of the story of gift giving, one that gives the meaning of life and death to the members of the community.

Lévi-Strauss calls the direct and reciprocal exchange 'restricted exchange', one which is limited to two parties between A and B (not individuals, but groups). In contrast, he calls an indirect and unidirectional circular exchange, 'generalized exchange', one which circulates among three parties, from A to B, and then to C, and then back to A (Lévi-Strauss 1969/1949). In the case of 'restricted exchange', the giver and the receiver alternate and, therefore, the party who shoulders the sense of indebtedness alternates. By contrast, in the case of 'generalized exchange', B does not return gratitude directly and, therefore, the sense of indebtedness to A remains. This, however, is not limited to B, but is commonly experienced among all the members who participate in exchange. A also receives a gift from another partner who is different from the one to whom A gave a gift and, therefore, A retains the sense of indebtedness to his partner. In this way, in general exchange, all the members who participate in exchange cannot get rid of the sense of indebtedness, and hence, a circle of exchange continues eternally.

As the Japanese expression, 'returning *On*', implies, the later generation cannot fully return gratitude to their parents, and much less so to their ancestors. Therefore, the sense of indebtedness continues. As we saw in Nietzsche above, the later generation does not return the debt directly to the former generation for their gift giving, and hence, it may seem that the give and take between the two parties is not that of exchange. This, however, can be conceived as a general form of exchange, one in which the presence of the ultimate receiver is postponed until the end of the temporal process of reciprocation. Here we can see the way in which teaching of an ancestor's sacrifice and achievements is passed down to the later generation. This is driven by the sense of indebtedness carried by the members of a community. In this act of teaching in a community, we can find the event of gift giving. The act of teaching in a community, however, is not a pure gift giving by the first teacher: it is a return of gratitude based upon the sense of indebtedness to gift giving. More correctly, it is a part of a phenomenon called the 'exchange of the gift'.

As we have seen so far, even in education originated in a community, a stroke of gift giving constitutes its starting point. Though the stroke is extra-ordinary, it will in due course be systematized and become assimilated into the system of exchange with the return of gratitude. Thus a stable system of exchange of gift giving is established. In this sense, the original stroke of gift giving by gods and ancestors provides the momentum to continue the sense of indebtedness on the part of the offspring. It is this sense of indebtedness to the dead that continues to drive education within the community. At the same time, education based upon the sense of indebtedness justifies an idea of justice, one which is conditioned by revenge (as exchange), as in the idea of 'an eye for eye'. It transmits an idea of morality based upon the sense of indebtedness as energy. This is the principle of exchange as it is embodied in the idea of repaying a gift giving and revenging an injury – an underlying principle that conditions the morality of a community.

## National Education Derived from the Sense of Indebtedness to the Sacrificed

We need, however, not only to reconsider the origin of the initial model, but also to further examine the relationship between community and education. So far a community has been understood at a trans-historical level to be based upon the exchange of gift giving (which is to say, reciprocity). This, however, is not sufficient to clarify the tasks and limits of post-war education and post-war pedagogy in Japan, and to respond to the contemporary issues of education. Therefore, for further clarification, I shall introduce Kojin Karatani's concept of 'nation' as a manifestation of modern community.

Based upon work such as that of Michael Polanyi, Karatani attempts first to reconsider the system of capitalism not as a mode of production but as that of exchange. He divides the mode of exchange into four types: (1) reciprocal exchange, (2) capturing and redistribution, (3) the exchange of commodities, and (4) the exchange, 'X', as an anonymous ideal. Karatani then matches these dominant modes of exchange, one by one, to the constitutive bodies of a capitalist society: the nation corresponds to reciprocal exchange (1), the state, to capturing and redistribution (2), and capital, to the exchange of commodities (3). This is how he interprets the constitutive bodies of a capitalist society as a unit (or a circulation) between capital, the nation and the state (Karatani 2006, p. 38). The last mode of exchange, X, corresponds to 'association'. X is a mode of exchange that is opposed to the other three modes, and hence, association is opposed to the other three constitutive bodies of a capitalist society. In association, therefore, Karatani finds the possibility of opposing other constitutive bodies of capital, the nation and the state. A correspondence between X and association is deeply related to the notion of the pure gift, to which I shall return later. For the moment, the focal point of the discussion is Karatani's interpretation of nation.

According to Karatani, in modernity, agricultural community was dismantled by a monetary economy, and restored 'imaginatively' as a nation. What is relevant to our discussion here is the following passage from Karatani:

> One more thing, however, needs to be added. That is the fact that along with the erosion of community, the generational time that was supposed to guarantee the 'eternity' entailed by community was inevitably lost. In the economy of an agricultural community, mutuality was supposed not only among living people, but also between the dead (or ancestors) and those who were going to be born (offspring) in the form of mutual exchange. For example, the living took action in view of their offspring, and the offspring appreciated their ancestors for the consideration they had given to them. Along with the erosion of an agricultural community, the idea of eternity, obtained by locating oneself between ancestors and offspring, became extinct. Though world religion may eternalize the individual soul, the eternity of community will not be restored. It is the nation that will allow us to restore it on an imaginative level. The nation accommodates not only the people who exist in the present, but also those members in the past and the future. (Karatani 2004, pp. 66–67)[1]

If we read these sentences in association with the quotes from Nietzsche above, we shall find in both the principle of the exchange of gift giving as driving education within the nation as a community. To guarantee eternity to the members of community is to found the common meaning of life and death, that is to say, the story of community. Such a story is a 'story of gift giving' bequeathed by the ancestor or the dead. The same thing happens at the level of the nation. The story of nation, however, is not based upon the daily, concrete relationship of the exchange of gift giving as is observed in an agricultural community and, therefore, the story needs to be constituted at the 'imaginative' level, such as through the promotion of the idea of 'the same race', 'the same language' and 'the same culture'.

A teacher of national history should teach first and foremost the story, history and language of the origin of the nation state. The nation state provides the teacher with the authority and power, and gives value to what he or she teaches at school. The story of the origin of nation guarantees the legitimacy of the nation as well as education – whether it is the mythological theory of a race based upon the Imperial family, the stories of independence of America or India, or the stories of revolution of France, the former Soviet Union and China. The voice of a teacher as the agent of the nation state is different from his personal voice, and represents the voice of the nation state. As with the voice of the minister in the church, his voice is uttered with authority. It is through such voice that the sense of appreciation (or returning of gratitude) is taught repeatedly at school – reciprocation by the whole race to ancestors, warriors fighting for the reformation of the nation, heroes of the War of Independence, the Founding Fathers, leaders in revolution, and the unlimited number of people who were sacrificed as symbolized by the tombs of anonymous soldiers (see: Nishibe 2000). Sharing the sense of gratitude to the sacrificed, people come to be formed as the entity 'the nation' – even if they are not engaged with each other in direct, reciprocal exchange, and despite the difference in their circumstances.

In order to give national identity to the amorphous state of child, the teacher tells this sacred 'story of gift giving' to the child. More specifically speaking, 'imagined communities' (Anderson 1983) are born through education in a 'national language',

---

[1] All translations from the Japanese are by the editors, unless otherwise indicated.

which has been allegedly passed down successively by ancestors – first, through a history (or story) of the 'unyielding race and nation that have overcome difficulties despite a series of crises', and second, through a selecting from the innumerable classic texts a cluster that has allegedly formed the culture of nation state and its transmission (Suzuki and Shirane 1999). To the nation as an 'imagined community', the 'story of gift giving' is indispensible as an account of the origin of the race and nation. The nation state aimed to control life as a whole by giving meaning not only to the life of the people [*kokumin*] but also to death. Without this sacred story of gift giving, the nation cannot dedicate their lives to their homeland, and it is impossible to execute the war (Anderson 1983).

Irrespective of the political system – whether characterized by ultra-nationalism, socialism or democracy – 'the nation' is a constitutive body of society in the modern nation state. In Japan, the post-war nation carried as its shared emotion the sense of indebtedness to those sacrificed in the Second World War. In this context, post-war pedagogy was born from the experiences of that war, and has been motivated by the sense of indebtedness to those sacrificed. Such pedagogues as Arata Osada and Seiya Munakata, who had been active since the pre-war period, criticized themselves, regretful that they had colluded with war. Their educational thoughts are permeated by mourning towards the dead in the war. This is not limited to pedagogues: teachers in the post-war educational context shared this. For those involved in education, the slogan, 'Do not send your students to the battlefield again!' had a strong effect. Not so much due to an aspiration towards peace as due to the sense of indebtedness and regret many teachers felt towards the sacrificed (the dead) (Oguma 2002, pp. 386–387). These teachers came to carry a sense of mission with respect to teaching.

The sense of indebtedness to the sacrificed in the war receded from the scene of schooling as, over time, the post-war pedagogy lost its momentum. From the 1970s onwards, the number of teachers who had experienced the war decreased more rapidly, and the idea of teaching came to lose its underpinnings in the ideology of the sacrificed. In 1995, however, the year of the fiftieth anniversary of the end of the war, Manabu Sato, in a prologue entitled 'Lending an ear to the voice of the dead' in his book, *Learning: Its Death and Revival*, symbolically discussed the necessity of 'education that resuscitates the gaze and voice of the 'dead'' concerning the relationship between education and those who died in the war (Sato 1995, p. 12).

At the moment when the sense of the debt to the dead was lost, the post-war education and post-war pedagogy in the narrow sense disappeared from the scene. Today, however, education based upon the sense of indebtedness to the war sacrificed is being reborn in the context of a concern for the unification of national space, and thus reaffirmation of 'the nation' in response to globalization. Of course, in the areas of politics and economics, various forces have been operating to affect education. It is, however, the sense of indebtedness to the dead that has been a significant source of power in the shaping of education. Education and pedagogy driven by the sense of indebtedness to the dead, just like morality driven by the sense of indebtedness, gives a meaning of life and death, and thereby a sense of belonging to the nation as a community, to the educated. It, however, will close out the way towards outside the community or others by subordinating our lives. As an alternative possibility for education, one that does not depend on the sense of indebtedness to the dead, we can consider instead education based on pure gift giving.

## Education as Pure Gift Giving and the Role of Pure Gift Giver

As I elaborate in 'Notes', there has been another strain of education, one that is different from the model originated in the inside of community. This is education as pure gift giving by 'the original teacher' – one who is represented by Socrates, Buddha, Jesus or Nietzsche's Zarathustra. He arrives from the outside of 'the principle of community', bequeaths his teaching (or a question) as pure gift giving, one which never expects a return, and presents his death as his last and greatest gift to his disciples. In terms of the driving force of transmission, we can think of two models of disciples, depending upon how they receive gifts from 'the original teacher'.

One is the model of disciples who are overwhelmed by the excessive and the most intensive form of gift giving – the death of the teacher. In this case, disciples become inheritors of the teaching of the teacher from the sense of indebtedness to him that is impossible to reciprocate. As a result, disciples become the narrators of the word of the teacher. They accept the death of the teacher as a sacrifice for which it is no longer possible to return gratitude. They compile the sayings of the teacher as the mythologized 'story of gift giving', justify themselves as dutiful successors of his teaching, and relay the idea of 'gift giving as sacrifice', one that is contaminated by the oppressive and dark sense of owing. Those who participate in this relay are not different from people who transmit the codes of the community in that both rely on the sense of indebtedness as the motive for teaching. This can be said even in the case where the idea passed down to them by the teacher is the idea of pure gift giving, one which tries to overcome the notion of 'gift giving as sacrifice' based upon the sense of indebtedness. The disciples build a closed clan with identity, and become holy servants who preserve and transmit the teaching of their teacher (Yano 2003).

In another model, disciples do not assimilate the event of gift giving from the teacher into 'the story of gift giving' or mythologize it. Instead they receive it as an unsayable myth or an unanswerable question. They make the event of gift giving the source of their own lives, and live a path of life that is opened through gift giving. These disciples do not become ones who relay 'gift giving as sacrifice', but they turn themselves into pure gift givers, and participate in pure gift giving. In other words, they themselves become the 'original teachers'. In the way these 'original teachers' exist and the way the disciples themselves become the 'original teachers' through the encounter with their 'original teacher', we can find a new possibility of ethics for life. Such ethics is different from the morality of justice in a community based upon exchange, as represented by the idea of 'an eye for an eye'. Rather it is made possible by love and forgiveness, which transcend the morality of community. The death of Socrates leaves his disciples with the riddle of who philosophers are, and simultaneously gives them the courage to move towards death. Here the dead, who represent the gift giving of death, have a major impact upon those who receive the gift, but what happens is not the relay of gift giving as sacrifice, but that of pure gift giving. The dead keep inspiring the living to further gift giving.

As referred to above, according to Nietzsche, Christian morality (which is different from the ethics of Jesus) is driven by resentment produced by the sense of indebtedness. Monks are driven by resentment, and transmit the morality of resentment to people.

Here these monks are prototypes of institutional teachers. By contrast, the transmission of the ethics of formation is driven by pure gift giving. Zarathustra's gift giving is the teaching of an overflowing life, one that does not depend upon resentment, and begins as an extravagant and generous act of pure gift giving. Pure gift giving as the way of transmission itself conveys to us directly what the ethics of formation is. In the pre-modern community as well as in the modern nation, it was the dead who monitored the stagnation of the exchange of gift giving and who governed its flows: it was the ancestors as the sacrificed and the dead in the nation as a community who motivated teachers towards teaching. In that sense, 'education as formation' is similarly driven by the 'original teacher' who died in sacrifice. Such death as pure gift giving, however, creates the event of pure gift giving, and opens the possibility of converting disciples to gift givers.

## Destroying the Sense of Indebtedness to the Dead: A Lesson from Dying

A diagram of interpretation that supports the morality of community breaks down when an excessive 'stroke of inquiry' arises from outside of the meaningful world of community – as in the case of Socrates' inquiry. This is a stroke of inquiry as an excessive gift giving. Once one encounters this event, it becomes an unforgettable and inescapable agenda for life. A stroke of gift giving threatens the human being who has lived comfortably the life of exchange within the community, by depriving him of the ground of his life. Simultaneously it opens his life towards outside the community and exposes him to the experience of vital life.

When gift giving as the excessive force of dynamic life is embodied in a specific person, the person is called the 'original teacher'. The 'original teacher' is born into the experience of death, which is the experience of non-intelligence, and turns such experience of his own into gift giving. By so doing, the teacher conveys his experience to his disciples. The 'original teacher' is an initiator who gives the experience of death as a gift, and who contributes to the creation of an individual. In addition, through the lesson of pure gift giving, which is the lesson of death, the teacher embodies the type of individual who dares to dive into the innerness of his own self. It is through this act of diving that the teacher himself undergoes the experience of his own death.

'Gift giving as an event' brings forth the experience of non-intelligence, violates the code of community based upon utility, and disturbs the order of community. By contrast 'the story of gift giving' lures us into transitory excitement, produces the transitory sense of solidarity and unity among the anonymous members of community, and assimilates gift giving as an event, in the form of the beautiful story of sacrifice, into nation as a community. Gift giving that is turned into a story brings the 'experience of expansion', one that expands the 'I' into the 'we' (Sakuta 1993, p. 112). Despite the reality of inequality and exploitation, it reinforces the sense of solidarity and fraternal love among members of nation as the 'we' community, and intensifies devotion to the nation state as a historical existence, one that transcends the finite life of an individual. In this process, the order of the nation as a community is sanctified (Anderson 1983, pp. 17–19).

Many beautiful stories narrated in lessons on morality at school create the experience of expansion. When volunteer activities are called the 'experience of volunteering' by the Japanese Central Council for Education, the experience is aimed at producing effects of expansion. Besides the story of 'self sacrifice' lie such stories of gift giving as 'the sense of loyalty' and 'patriotic mind', those stories that are aestheticized by the nation. Principally, both types of stories are not that far from each other. 'The aesthetization of death' is a locus in which the ideas of gift giving and exchange struggle against each other.

It is in that very locus that a 'pedagogy geared towards limits' must disclose the nature of beautiful stories of gift giving, and defend the lesson of death that presents the process of gift giving as an event. Moreover, the lesson of death resists the turning of gift giving into a story (i.e. the process of aestheticization), and displaces the 'imagined communities' of the 'we'. The lesson of gift giving (which is the lesson of death) is one in which the experience of non-intelligence takes place. This experience is the one through which we encounter the other, going beyond discrimination and exclusion created in the name of the 'we' as opposed to the 'they'.

The act of teaching becomes a self-aware act by 'the teacher of humanity'. Through the emergence of the 'original teacher', our reflection and awareness of teaching has been deepened. Teachers in the ancient and middle ages, in many cases, relayed 'gift giving as sacrifice', as they conceived the 'original teacher' as their own exemplar. The demonstration of Stoic courage that follows the example of Socrates can be said to be one of those historical scenes. Modern school teachers have been the agents of the nation state, while at the same time they are ones who have received a gift from the 'original teacher'. This lends a subtlety to the way of being a teacher, one which cannot be captured in terms of his role simply as an agent of the nation state. This essay has been trying to clarify the driving force of education that does not rely on the sense of indebtedness to the dead. It encourages us to remember the presence of the 'original teacher' in the genealogy of education, and opens up a way towards turning ourselves to the 'original teachers' and towards becoming participants in the relaying of pure gift giving. This ideological attempt, I believe, is significant so that we can locate the source of the power and thus problematize the movement of forming national identity based upon the sense of indebtedness to the dead.[2, 3]

---

[2] This chapter corresponds to the tradition of the Kyoto School of anthropology in the following two points. First, in terms of a methodology, it understands anthropology not only on the dimension of ontology, but also in the dimension of social being, that is to say, in an ontic and ontological way. More specifically, an effort of constructing anthropology by introducing the sociological and anthropological wisdom of the Durkheim school inherits an attempt of the pre-war Kyoto School of philosophy. Second, in terms of a view on human being, it is based upon the experience of touching nothingness in the ideas of Kitaro Nishida, following the principle of negativity. The original sources of the modern thought including the genealogy of Nietzsche and Bataille's theory of gift giving are reconceived under the ideological tradition of the Kyoto School of philosophical anthropology, and on that ground the discussion on pedagogy has been constructed.

[3] The original version of this Chapter was published, in Japanese, as 'Shisha no oime to zoyo to shite no kyoiku' (The sense of indebtedness to the dead, education as gift giving). In *Kindai Kyoiku Forum (Forum on Modern Education)* (History of Education Thought Society), Vol. 16 (2007): pp. 1–10.

# References

Anderson, B. (1983). *Imagined communities: Reflections on the origin and spread of nationalism*. London: Verso Editions.

Asada, A. (1983). *Kozo to Chikara: Kigo-ron o Koete* [Structure and power: Beyond the theory of sign]. Tokyo: Keiso-Shobo.

Benedict, R. (1946). *The chrysanthemum and the sword: Patterns of Japanese culture*. Boston: Houghton Mifflin.

Benjamin, W. (1986, c1978). *REFLECTIONS. Essays, Aphorisms, Autobiographical Writings*. Edited and with an Introduction by Peter Demetz. Translated by Edmund Jephcott. New York: Schocken Books.

Karatani, K. (2004). *The collected essays of Kojin Karatani [Teihon: Karatani Kojin shu]: Vol. 4. Nation and aesthetics (Nation to Bigaku)*. Tokyo: Iwanami-shoten.

Karatani, K. (2006). *Sekai-Kyowa-koku: Shihon-Nation-State o koete* [Towards the world republic: Beyond the capital as nation as state]. Tokyo: Iwanami shoten.

Lévi-Strauss, C. (1969/1949). *The elementary structures of kinship (Les structures élémentaires de la parenté)*; translated from the French by James Harle Bell, John Richard von Sturmer, and Rodney Needham, editor (Rev. ed.). London: Eyre & Spottiswoode.

Mauss, M. (1925/1966). *Sociologie et anthropolgie*. Paris: Presses universitaires de France.

Nietzsche, F. (2007). In K. Ansell-Pearson (ED.), *On the genealogy of morality* (C. Diethe, Trans.) Rev. student ed. Cambridge: Cambridge University Press.

Nishibe, S. (2000). *Kokumin no Dotoku [The morality of the nation]*. Tokyo: Sankei-Shinbun-Sha.

Oda, M. (1994). *Kozo-Jinruigaku no Field [The field of structural anthropology]*. Kyoto: Sekai-Shiso-Sha.

Oguma, E. (2002). *'Minshu' to 'Aikoku': Sengo Nihon no Nationalism to Kokyosei* ['The democratic' and 'the patriotic': Nationalism in post-war Japan and publicity]. Tokyo: Shinyo-sha.

Sakuta, K. (1993). *Seisei no shakaigaku o mezashite: Kachi-kan to seikaku* [Towards the sociology of formation: A sense of value and character]. Tokyo: Yuhikaku.

Sato, M. (1995). *Manabi: Sono shi to saisei* [Learning: Its death and rebirth]. Tokyo: Taro Jiro sha.

Suzuki, T., & Shirane, H. (Eds.). (1999). *Sozo sareta koten: Canon keisi, Kokumin Kokka, Nihon Bungaku* [Classics being created: Formation of canon, nation state and Japanese literature]. Tokyo: Shinyo-sha.

Yano, S. (1998). Kyoiku no Kigen nitsuite no oboegaki [Notes on the origin of education]. *Kindai Kyoiku Forum* [Forum on modern education], 7, 53–62. Tokyo: Society of Educational Thoughts and History.

Yano, S. (2003). 'Sensei' to shiteno Soseki: Shitei Kankei no Kyoiku Ningengaku teki kosatsu [Soseki as 'teacher': Examination on master-disciple relationship from the perspective of educational anthropology]. In Y. Takaya (Ed.), *Oto suru Kyoiku Tetsugaku* [Philosophy of education in response]. Kyoto: Nakanishiya Shuppan.

# Index

## A
Absolute nothingness, 7, 11, 57, 58, 66, 69–71, 74, 104, 112, 197, 198, 205
Acting-intuition, 11, 82–87
*Aesthetic Letters*, 10, 66–67, 70, 72
Aesthetics, 10, 13, 25–26, 30, 31, 47, 51, 57, 58, 65–75, 113, 115, 116, 121, 127–129, 158, 165, 170, 171, 174, 176, 177, 179
American philosophy, 12, 110, 204
American transcendentalism, 9, 12, 157–166

## B
Benjamin,W., 222
Beyond skills, 149–151
Buddhism, 6, 7, 19, 21, 22, 24–26, 57, 58, 65, 74, 78–79, 91, 92, 97, 98, 102

## C
Cavell, S., 9, 13, 25, 26, 158–166
Cognitive science, 118, 122
Cohen, H., 44–46
Consciousness, 2, 13, 20, 21, 44–49, 51, 52, 68, 69, 79, 82, 85–87, 91, 101, 103–106, 115, 117, 125, 153, 164, 169, 171–174, 177–179, 191, 197, 198, 205, 223
Conversion, 35, 38, 97, 99–102, 163, 166, 198
Critical thinking, 20

## D
Deliberation, 50, 118, 120–127
Derrida. J., 7, 9, 22, 24–26, 198
Developmental psychology, 12, 134, 137–139, 144
Dewey, J., 33, 111, 113–117, 119–121, 124, 126–129, 161, 175, 211
Dogen, 79–80
Double eyes, 12, 151, 153–155
Dramatic rehearsal, 120, 124

## E
Eastern philosophy, 12, 79, 82, 119, 147, 155, 197
Ecological, 11, 84, 118, 120, 121, 123–129
Ecological imagination, 11, 12, 109–129
Ecology, 118, 121, 122, 157
Educational anthropology, 40, 63
Environment, 13, 42, 43, 62, 84, 85, 111, 118, 122, 127, 140, 144, 158, 159, 164, 175, 215, 216
Environmental education, 109–129, 157–158
Environmental ethics, 115, 121
Environmentalism, 13, 157–159
Environmental problems, 109, 110, 129
Ethics, 6, 19, 114, 115, 121, 123, 126, 228, 229
Exchange, 4, 221–226, 228–230
Experience, 5, 9, 11, 13, 14, 19–26, 43, 44, 46, 48–52, 60, 62, 68, 72, 74, 75, 77–87, 91–105, 110, 112, 113, 115, 117–121, 126, 136, 139, 141, 142, 147, 149, 151, 153, 161, 166, 169–179, 192, 197, 203–217, 221, 224, 227, 229, 230

Printed by Printforce, the Netherlands